EMINENT MUSSALMANS

EMINENT MUSSALMANS

G. A. NATESAN

GYAN

Published by

GYAN

Gyan Publishing House
5, Ansari Road
Daryaganj, New Delhi-110002
Phone: 011-47034999, 9811692060
E-mail: books@gyanbooks.com

Distribution Network
gyanbooks.com
India, USA, Canada, UK, Australia

ISBN: 978-93-7225-449-5 (PB)

First Published, 1926

2nd Impression 2025

Printed at: Gyan Press, Delhi.

EMINENT MUSSALMANS
Author: G. A. NATESAN

Eminent Mussalmans.

EMINENT MUSSALMANS

CONTENTS

NOTE

THIS book is a welcome addition to the biographical literature now extant in India touching the lives and achievements of many Mussalman patriots who have in recent years contributed to the intellectual and social advancement of their countrymen. In the building up of our composite nationality Mahomedans no less than Hindus and Parsis have taken a leading part and an attempt is made in this volume to put on record not only the lives and doings of many leaders of Muslim thought in India but also to mark their distinctive contribution to the evolution of Indian polity and culture. Among such leaders have been men of marked eminence in diverse ways—reformers, statesmen, judges, lawyers, educationists, poets and politicans. Commencing from Sir Syed Ahmed, the story is brought down to this day.

THE PUBLISHERS.

P. 1.

SIR SYED AHMED

SIR SYED AHMED.

INTRODUCTION.

SIR SYED AHMED KHAN was perhaps the greatest leader of the Indian Mussalmans in the nineteenth century. He was for more than five decades at the helm of Muslim affairs in India, occupying more or less the position of teacher and dictator and utilising his marvellous powers for the benefit of his countrymen. His brilliancy of wit, charm of expression, his strength of opinion, his subtle mental powers, and the unique union of qualities in him as reformer, orator, man of letters, philosopher and leader have rarely, if ever, been found elsewhere in such happy combination.

He was a remarkable product of Oriental learning. Whatever noble work Raja Ram Mohan Roy, Vidyasagar, Keshub Chundra Sen, Ranade and Dadabhai Naoroji have done in the cause of India in their respective spheres is not, in one sense, a matter for great surprise, for they were masters of the English language and had drunk deep at the fountain of Western civilization and culture. In Sir Syed it was different. It is certainly to his credit that, although ignorant of English and other European languages, he mastered the principles of the British Constitution and the principles of occidental jurisprudence so perfectly. Brought up as an Oriental scholar, he rose to be the apostle of English learning amongst his co-religionists. He was not only an educational and moral force but a political force of no mean importance as well. In fact, he was a supreme factor in inspiring, restraining and guiding his community and country—the interests of both of which claimed his sympathies at many decisive moments. His work as a regenerator of his fallen community can be best judged if our readers are made acquainted with the important events of his life. It is here proposed to mention very briefly some important phases of his life which bridged the long span of 82 years.

HIS ANCESTORS.

Sir Syed was born in the imperial city of Delhi on the 17th April, 1817.- He was a Syed by birth on his father's as well as on his mother's side. Paternally, he was descended from *Hazrat* (Lord) Hussain, the grandson of the Prophet Mahomed, in the 36th degree. Being persecuted by the Ommiades and Abbassides, the Beni Fatimites found their lives in great peril and consequently left their hearths to settle down in the distant countries of Asia, Africa and Europe. Some of the Fatimite families migrated to Egypt, some to Berber and Spain and some others again to Persia, Afghanistan and India. Sir Syed's ancestors, escaping from the tyranny of the Ommiades took refuge in Damghan and finally settled down in Hamadan and Herat. It was in the reign of Shah

Jahan that the members of the family came to India and were appointed to posts of trust and responsibility by that Emperor, and their connection with the Moghul Court continued down to the end of the nominal rule of Bahadur Shah (1857). They held important *mansabs* under the Moghul Government. His paternal grandfather, Syed Hadi, was a man of great influence at the Court of Alamgir II, who bestowed on him the honoured title of Nawab Jawad-ud-daula. His father, Mir Taqui, held independent views and was much respected by the Court and by the gentry of the city. Mir Taqui had been offered the post of Prime Minister to Akbar II, but refused this and other coveted honours. Sir Syed's mother, Aziz-un-nissa Begum, was the eldest daughter of the Minister who was acknowledged to be the best Oriental scholar of his time. She exercised the most wholesome influence on his character. He received an excellent training under her fostering care. He lost his father when he was quite young. His father's pension ceased and the family was thrown on the mother's resources. She was a remarkable woman. Throughout her life, she lived frugally and managed the household affairs ably. It was from his mother that Sir Syed received the incentive to exertion. Physically he possessed superior weight and size as well as a tough and strong constitution which distinguished him from his fellows.

HIS EARLY EDUCATION.

The beginning of the nineteenth century had seen the politico-religious decay coincident in the

Islamic World with social and intellectual deterioration. Rank superstition and dire ignorance had taken hold of the people's mind. The forces which had sustained the existence of society—and an empire—were fast ebbing away. The remnants of the Moghul civilization were crumbling to decay at Delhi and Lucknow. There was hardly a seminary of good repute where the sons of noblemen and the middle classes could proceed for their education and training. Sir Syed was therefore educated at home by his mother, who was one of those Mahomedan ladies who, though not educated in the English fashion, are nevertheless cultured and not infrequently speak two or three Oriental languages and possess a good knowledge of their poetry also. She was singularly free from the grovelling superstitions which have eaten into the vitals of Muslim society. Early religious training at her hands enabled him to shake off the trammels of those superstitions which had crept into the faith of his compatriots and which he so successfully combated in later years.

He was one of the most well-read men of his time in Persian, Arabic, Muslim theology and law and contemporary history. He had to leave his studies at the early age of 18 and seek service under the East India Company. He enjoyed the best society of Delhi of those days and moved freely in the company of the great poets, *Sahbai*, *Ghalib* and *Azurda*.

(1838—1857.)

After his father's death, his mother's income proved insufficient for the maintenance of the family, consisting as it did of five or six souls; and as the Maafi lands had also been confiscated by Government, he severed his connection with the Moghul court and started life as a Sherishtadar at Delhi. In 1839, he became Naib Mir Munshi to Mr. (afterwards Sir) Robert Hamilton, Commissioner of Agra. He passed the Munsif's Examination with credit and was posted to Mainpuri in 1841. His reputation as a civil judge reached the Moghul Court, which was not slow to confer on him the family title of *Nawab Jawad-ud-dowla.* From 1846 to 1854, he remained at Delhi as Sadr Amin. Here he resumed his studies and wrote his famous work, ***Asar-e-Sanadid,*** on the ruins, architecture and mausoleums of Delhi. It is the standard work on the subject and is recognized as such by European *savants* and drawn upon by modern authors in writing the history of Delhi. A copy of this historic work was presented to the Royal Asiatic Society by Mr. Roberts, the then Collector of Delhi, who attempted an English translation of the same but left it unfinished. The celebrated French Orientalist, M. Garcon of Tassy, published a French translation of it in 1861. This attracted the attention of the Royal Asiatic Society, which marked its sense of his antiquarian researches by electing him an honorary member of its body. This period of 8 years was one of incessant literary activity on the part of Sir Syed.

In this period he wrote some important religious works also, which will be briefly alluded to elsewhere.

In 1855, he was transferred to Bijnour as Sadr Amin. Here he found time to edit the *Ain-i-Akbari* and corrected many a mistake which had crept into that celebrated work of Abul Fazl. Mr. Blochmann, the translator of *Ain-i-Akbari* in English, has paid a glowing tribute to his capable editing of that famous work.

1857 TO 1868. MUTINY AND AFTER.

Sir Syed was stationed at Bijnour, when the Mutiny of 1857 broke out in the North. The sad episode of the Mutiny may fitly be described as a turning point in the life of Sir Syed, as it brought into relief the great qualities of his head and heart. In those troublous days he saved the lives of many Englishmen and women. Although he saw a great rising enveloping his, as well as the adjacent districts, his implicit and unflinching confidence in the durability of British Rule never forsook him for a moment during those stormy days. There were not a few sons of India who firmly stood by England in this dark hour of her trial. The after-effects of the Mutiny are too terrible to dwell upon. The Government began to punish ruthlessly the mutineers and those who were supposed to have joined hands with them. Thousands of innocent persons suffered owing to the personal animus or grudge of an informer; but Sir Syed helped the authorities to differentiate between the guilty and the innocent and saved many families from destruction. He had the just satisfaction of exercising his influence in the direction of tempering justice with mercy. Big fortunes were made by many an Indian, when the estates of rebel chiefs and zamindars, which were confiscated after the Mutiny, were awarded to them for little or no service done. A big Taluka, yielding an annual rental of $1\frac{1}{2}$ lakhs of rupees, formerly owned by a rebel chief, was recommended by Mr. Shakespeare, Collector of Bijnour, to be awarded to Sir Syed Ahmed for his loyal services during the Mutiny but he firmly and boldly refused the offer, as his conscience did not permit him to enjoy an estate the price of which was the blood of his countrymen.

At last British prestige was re-asserted and a general amnesty was proclaimed and the great Proclamation of Queen Victoria restored peace and order in the country. But to Sir Syed the prospect did not appear cheerful at all. He despaired of the regeneration of Muslim India and once entertained the thought of emigrating to Egypt. His love of his community and the country, however, could not permit him to take that extreme step, for he deemed it the greatest crime to forsake his countrymen at such a sad and critical juncture and to seek repose and comfort in a foreign land.

It was at such a time that he set before himself the Herculean task of regenerating his fallen community and of making Indians and Englishmen understand each other. He firmly believed that the existence of the great gulf between the rulers and the ruled was wholly responsible for the calamity into which the country had been plunged in 1857. In 1858, he wrote the famous pamphlet on the *Causes of the Indian Mutiny*, which was not published till 1863, when the storm of anger and rancour swelling in the breasts of Englishmen had abated. This important brochure was translated into English by his old friend, Mr. (afterwards Sir) Auckland Colvin, Ex-Lt.-Governor of the United Provinces. He is the first Indian who wielded his pen for the noble cause of dispelling the wrong notions of Englishmen on the causes of the Indian Mutiny. He boldly expressed his opinion on the subject. No apology is needed to make the following extracts from that pamphlet to show the trend of his political views in those days :—

As regards the rebellion of 1857, the fact is, that for a long period, many grievances had been rankling in the hearts of the people. In course of time a vast store of explosive material had been collected. It wanted but the application of a match to light it, and that match was applied by the Mutinous Army.

The original cause of the outbreak was the non-admission of a native as a member into the Legislative Council.

I believe that this Rebellion owes its origin to one great cause to which all others are but secondary branches so to speak of the parent stem. I do not found my belief on any speculative grounds or any favourite theory of my own. For centuries many able and thoughtful men have concurred in the views I am about to express.

Most men, I believe, agree in thinking that it is highly conducive to the welfare and prosperity of Government, indeed it is essential to its stability, that the people should have a voice in its councils. It is from the voice of the people only that Government can learn whether its projects are likely to be well-received. The voice of the people can alone check errors in the bud, and warn us of the dangers before they burst upon, and destroy us. ... ...

To form a Parliament from the natives of India is of course out of the question. It is not only impossible but useless. There is no reason however why the natives of the country should be excluded from the Legislative Councils, and here it is that you come upon the one great root of all this evil. Here is the origin of all the troubles that have befallen Hindustan. . . .

The evils which resulted to India from the non-admission of natives into the Legislative Council of India were various. Government could never know the inadvisability of the laws and regulations which it passed. It could never hear as it ought to have heard the voice of the people on such a subject. The people had no means of protesting against what they might feel to be a foolish measure or of giving public expression to their own wishes. But the greatest mischief lay in this that the people misunderstood the views and intentions of Government. They misapprehended every act and whatever law was passed was misconstrued by men who had no share in the framing of it, and hence no means of judging of its spirit. At length the Hindustanees fell into the habit of thinking that all the laws were passed with a view to degrade and ruin them, and to deprive them and their fellows of their religion.................. .. .. I do not wish to enter here into the question as to how the ignorant and uneducated natives of Hindustan could be allowed to share in the deliberations of the Legislative Council: or as to how they should be selected to form an assembly like the English Parliament. They are knotty points. All I wish to prove here is that such a step is not only advisable, but absolutely necessary, and that the disturbances are due to the neglect of such a measure.

The outbreak of the rebellion proceeded from the following five causes:—

1. Ignorance on the part of the people: by which I mean misapprehension of the intentions of Government.

2. The passing of such laws and regulations and forms of procedure as jarred with the established customs and practice of Hindustan and the introduction of such as were in themselves objectionable.

3. Ignorance on the part of the Government of the condition of the people; of their modes of thought and life; and of the grievances through which their hearts were becoming estranged.

4. The neglect on the part of our Rulers of such points as were essential to the good government of Hindustan.

5. The bad management, and disaffection of the Army.

I would here say that I do not wish it to be understood that the views of the Government were in reality such as have been imputed to them. I only wish to say that they were mis-

construed by the people, and that this misconstruction hurried on the rebellion. Had there been a native of Hindustan in the Legislative Council, the people would never have fallen into such errors.

Every passage in the famous pamphlet on the "Causes of the Indian Revolt" is important. Sir Syed, proceeding to consider the five causes of the Indian Revolt, refers to unwise interference in matters of religion. It was believed by the ignorant as well as by the educated, that the British Government were bent on interfering with their religion, and with their old established customs. They believed that Government intended to force the Christian religion upon the Hindus and Mussalmans alike. Events had happened which increased and strengthened this conviction. He refers to the step which was taken in the famine of 1859 of rearing orphans in the principles of the Christian faith. This was looked upon throughout the N. W. P. as an example of the intentions of Government in this connection. As another example of the misapprehension on the part of the people, he mentions that it was commonly believed that Government appointed missionaries and maintained them at its own cost. It was supposed that Government and the officers of Government contributed large sums of money to proselytize the poor people. Many covenanted officers and many military men assumed the missionary functions and used to talk to their subordinates about religion and directed them to listen to the preaching of missionaries. For the first time in India, the Gospel was preached in places of public resort and at markets and fairs. The establishment of missionary schools and the fact that the covenanted' officers attended examinations at those schools kindled the fire that was smouldering. Village schools were looked upon with suspicion as the general belief was that they were instituted solely with the view of spreading the doctrines of Jesus. Unnecessary alterations in the usual system of education in large colleges formed another instance of the alleged interference. In the beginning of the nineteenth century, when colleges were established, Arabic, Persian, Sanskrit and English were equally taught. The "Fiqha" (theology), "Hadi" (traditions) and other such books were also read. Examinations were held in the "Fiqha" for which certificates of proficiency were given. Religion was not in any way thrust aside. But all was changed in the forties. The study of Arabic was little thought of. The "Fiqha" and "Hadi" were suddenly dropped and Persian was almost entirely neglected. All this tended to strengthen the idea that Government wished to wipe out the religions which it found in Hindustan.

Taking the second cause, Act XXI of 1850 was, without doubt, prejudicial to the professors of other creeds. This Act was thought to have been passed with the view of advancing Christian interests. Sir Syed remarks:—

The Hindu faith, as it is known, allows of no converts. To the Hindus, therefore, this Act brought no benefit. If a man again became convert to Islam, he is forbidden by the laws of his new religion, from inheriting property left to him by men of

another creed. No Mahomedan convert, therefore, could profit by this Act. To such men, however, as became Christians, it offered great advantages. Hence this Act was said not only to interfere with people's religions, but to hold out strong inducements to conversion.

Act 15 of 1856, relating to Hindu widows was put forward as another example as it was opposed to the practice of the Hindu religion. However noble and humane, it allowed Hindu widows to remarry. The ignorant masses believed that it was intended to give liberty to females. Moreover, certain acts and laws were passed which led to decisions, in the civil courts opposed to the religious practices of the litigants. Sir Syed would not have the Government show a partiality for any creed whatever. The laws, providing for the resumption of Revenue Free Lands, the last of which was Regulation 6 of 1819, were most obnoxious. Sir Syed remarks:—

> It is a remarkable fact that whenever the rebels have issued proclamation to deceive and induce the people, they have mentioned two things: the one, interference in matters of religion; the other, the resumption of revenue free lands. It seems fair to infer that these were the two chief causes of the public discontent. More especially was it the case with the Mahommedans on whom this grievance fell far more heavily than on the Hindus.

Public sales of zamindari rights were most objectionable, as bankers and money-lenders availed themselves of it to advance money to landlords, resorting to every kind of trickery and roguery to rob them of their property. Sir Syed was rather strong on the question of heavy assessments of lands. In many districts, every settlement that was made pressed heavily, and landlords and cultivators were alike reduced to straits. "The assessment imposed by the English Government have been fixed without any regard to their various contingencies." The abolition of Talukdari rights, particularly in the Province of Oudh, and the introduction of stamp paper were entirely opposed to the spirit of Hindu customs.

This brings us now to the third cause, *the ignorance of Government of the state of the country and their subjects.* Government was but slightly acquainted with the unhappy state of the people. Let us quote in *extenso* some important passages on this heading :—

There was no real communication between the governors and the governed, no living together or near one another as has always been the custom of the Mahommedans in countries which they subjected to their rule. Government and its officials have never adopted this course without which no real knowledge of the people can be gained. . . . .

The people again having no voice in the Government of the country could not well better their condition, and if they did try to make themselves heard by means of petitions, these same petitions were seldom attended to and sometimes never even heard.

Government, it is true, received reports from its subordinate officials, but even these officials themselves were ignorant of the real thoughts and opinions of the people, because they had no means of getting at them.

Now Government, although in name only a Government subordinate to a Higher Government, was in reality the real Government of this country, and as such, it ought to have received the complaints and petitions of its people direct and not as it did invariably by reports from its District Officers. These are some of the reasons why the real feelings and ways of its people, why the action of new laws passed for that people, their working for good or for bad, for the prosperity or otherwise of the countrymen were unknown or slightly known to Government. The people were isolated, they had no champion to stand up for their rights and to see justice done to them, and they were constrained to weep in silence.

As regard Cause IV, the following quotations set out what Government ought to have done :—

I maintain that the maintenance of friendly relations between the Governors and the governed is far more necessary than between individuals, private friendships only affect a few, friendship and good feeling between a Government and its subjects affect a nation. . . *The people and the Government* I may liken to a tree, the latter being the root, and the former the growth of that root. As the root is, so will the tree be. What! Was such intimacy impossible under this Government? Most certainly not.

* * * * *

Government has hitherto kept itself as isolated from the people of India as if it had been the fire and they the dry grass, as if it thought that were the two brought in contact, the latter would be burnt up. It and its people were like two different sorts of stone, one white and the other black, which stones too were being daily more and more widely separated. Now the relations between them ought to have been close like those between the streaks of white and black in the stone called Abri in which we see the former close alongside of the latter, the one blending with the other.

Sir Syed clearly points out that, although the blood of the Mahomedan conquerors and that of the people of the country were not the same, they still became friends. The history of Muslim India shows that, in those times, as long as cordiality was not *observed* by the reigning powers, tranquillity was not established. Treating the Indians with contempt also alienated the feelings of the people against their Rulers.

Contempt is an ineradicable wrong. Being treated contemptuously sinks deep into a man's heart, and although uninjured by the same as to his wordly goods, he still becomes an enemy. The wound rankles deep and cannot be healed. That given by a sword can be healed but that inflicted by a contemptuous word can *not* . . . . . .

Now in the first years of the British Rule in India, the people were heartily in favour of it. This good feeling the Government has now forfeited and the natives very generally say that they are treated with contempt. A native gentleman is in the eyes of any petty official, as much lower than that official as that official esteems himself lower than a Duke. The opinion of many of these officials is that no native can be a gentleman.

However good the intention of Government with regard to its subjects may be, unless these same officials give practical proof thereof by kind treatment of the natives, the people will not believe in them. Theory and practice are not one and the same In these days, or rather within the last few years the feeling of officials towards natives is not nearly so favourable as was formerly the case. In olden days natives were treated with honour and in a friendly manner by these officials, and consequently to use a native expression, "they carried their (natives') hearts in their hands."

Sir Syed mentions, as another reason, the exclusion of natives from high appointments.

HIS PRACTICAL WORK.

In his "*Cause of the Indian Revolt*," Sir Syed tried to solve the question of the sympathetic administration of the country. He essayed in a practical manner, to remove the general aloofness which existed between the rulers and the ruled. He did not believe in the imperialistic poet's oft quoted line, "East is East and West is West, etc." He was an ardent believer in, and a staunch advocate of, substantial union between the Orientals and Occidentals. His work in that direction was an uphill one. At first, he commenced his work amongst his own men. He had seen that ignorance, superstition and narrow-mindedness reigned supreme throughout Muslim India. He therefore prepared himself to fight these giants of superstition and ignorance and to open the eyes of his countrymen and co-religionists to the new situation in India. He fully knew what great harm the extensive hierarchy of bigoted Mullahs had done in keeping back his co-religionists from educating themselves in the new subjects of Western lore. He raised his voice for the assimilation of Western arts and sciences in his own community. From 1861 to 1875, he strove hard to prepare the minds of his co-religionists for the reception of new ideas. We may designate this period as a period of religio-social reform. From 1875 till his death in 1898, education engrossed all his attention. The early seventies saw him promoted to the post of a Subordinate Judge. Notwithstanding that the duties of his post were very arduous, he found time to do other useful and philanthropic work which deserves our gratitude. Among the literary products of this period (before his visit to England) may be mentioned a "History of the Mutiny in the Principality of Bijnour," an "Inquiry into the Causes of the Indian Revolt," a "Commentary on the Bible and Essays on Islam" and a "Life of the Prophet Mahomed," and a vigorous reply to Dr. Hunter's Book, "Are the Mussalmans of India Loyal ?" Each of these brought a feather to his cap. But he was destined to do still greater deeds.

THE SCIENTIFIC SOCIETY.

In 1863, when he was stationed at Ghazipur, he developed the idea of establishing a Literary and Scientific Society with a view to reconcile Oriental and Occidental ways of thought by translating standard English works into Urdu, so that Mussalmans who foolishly had not taken to English education might get a glimpse of European thought and culture and thus cultivate liberal ideas which Islam, in the first three centuries of the Hejira Era had so successfully inculcated. The Society was established at Ghazipur and Aligarh was made its headquarters when its founder was transferred to that district. It was an honest attempt on the part of Sir Syed to bring Hindus and Mahomedans on one common non-controversial platform. Hindus were invited to join it and they did not join it in very large numbers. The Society also undertook the work of translating such old works of Indian authors as might be deemed instructive. The Duke of Argyle, then Secretary of State for India, accepted the Patronship while the Lieut. Governors of the Punjab and Bengal became its Vice-Patrons. The then Maharaja of Patiala royally supported the Scientific Society. It became very popular and some important treatises were compiled by its members on various subjects, such as History, Agriculture, Biography and Political Economy. Syed Ahmed was able to locate it after a few years in a handsome building which has been recently converted into one of the Boarding Houses of the Aligarh College.

ESTABLISHMENT OF ENGLISH SCHOOLS

After the Mutiny, about 1861, he established an English School at Moradabad, which was amalgamated with the District Board School later on. When he had become convinced of the utility of the assimilation of the Western arts and sciences by the Mussalmans of India, he sketched out a rough plan of inaugurating an Anglo-Oriental programme of universal education for the Indian Mussalmans. In 1864, two months after the establishment of the Scientific Society, he laid the foundation-stone of an English School at Ghazipur, now known as the Victoria School. On that occasion he delivered a very vigorous speech in the course of which he said:—

The work to be inaugurated to day is portentous. We are laying foundation to-day of spreading the light of learning amongst our countrymen and removing the clouds of darkness and ignorance which were enveloping us and this great country. This noble work will be not only profitable to ourselves and our contemporaries but to the coming generations, our sons and sons' sons. What gives me greater happiness and an occasion to congratulate you is the fact that the inauguration of this School originated from amongst you without outside help and you, of your own accord, and without asking other's help, have started this School with your donations and subscriptions.

After showing what benefits English education was destined to bring to its students, he remarked:—

You will always bear in mind, gentlemen, that Her Most Gracious Majesty, Queen Victoria, has proclaimed (in this country) that her European and Indian subjects are on an equal footing and this assurance is not a mere matter of form but a reality. Those of you who have gone recently to Calcutta will see an Indian Judge, Babu Shamboo Nath, adorning the Bench of the Calcutta High Court. This Indian Judge possesses all those privileges and rights which the English Judges are possessed of.

Further on, in the course of the same address he remarked:—

The admission of Indians to the Supreme Legislative Council is a beginning of the advancement of India. You remember my proposition that the day is not far off when I trust that the Council will be composed of representatives from every Division or District and that the laws will be enacted by you and abided by you also. So ponder well how necessary it is for the people to advance in education and experience. I once had a conversation with a high Official on this very subject, and he said that Government will be only too glad to act upon the scheme as sketched above, but he felt doubtful, if it were stated that there were qualified men in every Division, Government would gladly avail itself of their knowledge and give them seats in Councils. I knew this only too well and felt ashamed that such was the case. The object (of this discourse) is to inculcate on your minds the great fact that Her Gracious Majesty wishes all her subjects to be treated alike, irrespective of their religion, race or colour and has opened the doors for all; the only way to avail ourselves of the great opportunity is to advance ourselves in the arts and sciences.

THE BRITISH INDIAN ASSOCIATION.

He was instrumental in establishing on the 10th May, 1866, the famous "British Indian Association"—which was the fore-runner of the Indian National Congress—with a view to keep the Association in touch with the Members of the House of Commons. The address he delivered on that occasion is a memorable one in the history of Indian politics. After showing the necessity of Indian affairs being more prominently brought before Parliament and of forming an Association for the purpose, he compared British Rule with that of former Emperors and Rajahs of India thus:—

The rule of the former Emperors and Rajahs of India was based upon nothing but tyranny and oppression. The law of might was in force in those days; the strong and turbulent kept the feeble and the poor under their thumb and usurped all their privileges with impunity and force for their own luxury and comfort. It is only therefore by such usurpers and turbulent spirits that a despotism, such as flourished in Hindustan for many long centuries, is at all to be desired.

In the course of the same address, he regretted the indifference with which the affairs of India were treated in Parliament and laid the blame of it to a great extent upon the shoulders of his own countrymen. He was also grieved to see that India looked on Parliament with a dreamy, apathetic eye. He exhorted his countrymen to discontinue their apathy and entreated them to secure the proper representation of their interests in the Imperial Legislature of the British nation. He appealed to them to co-operate with the London Association formed for that purpose. He warned them as follows:—

> You will have only yourselves to reproach when in after years you see the European section of the community enjoying their well-earned concession while your wants remain still unredressed. ... ... I am afraid that you entertain a fear that the Government which protects your lives and properties or the District Officials would esteem you factious and discontented (were you to inaugurate this Association)............. ... .Believe me that it is your folly and cowardice. Your apprehension is unfounded and that there is not an Englishman of liberal turn of mind in India who would regard it with feelings other than those of pleasure and hope.

Regretting that Indians have little or no voice in the management of the affairs of their country, he deplored very much the fact that, whenever any measure of Government proved objectionable and obnoxious to them, they always brooded over it, looking apparently well-satisfied while really discontent rankled in their hearts.

> I may be pardoned if I say that the natives are in the habit of inveighing against such measures in their homes but when they meet the Europeans, they represented that they were satisfied with the justice and wisdom of the measures.

To his mind such a state of affairs was inimical to the welfare of the country. Such associations as the London Association, he was of opinion, should deem it their duty to express their frank and honest opinion as to the justice or otherwise of the acts of Government. One should bear in mind that Sir Syed made this important utterance when he was in Government Service.

He thus educated the people and exhorted them to avail themselves of the means of educating themselves in every way. On the 6th October, 1873, he was invited to Calcutta by Nawab Abdul Lateef, where he delivered an important address before the Mussalmans of Bengal, in Persian, on the benefits of English Education. Here we have the unique example of a man who, though not possessing the advantages of an English education and having never acquired great colloquial facility in that language, yet by extensive reading and culture, eagerly grasping the dire necessity of getting his co-religionists out of the groove of the old orthodox Mahomedan education and making them acquainted with the results of modern science and thought.

HIS VISIT TO ENGLAND (1869-70).

In 1869, the Government of India selected his second son, Mahmood, (Justice) for a state scholarship to proceed to England for his education. Sir Syed had long wished to visit England, with the view of obtaining by personal observation a more thorough insight into the manners and customs, and the religious, educational and political institutions of Europe. He accompanied Mr. Mahmood to England and carefully studied the system of education prevailing in England and determined to introduce it in a suitably modified form in his own country. He wrote descriptive accounts of his voyage to, and his sojourn in England to his old friends, Nawab Mohsin-ul-Mulk and Moulvi Zair-ul-Abedin. He stayed in England for full 17 months and strenuously studied the educational system of the great English Universities. One of his objects in proceeding to England was to collect materials for the publication of a comprehensive rejoinder to Sir William Muir, whose criticism of the Life of the Prophet Mahomed necessitated such a reply. For months he searched the shelves in the Oriental Library of the British Musuem and collected materials for the rejoinder. His renowned "Essays on the Life of Mahomed" were published in the beginning of 1870. They met, particularly among others, the criticism of Sir William Muir by well-reasoned arguments and substantive quotations. It is an open secret that Mr. Mahmood was responsible for the translation of these Essays into English. The work had a very large sale in England and was favourably noticed by the British Press and by European Orientalists. It is now universally recognized as a standard work on the subject.

Sir Syed led a very busy life in England. Every week he had one or two engagements and exchanged visits with his old English friends and the new acquaintances he formed in the British Isles. His enlightened opinions, suavity of manners, dignified bearing and, above all, catholic sympathy attracted much attention. He visited all the important

English and Scottish Universities and minutely examined their working and curriculum of studies. Often he would sit in his rooms brooding over the causes of England's intellectual ascendency and India's backwardness. He made up his mind while in England to establish a Mahomedan residential college on the lines of the Oxford and Cambridge University Colleges which he admired most. The very plans of the College rooms and the various Boarding Houses and the Hostels were sketched by him in England. His son, Mr. Mahmood, was very helpful to him in preparing all the schemes which he put into effect on his return from England.

HIS THREE SCHEMES.

Sir Syed had now become fully convinced that, along with the Persian and Arabic Literatures, which are in truth the pride of Mussalmans, Western arts and sciences should be made popular amongst the Mahomedans of India. Before returning to India he set to work to outline three schemes in connection with Muslim Education in India; *first*, to consider the measures necessary to remove the prejudices of Mahomedans against the study of Western arts and sciences, which, they considered, were the means of making them infidels; *secondly*, to make Mussalmans consider why they were not availing themselves of Western education; and *thirdly*, to collect subscriptions and donations for the establishment of a College at Aligarh, a small town in the United Provinces which he had selected while in London for locating his College.

THE TAHZIBUL AKHLAQ OR SOCIAL REFORMER.

It may not be out of place to mention here that his time in England was fully occupied. He was presented to the late Queen Victoria, and Her Majesty presented him with two copies of Her works with Her royal autograph signature. He received the decoration of the Companionship of the Order of the Star of India at the hands of the Duke of Argyle. The Athenæum Club elected him to be an Honorary Member on its august rolls. He returned to India towards the close of 1870 and began to put into practice the plans he had formed while in England. During his sojourn in England he was greatly struck with the influence of newspapers in England. He at once started a monthly periodical called the *Tahzibul Akhlaq* or *The Social Reformer* in Urdu, which soon revolutionised Muslim India. The *Tahzibul Akhlaq* did for Muslim India what the *Tatler* and the *Spectator* of Steel and Addison had done for the people of England in the early part of the 18th Century. The Journal was edited and published by Sir Syed, assisted by a small committee of his friends. It was started to improve and widen the religious thoughts of Mussalmans and induce them to turn to Western education the attainment of which would bring them to their former prosperity and glory. His idea was to bring about a great reformation in his community. It dealt with religious, socia and educational subjects on which Sir Syed, Mohsin-ul-Mulk, Viqar-ul-Mulk and Moulvi Chirag Ali wrot in a free and courageous spirit. The paper exercised a great influence on the minds of a select but thoughtful body of readers for whom it furnished a variety of intellectual food. The opposition which it created in conservative circles advertised its propaganda far and wide and one can say, with justice, that it succeeded in reforming thousands of Mussalmans, who readily flocked to the banner of rationalism unfurled by Sir Syed. Muslims and Hindus devoured its articles. Verily a new light had appeared on the horizon of Muslim India, beckoning Mahomedans to take heart and march onwards on the path of progress and refinement. It asked Muslims to revivify their character, improve their customs and manners and to aim at national ideals. It tried to remove the false notions of Mussalmans about those matters which had nothing to do with their religion, to refute the charges of the Christians that Islam was antagonistic to science and reform, to show them what causes had led their ancestors to believe in such notions, to make them hate and give up injurious and unwholesome customs, to bring home to their minds the extent and magnitude of their adversity, to purify Mullah-clogged Islam, to revive amongst them the memories of their great ancestors and to enable them rise to their former position. The *Tahzibul Akhlaq* was the great vehicle for spreading his views amongst the masses. His voice was heard, through its pages, throughout the length and breadth of the country, and not only opened the sleepy eyes of his indolent co-religionists but inspired them with new hopes and aspirations, aroused the inactive to activity and infused a new and vigorous life into the dying nation. His was a very ambitious programme but the success that he has attained is the true measure of his greatness.

MAHOMEDAN ANGLO-ORIENTAL COLLEGE.

Finding that the time was now ripe for formulating a scheme for the education of Mussalmans, on Anglo-Oriental lines, he organised an Educational Board, of which he became Secretary, to take this work in hand. Mr. Mahmood drew up the constitution of this Board and published the synopsis of questions put to Mussalmans of light and leading as to the best mode of regenerating their fallen community. A comprehensive report was drawn up by the Board, foreshadowing the establishment of a Central Institution. It clearly pointed out the prejudices entertained by conservative and orthodox Mussalmans as absurd and detrimental to the best interests of the community. It also found that the number of Mussalman students reading in Government Schools and Colleges was infinitesimally small and that most of the causes which conspired to dissuade parents from sending their childern to Government or missionary schools, had a substratum of reason and that State institutions did not fulfil the educational requirements of Mussalmans. It finally brought home the conviction how necessary it was to rescue ancient Mahomedan learning from oblivion, to imbibe the new arts and sciences and to place the work of Mahomedan education into purely Mahomedan hands in view to training Muslim children in the best tradition of Islam.

In 1872, a Committee, by the name of the "Mahomedan Anglo Oriental College Fund Committee," was formed at Benares with a Sub-Committee at Aligarh. On the 10th of February, 1873, the late Mr. Justice Mahmood issued a circular letter addressed to the members of the Committee, submitting a scheme, rich in details, for the creation of a Mohamedan University.

One remarkable thing strikes us in the eventful life of Sir Syed. He was the first Indian who taught us the principle of self-help. When his prophetic vision recognised the needs of his people he did not resign himself to fate or appeal helplessly to Government for aid. He knew that the reforms he aimed at, if they were to be accomplished at all, must be accomplished by the people themselves. With characteristic energy, Sir Syed threw himself heart and soul into the task of raising subscriptions for his College. In less than two years, he collected sufficient funds to establish the M. A. O. School, which was to develop into a Residential College, on the 24th May, 1875, being the auspicious day of our beloved Queen Victoria's birth.

In June, 1876, Sir Syed retired from Government Service and personally looked after the Institution by settling down at Aligarh. Sir John Strachey, then Lieut-Governor of the United Provinces, secured the present site for the Aligarh College. His Excellency Earl Northbrooke took great interest in this Institution and was to have laid the foundation stone of the College, but His Lordship resigned the Viceroyalty shortly afterwards. He was the first big donor, of Rs. 10,000, to the College. On the 8th of January, 1877, Lord Lytton came to Aligarh and laid the foundation stone.

THE PROGRESS OF THE COLLEGE.

In 1878, F. A. Classes were opened; in 1881, B.A., and M.A., Classes were added. The College was at first affiliated to the Allahabad and Calcutta Universities and subsequently to the Allahabad and Punjab Universities. In the beginning of the early eighties there were 50 students in the College Classes and two incomplete Boarding Houses. The Institution now accommodates 1,000 Boarders and has 10 Boarding Houses. Sir Syed was as careful of the morals, breeding and discipline of his pupils as he was of their success in Examination. He insisted that boys should learn to play as well as learn to work and attached great value to games. Football and cricket became very popular. The Aligarh Cricket Team won the distinction of being the champion team after defeating the Patiala, the Parsee and the best English teams in India. It was one of the foremost objects of the College to impart religious instruction along with secular subjects, as he firmly believed that secular education without religious training was "comparatively futile and ineffectual work." He laid it down as an axiom in the working of the College that all the European professors on its staff should live in the very compound of the College and he erected bungalows for their residence.

The history of the College from the time of Lord Lytton's visit onwards, is one unbroken record of steady progress, achieved in the face of gradually diminishing opposition on the part of old conservatism. One who has not been inside the College compound, can hardly form an adequate idea of its structural grandeur and scholastic importance.

Let it be understood that all this was not accomplished at once. It took up not less than 25 years to bring the College to a high pitch of efficiency. Syed Ahmed had to travel throughout the length and breadth of the country at his own expense, exhorting his co-religionists to give pecuniary help to the new institution and creating an interest in Western education. He cheerfully underwent all worries and troubles for its sake. His earnestness succeeded in the long run and money began to pour in.

Before we pass on, we must commend with real pleasure the catholic spirit of the founders of the College in opening its doors to Hindus, Christians and Parsees along with Mussalmans. Unlike the Madras Pachaiyappa's College and the Benares Central Hindu College, the Aligarh College admits students professing different religious beliefs. Except that there is no Temple or Church for non-Mahomedan Boarders, there is every facility and comfort for them at Aligarh.

IN THE LEGISLATIVE COUNCIL (1878 TO 1883).

Lord Lytton, who was Sir Syed's guest at Aligarh in 1877, was much impressed with his personality and vast learning and appointed him a Member of the Imperial Legislative Council in 1878. This was a very happy period of his life, as he realised in his own person the desire expressed in 1858. He was re-appointed in 1881 by Lord Ripon and sat in the Council for 5 years. He was the first Indian who was permitted to introduce private bills, which eventually found place on the Indian Statute-Book. The Vaccination Bill and the Kazi's Act were passed at his initiation; the former in the teeth of opposition by the then Lieut-Governor of Punjab. It was then that he made a memorable speech, every word of which has been rendered true by the events of the next quarter of a century. On the 12th of January, 1883, in the course of a discussion on the Central Provinces Local Self-Government Bill, he objected to the introduction of the principle of election in India. Sir Syed favoured compartmental elections which for good or ill, have been incorporated in the Montagu-Chelmsford Reforms :—

The system of representation by election means the representation of the views and interests of the majority of the population, and, in countries where the population is composed of one race and one creed it is no doubt the best system that can be adopted. But, my Lord, in a country like India, where caste distinctions still flourish, where there is no fusion of the various races, where religious distinctions are still violent, where education in its modern sense has not made an equal or proportionate progress among all the sections of the population, I am convinced that the introduction of the principle of election, pure and simple, for representation of various interests on the Local Boards and District Councils would be attended with evils of greater significance than purely economic considerations. So long as differences of race and creed, and the distinctions of caste form an important element in the socio-political life of India, and influence her inhabitants in matters connected with the administration and welfare of the country at large, the system of election, pure and simple, cannot be safely adopted. The larger community would totally override the interests of the smaller community, and the ignorant public would hold Government responsible for introducing measures which might make the differences of race and creed more violent than ever.

On the occasion of the introduction of the Ilbert Bill, Sir Syed made a vigorous speech in support of that Bill. Sir Syed and Kristo Das Pal were the only non-official members who supported the Bill.

THE EDUCATION COMMISSION

His prominent position among the Educationists of the country induced Lord Ripon to offer him a seat on the famous Commission of 1882, which he gratefully accepted; but hardly had he toured with the Commission in one Province when, owing to a pressing call from Aligarh, he resigned the membership which was offered by Lord Ripon subsequently to his distinguished son, Mr. Justice Mahmood.

HIS TOUR IN THE PUNJAB

In the beginning of 1884 he made a tour in the Punjab for the purpose of collecting funds for his College. In that tour valedictory addresses were showered upon him. Hindus joined Mahomedans in honouring their great leader. Among others, his two speeches at Gurdaspur and Lahore are too important to be passed over without a reference here.

HIS VIEWS ON INDIAN NATIONALITY

In his speech at Gurdaspur on the 27th of January, 1884, he said:—

We (*i.e.*, Hindus and Mahomedans) should try to become one heart and soul and act in unison, if united, we can support each other. If not, the effect of one against the other would tend to the destruction and downfall of both. (Cheers) In old historical books and traditions you will have read and heard, and we see it even now, that all the people inhabiting one country are designated by term one *nation*. The different tribes of Afghanistan are termed one nation, and so are the miscellaneous hordes peopling Iran, distinguished by the term Europeans, though abounding in variety of thoughts and religions, are still known as members of one nation, though people of other countries also do come and settle with them, but being mixed together they are called members of one and the same nation. So that from the oldest times the word nation is applied to the inhabitants of one country, though they differ in some pecularities which are characteristic of their own. Hindu and Mahomedan brethren, do you people any country other than Hindustan? Do you not inhabit the same land? Are you not burned and buried on the same soil? Do you not tread the same ground and live upon the same soil? Remember that the words Hindu and Mahomedan are only meant for religious distinction--otherwise all persons, whether Hindu or Mahomedan even the Christians who reside in this country, are all in this particular respect belonging to one and the same nation. (Cheers.) Then all these different sects can only be described as one nation; they must each and all unite for the good of the country which is common to all.

Again, in a speech at Lahore in reply to the Address of the Indian Association he said:

Even granting that the majority of those composing this Association are Hindus, still I say that this light has been diffused by the same whom I call by the epithet of Bengalees. I assure you that Bengalees are the only people in our country whom we can properly be proud of and it is only due to them that knowledge, liberty and patriotism have progressed in our country. I can truly say that really they are the head and crown of all the different communities of Hindustan. *

I myself was fully cognizant of all those difficulties which obstructed my way, but notwithstanding these I heartily wished to serve my country and my nation faithfully. In the word Nation I include both Hindus and Mahomedans because that is the only meaning which I can attach to it. * * * *

With me it is not so much worth considering what is their religious faith, because we do not see anything of it. What we do see is that we inhabit the same land, are subject to the rule of the same Governors, the fountains of benefits for all are the same, and the pangs of famine also we suffer equally. These are the different grounds upon which, I call both those races which inhabit India by one word, *i.e.*, *Hindu*, meaning to say that they are the inhabitants of Hindustan. While in the Legislative Council I was always anxious for the prosperity of this nation,

THE MAHOMEDAN EDUCATIONAL CONFERENCE.

The M. E. Conference which he founded in 1886 is another important work of Sir Syed Ahmed Khan, which has played an important part in the amelioration of Indian Mussalmans. The scheme of the Conference, as promulgated by him, was to hold an annual deliberative assembly of Mahomedans from all parts of India, exclusively devoted to discussing the problems of Mahomedan education. Owing to want of uniformity of action, the energies of workers in the cause of Muslim Education were much frittered away. Provincial leaders of different Provinces in India worked according to their own lights, but they had no settled programme for their guidance. The main object of the Conference was to bring such men together and to decide upon a uniform educational programme.

The Conference has done immense good to the community because, wherever its Sessions have been held, a change for the better has crept over the people

3

of that Province. In short, the Conference has delivered the intellectual message of Aligarh to the remotest corners of the Empire.

THE PUBLIC SERVICE COMMISSION.

In 1887 Lord Dufferin appointed Sir Syed a Member of the Public Service Commission and he was able to do very useful service to his country. He vigorously advocated the retention of the Statutory Civil Service whereby Indians, without being appointed to the Civil Service Commission in England might aspire to rise to the highest posts in India.

HE OPPOSES THE NATIONAL CONGRESS.

The year 1887 marks that decisive turn in the public career of Sir Syed which gave a wholly new trend to Muslim thought. It may not be out of place to mention here that in May, 1884, when Babu Surendranath Bannerjee was touring in Upper India in connection with the Memorial to the House of Commons to raise the age of the Civil Service candidates from 19 to 21, Sir Syed presided at the Aligarh meeting and paid a high tribute to the disinterested services of Babu Surendranath. In 1885, the Indian National Congress was established and attracted to itself a good deal of public attention. Sir Syed however refrained from joining the movement and in a speech at the Mahomedan Educational Conference in Dec. 1887 dissuaded his community from participating in it. He preferred a more respectful tone towards the Government than the congress was disposed to adopt in its protests against bureaucratic actions.

Towards the end of his life, Sir Syed felt the justice of the Congress demands. He realised with bitterness the disadvantageous position of his countrymen in the councils of the Government and went so far as to despair of equality of treatment between the "conquerors" and the "conquered", even in the distant future. He wrote in connection with the forced retirement of his son, Justice Mahmood :—

"In my opinion the time has not come yet, and perhaps will never come, when our European friends, conquerors of this country, and naturally full of pride of their conquest, will condescend to sit on the same Bench with a conquered and naturally hated Indian, who is desirous of performing his duties with equal honour and respect requisite to his high position. If the Indian wants to keep up his self-respect as an honest and well-bred gentleman, his life becomes unbearable. On the contrary, if he yields to his European colleague who, on account of his being a member of the conquering race, regards himself as an altogether superior person, or if he acts on certain directions he can be happy. But if an Indian desires to obey the dictates of his conscience, and if there is even a little blood of his ancestors in his veins then he cannot perform his duties. It is no secret that the treatment which English people accord to their own countrymen and that which they accord to the Indians are as different from one another as black is from white. People might brag and contend that it was otherwise, but the wise alone know the whole truth of the matter."

SOCIAL REFORM.

Sir Syed held very liberal views on social questions. He was in favour of reforming many a ceremony, provided it was cautiously and peacefully done, and one of the main reasons why he valued English education was that it would open men's eyes to the social evils which existed. He earnestly believed that it was high time for Mussalmans to set on foot systematic social reform. He believed that it should proceed without affecting Islam. He always remarked that it was their own fault that Mahomedans allowed religion to enter into every social matter. He wisely discriminated between religion and society. He showed great moral courage in breaking the barriers of hollow customs which did not permit interdining between Mussalmans and Englishmen. As early as 1866, he had received interrogatories from a Moulvi asking him whether it was permissible for Mussalmans to dine with Englishmen at the same table if there be no forbidden dishes. He replied in the affirmative, strengthening his position by quoting verses from the Koran and reliable traditions. Later on he wrote a booklet on the same subject and practised what he preached. He mixed in English society very intimately. Englishmen dined at his table and he accepted their hospitality on condition that no wines and forbidden dishes would be served. This act of Sir Syed enraged the Ulema party, who excommunicated him and sent special messengers to Mecca to get *futwahs* of *Kufr* (infidelity). He was earnestly anxious that Muslim girls should be brought up and educated in a proper manner. But any scheme contemplating the education of girls through the medium of public schools was with him as yet premature. He was of opinion that the current system of home education which prevailed in the educated society of the North, was beneficial to the community in that stage. He was an advocate of female education on the lines of least resistance and condemned *the Anglicising* of Muslim girls. He went so far as to say that mixed marriages were a curse to the country.

In 1889, he was decorated with the K. C. S. I.

CONCLUSION.

Sir Syed was the foremost Indian Mahomedan of the nineteenth century as regards force of character, influence over his co-religionists and literary ability. His patriotism and intellectual gifts were of a high order. He was a man of marked suavity of manners and of catholic sympathies. The Mahomedan Anglo-Oriental College will for ever stand out as the greatest monument of his educational activities. Throughout the length and breadth of the country, he was recognised by Mussalmans as a towering personality and a power and influence for good.

Himself uneducated in English, he became one of the greatest promoters of English education in India. Through it, he wished to raise his co-religionists to a position of social efficiency, moral and spiritual greatness and political power.

He died on 28th March, 1898, full of honours and was buried in the Mosque of the College. Mr. Theodore Morison, in one of his addresses delivered on Founder's Day in the Aligarh College, spoke of Sir Syed as a hero-prophet; but to our mind his mission in this mortal world was that of a hero-reformer, for, his mission was to elevate and ennoble his co-religionists.

SIR SALAR JUNG.

INTRODUCTORY.

FORTY years have gone by since Sir Salar Jung, who made the state of Hydrabad what it is today died at the very zenith of his influence and popularity. Since then there have been several changes in the Ministry at the Nizam's Court: but public opinion, as to the genius and statesmanship of Sir Salar Jung, has neither wavered, nor diminished in its fervour and enthusiasm. Some critics have extolled him as "the Saviour of India." One European administrator considers that as a man of business especially in Finance, Sir Salar Jung has not been surpassed by any native of India. Another declares that India is not likely to produce two such men as Sir Salar Jung and Sir T. Madhava Row more than once in two or three centuries. While a third shrewdly remarks that Sir Salar Jung by his diplomatic and statesmanlike skill became one of the foremost administrators in India, and by his noble endeavours contributed to the prosperity of Hyderabad.

HIS FORBEARS.

Since the last days of the Bahmini Kingdom, the family to which Sir Salar Jung belonged had taken a leading part in the affairs of the Deccan. Their loyalty first to the Adil Shahis, then to the Moghul

Emperors, and lastly to the Nizams, was as unflinching as it was sincere and true. The ancestors of Salar Jung belonged to a noble family of Medina. Shaikh Ovais Karani was the first of the line to leave his native country and settle in India. His son held high and responsible offices in the Bijapur Court. It was the time when the Moghul Emperors were forcing their way to the Deccan; the Shaikh's grandson offered his services to the Emperor of Delhi, who appointed him to the Dewani of Shajahanabad and Kashmir. His son, Mohamed Taki, was the first representative of the family to come in contact with Asaf Jah Nizam-ul-Mulk who, at the dissolution of the Moghul Empire, was trying to found a kingdom for himself in the south. Mohammed Taki's son, Shamsuddin, was a great favourite of the first Nizam; his command was in the time of Nizam Salabat Jung increased to 7,000 foot and 7,000 horse with the title of Nawab Munir-ul-Mulk. He was subsequently made the Dewan for the Subahs of the Deccan. Shamsuddin's grandson, Munir-ul-Mulk II married the daughter of Mir Alum, who was the Prime Minister to Nizam Sikandar Jah from 1804 to 1808, and who led the Hyderabad contingent forces to Seringapatam in 1799. On Mir Alum's death in 1808, Munir-ul-Mulk II became the Prime Minister, and held office for 23 years. He had two sons, of whom the elder was Sir Jalar Jung's father; the younger son, Seraj-ul-Mulk, was Prime Minister of Hyderabad from 1851 to 1853. And when he died,

Salar Jung was elevated to the position held by many of his ancestors in Hyderabad at the early age of 24.

EARLY LIFE.

Nawab Mir Turab Ali Khan, Salar Jung, Siraj-ud-Dowla, Mukhtar-ul-Mulk, D.C.L., G.C.S.I., (to give him his full name and titles) was born on the 2nd January 1829. While an infant he lost his father, and when four years old his grandfather, Munir-ul-Mulk II, died leaving the boy in sole charge of his second son, Seraj-ul-Mulk. There is a story related which shows the great affection which Munir-ul-Mulk II had towards young Salar Jung. The latter had an attack typhoid fever, and for many days his condition was considered to be critical. Thereupon his grandfather, like Baber of old, performed the ceremony which is known among Mussalmans as Tassaduk, and prayed that any evil which might befall the child might be transferred to him, and that if it was the will of God that Salar Jung should die, be prayed that his own life might be taken. Strange to say the boy recovered and the grandfather fell ill and died. The guardianship of the boy therefore fell on his uncle, Seraj-ul-Mulk.

Salar Jung's education till he was thirteen was not regular and continuous. His early training can scarcely be said to have made him fit for the high and responsible position which he was called upon to fill in after life. He was weak, and the pecuniary and other troubles of his family apparently obscured all his future hopes. His grandfather, Munir-ul-Mulk

II had left debts to the extent of 25 lakhs and the then Nizam, H. H. Nasir-ud-Dowla, paid off the debts of his Minister, and took possession of the greater portion of the family estates as security. However Seraj-ul-Mulk cheerfully performed the trust confided to him and gave his nephew such education as was thought fit for a scion of a noble family at Hyderabad. Salar Jung read Persian and Arabic under a private tutor for nearly seven years. The teaching of English was not then in vogue at Hyderabad; and Salar Jung began to learn this languge when he was 19 years. He worked at it for half an hour every day under an Eurasian private teacher, later on he pursued the study so assiduously till he came to know English as well as his mother-tongue. Towards the end of his life he became a good English speaker, and the testimony borne by Sir Monier Williams is well worth repeating here:—"I conversed with both these great Ministers (Sir Salar Jung and Sir T. Madhava Row) not long since in their own houses and found them capable of talking on all subjects in as good English as my own."

As a boy Salar Jung was fond of riding, and had had many narrow escapes. His uncle had a pet giraffe, and it was Salar Jung's delight to bestride it to the great astonishment of his awe-struck attendants. From his early days, Salar Jung imbued business habits of a very high degree through the exertions of his grandmother. The accounts which the old lady received from her Jaghir villages were sent to Salar Jung, and he had to verify them with the help of the clerks and explain everything in detail to his grandmother—a task which young Salar found by no means easy.

In 1847, Salar Jung was appointed as the Taluqdar (Collector) of some Telingana Districts, which till then were managed by an Englishman named Mr. Deighton. He was thus early brought into contact with the administration of the State, and he found no difficulty in mastering the system of land revenue introduced by his predecessor, and worked it out satisfactorily during the eight months he was in office. By this time the Nizam restored some of the family Jaghirs to Seraj-ul-Mulk, who lost no time to appoint Salar Jung for looking after them. For five years he worked hard to improve the condition of his estates while at the same time to increase their revenue. When in independent charge of his family Jaghirs, he moulded and shaped the high administrative capacity, which he showed in such unmistakable manner in after life.

PRIME MINISTER.

Seraj-ul-Mulk died on 26th April 1853, and as is usual in the then Hyderabad affairs, a political *impasse* intervened. The choice of a Minister became a matter of perplexity to the Nizam. Of the available candidates, the one whom the Nizam least favoured was Salar Jung. The latter was only 24 years old, and he was the nephew of the Minister who negotiated and concluded the treaty by which Berar was transferred to the English control. Salar Jung's candidature was however supported by Lala Bahadur (the State Record-Keeper) and two other favourites of the Nizam. "It is not a Minister," they said to the Nizam, "but your prestige that governs. Siraj-ul-Mulk conducted the administration through the subordinate departments. Lala Bahadur, who did every thing, will as before conduct the affairs of the administration for Salar Jung." Such arguments did not miss the mark, and the favourites won the day. Salar Jung was invested with the office of Minister in full Durbar on the 31st of May 1853. How well Salar Jung knew the difficulties of his new position is seen from the following extract from a letter to a friend of his in England on his accession to power:—

> Without any solicitation on my part or my grandmother's His Highness was pleased to confer the office of Dewan on me at the Durbar the day before yesterday (31st May). I should have been quite content to remain in unmolested possession of my uncle's Jaghirs were it possible without the cares which such an office would impose upon me, especially in the present critical state of affairs here, and I was advised by friends, European and Native, and with too much appearance of truth to reject the advice, that if I declined the office, myself and family would be utterly ruined . . . I shall therefore do my best with God's help to restore some order in the affairs of this country, and endeavour to extricate the government from its embarrassments.

The country was indeed in a deplorable state. The preceding ten years were marked by a series of administrative and financial adversities. Salar Jung's predecessor left a heritage which no statesman could envy. The administrative capacity of the man was put to the greatest test, and it may be affirmed that the new Minister successfully tided over the strain and worry attendant on those who bring order out of utter confusion.

Since his accession to power up to the outbreak of the Sepoy Mutiny in 1857, he found means to introduce many reforms in the State, and this made him very unpopular with those who counted that his youth would be a safeguard for their own private aggrandizement. The very first to quarrel with the young Minister was Lala Bahadur who, experienced as he was in Hyderabad affairs, tried his best to oust him from office. Again and again the prospect of dismissal seemed imminent: but the Nizam had no other subject as capable, upright, and loyal as Salar Jung. As Mr. Sorabji Jehangir has pointed out in his *Representative Men of India:*

> Sir Salar Jung had to wage amidst unparalleled difficulties, prolonged and at times disheartening battles with abuses which had grown hoary with age and whose dimensions were in proportion to the extent of the unwiedly state in which they existed, demanding all the resources of a superior and acute intellect, a conciliatory but firm disposition, administrative prudence and foresight of the highest order. and an intimate acquaintance with human nature, Sir Salar Jung was endowed with these attributes in such a marked degree as to stamp him as an Indian statesman of the highest eminence.

Nor were opportunities for the exercise of his statesmanship wanting.

THE SEPOY MUTINY, 1857.

For in May 1857, the great Sepoy Mutiny broke out near Delhi, and all Mussalmans in Southern India turned their eyes towards the Nizam's capital. The rebellion spread like wild fire in the North. Hyderabad filled with a large population who had only recently been brought under one settled government, and who cherished the memory of the great Imperial House of Baber, was showing its sympathy with the Sepoys, who espoused the cause of the Moghul Emperor at Delhi. Wildest rumours of the dire peril, to which the British were exposed in Hindustan having reached Hyderabad from the north, the city Mohammedans were plunged in a state of intense excitement. Some openly manifested their displeasure to the British Government. The city people assembled in large numbers in the streets clamouring for war against the English.

At such a critical moment the Nizam Nasir-ud-Dowla died; and great fears were therefore entertained in responsible quarters regarding the issue of events at Hyderabad. Salar Jung was then only four years in office, and he so well gauged the situation that he firmly and persistently adhered himself to the definite policy of seeing that Hyderabad did not join in the general revolt, and thus extend the disaffected area far down to the south. He was a Mohammedan and serving a Mohammedan State: to him it was "a trial, the tension and force of which could never be understood by a European and a Christian."

A new Nizam was placed on the Masnad without any loss of time; and the Resident on returning from the installation ceremony found a telegram from the Governor-General announcing the fall of Delhi. He sent for Salar Jung at once, and communicated the news to him. The Minister replied that the news had been known in the city three days ago. To many unacquainted with British resources, the fall of Delhi was synonymous with the destruction of the British *Raj* in India. If Salar Jung had ever wanted to be disloyal to the British Government, he had the best opportunity of disclosing his motive when information reached him about the success of the mutineers at Delhi. What would have been the fate of the British officers assembled in the Nizam's palace on the Durbar day if Salar Jung had only given any sign to show that he sympathised with the mutineers!

The Minister, however, could not keep in check the excited mob in the city. On June 12th, there were found posted on the walls of all conspicuous places, placards with incitements to sedition signed by orthodox Moulvies calling upon the Faithful to be ready to fight against the English. The next day a coloured flag was hoisted at the chief Mosque of the city, and the excited people mostly of the lower orders gathered round it. Two men tried to make a stir by interrupting the preacher, and shouting out: "Why do you not preach the rising of the holy standard?" upon which the cries of "Deen," "Deen" (for the Faith) were heard, and it had no response as the respectable people held aloof from such a scene. The Moulvie was arrested, and the crowds were dispersed by the Minister's orders. A fakir, while openly preaching a Jihad against the English, was promptly arrested and placed in confinement with the aid of a few faithful Arabs, who maintained order in the city, and strict instructions were issued to the guards at the city gate to fire on anyone who attempted to incite the people against the English. "These energeitc measures," says a military officer, "saved South India, for had the people at Hyderabad risen against us, the Mohammedan population of Madras would, it was well-known at the Residency, have followed their example."

The situation was so critical that the Governor of Bombay telegraphed to the Resident at Hyderabad: "If the Nizam goes, all is lost." There was certainly a panic in the above message, but Englishmen in India felt a keen sense of relief when it was found that the Nizam did not and would not go. "Had the Nizam," says Colonel Briggs, "untried as he then was, sided the movement or even openly avowed his sympathy with the mutineers, there can be no doubt that the whole of Southern India would have been in a blaze." But wiser counsels prevailed at the Nizam's Durbar, and Salar Jung's statesmanship saved the situation.

The British Residency at Hyderabad is situated very near the busy quarter of the city and is far removed from the cantonment of Secunderabad. A body of 500 Rohillas with 4,000 disaffected people led by two leaders, Torabazkhan, and Allauddin, marched and attacked the Residency, which was not then protected by any fortifications. The Minister knew of the projected attack, and gave a timely warning to the Resident, Colonel Davidson, who at once ordered for some reinforcements from Secunderabad. On their arrival, they were joined by a party of Arabs sent by Salar Jung. These troops repulsed the mutineers' attack: one of the leaders was shot dead, and several others taken prisoners and deported. Some of the ringleaders were executed, and others fled to Hyderabad with the hope that the Nizam's government would protect them. But the Minister issued orders to hand over the mutineers to the Resident for necessary punishment. A large concourse of people assembled at the chief Mosque with a view to send a deputation of some Moulvies to the Nizam to expound the duties of a Mussalman Sovereign, and persuade him to order the release of all the sepoys who had been imprisoned for attacking the Residency. But it was soon dispersed; a mob collected near the Residency, and broke open two of its gates. Before further injury could be done, fire was opened on them and they were driven away.

Much criticism was levelled against the Resident, Colonel Davidson, for his continued occupation of the Residency in these critical times. But like a true Englishman he said: "I have taken a fancy to lay my bones at Hyderabad. If open force be used I will fight to the last." Besides he added that the non-occupation of the Residency at that time "would have been looked upon as a sign of fear, and the loyal Minister, Salar Jung, would have been left to his fate." But many years after the mutiny, Salar Jung said with characteristic modesty that, but

P. 49.

SIR SALAR JUNG

for the courage and hope given by the Residency Officers, he would not have triumphed over the crisis so successfully.

I have often been complimented as the Saviour of India, he wrote, "but if I was able to be of any use to my Sovereign, and to Her Majesty's Empire in India, the credit of it is entirely due to General Thornhill. Had not General Thornhill been at Hyderabad, I tremble to think what might have become of the Nizam, of the Residency, and of myself. Colonel Davidson was an excellent man and was in every way fitted for the high position he held; but the magnitude of the emergency had taken him so completely by surprise that had it not been for the strong will and stout heart of General Thornhill, he would never in my opinion have tided over the troubles. As for myself, it was entirely General Thornhill's constant counsel and support that kept up my courage and enabled me finally to triumph over the disaffection with which the whole city seemed to be enveloped to an extent which few British officers have any conception of. Next to General Thornhill, though not to be compared with him in point of importance, were the services of General Briggs. His strong arm and undaunted courage were of the greatest service in saving the Residency when it was attacked by the mutinous rabble. I never felt so discouraged in my life as when I saw the services of these two officers passed over without notice.

Sir Richard Temple characterised his services to the British Government on this occasion as "simply priceless." The Governor-General in Council informed him that "the ability, courage, and firmness with which he had discharged his duty to the Nizam and to the British Government entitled him to the most cordial thanks of the Government of India."

In July 1860, the Nizam was presented with British manufactures valued at a lakh of rupees, and his minister articles worth thirty thousand. The districts of Raichur and Dharaseo were restored to the Nizam, and the petty State of Shorapur was added to the Nizam's territory.

INTRIGUES AGAINST HIM.

The attitude which Sir Salar Jung wisely followed during the Mutiny brought on him much unpopularity. A determined attack on his life was made on March 15th, 1859, when he was leaving the Nizam's Durbar Hall with the Resident. A Rohilla, said to have been from Hindustan, discharged a loaded carbine which, though missing the mark, hit one of the Minister's retinue. The assailant then rushed on the Minister with a drawn sword; but fortunately he was overpowered by the Nizam's guards who cut him down immediately.

Salar Jung's passion for reforms in the administration of the State was well-known. But Hyderabadees were slow to recognise it: he grew more and more unpopular with them. In 1861, an attempt was made to remove him from office. The Nizam was made to believe that the Resident was anxious to dismiss Salar Jung. The Nizam in an interview with the Resident made him understand that he would gladly dismiss the Minister. The Resident was surprised to hear the proposal, and dissuaded the Nizam from entertaining any such idea. The conspiracy against Salar Jung was exposed, and the Minister was once again in the good graces of his master. It is said that the Nizam's harem contributed not a little to this change of attitude between His Highness and his Minister. These ladies were, since Salar Jung was made Minister, getting their pensions and allowances regularly—a fact of very rare occurrence in the administrations of the previous Ministers. They in a body petitioned to His Highness pointing out how successful Salar Jung had been as a Minister and threatened in the event of a change some violence to his successor. That Salar Jung had been restored to confidence was evidenced by the presentation of some fine jewels to him by the Nizam at the Ead Durbar; and when the Minister had a fall from his horse, the Nizam was so glad of his recovery that he caused a large some of money to be given away to the poor as a thanks-offering.

In 1866, Her Majesty Queen Victoria conferred upon him the title of the Knight Commander of the Star of India. A year later, once again the relations between the Nizam and his Minister were strained. The Government of India proposed a treaty for the mutual extradition of certain criminals. The Nizam suspected that it was an encroachment on his power, and believed that the Minister was responsible for it. He made no secret of his dissatisfaction with him. At this time one of the two officials whose business it was to act as confidential Vakil between the Nizam and his Minister died. His Highness lost no time in appointing Laskar Jung, a bitter personal enemy of the Minister, to the post. Salar Jung resigned: and the Resident, Sir George Yule, sought an interview with the Nizam, who was much perturbed at what he called his Minister's pride. The Minister threatened to resign more than once, and this His Highness could not stand. He wished that Salar Jung had been more humble and acted as his servant. Salar Jung being persuaded to apologise in a most humble way did so, much to the gratification of his Highness who permitted him to continue in office.

Salar Jung had to clear his course in "the face of a permanent opposition offered by jealous and powerful enemies, and of the most vexatious and senseless interference on the part of his sovereign." "He was kept by the Nizam," writes Sir Richard Temple,

> in a state of thraldom and was almost a prisoner in his own house, unable to move beyond the outer gates of his court-yard without his master's permission. If he wished to give a social entertainment in his summer house outside the city, or attend a parade of British troops, or have an interview with the Resident, he must ask leave, not as a mere formality, but as a request that might be refused or which would be grudgingly granted. I had much business with him, and its transaction was difficult, because to have seen him often would have renewed the Nizam's jealousy, and to have sent him papers in despatch boxes would have been open to the same objection. He did not seem to regard this in the light of a personal grievance as he shared the reverence his countrymen felt for their master. He was seldom admitted to the Nizam's presence, and when he was, he used to be almost pale from agitation. He must have been quite hopeless of conciliating his master, yet he was perfectly loyal, and would have undergone any labour for the welfare of his liege.

In January 1868, another attempt was made on the Minister's life while he was proceeding to the Nizam's palace to attend the Ead Durbar. Two shots were fired at him—one of which went so close as to graze his turban, and the other wounded an attendant. The Nizam warmly congratulated his Minister on his escape, and issued strict orders regulating the possession of firearms by the people.

The would-be assassin proved to be one who had been prejudiced by Salar Jung's administrative measures.

VISIT TO EUROPE.

In 1875, His Royal Highness the Prince of Wales (afterwards King Edward VII) came to India: and among the nobles that formed his suite was the Duke of Sutherland. The Duke paid a visit to Hyderabad as the guest of Sir Salar Jung. When leaving he pressed the great Minister to visit England Salar Jung accepted the invitation and visited Europe in the summer of 1876. He could not have been quite ignorant of the sort of reception he would meet in England. People would not forget his invaluable services during the Mutiny: his administrative ability and statesmanship were wafted across to distant lands: and his kind and genial personality made him an acceptable friend to many an Englishman.

Lord Lytton, who had succeeded Lord Northbrook as Viceroy of India, landed in Bombay on the 7th April 1876. Salar Jung was present at his reception at the Bombay Dockyards. The next day he sailed for Europe, reaching Rome on the 5th of May. Sir Salar paid a visit to the late King, Victor Emmanuel, at the Quirinal. Three days later, the Pope received him in audience at the Vatican and expressed his gratitude for the facilities allowed to Catholics in the Hyderabad State. After visiting Rome, Naples, and some of the other chief cities of Italy, the party reached Paris on the 13th of May.

Here, Sir Salar was detained for nearly a fortnight owing to an unpleasant accident. On the very evening of his arrival at the Grand Hotel, he slipped on the stairs which resulted in a fractured thigh bone. He suffered great bodily pain not to speak of the vexation of an enforced stay in his rooms, but in spite of it he persevered, says a visitor to him,

> with the equanimity and resignation characteristic of men of his stamp, nationality and faith; but the frustration of his plans would have affected the nerves of any other man . . . Nothing however in Sir Salar Jung's countenance betrayed either pain or anxiety of any kind. Since Sir Salar Jung has kept to his room, none of his attendants (and they were 52) has gone outside the Hotel—not that they are indifferent to sight-seeing, for at Naples, Rome, and Venice they went to look at everything in spite of the crowds which followed and incommoded them. One of them told me that since Sir Salar Jung's arrival in Paris, he has been receiving 20 letters a day in French and English making the strangest applications. Some beg for alms giving a long narrative of more or less voracious misfortunes; others offer all sorts of inventions, merchandise, articles of luxury and fancy; others again ask for an interview; others forward gushing verses expressing regret at his accident; others offer him amusements and recreations of all kinds; not to speak of tailors, shirt-makers, hatters, and shoemakers who not satisfied with writing are constantly stepping into the corridors forcing their cards, prospectuses and samples into the hands, the pockets and almost the turbans of the servants they encounter. Their recital much amused Sir Salar Jung, who however exhibited great satisfaction when informed that this was a Parisian persecution from which he would be free in London. He appears impatient to arrive there, and listens with great interest when the conversation turns upon London or England.

By the end of May he recovered so far as to travel and on 1st June 1876, he left Paris for England and landed at Folkestone, where the Duke of Sutherland was the first to welcome him to the English shores. Sir Salar who was still unable to walk was carried ashore by a party of English sailors, and the Mayor of Folkestone read an Address of Welcome. From that day till he left England invitations, honours and addresses poured thick on him: and the English Press kept up a never-ending chorus of praise of the worth of the great Indian on a visit to England. One of the leading London journals remarked:—

> Our new guest is the man who, when Delhi had fallen, and our power was for a moment in the balance, saved Southern India for England. Even if Southern India had revolted it is possible that by profuse expenditure of men and money we might have conquered it back again, and all the rest of India as well. But, Sir Salar Jung spared us the expenditure of countless lives, and countless millions; and if there was a clear occasion for acknowledging in a fitting manner an inestimable service, such an occasion is presented by the arrival in England of the Prime Minister of the Nizam.

But his stay was made less pleasant owing to the unfortunate accident at Paris, and while confined to his rooms at London, he was visited by the Prince of Wales (King Edward VII), and other members of the Royal Family. On June 20th, the Prince of Wales gave a banquet in Salar Jung's honour when the leading noblemen, statesmen, and old Indian officials were invited to meet him. Next day he went over to Oxford, where the honorary degree of D. C. L. was conferred upon him by the University. On July 3rd, Sir Salar Jung was presented to H. M. Queen Victoria by the Marquis of Salisbury at the Windsor Castle, where he dined with the Queen and other members of the Royal Family. He spent the next day in visiting the Woolwich Arsenal and the

London Docks. On 5th July Sir Salar Jung and his suite attended the State Ball at the Buckingham Palace, and the next day the Marquis of Salisbury (the then Secretary of State for India) entertained him at dinner. Later on Sir Salar had the honour of giving a dinner party at his temporary residence in Piccadilly to H. R. H. the Prince of Wales. Before Sir Salar Jung left London for Trentham, the East India Association presented him with an address recounting his services during the Mutiny and expressing satisfaction at the way in which the various reforms were introduced by him in the Nizam's State. After spending a pleasant week at Trentham Hall with the Duke of Sutherland, Sir Salar Jung travelled over to Scotland, where he received deputations from the Town Councils of Inverness, Dingwall, Tain and Wick. Later on he went to Edinburgh where he and his party drove through the streets seeing all the places of interest in that ancient city.

He returned to London on the 22nd and three days later a special meeting of the Court of Common Council was held at the Guildhall to present Sir Salar Jung with the Freedom of the City of London. The Lord Mayor proposed the toast of Sir Salar Jung and eulogised his services to the Nizam and the English. On July 26th, Sir Salar received deputations from the Manchester Corporation and the Manchester Chamber of Commerce, and owing to ill health had to decline invitations to visit Liverpool and Manchester. His tour in England was like a triumphal march and as one writer says:

> He was entertained by the highest in the land, and yet his success does not seem to turn his head in any way. The house he hired for the occasion, his servants and the whole establishment have been kept up on an almost princely scale but without the slightest ostentation or attempt at vulgar show. His manner is so like that of a well-bred English gentleman that many people cannot understand how or where a native of India who has never been in England seems to have picked up what seems to have been a kind of second nature with Sir Salar.

Salar Jung after a stay of two months in England left London for Paris on his return journey. He was much struck with the marvels of the French capital: but the severe aspect, and the incessant activity of London (as contrasted with the pleasures of Paris) appealed to his imagination.

Leaving Paris on the 3rd August, Sir Salar visited Turin and Milan and took the steamer to India from Brindisi, and arrived at Bombay after an absence of nearly four months. He was not quite recovered from the effects of his accident, and so he was helped over the side of the steamer, when the crew and the passengers cheered him to their utmost capacity. How much the English sailors of the day knew and appreciated Sir Salar is evidenced by the following incident: the steamer conveying Salar Jung and his suite passed a troopship. As soon as the soldiers and sailors knew who was on board they swarmed on to the deck and into the rigging and "three cheers for Salar Jung, the Saviour of India" was the cry followed by such enthusiastic hurrahs which took a long time to subside.

He arrived at Hyderabad on the 26th of August, and was received with the liveliest demonstrations of affection by all classes of people.

THE BERAR QUESTION

H. H. The Nizam Afzul-ud-Dowlah died on the 26th February 1869, and his son Mahbub Ali Khan aged about three years, was placed on the Masnad. Salar Jung and Shams-ul-Umarah—the premier noblemen of the State—were made co-Regents during the minority of the Nizam, and there seemed every prospect of a smooth sailing in the State's progress towards administrative efficiency. But Sir Salar's attitude towards the Berar question brought him in conflict with more than one Viceroy. He fostered so passionate a desire for the restoration of Berar to the Nizam that he expressed his object in a letter to Lord Northbrook:—"Either I must recover Berar or I must be convinced of the justice of the reasons for withholding it or—I must die." Berar had been nominally in the Nizam's possession since 1724, and the dimensions of the province were repeatedly curtailed by grants to the Peshwas of Poona, who laterly were even empowered to collect taxes from the people. Since 1804, the Nizam had the sole authority over the country, but owing to its unsettled state it remained the rendezvous of the lawless. It had dwindled with every political change till in the middle of the last century it was not the Berar of the early Nizams, far less the Imperial Subah of that name. In 1853, upwards of 45 lakhs of rupees became due to the British Government for the maintenance of the Hyderabad contingent. Lord Dalhousie, the then Governor-General, instructed the Resident to ask the Nizam territorial guarantee for the regular payment of the contingent charges, and the liquidation of the debt. After much negotiations a treaty was drawn up, by which districts yielding an annual gross revenue of 50 lakhs were assigned to the British. These included Berar, the Raichur Doab and Dharaseo district. The treaty was signed on the 21st April 1853; and two weeks later Salar Jung was appointed Prime Minister. Ever since he was not at ease over this subject and had two motives to guide him. "The solemn injunctions of his two last sovereigns," says a writer, "had made it a duty of the most sacred obligation upon him to seek its accomplishment. The assignment which was effected in the last hours of his uncle (Nawab Seraj-ul-Mulk) had left a reproach on his family in the eyes both of the sovereign and the people of the country."

In 1866, the Minister addressed a communication to the British Government on behalf of the Nizam claiming the restoration of Berar. The request was not complied with, and Salar Jung was told that "the spirit of extravagant assertion which pervades Sir Salar Jung's letter, unworthy alike of his princely master's dignity and of his own reputation for enlightened statesmanship, leaves the Governor-General in Council no alternative but to require that the future communications of the Hyderabad Durbar shall be framed in a tone more serious and circumspect." There was still hope, and it was based on the statement of the Government of India that the restitution of Berar must remain an impossibility so long as satisfactory arrangements were not made for the regular payment of the Hyderabad contingent from some other source. When the Minister had effected many administrative reforms in the State, he was able to point out "a source" to the British. In 1872, Salar Jung offered to deposit with the Government of India in lieu of Berar, the sum of 12 crores of rupees, the interest on which would be sufficient to meet the cost of the contingent. The Minister noted that this scheme will not only furnish a proper security but also be a deposit of His Highness' treasure, which would enable the Government to carry on some public works out of that source, and also reduce the cost of management. The Government of India were unable to entertain such a proposal since "a territorial guarantee was the fundamental principle of the treaties of 1853 and 1860." After much correspondence, Salar Jung was informed that the Resident would not receive for transmission any correspondence on the subject in future. Whereupon the Regents forwarded an appeal direct to the Secretary of State for India. While in England it is said that Salar Jung influenced a number of British politicians to recognise the justice of his claim. The Secretary of State (Lord Salisbury) affirmed that Berar was not ceded to the British, and that the Nizam's sovereignty over the assigned districts remained unimpaired. His despatch to the Viceroy concluded as follows :—

> Your Excellency has noticed the inconvenience of discussing questions of this kind while the Nizam, on whose behalf they are professedly raised, is himself a minor. In this opinion I entirely concur.

Early in 1877, the co-Regents declared in writing that "they fully accepted the decision of the Secretary of State as conveyed in the above despatch, and would take no steps whatever in the matter during the minority of "His Highness." But Salar Jung was not spared till the young Nizam Mahbub Ali Khan came of age and assumed the reins of government. The subject was therefore shelved till it was re-opened in 1902 by Lord Curzon, when by a new treaty Berar was ceded in perpetuity to the British Government on the latter paying to the Nizam 25 lakhs of rupees per annum.

HIS REFORMS

To sketch the reforms introduced by Sir Salar Jung in the State, is to describe the history of Hyderabad for nearly thirty years. The State at the time of his accession to power had been compared to the England of the Stuarts. The Revenue Administration was in the most deplorable state and the accounts showed a sum of only 18 lakhs of rupees as the net revenue available to the government after paying the troops in the State service. The collection of revenue was carried on what was known as the contract system. The territory was parcelled out for a certain period among contractors called Taluqdars, who were paid at a definite rate for the cost of management. Their sole aim was to make as much money as possible when in power, and therefore much oppression and mismanagement prevailed. Besides certain districts where in the hands of Arabs who had advanced money to the State, and who were empowered to collect the revenue of those districts in repayment of the loans made.

Sir Salar Jung's attentions was first drawn to the maladministration of the Revenue Department. A court was established to adjudicate the claims of the Arabs: and all turbulent men were arrested and punished either by deportation or imprisonment by the Arab *Zamindars*, whose support was an asset to the youthful Minister. As much of the debts as the finances of the State could allow were disbursed to the creditors. By 1854, Salar Jung was able to recover mortgaged lands yielding a revenue of 40 lakhs, and to disband nearly 4,000 Arabs and Pathans from the State service. The old Taluqdars were forced to submit their resignations, and trustworthy persons were appointed in their places.

In 1856, a Central Treasury was established at Hyderabad, to which all Revenue collections were transmitted. Vexatious transit duties and other minor taxes were abolished. The country was for administrative purposes divided into four parts; and Salar Jung took under his charge the largest division yielding 60 lakhs of revenue.

The traffic in Mahomedan and Hindu children had been going on for a long time, and in 1856, Salar Jung issued a proclamation forbidding the practice under pain of punishment. There were daily robberies and dacoities in the districts; and villages were in many cases looted by armed men. More than once a body of the contingent troops were requisitioned to scare away the besiegers. A special Rohilla Court was established at Hyderabad to try such cases, and several gangs of robbers were imprisoned. There was famine in 1862 and 1866, and Salar Jung took effective measures to relieve the poor and the distressed. In 1867, the Zillabandi system was introduced, and the State was parcelled out into five divisions and seventeen districts.

There was a thorough re-organization of the Judicial, Public Works, Medical, Police and Educational Departments. In the Telugu districts the system of payment in kind was the rule. The Minister abolished it to the great satisfaction of the ryots, and sent a memorandum on the disadvantages of this system to the Famine Commission.

In the beginning of 1882, Salar Jung drew an elaborate scheme for the general management of the administration. This was the last and in some respects the greatest undertaking of the Minister for the benefit of the State. This system was adopted practically *in toto* by his successor, and still remains the basis of administration in the Dominions. To help the Minister, four Moin-ul-Mahams (Departmental

Ministers) were appointed, and elaborate details regarding the powers and working of the Ministers and Secretaries were framed. The Government of India, after a careful and close examination of the scheme, gave it their most hearty and cordial appreciation.

Before Salar Jung's time there were no regular courts throughout the dominions. The Minister established a Court in Hyderabad with a Chief Judge, and four assistant Judges having full powers to try civil and criminal cases. To suppress crime in the districts, *Zilladars* with a fully equipped force were appointed, who either captured or imprisoned all turbulent Rohillas. A special Court to try Thuggee and Dacoity cases was instituted. In 1860, a Court at Hyderabad with a Hindu as its presiding Judge was established to try civil cases among Hindus. Government stamped paper was also introduced; and a stamp office was established in the capital.

Before Salar Jung came into power, the village servants acted as the police; and military troops arrested thieves and dacoits when called upon to do so. Cases of torture were very frequent. In 1865, Salar Jung re-organised the police department. At the head of the administration there was the Inspector-General of Police with *Mohatamims* (Superintendents) and Amins (Inspectors) in charge of districts: the Jamadars and Dafadars worked under them. A Kotwal (Commissioner of Police) was appointed for the Hyderabad city, and the Police Code revised and amended.

In 1875, the Survey department was established on the lines followed in the Bombay Presidency. Education in Hyderabad had been carried on, on the old lines: boys were only taught the Koran and to read and write Persian or Arabic. In 1855, Salar Jung established an Oriental College, where English was taught as an optional subject. Some years later a school was opened in the chief village of each Taluq and one at the headquarters of each District. The department was brought under an Educational Secretary and a Director of Public Instruction. A Civil Engineering College and a Medical School were opened. In a short time the educational charges of the State rose to nearly a lakh and half. In 1880, the school at Chadderghet (in Hyderabad) was raised to the status of a College, and affiliated to the Madras University. With a view to encourage the nobles of the State to study the English language, the Madras-Aliza was instituted which was subsequently re-organised and named the Nizam's College. To train teachers for schools, a normal school was established; and five divisional inspectors were appointed for supervision of the schools in the district.

There was also a re-organization of the Public Works Deparment. Many tanks were repaired, roads and district communications were improved, and several government buildings were erected. In 1874, the Hyderabad-Wadi Railway was completed, and to Salar Jung thus belongs the credit of connecting the Nizam's capital with Madras and Bombay. In 1862, regular postal communication between the capital and the districts was established. There were many mints in the State, but Salar Jung withdrew all the coins and established a State mint at Hyderabad. The Abkari Department showed an increased revenue owing to the suppression of illicit manufacture, and the income of the Customs Department rose to nearly 40 lakhs. Municipalities were established at Hyderabad, Aurangabad, Raichur and Gulburga, where the management was effected by a Council consisting of official and non-official members. When Salar Jung became Prime Minister, the military cost of the State per annum was nearly 80 lakhs; but at the time of his death it was reduced to nearly 20 lakhs. Indeed it would take us far afield to measure all the reforms he introduced in remodelling a State like Hyderabad. Suffice to say that he is in a sense the maker of the modern Hyderabad.

A DAY'S WORK

The public are generally ignorant of the way in which great Indians spend their time when in harness: much less do they know of their private lives. But the following description of how Salar Jung spent a day given by a European Military Officer will be read with great interest:—

> He rises about 6 A.M. and after a bath and a cup of tea proceeds to business. The Daroghas of the Feel Khana (superintendent of elephants) etc., first wait upon him and make their reports. A public Durbar is then held to which the poorest of the people have free access, and opportunity given them for

making their representations. The various Jamadars (Officers) of the Troops attend this Durbar and make their reports.

The Minister then proceeds to his private sitting room, where he inspects the accounts of the treasury receipts, and disbursements, and the Munshi of Daroolinshan (office of correspondence) waits upon him with official letters for his approval and signature, and to receive communications respecting unanswered letters. The Nizam (dispenser of justice) of the Adawlut is then granted an audience. By the time the above business is gone through it is half past ten o'clock when the Minister goes to breakfast which does not detain him above a quarter of an hour. He is now waited upon by the Munshi in charge of Urzikhana (office where petitions are received) who submits summaries of all petitions received the previous day and receives orders thereon. The rest of the time till half past twelve is occupied in attending to business of a miscellaneous nature, in receiving visitors, etc. At half past twelve o'clock, the noblemen and other courtiers from His Highness the Nizam's palace with the Kotwal (Magistrate's deputy) of the city attend to pay their respects. They are received in durbar, and the representations listened to, which any of them may have to make. They are usually dismissed in about ten minutes, but to such of them as desire it, private interviews are granted by the Minister in his sitting-room; afterwards His Highness' Hurkarrahs (messengers) attend and make their reports and the correspondence from the Residency is attended to. The Minister then takes his siesta for about half an hour if there be no other pressing calls on his attention.

It is now about two o'clock P. M.; after the afternoon prayers the undermentioned officers of government are received, and their business is gone through in succession, namely, the Dufterdars (Record-keepers) and their Mutseddies (clerks) the Jamadars (officers), and Serishtadars (accountants) of the different corps and the Taluqdars (local Collectors) and others. The Sowcars (bankers) also attend at this time of the day and have audiences granted them. Afterwards various accounts are looked into and orders given; the Resident's letters are received, the Nizam's Vakils (confidential agents) also generally attend. The Minister is thus occupied till half-past five or six o'clock when he goes into his garden and either rides, drives or walks for half an hour. The Nizam's horses as well as the Minister's are brought out for inspection at this hour.

The Minister returns to his private sitting room; and after evening prayer goes to dinner for about half an hour. After dinner the letters received from Taluqdars (Collectors) are perused and answers to them endorsed. He signs letters prepared; examines also district accounts or drafts letters of importance to the Resident; all this occupies until about half past ten or eleven o'clock when he retires to rest.

CONCLUSION

In 1871, the Government of India bestowed on Salar Jung the distinction of the Grand Commander of the Star of India; and he received at the Imperial Assembly at Delhi on 1st January 1877, a salute of 17 guns as a mark of personal distinction. Nawab Shams-ul-Umarah died in 1879, and Nawab Vikar-ul-Umarah became the co-Regent, whose death two years later left Sir Salar Jung as the sole Regent of Hyderabad.

In the summer of 1882, Sir Salar Jung paid a visit to Simla to discuss in person certain administrative questions of the State and to arrange for the tour of the young Nizam to Europe in the following year. His stay was very brief not exceeding eight days, and yet he left behind him a very good impression in the highest society that was gathered together in the summer capital of the Government of India. In January 1883, the Regent accompanied the young Nizam on a tour to Raichur, Gulburga and Aurangabad. On return to Hyderabad, arrangements were being made for the forthcoming visit of H. H. the Nizam to Europe: but to the great sorrow of all, Sir Salar Jung died of cholera on the 8th February 1883.

Telegrams and letters of condolence poured in from different parts of India and the United Kingdom. His Excellency Lord Ripon telegraphed a message from the Queen expressive of Her Majesty's grief at the sad news, and also added an expression of his own sympathy. The news of Sir Salar's demise was published in an extra-ordinary issue of the *Gazette of India* edged with a deep black border: "With a feeling of deep regret the Governor-General in Council announces the death on the evening of the 8th instant from cholera of His Excellency Nawab Sir Salar Jung, G.C.S.I., Regent and Minister of the Hyderabad State. By this unhappy event the British Government has lost an exprienced and enlightened friend, H. H. The Nizam a wise and faithful servant, and the Indian community one of its most distinguished representatives." How deeply his loss was felt by all classes of people is to be seen from the following extract from the Resident's letter to the Government of India:—

> I do not know how to express the concern and sorrow which Sir Salar Jung's death has caused to every one here. At present the sense of personal bereavement seems to outweigh the feeling of public loss. Every British Officer who has had the honour of his acquaintance feels his death as he would that of a friend of many years. Those who had the pleasure to serve under him will mourn the kindest, the most considerate of masters. The British Government will lament the death of one whose loyalty and attachment to it, based as they were on an intelligent appreciation of the true interests of the Hyderabad State, were only second to his loyalty and attachment to his own sovereign. Most of all, His Highness for whom Sir Salar Jung had so laboured must grieve his loss. No master had ever a more devoted servant. It seems so hard that he should have passed away before he could see the sovereign whose interests he had so striven for, on the throne.

Sir Salar Jung's appearance was very striking. He was of medium height and slenderly built, and yet he had a commanding presence. His frame though not robust was wiry. He was simple in his habits. His dress was never gaudy, and in his time he was known as the best dressed Indian. He was unostentatious and seldom wore jewellery save on State occasions. He was of free and easy manners, and was easily accessible. Though a Shiah, he did not evince any partiality to one sect or another, and was a thorough liberal with respect to religion. He did not however omit any of the more binding injunctions of the Muslim faith, and it was very seldom that he neglected his daily prayers or the fasts prescribed to be observed in the month of Ramzan.

The Minister left two daughters, and two sons—Mir Liak Ali Khan, and Mir Saadut Ali Khan: the former was the second Salar Jung, and was the Prime Minister of Hyderabad from 1884 to 1887, and the latter a Member of the Council of State and an acting Prime Minister during his brother's absence on tour. His son, Nawab Mir Yusuf Ali Khan Salar Jung III succeeded to the post held so brilliantly by several of his ancestors in 1912, soon after the accession of the present Nizam to the throne of Hyderabad. He however resigned his high office on the 1st of December 1914, that he might take a trip to Europe for the sake of his health. The office of Ministry has since been retained in the hands of H. H. the Nizam himself.

Nawab Mohsin-ul-Mulk

SIR Syed Ahmed Khan gathered around him a band of devoted workers, inspired by his own reforming zeal. The greatest name in that noble band is perhaps that of Nawab Mohsin-ul-Mulk, a brief sketch of whose inspiring life and career is here attempted.

EARLY LIFE

Syed Mehdi Ali, Nawab Mohsin-ul-Mulk was born at Etawah on the 9th December 1837. His father, Mir Zamin Ali, belonged to the famous Syed family of Etawah, while on his mother's side he was connected with the Abbaside family of Shaikhapur (Farrukhabad). In common with so many other distinguished men of the world, he was born of poor parents, whose sole asset was their noble lineage which they prized above all things. He could not, therefore, enjoy any of the advantages which wealth and riches offer; but he possessed in an abundant measure the advantages derived from good breeding and good society. In spite of the adverse circumstances under which his family laboured, due care was given to Mehdi Ali's early education. He was taught Persian and Arabic first at his own house and then when he gave proof of singular intelligence and taste for learning, he was sent to

Phapund, a place near Etawah, to receive his education from Moulana Inayat Husain, a scholar of repute. He fully availed himself of the teaching of his learned master and made considerable progress in his studies, with the result that every one formed a high opinion of his intellectual attainments.

ENTERS GOVERNMENT SERVICE

Soon after, he was forced to give up his studies and to seek some means of livelihood. He got employed under the East India Company as a clerk on only Rs. 10 per month. This was a death-blow to all the high hopes that were entertained about him, for such a poor reward was not expected for talents and learning like his.

Mehdi Ali, however, was not discouraged ; he did his duties with great pains and care. He was in consequence made an Ahalmad in the memorable year of 1857. It must be mentioned here that he and his family remained perfectly loyal to the British Government during the troublous times of the mutiny. There were strong temptations for him to act otherwise, for Etawah had passed for some time into the hands of the mutineers. But he successfully resisted these temptations and his devotion to his masters remained unshaken.

After the mutiny was over, he was made a Paishkar and subsequently a Sherishtadar. In 1861 he was appointed Tahsildar of Etawah in which position he gave much of his time to the improvement of the place. His untiring energy had a considerable share in the erection of the beautiful Government buildings and other public works which are found in the town. During this period he also compiled "the two well-known Vernacular works on Criminal and Revenue Laws." His work so much pleased Mr. Hume, the Father of the Indian National Congress, who was then Collector of Etawah, that he is reported to have said that Mehdi Ali had enough administrative capacity to be entrusted with the charge of a district.

Two years later he sat for the competitive examination for Deputy Collectorship along with many European candidates, and was able to secure the first place. In 1867, he was appointed a permanent Deputy Collector and posted to Mirzapur. In addition to this he also acted as Superintendent of Dudhi and Rai-Bareilli estates. It is needless to say that he performed these duties with his usual ability and care and established a name for himself in the service to which he belonged. One testimony only need be quoted here. When later he got employment in Hyderabad State, Sir William Muir, the then Lieut.-Governor of the United Provinces of Agra and Oudh, wrote to him :—

When I heard of your transfer to Hyderabad, I felt sure from my experience of your intelligence and ability in your office at Mirzapur that you would distinguish yourself in your new sphere.

How he justified these hopes will be presently seen.

SERVICE IN HYDERABAD STATE

His fame travelled from the North to the distant South and attracted the notice of one of the greatest statesmen that India has ever produced—we mean Sir Salar Jung, the Prime Minister of Hyderabad, Deccan. Sir Salar had a peculiar insight into the character of men and his discerning judgment seldom failed to form a correct estimate of any man with whom he came across. By this remarkable gift he was able to gather around him the ablest men of Northern India, men like Mehdi Ali, Mushtaque Husain and the Bilgrami brothers. Among these men of fine talents the greatest perhaps was Mehdi Ali. He reached Hyderabad in the year 1874.

Here he had before him a vast field for the exercise of his abilities which had hitherto been allowed only a limited scope to manifest themselves. He was first appointed Inspector-General of Revenue and after some time Commissioner of Settlement and Survey Department. In both these capacities he earned the well-merited admiration of his superiors who were deeply impressed by the able manner in which he conducted the business committed to his charge. He did work of lasting good to the state by ensuring the fixity of tenure to the cultivators and by assessing fair rates on all lands. Writing to the Nawab, in 1886, the Hon'ble Sir Stuart Bayley, Lieutenant-Governor of Bengal, said:

> Of your administration work in introducing the survey and settlement and in putting the revenue system of the country on an exact and stable business I can only say that therein you

have rendered services to H. H.'s Government, second only to the Minister himself, and I regard the fact that under the present trying circumstances the daily work of administration both here and in the interior goes on without any serious strain is to a great extent due to your judgment, steadfastness, and capacity."

It was he who introduced Urdu in place of Persian as the court language in the capital and the mofussil. The Legislative Acts of the State bear testimony to the amount of work he did as a Legislator. During this period, he induced the late Mr. Justice Mahmood to come to Hyderabad and give the final touches to the proposed legislation. Mr. Mahmood accepted the offer and drafted many an important Act of the State and Legislature. Two years later Sir Salar Jung made him his own Revenue Secretary in which position he proved to be of great help to him and gained his full confidence. In 1884, he rose to be the Financial and Political Secretary on a monthly salary of Rs. 2,800. As a mark of recognition of the remarkable services which he rendered while in his office, he was awarded the title of Munir Nawas Jung Mohsin-ud-Dowlah Mohsin-ul-Mulk. Henceforth his own name went into the background, and he was known to the world by his last title, *viz.*, Mohsin-ul-Mulk.

He was subsequently entrusted with the delicate task of appearing before a Special Committee in London in Sirdar Diler Jung's case, and he acted with such admirable prudence and discretion and so fully justified the confidence placed in him that he gained the goodwill and pleasure of H. H. the Nizam.

While on this duty, he got an opportunity to see all the great Englishmen of the time upon whom he made a very favourable impression. Mr. Gladstone was so charmed with the talent of this Indian Mussalman that he continued his correspondence with him as long as he lived.

The following extract from a letter of Salar Jung II, which we are enabled to insert through the courtesy of a relative of the late Nawab Mohsin-ul-mulk, will show the extent of the influence and confidence which he enjoyed with that great minister, Sir Salar Jung, and his son. His words translated into English run as follows:

> The value of the services which you rendered to my late father during the period when he was minister, and of the assistance which he received from you, was known only to him. He regarded you as his true friend and sincere well-wisher. He had so much confidence in you that he mentioned your name in his will. There can be no greater mark of confidence. Whatever you did during my time and the honest and truthful assistance which you rendered me was such as I could not have expected even from a very near relation of mine. I am and will for ever remain thankful to you and will never forget your services.

After his return from England he continued in his office till the year 1893 when he had to leave Hyderabad under circumstances which so largely govern the destinies of the people in Native States. He fell a victim to the factitious designs of some interested persons, and the consequence was that the State lost one of its most able officers. But the loss of Hyderabad was the gain of the entire Muslim community. He got a pension of Rs. 800 a month and settled at Aligarh which was to be the scene of his future labours. He now devoted all his time and energies to the cause of Muslim progress in India.

HIS CONNECTION WITH SIR SYED AHMED

It must not, however, be supposed that it was only after his retirement from service that he gave his attention to the welfare of Indian Mussalmans. On the contrary, their welfare and advancement were ever present in his mind long before he finally settled at Aligarh, and he was giving all possible help to Sir Syed in all the schemes which he undertook for the uplift of his backward community. To trace his connection with the mission of Sir Syed, one has to go back to the year 1863. It was in this year that Sir Syed Ahmed published his commentary on the Bible which raised a storm of indignant criticism amongst the orthodox circles of the Mussalmans. Mehdi Ali also wrote a letter to Sir Syed in which he went so far as to call him an apostate. After some months he had occasion to see Sir Syed, and was so profoundly impressed that a considerabie change came over the ideas which he had entertained about him, and Mehdi Ali was entirely won over to the side of the man whom he had not hesitated to call an apostate. A few visits more had strengthened that bond of friendship between these two great men which lasted for life.

His love and respect for the great reformer grew with the lapse of years and he came to be regarded as his chief disciple. Sir Syed also had a very high opinion of the talents of his friend and looked upon him with feelings of love not unmingled with respect. The nature of the relations which existed between them can best be realised by some letters of Sir Syed which he wrote to his friends from time to time. They give evidence at once of the love, the admiration and the respect which the great Syed felt for his devoted friend. In an article in the *Tahzibul-Akhlaq* (the "Social Reformer"), Sir Syed wrote as follows :—

> Moulvi Mehdi Ali's learning, personal merits, charming conversation, sincerity, honesty and eloquence are such that our community, had not its mind's eye been blind, would have been proud of him.

That this friendship proved of immense value to the community is beyond question. Mehdi Ali shared with Sir Syed all the anxious cares which beset him in his great task. He came forward to help him with money whenever it was needed for his many schemes for the welfare of Mussalmans. For this purpose he neither spared his purse nor hesitated to make a demand on that of his friends. Specially his efforts to secure for the M. A. O. College a handsome annual donation from the Hyderabad State will ever be remembered with gratitude.

We may quote here the words of Shamsul Ulema Altaf Husain Hali, the famous poet and biographer of Sir Syed, in which he bears testimony to the valuable assistance which Mohsin-ul-Mulk rendered to Sir Syed. He says :—

> If we omit on this occasion to make mention of one who proved of immense help to Sir Syed in all his works, we will leave an important secret of Sir Syed's success undescribed. Need we say we refer to Mohsin-ul-Mulk on whose shoulders has, by the unanimous consent of the whole community, fallen

the mantle of Sir Syed. It was he who was the first to understand Sir Syed and to realise the sincerity of his mission. It was he who fathomed the depth of his ambitions and realised the greatness of his aims. He sided with him when there was none to stand by him, and he helped him when there was none from whom he could except help; in England Sir Syed was writing the "Essays on the life of Mohammed"; in India, Mehdi Ali was collecting material for the same. While the former was getting the book printed in England, the latter was collecting in India and sending him contributions for the expenses of publication. While on his return from England, Sir Syed desired to form a committee for the purpose of the educational advancement of the Mussalmans, he was in a state of utter despair, because there was no hope of the realisation of the dreams which he had cherished. Mehdi Ali went from Mirzapur to Benares and was the means of restoring Sir Syed's drooping spirits, the consequence being that the committee was successfully formed. When in order to ascertain the reasons why the Mussalmans did not avail themselves of the Government Schools and Colleges, the Committee advertised prizes for the best three essays on the subject, Mehdi Ali with great labour wrote a lengthy essay which was regarded to be the best of all He however, refused to take the prize which was worth Rs. 500, and it was awarded to the writer of the next best essay.

AS A WRITER

The help which Mehdi Ali rendered through his pen had a considerable share in the success of the cause advocated by Sir Syed. It dates from 1870. It was in this year that Sir Syed Ahmed started his famous paper, the *Tahzibul Akhlaq* (the "Social Reformer"). The objects of the journal were to promote reforms in the social life of the Mussalmans and to present Islam in its original state of purity and simplicity freed from the superstitious ideas that had crept into it through centuries of ignorance. Besides, the literary style of the paper was also a great improvement on what then commonly existed. In fact, it was a distinct landmark in the history of Urdu literature, for it might be safely said that it was this journal which laid the foundations of modern Urdu literature.

SIR SYED AHMED

The achievement of these objects was full of difficulties, for it was no easy task to uproot the long cherished passions and prejudices of the people and to introduce them to novel ideas in a novel fashion. In this difficult task, Sir Syed received the greatest help from Mohsin-ul-Mulk. His brilliant articles formed one of the most attractive features of the journal. They were mainly religious or historical and displayed in an abundant degree the vast knowledge possessed by the writer. His chief concern was to show to the Mussalmans those noble features of Islam which had been suppressed on account of ages of ignorance and bigotry. Any one who reads his writings is sure to be struck with the scholarship and breadth of view which characterised them. In his style are found singular force, ease and beauty. He has a fine gift of making himself clear by means of choice metaphors and similies. As a result of these contributions to the *Tahzibul Akhlaq* he has secured for himself a unique place in modern Urdu literature.

It will be of interest to know that the style adopted by him in these articles was entirely different from that of his earlier writings. His older style was that which was so common prior to the establishment of the *Tahzibul Akhlaq.* It abounded in flowery language and was full of bombast and tinsel

NAWAB MOHSIN-UL-MULK

which were indulged in at the sacrifice of sense and meaning. The later style presents a marked contrast to the old. It is simple, elegant and graceful. In fact, on comparing the two, one wonders how the same man could have written in styles so widely different.

Hali, the biographer of Sir Syed, has the following with regard to the writings of Nawab Mohsin-ul-Mulk:

> In his writing Sir Syed always used to rebuke and reproach the Mussalmans and to point out the mistakes of the old Ulema. He committed his views to paper without corroborating them with the sayings of the men of old. On the contrary, Syed Mehdi Ali stimulated the hearts of the Mussalmans by describing to them the achievements of their ancestors. Whatever he wrote in support of Sir Syed, there was in it reference to the standard and reliable authorities of old. Most of his articles are treatises of fairly considerable size, which have been written with great research and labour.

The late Moulana Shibli, the greatest Muslim historian of Modern India, says:

> In the field of literature he can claim to equal the most renowned writers. His is a style of writing which is peculiarly his own.

These are testimonies of no mean value, and they give us a fair idea of his eminent position in the realm of literature.

It is a pity that a writer like him should not have left us any great work except these occasional articles. The only book written by him is "Aayat Bayyanat," which deals with a controversial subject of the Islamic faith. It will not be too much to say that his scholarship and power of expression were such that if he had devoted more of his energies to this department of activity only, he would have remained second to none amongst the renowned authors of modern India. His other pursuits, however, did not allow him to give much of his time to literary labours. Several books, however, were written or translated from other languages into Urdu at his instance. It may be interesting to know that we are, in a way, indebted to him for the very remarkable Urdu translation of the "History of the Conflict between Religion and Science," which Mr. Zafar Ali Khan did at his instance.

ACTIVITIES IN THE CAUSE OF MUSLIM EDUCATION.

In 1893, as we have said, he finally settled at Aligarh. From this date onwards one could see Mohsin-ul-Mulk taking an active part in all the communal movements. He revived the *Tahzibul Akhlaq* which was dead, and infused a new life into the *Aligarh Institute Gazette.* He tried to raise the tone of the institution by freely mixing with the students of the College and discussing with them various topics of interest. He was a familiar figure in the College Debating Society, where he took part in the debates of the students, and by his example set before them a high ideal of speaking. His greatest work, however, consisted in the popularizing of what is known as the Aligarh Movement. It was through the Mohammedan Educational Conference that he did this missionary work. His fine eloquence served him here in very good stead. He first made his mark as a speaker in 1890 at the fifth Annual Session of the Educational Conference held at Allahabad, at which the late Syed Mahmood welcomed him in a Persian poem. Before this it was not generally known that he had in him the gift of public speaking in so eminent a degree. He was twice elected to preside over the deliberations of the Conference, an office in which he acquitted himself with great tact and ability.

After the death of Sir Syed he infused a new life into the Conference, which seemed to have also breathed its last with its founder. He carried the torch of learning to distant parts of the country such as Calcutta, Bombay and Madras. He removed from the popular mind all misconceptions as regards its objects and secured public confidence and sympathy. The religious views of Sir Syed were responsible to a large extent for the antagonistic attitude which the orthodox Muslim Ulema adopted against this body. Sir Syed did not care to bring them over to his own side, but Mohsin-ul-Mulk was more tactful and conciliatory in this respect. He believed that their support was extremely necessary in order to secure for their great work the sympathies of the Mussalman public in general. On one occasion he expressed his views on the subject in the following words:—

Gentlemen! Remember and remember well that we can never secure any appreciable amount of success in our endeavours without the help of that revered and respected body of Ulema (the learned of the old type). Our feeble efforts alone cannot be of any great avail to our community. Whatever we are doing in our present state and have been doing since a fairly long time, have affected only a limited number of people. Only a few persons have begun to share our views and our efforts.

. . A large majority of our community does not listen to our voice, and we have no means of introducing the enlightened ideas to the masses. But the voice of that body of men who hold sway over the hearts of the entire community, will be listened to by every Mussalman, from Peshawar to Burmah, and from Kashmir to Madras. Gentlemen! There can be no doubt that Mussalmans, however ignorant and imprudent they might be, have a heart which is full of love for Islam and a temper which is inflamed with religious fervour. They will never do anything which will appear to them contrary to Islam and will never walk on the path which, in their opinion, leads to a direction opposite to their faith. And to them Islam is nothing but what is expounded by the Ulema. Therefore, if we really wish for communal progress, our first concern must be to make them share our views and to keep them in the fore-front.

Now that the essential necessity of Western education is recognised on all hands, it is impossible to convey an adequate idea of the difficulties which he had to encounter in this respect. He had to deal with a body of men who were nourished on the strongest possible prejudices and who refused to listen to the voice of reason. They moved within a narrow world of their own and had no desire to get beyond that. They urged with all the vehemence at their command that English education would lead the Mussalmans to disaster and unhesitatingly declared its promoters infidels. Wherever he went Mohsin-ul-Mulk was greeted with fatwas of Kufar (infidelity) and every attempt was made to make his mission a failure.

This active antagonism continued as late as 1904, when the annual session of the Mohammedan Educational Conference took place at Lucknow under the presidency of Sir Theodore Morison, former Principal of the M. A. O. College. Here, Moulvis of both the sects of Islam, Shias and Sunnis, for once combined to alienate the sympathies of Mussalmans from the Aligarh Movement. Mohsin-ul-Mulk, with the tact and persuasion that were entirely his own, explained the whole truth to the leading Moulvis, many of whom were convinced of the error of their ways and gave up the opposition. Henceforth all opposition died away and the difficult task of enlightening an influential and bigoted section of the public was completed.

In a speech on the "Causes of the Decline of the Mahommedan Nation" Mohsin-ul-Mulk pointed out that his community could hope for no progress so long as they merely gloried in the achievements of their ancestors and did not strive to emulate the Hindus in their eagerness to acquire the new knowledge of the West. He condemned this habit of "living in the past," this "too exclusive, too superstitious" pride.

> Not so has it been with the Hindu. The Hindu also has a glorious past. It was the ancestors of the Hindu who first conquered this great peninsula; it was the ancestors of the Hindu who left behind a literature which excites the interest of learned men everywhere. But the Hindu has not rested content with the relics of the past: as soon as the advantages of learning were offered to him, he was at once ready to seize them and to make the most of them. Bigoted and exclusive though he is in religion, the Hindu does not allow religious scruples to interfere with the acquisition of knowledge. The Brahmin will not only sit on the same college bench as the Sudra, but he will go through his course of lectures in a Christian school, where Christianity is openly taught, and where the Bible forms one of the subjects of study. The conseqnence is that, quite unnecessarily, we have allowed the Hindu to outstrip us in the intellectual race; and now-a-days it is intellect that rules the world.

AS HONY. SECRETARY OF THE M.A.O. COLLEGE.

In 1897, the Muslim community suffered a great loss in the death of Sir Syed Ahmed and all eyes turned towards Mohsin-ul-Mulk for the realisation of the dreams cherished by the veteran leader. After a short time during which Syed Mahmood acted for his father, the Board of Trustees of the M.A.O. College, Aligarh, elected Mohsin-ul-Mulk as their Honorary Secretary. The brilliant record of his achievements proved that their choice could not have fallen on a better man. The disciple not only kept up the traditions of his master, but added more lustre and glory to them.

The time when he assumed office was perhaps the most critical in the history of the College. On account of the embezzlement by a manager of the office of more than a lakh of rupees which had occurred in the last days of Sir Syed and which had told greatly upon his health, the finances were in a shattered condition. The differences between the trustees themselves had risen to the highest pitch. The death of Sir Syed at such a juncture brought the College very nearly to the verge of ruin. Mohsin-ul-Mulk boldly met the situation and with his characteristic zeal and ability set matters aright. The clouds which had threatened the existence of the College soon melted away and there dawned an era of progress and prosperity. The financial crisis was averted, as he was able to secure by his tact and eloquence the patronage of men like H. H. the Aga Khan and Sir Adamji Peerbhoy and the sympathy of the public in general and to put the College on a sound financial basis.

One is struck with the progress which the College made in every direction during his term of office. In 1898 the number of students was 343 and the annual income was Rs. 76,747-5-4. At his death (1907) the number of students had risen to 800, and the annual income to Rs. 1,53,655-12-5. These figures speak for themselves and need no comment. The College was graced by the visits of some of the most distinguished personages, *e.g.*, H. R. H. the Prince of Wales and H. M. the Amir of Afghanistan. In short, he considerably raised the position of the institution and proved himself in every way a worthy successor of Sir Syed Ahmed.

Mention must be made here of his strenuous labours in connection with the proposed Mohammedan University. On the death of Sir Syed, he preached it far and wide that the best monument that the community could erect to the memory of its great benefactor was to turn his long-cherished dream into an actual fact by raising the M. A. O. College to the status of a University on the lines of Oxford and Cambridge. Though that great dream is still unrealised, Mohsin-ul-Mulk did his part of the work by familiarising the people with the aims and objects which the promoters of the movement had in view. Whenever the time may come to see the fruition of these efforts, Mohsin-ul-Mulk's name will deserve to be remembered for paving the way for the successful achievement of the end.

HIS SHARE IN POLITICS.

Mohsin-ul-Mulk's efforts for the well-being of the Mussalmans were not confined to matters educational only; he contributed no small share to the political activities of the community also. Soon after the death of Sir Syed, there arose a question which was of great political significance for the Mussalmans. It was the Urdu-Nagari question which assumed serious proportions on account of a resolution of the Local Government which seemed to deal a death-blow to the native tongue of the Mussalmans. Mohsin-ul-Mulk took an active part in the well-meaning agitation which followed and called together a representative meeting at Lucknow to enter a strong protest against the action of the Local Government. He delivered a remarkable speech as chairman of that meeting and tried to describe in as clear a manner as possible the point of view of the Muslim community.

His participation in these proceedings was not, however, favourably viewed by Sir (now Lord) Antony Macdonell, the then Lieutenant-Governor of the United Provinces of Agra and Oudh; whose attitude towards the College became ominous. Matters went so far that Mohsin-ul-Mulk desired to resign the Honorary Secretaryship of the College that its interests might not suffer. Before very long, however, the reins of the Government passed into the hands of the sympathetic Sir James La Touche and everything resumed its normal condition. In justice to Mohsin-ul-Mulk, it must be said here that his silence at a later stage of the agitation was due not to any weakness of his own, as some said at the time, but to his anxiety that the interests of the College might not suffer.

ALL-INDIA MOHAMMEDAN DEPUTATION

His second appearance in the arena of politics was attended with more favourable circumstances and with more favourable results. It was in connection with the historic All-India Mohammedan Deputation to His Excellency Lord Minto, with H. H. the Aga Khan as its head (1906). The idea originated from Mohsin-ul Mulk who organised the deputation and to him was due all the credit of the success achieved. As a result of this deputation, the importance of the Muslim community was recognised by the Government, and it was no longer to be considered as a negligible quantity in the affairs of the State.

Apart from the recognition of their rights, the Deputation proved to the Mussalmans of immense importance in another way. It awakened them to the necessity of political activity from which they had hitherto strenuously kept aloof. As a result of this awakening came to existence that well-known organisation, the All-India Muslim League, which has since then served as an exponent of advanced Muslim opinion in India. In the formation of this League also Mohsin-ul-Mulk gave much valuable assistance.

HINDUS AND MUSSALMANS

These political movements of the Mussalmans were subjected to much adverse criticism in some quarters. They were regarded as highly detrimental to the interests of the country in as much as they tended to widen the gulf which unfortunately existed between the Hindus and the Mussalmans. This is no place to enter into a discussion on the correctness or otherwise of this idea; but we feel it our duty to say that the real intention of the promoters of these movements was not, to create or accentuate differences between the two sister communities of India. They aimed at no other object than to secure for the Mussalmans what was their due. With regard to the relations of the two communities, it was their firm belief that in the union of the two races lay the salvation of India. The views expressed on the subject by Mohsin-ul-Mulk who took so prominent a part in all these movements will, we trust, be read with interest. At the Madras Session of the Educational Conference, he said:—

> As long as the Hindus and Mussalmans of India are not sympathetic towards each other, and as long as they will not maintain friendly relations between themselves and treat each other with generous and unprejudiced feelings, they will not deserve the title of fellow-countrymen. He, be he a Hindu or a Mussalman, who does not strive to maintain and improve mutual friendly relations, sins against his community and his country.

On another occasion he observed:—

> I go so far as to say that the importance of co-operation is confined not only to Hindus and Mussalmans; it extends equally to the Christians also. As long as these three do not make equal efforts to devise ways for the progress of the country, India will not be a Heaven but will be a Hell on earth.

MOSLEMS AND THE KHALIFA

It is interesting in these days to recall the words of Nawab Mohsin-ul-Mulk regarding the proper relation of Indian Moslems to the Khalifa, who in those days was also the Sultan of Turkey. The Nawab was a devout Mohammedan but his loyalty to the Government established by law in India was not to be shaken. He defined the correct attitude of Indian Moslems in regard to Turkey in words which are even truer to-day than when he wrote them in the columns of the *Englishman* of June 26, 1906:

It is impossible for any man of even very common understanding, to think that the Sultan of Turkey is the Khalifa of the Indian Mussalmans or that the Mohammedans of India can call him their Khalifa in the real sense of the term. Evidently the Sultan cannot exercise any of the powers and prerogatives of the Khalifa over the Mohammedans of this country, nor are they in any matter bound by their religion to obey the Sultan. They are subjects of the King-Emperor and owe their allegiance to him alone. The commands of the King-Emperor religiously bind upon them, and I think that there is hardly any single Mohammedan who thinks or wants to act as though it were otherwise. * * * * *

But by denying the Khalifat it does not follow that the Indian Mussalmans have no love for the Sultan of Turkey and that they do not care for the safety of the Turkish Government. On the contrary the truth is that all the Mohammedans have great sympathy and love for the Sultan. They all wish with one heart the stability of the Turkish rule and earnestly pray to God that friendly relations between their Government *i. e.*, the British Government and the Sultan may be firmly established. Those of us who say that they do not care a bit for the Sultan and for Turkey, are either cringing flatterers of the British Government whom it is certain, the Government will never believe, or they have no love for religion; they also go against the natural law.

It should be remembered that sympathy for a religion and for a community is quite distinct from political relations. It is not necessary that those who love the Sultan because he is of the same religion should not be loyal and faithful to the British Government under which they live. Nor does it follow because we are subjects of the British Government that we should not wish for the safety of the Sultan or other Mussalman Ruler and be sorry for them if anything happens to them. Loyalty to our Government does not exclude the idea of sympathy with one's co-religionists. Those who think that the two are exclusive of each other, are ignorant, both of their religious duties and their political relations.

LAST DAYS.

Mohsin-ul-Mulk's last days were disturbed by the unfortunate students' strike due to the tactlessness of a new Principal. His health was none of the best, shattered as it was by the heavy strain of work which he had to bear in his old age. He was at Simla when he was overtaken by his last illness. The object of his visit was to have a private conference with the Viceroy about the interests of the Mussalmans involved in the then proposed scheme for the Reform of Councils. No pains were spared to secure the best medical aid; the Viceroy was pleased to appoint his own Surgeon to attend on him. Alarming symptoms, however, soon developed themselves, and it was recognised that the end was near at hand. Two days before his death, he recited the Formula of Testimony and said: "Whatever I did for my community and country, I did with the best of intentions. If there was anything wrong, I should not be blamed for that, because my intentions were good and God knows them well." Then he asked his friends to take him or his remains to his home at Etawah to be laid in the dust beside his ancestors. On the 16th October 1907, he breathed his last and left behind him an entire community to mourn his loss. With considerable difficulty, the Trustees of the College secured the permission of his relatives to bury his remains at Aligarh. There in the compound of the College Mosque he sleeps his last sleep by the side of his illustrious predecessor, Sir Syed Ahmed.

CONCLUDING REMARKS.

A word may be added with regard to his personal qualities. Mohsin-ul-Mulk combined in himself many qualities which contributed to his success. He had a very high sense of duty and always did his work in a manner which gave entire satisfaction to his superiors. He was entirely a self-made man, for it was through his own exertions that he rose from a very humble position in life to the summit of greatness. His assiduity and capacity for work were astonishing. He was a lover of knowledge for its own sake, for, notwithstanding the pressure of work which his duties entailed upon him, he always found time to read books which included a wide range of subjects. He was extremely lavish with his money and gave much of it either to works of charity or to his relatives. In fact, he was generous to a fault.

He was a man of broad views and liberal ideas. By renouncing certain religious views of his forefathers, he had early in life given proof of his rare courage and shown to the public that he was determined to carry out his convictions. As soon as he was convinced of the truth of a thing, he did not hesitate to declare his adherence to it, without caring for what other people would say or think of him.

A robust optimism pervaded his whole life—both private and public. Cheerfulness was a habit of his mind which went a long way towards recuperating his otherwise broken health. All his public utterances were marked with a spirit of optimism which refused to take notice of the dark side of the picture.

The secret of his success in public life lay in the winning manners and the charm of expression which he possessed in so remarkable a degree. His cheerful conversation charmed his hearers and stole away their hearts. Once a man came under his magic influence, he was sure ever to remain an admirer of his. It is impossible to omit to mention here the case of H. H. the Amir of Kabul. He came to visit the College with very strong prejudices, for he had heard all sorts of rumours against the education imparted there. Thanks, however, to the tact and charming conversation of Mohsin-ul-Mulk, he was extremely pleased with all that he saw and went away with a very favourable impression of the Institution having made a handsome annual grant to it.

He had a large circle of personal friends not only among the Mussalmans, but also among the high European officials of the State. He always used his private influence with them for the good of his community. This was the one guiding idea of his life ever since his connection was severed from Hyderabad. He cared little for personal comfort. His attentions were all centred on what is known as the Aligarh Movement and regarded the students of the College as his own children. The letters written by him to the students during the strike are a true index of his feelings. They give vent, in his own peculiar way, to the sincere love which he had for them and to his extreme anxiety for their welfare.

As regards his unrivalled gift of public speaking, it need only be said that he was a born orator. He could move his audience to tears or laughter, as it suited his purpose. Some of his speeches have been collected and published in the form of a book. They are precious gems of eloquence likely to prove of inestimable value to one who wishes to study the art of Urdu oratory. Two of his lectures in which he has described the past civilisation of the Mussalmans and the causes of their downfall, deserve special mention. "Either we must die out entirely" he said "or else we must acquire other habits of energy and work adapted to the times and circumstances in which we live." And he went on to condemn the indolence and profligacy of the wealthy classes and concluded with a remarkable peroration :—

> To me it seems that as a nation and a religion we are dying out; our day is past, and we have but little hope in the future. It reminds me of the story of the old man who went to consult a Doctor. "Doctor," he said, "I cannot sleep!" "That is owing to old age," was the answer. "I cannot walk well:" "Old age." "My appetite is gone." "Old age." "My sight is failing and I am getting deaf" "all due to old age." "What!" exclaimed the patient in a rage, "can you do nothing to help me, and only say "old age," "old age"? "Your being angry is also due to old age," was the reply. Our body, as a nation, is worn out by the diseases which have ravaged it for the last three or four hundred years. Small complaints have grown into chronic and deeply-rooted diseases which are now past cure. Unless a miracle happens, I see nothing which will raise us from the degraded state which we now occupy. It seems to me that the Mohammedans as a nation have been tried before the Judgment seat of God. They have been found guilty and judgment has been passed, but I trust, nay I feel, that the decree is not an absolute one, Like those that are passed in

the English divorce court, it is a decree *Nisi Prius*, and a date has been fixed on which "unless before" a reform takes place it will be made absolute. What that date is we do not know, but I fear it cannot be far off.

Unless a miracle of reform speedily occurs, we Mohammedans are doomed to extinction. and we shall have deserved our fate. For God's sake let the reform take place before it is too late.

In short, one is astonished to see how various and varied were his accomplishments which have a claim upon our esteem and regard. He was not only a brilliant and effective orator, an able journalist, a renowned theologian, a formidable debater and a classical writer ; his fame rests equally upon his being a capable administrator, a veteran educationist and a successful social and political reformer. He was a man whose example may well inspire men with noble aspirations and whose memory will ever be cherished by Mussalmans with feelings of love, respect, and gratitude. His name will ever live in the annals of Muslim progress in India. The Aligarh College is a standing monument to the exertions of that noble band of workers, of whom Mohsin-ul-Mulk was so prominent a member.

P. 97.

BUDRUDDIN TYABJI

BADRUDDIN TYABJI.

BOYHOOD AND EDUCATION.

BADRUDDIN TYABJI was born on the 8th October, 1844. His father was a wealthy Arab merchant settled in Bombay. Tyabji Bhai Miyan Sahib, who dealt extensively with foreign countries, was a very enlightened Muhammadan and though he was the religious head of his community who in those days thought it against their faith to learn English as a Christian language, sent all his six sons to Europe, following them there himself. Three of these sons, Shujauddin, Shamsuddin, Najmuddin, were merchants and extended their father's business in Havre and Marseilles, while the youngest, Amiruddin, remained a gentleman at large. One of them Mr. Camruddin was the first Indian to be articled as Solicitor in England and on his return to Bombay established a large and lucrative business, which is still continued bearing his name. Mr. Badruddin, the subject of this sketch was next in age. Like his brothers, Badruddin learned Urdu and Persian at Dada Makhra's Madrassa and subsequently joined the Elphinstone Institution. After a few years there he had to be sent to France for treatment of the eye. On being cured he went to London and joined the Newbury High Park College in his 16th year. He matriculated at the London University and entered upon higher studies, but these were interrupted by ill-health, in consequence of which he returned to India for a time. Even after recovery, he was pronounced unequal to the strain of University studies, so that, in the end, he became a law student at the Middle Temple and in April, 1867, was called to the Bar.

AT THE BAR.

In November of the same year he set up practice at the Bombay High Court, being the first Indian Barrister of the place as his brother had been the first Indian Solicitor. His initial difficulties must have been great, but they yielded to his ability and industry, backed as these were by the powerful help of his brother. Fluency of speech, choice though somewhat diffuse diction, lucidity of exposition, skill in cross-examining, above all, a perfectly dignified and earnest bearing, are qualities which would have ensured success in any case; but when they were combined, as in Mr. Badruddin's case, with high character, sweet manners, and single-minded application, they soon raised him to the front rank in his profession. Two anecdotes deserve to be remembered. A criminal case before Mr. Justice Westropp had ended, thanks to Mr. Tyabji's defence, in acquittal; but the *Bombay Gazette* characterised it in its legal columns as rigmarole and nonsensical. Next day as soon as Court began the Judge said to Mr. Tyabji:

> Mr. Tyabji, I am glad to see you here, and also the reporter of the *Bombay Gazette*, as I wish to make some observations upon the report of the case which was concluded yesterday. The paper represents you to have made 'a rigmarole and a nonsensical speech' in defence of your client. As these remarks are not only unfair but likely to do harm to a young barrister, I deem it my duty to observe that, in my opinion, there is not the slightest foundation for those remarks. I consider the case was most ably conducted by you, and that the acquittal of the prisoner was mainly due to the ability and skill with which you addressed the jury.

The other anecdote illustrates the strength of the man, the quality that has been generally acknowledged as characteristic of him both as barrister and as Judge. We take it from an appreciation that appeared in the *Bengalee*:

> It is some years since he appeared as counsel for an accused person in a criminal appeal before a Division Bench consisting of Mr. Justice Parsons and Mr. Justice Ranade. The case had excited some sensation at the time and it was during the hot days of May that the two Judges sat to hear the appeal. Mr. Tyabji began his argument with some prefatory remarks giving a general view of the case, and that occupied about half an hour. He then commenced reading the evidence. He had not gone on for more than ten minutes when Mr. Justice Parsons, who always liked a short argument, said:—'We have read the evidence, Mr. Tyabji.' Mr. Tyabji met the remark with a cool 'Yes' and went on reading the deposition all the same. Mr. Justice Parsons.—'What is the use of reading the depositions and wasting the time of the Court when we have read them all? Better confine yourself to such comments as you may have to make on the evidence' Mr. Tyabji: 'I dare say, my Lord, your Lordships have read the evidence but you have read it in your own way. I am here to make your Lordships read the evidence in my way and it is only then that you can follow my comments.' And Mr. Tyabji had it his own way. For two days he kept the Court occupied hearing his arguments, with the result that at last he secured an acquittal for his client, and the remark went round the Bar that Mr. Tyabji had given a good lesson on patience to the Bench.

As an advocate the case perhaps which will be most connected with his name is the case of Sahibzada Nasrulla Khan which he conducted with pre-eminent success. It has been said that in that case he exhibited forensic ability and eloquence of the most brilliant order, which reminded his hearers of the great feats of Erskine, and is by some regarded as perhaps the greatest feat of forensic eloquence in the annals of the High Court of Bombay.

PUBLIC WORK.

For ten years and more he allowed nothing to distract him from the pursuit of law, putting away the frequent solicitations of Messrs Mehta, Telang, and Ranade with "that sort of thing is not in my line". But soon thereafter he threw himself heart and soul in the work of promoting education among his co-religionists and remained devoted to that task to the end of his life. He became Secretary of the Anjuman-i-Islam of Bombay about 1880 and then president and raised the influence of that Institution to be one of the most powerful in the Bombay Presidency.

He also became President of the Bombay Presidency Association, which was another Institution with influence in the Presidency, and was followed in that office by Pherozeshah Mehta, Gokuldas Parekh, Narayen Chandavarker and D. E. Wacha. It was in 1879 that he definitely joined that illustrious band of patriots which was Bombay's unique boast. To that band he remained attached to the end. His maiden speech was against the abolition of import duties on cotton goods and brought him great applause. From this time he was in great request at every public meeting, and from the numerous speeches that he made, we may select for special mention those on the Indian Civil Service question, the Ilbert Bill and Lord Ripon.

Addressing a public meeting in Bombay in April 1883, Tyabji spoke on the Ilbert Bill controversy with his accustomed lucidity and exposed the pretensions of the opposition. He said:

> Further, gentlemen, what can be greater injustice to the whole Indian community than to declare even the ablest of our native magistrates and judges, no matter what their qualifications may be, as an inferior order of men, incapable of rising to that height of judicial excellence which is supposed to be necessary to try cases against Europeans? Gentlemen, I venture to think that the present state of the law is not only unjust, but it is insulting to us. (Cheers.) It is insulting to us, first because it brands even the ablest, the highest, and the most distinguished of our judicial officers with a galling and a perpetual mark of inferiority. (Renewed cheers.) It is insulting to us because it draws an invidious distinction between the European and the native members of the same Covenanted Civil Service. It is insulting to us because it exalts the European British subjects into such superior beings as to declare that even the highest of our judicial officers shall be incapable of imprisoning him a single day or fining him a single rupee; and it is insulting to us because it degrades our own countrymen to such a depth to declare in the very next breath that the same incompetent and unfit magistrates and judges, who are incapable of trying even the most trivial case of assault against an Englishman, are yet fit and competent to try milllions of our own countrymen for the gravest charges and even to condemn them to death? (Loud and prolonged cheers.) Gentlemen, the height of absurdity could go no further, and yet forsooth these are the arguments ostensibly put forward for the purpose of defeating this just, generous, and above all, extremely moderate and cautious measure.

Meanwhile the Local Self-Government measure of Lord Ripon had been carried into effect in Bombay in 1882, and Sir James Fergusson, the then Governor, nominated Mr. Tyabji to the Legislative Council. His work in connection with the Municipal and Local Board Bills was highly commended at the time and the Governor paid him the compliment of saying that he would have been listened to with rapt attention even in the House of Commons. Close reasoning, clear statement, and studied moderation, then as ever, distinguished his speeches. He shares with such men as Messrs. Hume, Bonnerjee, Naoroji, and others the rare privilege of having assisted at the birth of the Indian National Congress which met for the first time at Bombay in December, 1885. Calcutta had its turn in 1886, and when next year Madras had to welcome the delegates, the unanimous choice of the country for the place of President fell on Mr. Badruddin Tyabji.

CONGRESS PRESIDENT, 1887.

Never was choice better justified. Three speeches stand out in the memory as giving that Session of the I. N. C. its peculiar glory. Rajah Sir T. Madhava Rao's address of welcome was couched in diction which suggested the cunning of the Taj Mahal chisellers, and which an Anglo-Indian journal, broad-minded and generous in those happy days, declared was "such as few persons in the continent of Europe ever speak." For pure dash and brilliancy nothing in the whole range of Congress oratory can equal the short speech by which Mr. Surendra Nath Bannerjee (now, Sir) carried the Arms Act Resolution in the teeth of the opposition of such leaders as Messrs. Hume and Chandavarkar. Inferior to neither in weight or impressiveness, but superior to both in dignity and grace of delivery, was Mr. Tyabji's Presidential Address. The present writer still cherishes as one of his most precious intellectual possessions the memory of the scene where as a mere stripling, he stood behind a vast crowd, drinking in with rapture every word as it reached him, clear and apt, none so apt, he thought, and catching now and then a glimpse of the handsome countenance which beamed with earnestness, good humour, and perfect self-possession. He began by saying that he had accepted the office of President in spite of ill-health, not so much because it was the highest honour that the people could confer on an Indian, as because he was anxious to demonstrate in his capacity as a representative of the Anjuman-i-Islam, of Bombay, that there was nothing in the aims and methods of the Indian National Congress which could justify his co-religionists in keeping aloof from it. He then went on to impress on his audience the need for moderation, caution, and forbearance,—a need always present, but at that time of the infancy of the Congress most imperative.

Be moderate in your demands, just in your criticism, correct in your facts, and logical in your conclusions, and I feel assured that any proposals we may make will be received with that benign consideration which is characteristic of a strong and enlightened Government.

HIGH COURT JUDGE.

In 1895, he accepted a place on the High Court Bench—a promotion which, on a former occasion, ill-health had compelled him to decline. As a Judge he maintained his reputation for strength, judicial temper, and unfailing courtesy to the Bar. He cared more for equity and substantial justice than for legal abstractions so dear to the heart of those lawyers who are ambitious to be known as jurists. Once, indeed, he is said to have declared: "These law reports are becoming a cumbrous affair, and I sometimes wish we could manage to get on without them."

As Judge, the most remarkable features of his career were undoubtedly his fearless and absolutely independent character uninfluenced by any considerations of race or faith or self-interest, and the public felt before him as they perhaps felt before no other Judge that whether he was pitted against the Government or a great and powerful European Corporation or an ordinary litigant, justice would be given to him indifferrent of all considerations.

His behaviour, bearing and attitude was throughout most dignified and inspired respect.

His judgments were seldom if ever written out, and he generally delivered his most elaborate and lengthy judgments from a few notes. And perhaps the solemn, clear and decisive manner of his pronouncements, in a beautiful voice, were another feature of his tenure of the judicial office.

In his youth he had gone through a vast number of volumes of the Law Reports, and once well furnished with and grounded in the principles of the Law, in his later life he threw off his dependence on the law reports and chiefly trusted to the principles he had grasped.

Some nine months after his death was delivered in the famous case of Kessowji Issur against the Great Indian Peninsula Railway Co. (1907) what is a most remarkable judgment of the Privy Council in which their Lordships of the Privy Council held up the judgment of Mr. Justice Tyabji to admiration with repeated compliments, even going to the length of setting it up as an example to the learned Judges who had sat in appeal over him and reversed his judgment.

No judge could wish for a higher compliment from the Privy Council, but he did not live to see it.

WOMEN'S EDUCATION AND FREEDOM.

Perhaps, Mr. Tyabji's most solid work was done in connection with the Anjuman-i-Islam, of which he was at first Secretary and for some years before his death President. He held advanced views in regard to the condition of the women of his community and strove hard to weaken the power of the zenana system. Unlike many reformers who show their vehemence only in the denunciation of others, Mr. Tyabji, cautious as he was by nature, acted on his conviction in his own family circle. His daughters came out of the purdah and received their education in England. Indeed, the Muhammadans of Bombay owe much of their present prestige and enlightenment as a community to his watchful and unremitting labours on their behalf.

Mr. Tyabji contributed largely to the development of social life in Bombay and both Mr. and Mrs. Tyabji were distinct social centres round which began aided by Lady Reay, Lady Scott (wife of Sir John Scott) and Mrs. Peachy Phipson, that social intercourse in private houses, between the different communities, which has since their time developed the clubs and gymkhanas of Bombay. Mr. Tyabji was one of the founders and from the commencement the President of the Islam Club, and the Islam Gymkhana which both he attended almost daily.

Although himself not an athlete nor a sporting man he gave a most constant encouragement to all outdoor games, badmintion, tennis, cricket, riding and generally presided at the races and sports in Matheran.

He was himself a fine card and chess player but discouraged these in preference to the outdoor games among the young men holding that fresh air and exercise as much more necessary.

He set an example by introducing badminton and tennis in his family in 1887 when these games were hardly known in Bombay, by having courts in his own garden when he daily played a couple of games from that year every morning before breakfast, almost without exception, prevented only occasionally by reason of health, and his constancy of habits is exibited by another practice of his—walking from court with his carriage behind him throughout the year, in winter, summer, spring, and even actual rain did not prevent him, unless it was excessive.

On account of a defect in his eyes he often saw a double ball one on the top and another at the bottom, and he constantly hit the wrong one but this did not discourage him in his games.

On account of his eyes he was for many years unable to write or read much, and had to be read to and write by dictation. He had a peculiar characteristic in dictation. He dictated without ever changing or altering or stopping, but stopped to ascertain that the spelling was correct. At the end of the dictation he invariably had it read out, but those who wrote for him never know of any occasion when he made any alteration in his own word or phrase.

PRESIDENT OF THE M. A. O. E. CONFERENCE.

When he presided in 1903 over the Muhammadan Educational Conference held at Bombay, he made a powerful plea for the abandonment of the purdah system and for a liberal education for the women of his community. But the part of his address that will be most remembered by his countrymen is the one in which he declared his adhesion to the principles of the Indian National Congress,—a declaration which derives additional force from the circumstance that among his hearers on the occasion was the Governor of Bombay. One cannot help contrasting with it the miserable tone of apology that other Congressmen assume both when they are in the running for Government favours and long after they have secured them.

> Gentlemen, you are no doubt aware that, although the Conference has been in existence for several years past, I have not hitherto been able to take an active part in its deliberations. No doubt, there have been many reasons for this, to which it is unnecessary to refer. But there is one in regard to which I must say a few words. You are no doubt aware that I have always been a supporter of the Indian National Congress. In my younger and freer days, when I was not trammelled with the responsibilities imposed by my present office, and when I was, therefore, able to take a more active part in public life, and especially in the politics of the Empire, I deemed it my duty to support the Congress, and, as you may perhaps know, I had the honour of presiding at the Congress held in Madras some years ago. On that occasion I described my election as the highest honour that could be paid to any Indian gentlemen by his fellow-subjects of the Empire. Being of that opinion at that time and being still of that opinion now, you will readily understand that it was not possible for me to take any part in connection with any institution which had or could be supposed to have the slightest trace of being hostile or antagonistic to the Congress.

This must have been hard food to swallow for those among the audience who were endeavouring to represent the Muhammadan deputation to the Viceroy as being anti-Congress and anti-Hindu, and *on that account* entitled to the sympathy and countenance of Government.

LAST DAYS IN ENGLAND.

Early in 1909 he went to England for a cure of his eyesight which had begun to give serious trouble. He progressed remarkably well and felt strong enough to make long motor tours. He was even present at two great meetings and spoke with high usual candour and vigour. His theme at a meeting of the East India

Association in March was moderation and courtesy in politics and progress and enlightenment at home.

Although I have oftentimes in former days criticised the acts of Government, I would ask my young friends to remember whether they have not very much to be grateful for, although they have no doubt also many causes to complain; but, in looking at the acts of Government, it does not do either for young India, or, for the matter of that, middle-aged India, or old India, always to fix its eyes upon the faults of the Government, and entirely to forget these blessings which we enjoy under the ægis of the British Government. * * * *

Now, as regards the attitude of Government towards the Congress. Although we have been reminded that this is an occasion on which political views may be discussed, it must be borne in mind that in the position which I occupy at present, I am not at liberty to discuss any political questions of a controversial character, but I believe that Government perfectly understand and recognise that the Congrees is not a seditious body. I believe they recognise that the Congress does consist of a lage body of people speaking with authority upon the question, and although they do not like their acts to be criticised openly in the way that sometimes they have been, I believe that the resolutions of the Congress are really considered by Government in a sympathetic spirit; and as far as they think any effect can be given to them, I believe that they are desirous of giving effect to them and to the desires of the nation as expressed through the Congress. But after all—speaking for my own countrymen—I think we have to address ourselves more to the question of education and to the question of social reform. I am afraid that young India has fixed its attention too exclusively upon politics, and too little upon education and upon social reform. I am one of those who think that our improvement and progress lies not in our efforts simply in one direction, but in various directions, and that we ought to move side by side for the purpose of improving our social status and our educational status quite as much as our political status. It is no use labouring together for a representative Government of a very advanced type if the majority of our own countrymen are still steeped in ignorance.

ALIGARH UNIVERSITY

In July he attended a dinner of the Aligarh College Association, and expressed his deep sympathy with the movement. He was in favour of Aligarh becoming a university, and appealed to his brethren for active help.

It has been well remarked by Sir Thomas that one college, however good and important, cannot possibly be sufficient for the requirements of fifty or sixty million Mahomedans in India. We must have these institutions all over India, and it has always seemed to me of the greatest possible importance that the educational institutions we have in other parts of the country—some of them fulfilling the humbler mission of imparting primary education, and others teaching up to the high school standard, should be raised to or supplemented by collegiate institutions. The well-wishers of our community present to-night as guests will be pleased to hear that efforts in this direction are being made (and not without success) in other parts of India. If, as I hope, Aligarh develops into a university, it will become the centre of attraction educationally for all Mahomedans, not only from the various Mahomedan schools and colleges of India, but also, it may be, from other parts of the Mahomedan world. And it certainly is a very pleasant symptom that we have so recently seen, in connexion with the Royal visit, such large contributions made for the endowment of chairs at Aligarh, the donations including a lakh of rupees from a private Mahomedan gentleman in Bombay, and a large contribution from that very enlightened, most intellectual, and public-spirited nobleman, the Aga Khan, who, I may point out, is much more directly connected with Bombay than with Upper India. Having received so much help from Western India, our brethren in the North may permit me the friendly criticism that they seem to have greatly neglected the cause of female education. This is a reproach to men of their enlightenment, and I have noticed with the greatest pleasure that recently efforts have been made to remedy that state of things This is a reform in respect to which my Mussalman friends in the North may not despise to take a leaf out of the book of their Bombay co-religionists. I need only add a hope the college will develop into a real centre of Moslem education and enlightenment not merely for the North-West, but for all India. There is not a Mussalman in India, certainly not in Bombay, who does not wish all prosperity and success to Aligarh.

THE END

These were fated to be his last public utterances. To all appearance, he was in excellent health and being amongst his own children, enjoyed a degree of peaceful and contented joy that, perhaps, only an Indian parent can appreciate. But unsuspected, save by a doctor who kept his own counsel, an insidious affection of the heart was sapping his vitality and carried him away on the 19th August 1909 without pain. Among public men, he will be long remembered not merely for his sagacity and eloquence, but for his absolute fearlessness and fidelity to the popular cause.

SOCIAL LIFE IN BOMBAY

He was a man of remarkably handsome features and of a strikingly dignified, though severe and awe-inspiring bearing. His influence wherever he moved was almost decisive, and his opinion and will rarely failed to prevail.

In his presidential speech at the Mahomedan Educational Conference he expressed the opinion that the restrictions of the purdah were carried beyond the commandments of the Koran, and ought to be brought within them. This opinion was so hurtful to a large number of the audience that it was feared they might resort to violence, and there was a conspiracy to challenge his view on the next day of the Conference. On this day as he entered a man of stentorian voice rose amidst a band of bigots and challenged the interpretation of the Koran citing a passage.

Mr. Tyabji said: " Write down the passage and hand it over!" The man wrote and sent it over.

Mr. Tyabji then closely read it to himself and said: "This has nothing to do with the question".

The man began to argue and Mr. Tyabji with a powerful voice cried out, "Sit down Sir, sit you down." So full of authority and power and with such force was it said that the man dropped to the ground and with it the conspiracy. It is narrated that a certain number of notables tired and jealous of the respect which he monopolised and the attention concentrated upon him decided that they would not move or rise when he entered. But when he did they all rose up and each asked why the other did and the reply was: "what could I do, I tried my best but when he came I could not resist it." So it was when he as a young man visited the Anjuman School of which he was Secretary and the boys of the School would say that they had often risen up like drilled soldiers the moment he entered and had stood an hour without changing foot in his presence.

And perhaps it was this that made Lord Reay say "If there is one man I admire in India it is Bed-re-ed-din", as he used to call him; and His Highness the Aga Khan on the death of Sir Pherozesha Mehta thus spoke of him (Monday 6th December 1915.): Nothing finer or better could be imagined for a young Indian patriot than to take to heart and carefully study the life long principles and practice of three of India's greatest and soundest sons, each an example and inspiration to all this countrymen, and to his own community as well—Mehta, Gokhaleand Badruddin Tyabji."

RAHIMTULLA M. SAYANI

Rahimtulla Mohamed Sayani.

A fact which strikes even the casual visitor to Bombay is the remarkable position held, and deservedly held, by the Parsee community in that city. It is a singular proof of the many blessings of education and of the aptitude to assimilate Western civilization. Just as the Parsee community may rightly be called the leading native community of Western India, similarly the Khoja community may well be regarded, at least in some respects, as the foremost section of the Mahomedan community of the Bombay Presidency. If we analyse the causes of this unique position attained by this small community we find them to be the same that have raised the Parsee community to its present level, namely, energy and enterprise, education and self-reliance and last, but not least, a catholic spirit of charity and brotherly feeling towards the sister communities. The reason why we have referred to this matter is that the subject of our sketch, Rahimtulla Sayani, not only belonged to this community, but was one of those pioneers who, by precept and example, instilled the spirit of progress in it. That this was no easy task we shall see later on. For in the social world as much as in the physical world, the fact is true that it is much more difficult to set a heavy ball rolling than to continue its triumphant progress subsequently. All credit is therefore due to men like Tyabji and Sayani and the founder of Aligarh College and a few others, for laying the foundation of education and progress in the great Moslem community of India.

EARLY LIFE AND EDUCATION

Mr. Rahimtulla Mahomed Sayani was born in Bombay on the 5th of April 1847. His grandfather Sayani was a respectable merchant in the Cutch State, from which many of the ancestors of the Khojas have emigrated to other parts of the British India. Through vicissitudes of fortune worse days came on the family and one of the many difficulties encountered by Mr. Sayani during his school and college days was the necessity struggling against diverse adverse circumstances. Perseverance and steady industry which were his prominent characteristics kept him up, however, and when at last he entered his profession, his patience was amply rewarded. But this is the case with many students and want of material prosperity was not the chief obstacle encountered and successfully overcome by the late Mr. Sayani. Education has spread rapidly among the Khojas in these days, and whether in public life and public service, or in the liberal professions, the Khojas are to be found in good numbers. But fifty years ago the case was quite the reverse. Higher education was absolutely unheard of and even primary education existed in a very, very limited circle then. In fact two incidents of Mr. Sayani's school and college life, trifling as they are by themselves, show well the condition of the community and their attitude towards education in those days. Once when he was proceeding to the Elphinstone School he was followed by a band of ignorant Khojas who, with shouts "Infidel, infidel" assaulted him with stones. Subsequently, when failing eye-sight obliged him to put on glasses, he was again assaulted and followed with shouts of derision in the street! This often made it positively dangerous for him to walk alone in the streets. Conditions have fortunately changed entirely now and education has made a solid progress in this community.

When he passed his matriculation examination, young Sayani was asked by his father to discontinue further studies. But in spite of great discouragement and even opposition on the part of friends and near relatives, he decided to take higher education. By doing this he even incurred the displeasure of his father. But the blessings of higher education were soon made patent to the aged parent and he was easily persuaded to approve of the step taken by his son. After an eminently successful career at Elphinstone College Mr. Sayani passed his M.A. Examination in 1866. Owing to a technical difficulty however, he did not obtain his degree till 1868. He was not only the first Mahomedan who had obtained this honourable degree but no Mahomedan obtained it during the next twentyfive years. This fact throws an interesting side light on the backward condition of the Mahomedan community generally even during the closing years of the Nineteenth century.

During his college career Mr. Sayani was the recipient of many prizes and scholarships, and was eventually appointed a fellow of the college. His intimate familiarity with English literature enabled him to teach English successfully for the next four years. He was a favourite pupil of that distiuguished scholar, Sir Alexander Grant, who was the Principal of that college, and who, continued to watch sympathetically the rapid rise of his former young pupil, even after retirement to his home in Scotland.

In 1870 Mr. Sayani passed his LL. B. Examination and was within the same year appointed a Justice of the Peace and a Fellow of the Bombay University. Mr. Sayani was not only one of the foremost members of the Senate but also held various offices. He was a member of Syndicate, a member of the Board of Accounts (of the University), one of the Trustees of the premier College (Elphinstone) of the Presidency, and, in his younger days, was frequently appointed an examiner by the University. As the senior member of the Syndicate he often had the honour of presiding over meetings of the Syndicate and the Senate especially during the latter days of the Vice-Chancellorship of the late Justice Telang, who on account of ill-health was frequently absent. It may be incidentally remarked that the Syndicate, although a very small body at this time, contained no less than three judges of the High Court.

AS SOLICITOR

Mr. Sayani's professional career began in 1878 when he passed his Solicitor's examination through the firm of Leath and Leath. This firm is now represented by the highly respected firm of Messrs. Crawford & Co. He became a partner of the late Mr. Cumroodin Tyabji who was the first and only Mahomedan solicitor at that time. He was the elder brother of that distinguished lawyer and citizen, the late Justice Budruddin Tyabji.

After Mr. Tyabji's death he joined two other eminent solicitors in forming the firm of Payne, Gilbert and Sayani. Through the retirement of the two senior partners he became at the time of his death the senior member of the flourishing firm of solicitors styled as Messrs. Payne, Gilbert, Sayani and Moos.

OTHER ACTIVITIES

During the first fifteen years of his professional career he was largely practising as a pleader also. Had he wished during those days he might have obtained a seat on the High Court Bench. His professional and public career were more dear to him however, and prevented him from desiring it. If rumour speaks correctly Mr. Sayani's name was spontaneously mentioned more than once amongst those recommended as fit to sit on the bench.

His untiring energy and many-sided activities are evidenced by the fact that, in spite of great professional work he found time to work on the Board of Directors of various commercial companies, technical institutes, and other public bodies. This brings us to the most important part of his life-work especially from the public point of view, namely his public life.

IN THE CORPORATION

Mr. Sayani was first elected to the Bombay Municipal Corporation in 1876. From that year to the time of his lamentable death in 1902 he was not only the leading Mahomedan member but one of the foremost members of that body. He was subsequently elected a member of the Town Council (now called the Standing Committee) on which he served usefully for many years. His grasp of public questions, his disinterested zeal for the public good, and his unquestioned impartiality, always earned for him a patient and even respectful hearing. To mark their appreciation of his services to the city his colleagues elected him president of the Corporation in 1888. As might have been expected his tenure of Chairmanship was marked by a courteous but firm adherence to the rules of business and suppression of irrelevent discussion, which formerly used to cause waste of public time occasionally. The esteem in which he was held by the members, both European and Indian alike, is illustrated by an incident which occurred during his presidentship. A proposal was unanimously brought forward, suggesting that the President of the Corporation be styled the Lord Mayor of Bombay and that he be invested with the golden badge and chain of office, like the Mayor of London. On Government being approached with this view they negatived the proposal for certain reasons. But the fact that this was the first and as yet, the last occasion on which such a proposal has found general acceptance, shows in no uncertain manner, the high regard in which Mr. Sayani was held by all classes of the community. It may also be pointed out that he was the first Mahomedan who obtained the high honour of the Civic chair.

HIS SERVICES TO THE KHOJAS

In 1874 a Commission was appointed in order to recommend proposals with a view to amend the law relating to the Khojas. This community being governed partly by Mahomedan Law and partly by Hindu Law much confusion sometimes used to arise. The late Justice Sir Maxwell Melville, Judge Spencer, and Mr. Sayani, were appointed members of this Commission. Afterwards at the suggestion of Mr. Sayani, H. H. Aga Ali Shah and three other prominent Khojas were added as Members.

He was one of that small band of cultured Mohamedan leaders who brought into existence that very useful body known as the Anjuman-i-Islam, with its accessories of schools, hostels, gymkhana and club. No doubt the credit in this connection is largely due to the late Mr. Justice Tyabji. But Mr. Sayani's services in the cause of the Anjuman were also of no mean order. He was for many years Honorary Secretary of the Anjuman and also its Vice-President.

In 1885 Mr. Rahimtulla Sayani became the first Mahomedan Sheriff of Bombay. Genuine pleasure was felt at Government conferring this unique honour on a leading Mahomedan like Mr. Sayani, and he received a large number of congratulatory addresses from all parts of the Presidency.

Amongst the tokens of appreciation was a beautiful painting presented to the Khoja Reading Room and Library of Bombay in commemoration of this event. This painting constantly reminds posterity of one who was undoubtedly the chief founder of the educational and social progress of the community. This library is the first and only one of its kind in the Khoja community. It was largely due to the zealous assistance of Mr. Sayani that this library has been able to reach its present prosperous condition from a very small beginning. If has had its full share in encouraging education amongst the members of the Khoja community, and in providing a store of intellectual enjoyment to the rich and poor alike. From its foundation to the date of his death Mr. Sayani was the president and a zealous supporter of this usefull institution.

It may be said without exaggeration that almost all the institutions of organized philanthropy (among Khojas) that came into existence during the thirty years of the public activity of the late Mr. Sayani were either directly or indirectly due to his efforts. Urged by his shining example, many generous Khojas have come forward to establish charitable and educational institutions of every kind. The Khoja community is second only to the enlightened Parsee community in this respect. But the establishment of such institutions on a sound basis, and their progressive development may largely be traced to the versatile genius of the subject of our sketch.

MEMBER OF THE BOMBAY COUNCIL

Mr. Rahimtulla Sayani was first appointed a member of the Bombay Legislative Council in 1888. He was the first Khoja gentleman who obtained this high honour. His singleminded devotion, and exceptional grasp of public questions soon obtained for him a leading position in the Council and instances have happened of meetings of the Council being postponed to enable him to be present. In order to illustrate his views on burning questions of those days we shall quote here portions of some of his speeches delivered in the Council and elsewhere. In 1893 Mr. Sayani was called upon to preside over the Provincial Conference held at Ahmedabad. "The unanimous action of the Conference in calling the Hon'ble Mr. Sayani to the chair proved to demonstration that so far at any rate as educated and influential people of the various communities were concerned, there was to be no racial distinction, and that they were welded together into one community with common aims and aspirations for these advancement of the common interests of the various races inhabiting the country."

THE SURAT ANJUMAN

On the conclusion of the president's address, a letter purporting to be from the Secretary of the Anjuman-i-Islam of Surat to the effect that that body was against the movement was placed in the hands of the President. The President read the letter to the assembled delegates with the following pertinent remarks:—

> The Anjuman did not assign any reason for its opposition to this movement and such simple assertion as had been made did not become the prudence or position of any properly constituted body. Had they, and even now if they would, come and discuss with the Conference, their views would receive every attention, and should they be in a minority however small, due regard would be paid to the opposition of the Surat Anjuman who put themselves forward as representing the Surat Mahomedans. Whatever the Surat Anjuman might say, this much was certain that their brethren of the Bombay Anjuman, who were respected both by the people and the Government, had always been loyal supporters of the Congress and their President who had not long ago presided over the National Congress.

When these facts became known to the Mahomedans of Ahmedabad they spontaneously sent a letter influentially signed to the President of the Conference dissociating themselves from the Surat Anjuman and expressing their warm approval and sympathy with the Conference cause. During the course of their letter they said as follows:—

> We......give expression to our approval of your work in connection with the good and benevolent object of this Conference. We fully understand that the object of this your movement is not in any way disloyal towards Government and is calculated to profit the Hindus as well as the Mahomedans.

The inaugural address of the President was marked throughout by wisdom, moderation and oratorical excellence, and contained an eloquent and judicious appeal for concord between the Hindus and the Mahomedan communities.

MR. SAYANI AND THE CONGRESS

The good done by representative bodies like the National Congress and Provincial Conference is now recognised on all sides. There was a time, however when they were sometimes sneered at by certain people. Referring to the ironical remarks made about the National Congress in connection with the Bombay riots which took place a few months before the holding of the Conference Mr. Sayani said that

> it was lately stated, in jest of course, that in Bombay there was no necessity of calling out the Military—the National Congress could have met at Pydhownie, passed a resolution condemning the riots, and the rioters would have dispersed without any further ado. I admit that such a feat could not have been performed either by the National Congress or by the Provincial Conference, nay, even by the House of Parliament itself. For if such be the power and influence of deliberative assemblies, who would have ever heard about coercion Bills, and all about Ulster and Belfast and many other political events besides of the last seven years in Ireland. But such things would have been impossible if there had been a perfect harmony prevailing amongst all the members of both the large communities living in Bombay. That the contagion did not spread to the higher classes was due to the harmony prevailing among them. It is necessary to educate people in order to prevent them from resorting to disorderly behaviour.

In 1896 Mr. Sayani was unanimously chosen the President of the National Congress held at Calcutta. He was the second Mahomeden gentleman selected for this unique honour, the first being the late Justice Budruddin Tyabji.

His Congress address was a masterly exposition of the aims and objects of the Congress, and contained a reasoned appeal to the Mahomedans to join that movement. During the course of this speech, after quoting many great Englishmen, he said:

It will be observed from the above extracts that the people of England, possessing as they do a genuine admiration for their own constitution and jealous as they are for their own liberty, are not the people to view with disfavour the political aspirations of the people of India, aspirations forsooth, which the people of England themselves have deliberately inspired in the hearts of the people of India, by purposely educating them in the English language, by disseminating amongst them English ideals of political life and encouraging them to raise themselves by education, intelligence and integrity, so as to become qualified to occupy positions of importance and trust in the service of Government as also to take part in the administration of the country. Under the circumstances those persons—and I regret to say some such do exist among my community—who imagine that the people of England are at heart against the people of India are certainly doing a great injustice to the people of England. It may be that such wrong thinkers may have led into committing the mistake by the insular rigidity of England and by the stiff and stand off attitude of some Englishmen, and then sometimes rough refusal to budge or bend an inch. But surely such wrong thinkers should not be carried away by outward appearances or by false inferences derived from such outward appearances. If such people will go a little deeper into things, their minds will soon be disabused of these pure delusions. In fact a more honest or steady nation does not exist under the sun than this English Nation; and there ought to be no doubt whatever as to the ultimate concession of our demands founded as such demands are on reason and justice on the one hand, as on the declared policy and plighted word of the people of England on the other—provided always that the people of India are true to themselves. I repeat that there can be no doubt whatever as to these reasonable demands being ultimately conceded.

Referring to the unwillingness of the Moslem leaders to join the Congress movement, Mr Sayani quoted with approval a portion of a speech delivered by Sir Syed Ahmed Khan in 1866 at Aligarh:—

Syed Ahmed then urging his co-religionists to give up their apathy said that "if you will not help yourselves, you may be quite certain no one else will. Why should you be afraid? Here am I a servant of Government, speaking out plainly to you in this public meeting. My attachment to Government was proved as many of you know, in the eventful year of the Mutiny. It is my firm conviction on which I have invariably expressed both in public and in private—that the greater the confidence of the people of India in the Government the more solid the foundation upon which the present Government rests, and the more mutual friendship is cultivated between the rulers and yourselves, the greater will be the future benefit to your country. Be loyal in your hearts, place every reliance on your rulers, speak out openly, honestly and respectfully all your grievances, hopes and fears; you may be quite sure that such a course of conduct will place you in the enjoyment of all your legitimate rights, and that this is compatible, nay synonymous with true loyalty to the State, which will be upheld by all whose opinion is worth learning."

IN THE IMPERIAL COUNCIL

At the end of 1896 Mr. P. M. Mehta (now Sir Pherozshah) resigned his seat on the Supreme Legislative Council; the unanimous choice of non-official members of the Bombay Legislative Council then fell on Mr. Sayani. During the course of his two years' term of office several important matters came before that august body for disposal. Among them may be particularly mentioned the Epidemic Diseases Act, Amendment of the Criminal Procedure Code and Seditious Meetings Act. It is scarcely necessary to say that Mr. Sayani brought to bear on these discussions his unique experience, and clear grasp of these questions which earned for him an especial appreciation from H.E. Lord Elgin who was then Governor-General of India. His Budget speeches are also noteworthy.

Sir James Westland while replying to the debate also referred to Mr. Sayani's speech, as "very pregnant in suggestion and which it will be useful for us to read at leisure." We give below extracts from

Mr. Sayani's speech delivered during the discussion on the Financial Statement for 1898—99. Speaking about the combined affliction of famine, plague, war and earthquake Mr. Sayani said as follows:—

I may be permitted to remind the Council that at the last Budget Meeting I referred to the causes of famine and remedies against the same. In reference to my remarks your Lordship was pleased to say:—No one feels mere keenly than I that Government does not discharge the whole ot its duty even if it provides adequate funds for meeting calamities like that of this year and administers them well. These calamities are, I fear, inevitable in the circumstances of India. But Government is bound never to lose sight of the condition of the people, or fail to take any opportunities it can of ameliorating it. Sir John Woodburn mentioned the other day that the subject, and specially the indebtedness of the people, had been under our consideration. Our programme of work had been laid out; we have no intention of dropping the subject. I avail myself therefore of this opportunity and beg to remind your Lordship of the intended 'reforming legislation.' I hope that the programme, having been laid out more than a year ago, it has now been well advanced in 'sympathy with the people' and 'in earnest wish for improving the condition under which they live.' If your Lordship can see your way to make an announcement on the subject, your Lordship will be conferring an obligation on the country generally, and the Additional Members of your Lordship's Council, will on the dispersion of this Council and their consequent return to their respective homes, be enabled to carry your Lordship's message of goodwill to the people. The prosperity of this Country, My Lord, is capable of being vastly advanced. Under the British Rule based as it is generally on law and sympathy, and possessed as England is of the means of pouring British capital into this country to the mutual advantage of both, this country has a good chance of being materially developed. Nature has in its bounty provided us with a tolerably fertile land, good climate, and abundance of river water; the population is numerous and industrious. British Rule has given us peace and England can afford to lend us enormus capital. All the materials therefore, are thus procurable. Even manufactures can be materially increased, as England can teach us the methods and guide us in our endeavours. The only things wanted are to induce English capital to this country, and to guide operations and stimulate industry. The prosperity of this country will conduce to the welfare of both England and India. It will make the Indians prosperous and therefore contented and loyal. It will render India a field

for English capital, and a market for English goods. Indeed India is capable of becoming the greatest market for England.

In fact Mr. Sayani when in the Imperial Council represented not only Mahomedan interests but the non-official community of the Presidency of Bombay as a whole.

In his private life he was known as a gentle man of the old school but at the same time holding sufficiently advanced views. His simplicity of heart occasionally made him liable to be the prey of unscrupulous people in spite of his great abilities. Though during the last years of his life he held a very high place in the public life of this country, he was by nature of a very unassuming and unambitious character. There is reason to believe that he would have been the recipient of a K. C. I. E., while he was serving on the Imperial Council, had his own modesty not prevented him from coveting such titular distinctions.

One of his greatest titles to the gratitude of his own community consists in the fatherly encouragement he always used to give to his poor but deserving brethren. Several Khoja gentlemen who afterwards rose to some eminence and a fair amount of material prosperity, owed largely to the constant encouragement and pecuniary assistance timely rendered to them by the late Mr. Sayani.

The simplicity and piety of his life combined with his honourable and distinguished position, was remarkable. The only other gentleman of Western

India, with whose character and manner of living it could be well compared was that 'guide, philosopher, and friend' of the Deccan, the late Mahadev Govind Ranade. When he passed away on the 4th June 1902 there was a spontaneous outburst of grief in numerous Khoja homes and it was felt by many a person that he had lost a sincere friend who was, as it were,, a parent to him. It is gratifying to note that some of the best and kindest of condolence messages emanated from prominent members of the European community both official and unofficial.

Referring to the esteem in which Mr. Sayani was held one prominent journal wrote that Mr. Sayani's name had not figured in any despatches but was enshrined in the hearts of the people. Space does not permit us to quote many such instances. We shall therefore satisfy ourselves with quoting the reference of a distinguished Vice-Chanceller (Dr. Mackichan) during his convocation address, to Mr. Sayani's death:—

This is not the place to speak of the late Mr. Sayani's services to the public life of the city. I would only observe that he combined in a manner that is not common, the civic and the academic spirit. The latter lent refinement to his public life, while his experience as a public spirited citizen contributed in no small measure to the effectiveness of his services in the various offices which he filled in this University.

P. 129

SYED MAHMOOD

SYED MAHMOOD.

SYED Mahmood was, perhaps, one of the greatest Judges who ever presided over a chartered High Court in India. The second son of Sir Syed Ahmed, the famous Mahomedan patriot and worthy so well-known in connection with his work for the advancement of Moslem education in India, he was born at Delhi in 1850. He received his early education at Delhi and in the Queen's College, Benares and proceeded, (on a Government of India scholarship) in 1869, to England where he joined the Christ's College, Cambridge and had a successful academic career. He also distinguished himself by his knowledge of languages, European, Oriental and Classical. His illustrious father who had accompained him stayed in England long enough, to mature with his son's active aid and co-operation, his long contemplated scheme of Moslem education. The extent of help rendered by Syed Mahmood in this work to his distinguished father can never be easily set down. Though a student at Cambridge—his tutor was the late Mr. A. M. Bose, afterwards one of the most famous Presidents of the Indian National Congress—he proved of immense help to his father during the 17 months he stayed in England for planning out his life's-work. Syed Mahmood also assisted his father in searching up (at the British Museum and elsewhere) original materials for a re-joinder to Sir William Muir's sketch of Mahomed in his well-known *Life* of the Prophet. This rejoinder was published (by Sir Syed Ahmed) in 1870, under the title "Essays on the Life of Mahomed" and it is now an open secret that Mr. Mahmood was responsible for the translation of these Essays into English. The work attracted considerable attention both in England and in India, and in its English garb favourably impressed scholars in both countries. The valuable work he had done for his father in England in giving shape to the latter's educational ideas stood him in great stead when he was (about 1871) called upon by his father to draw up the constitution of the Educational Board he set up to evolve his scheme of an Anglo-Oriental College for the advancement of his country. Mr. Mahmood drew up the required constitution and published as well the synopsis of questions put to persons of light and leading as to the best mode of regenerating the country. The result was that, in 1872, a Committee called the M. A. O. College Fund Committee, was formed at Benares with a Sub-Committee at Aligarh. In 1873, Mr. Syed Mahmood issued a circular addressed to the members of the Committee, submitting a full-fledged scheme for the creation of a Mahomedan University. The Residential College soon after (1875) was set up and it is now the Aligarh University. To anticipate a little, it might be mentioned at this point that when Mr. Mahmood retired from the Bench he returned to his first love, education, and the M. A. O. College at Aligarh. He taught English in the College classes; he proved himself by far the ablest of its Trustees, later becoming its President, and the result of his connection with it from his under-graduate days was his *History of English Education in India*, a book as full of fecund thought as it is luminous in its treatment of a difficult, subject. Mr. Mahmood's connection with education was, in a word, a life-long one. It was fruitful in divers ways of good to his co-religionists and to Indians generally. If Sir Syed Ahmed was full of original ideas, his distinguished son, Mahmood, found the reasoning for them and what is more, gave them shape and brought round converts to them from the generality of the community. It is fair to put the position thus: the father and son, between them, made up what was exactly required for thinking out and bringing into existence the nucleus of an organization which has now blossomed into a full blown University of the most modern type.

AS A JUDGE.

Mahmood had a brilliant career in England and was called to the Bar at Lincoln's Inn in 1872. He returned to India in due course, and after a comparatively short period at the Allahabad Bar, was made a District Judge at Rai Bareli in 1879, and later raised to the N. W. P. (now Allahabad) High Court Bench. His first appointment to this post was an officiating one, made in 1882. After a reversion to the Bar, he was appointed permanently to it. This was the capacity in which he was best known to the public in India. Some of the judgments he delivered have become classical and have won for him an undying reputation. Sir Whitley Stokes, no mean judge of Judges, has recorded his opinion in his *Anglo-Indian Codes* that no judgments in the whole series of the Indian Law Reports are more weighty or illuminating than those of the Hindu Muthuswami Iyer or the Mahomedan Syed Mahmood. From the start, Syed Mahmood became what might firstly be called a *persona grata* with litigants. His broad-mindedness, his sense of equity, his keenness to do justice as between parties, became known not only to the practitioners in his Court but also to the general public outside. Sir Tej Bahadur Sapru, writing of him as a Judge, says:—

Perhaps the question to be asked in these days about a judge ought to be, does he do the justice which the law allows him to do? This is not altogether a reproach to modern law. For a greater degree of certainty of procedure and results is not purchased too dearly at the price of occasional miscarriages of justice, which are condemnable but all the same unavoidable. And, indeed, as remarked by one of the most eminent English judges—the highest justice consists in following law. We may now ask whether Mr. Mahmood was a just judge. I, for one, think, and I believe this is the general impression of the profession and litigants, that he always endeavoured to do justice—at least so much justice as our law is capable of allowing a judge to dole out. His innate sense of justice revolted against some of the absurdities and imperfections of our law, and though he did not deem himself at liberty to transgress the four corners of a statute, he could not at times forbear recording his protest against them. Indeed, whenever it was possible, he would endeavour to reconcile the inelastic language of codified law to broad principles of justice. I will give an instance of this. In the year 1891, the following question was, at his recommendation, referred to the Full Bench of the Court: "Can an appellant who is in jail, and who has presented his appeal through the officer in charge of the jail in which he is confined be said not to appear so that he may be heard within S. 423 of the Criminal Procedure Code, when by reason of his confinement in jail, he cannot appear, and is without means to instruct a pleader to appear for him." In a singularly able and exhaustive judgment which lays before us the innermost springs of his mind, he dwelt at length upon the maxims 'Audi alteram partem' and 'ubi jus ibi remedium,' showed that they were maxims of what he happily styled as 'human jurisprudence,' referred to Seneca and an Urdu poet to show that the absolute necessity of hearing an accused was as much a part of the Roman's creed as of the Indian's, and ultimately held that it was not enough that notices should be served on a prisoner but that it was also imperatively necessary that he should be heard in appeal, either in person or through a pleader. The Chief Justice, Sir John Edge, and Straight and Young, Justices, took a contrary view. I quote below a passage from his judgment, where the impassivity of the Judge warms up into the passionate eloquence of an advocate pleading for justice. "Having so far dealt with these aspects of the case, as they have appeared to me both in point of law and upon points which I think have even higher basis than that doubtful phrase; I think it is necessary for me to say that if it is true that the law of British India makes it possible for me, sitting here as a Judge, in the first place, by dint of my writ to order a person to be imprisoned, and tied by the chain, then in the next place to require the mockery of asking him to attend, when I, by dint of the exercise of my own power, have made it impossible for him to attend, and then have the solemn mockery of having his name called out; if this is the law of British India, I hope the sooner it is abrogated, the better." It is but too true that this is the law of British India, and that the hope so warmly expressed by him remains yet unfulfilled. It may not be without interest to note that Mr. Justice Hill, who was then a leading member of the Allahabad Bar and who appeared as *amicus curiæ* in the case from which I have quoted above, is reported to have lately from his seat on the Calcutta Bench, made similar observations with respect to the hardship of the lot of undefended prisoners, and that in England at least, a Bill for providing for the defence of poor prisoners is just now on the table of the House of Commons. One of the most cultured of English Judges, Lord Justice Bowen is reported to have observed in the course of a lecture at a meeting of the Law Society: "Law is the application of certain rules to a subject-matter which is constantly shifting. What is it? English life! English business! England in movement, advancing to a continuous future. National life, national business, like every other product of human intelligence and culture, is a growth—begins far away in the dim past, advances slowly, shaping and forming itself by the operation of purely natural causes." Of course he was speaking of England and English Law; but the same remarks may be, *mutatis mutandis*, applied to India and Indian life. It may be said that a Judge is neither a legislator nor a social reformer, that his proper business is to apply the law *as it is* to the facts before him. I think it is no longer considered a legal heresy to say that Judges do at times make law. The theory of judicial legislation would not have so clearly found its classification among the Fictions of Law, but for the bold exposition of Sir Henry Sumner Maine in his *Ancient Law*. That Mr. Justice Mahmood himself was prepared to take a broader view of his position as a Judge is to my mind apparent from many of his judgments. The legislature has guaranteed to the Hindus and the Musulmans the application of their respective personal laws in some matters, and it can be by no means easy to answer the question whether in a state of society which is entirely different to what it may have been, say some seven centuries back the ancient laws are to be applied, irrespective of any changes that may have come on during this interval. As to how Mr. Justice Mahmood would answer this question, I cannot do better than give a few characteristic extracts from some of his judgments. In one of his earliest judgments (Indar Kuar v Lalla Prasad Singh, 4 All., p. 541) he addresses himself to a discussion of the limits of a Hindu widow's powers of alienating the property to which she succeeds on her husband's death. After pointing out that the original Shastras knew no such thing as what is now technically known as Legal Necessity, he observes:—"But this extension of the original doctrine seems to have arisen from the exigencies of modern life rather than the precepts of Hindu law and to have originated in the principles of equity which could not be disregarded in administering an ancient law and *adapting its behests to the present conditions of life in British India.*"

A still more remarkable passage showing the attitude of his mind towards the manner in which ancient laws ought now to be interpreted occurs in another judgment which he delivered several years later. It is a fair sample of his style and erudition and it has been followed in other courts also. The question in the case was whether the widow of a Hindu son who had died in his father's life-time could sue her husband's brother who had inherited the property from his father for maintenance. After repelling the argument that there was no legal obligation on the defendant to give any maintenance to the plaintiff, he observes:—

"But because the case is not altogether free from difficulty and also because our judgment in this case will go very near the boundary of what is sometimes described as *judicial legislation*, I am anxious before concluding my judgment to refer to some considerations of good policy from which I confess my mind has not altogether been free in determining the question raised in this case. When I say 'good policy' I do not refer to any political exigencies of the population of the territories under the jurisdiction of this Court. I use the phrase in the sense in which such a phrase should be understood in judicial exposition of the law, that is, in the sense of those broad principles which ordain the basis of the rule of justice, equity and good conscience, upon which we, as Judges of the Court which exercises the combined jurisdiction of a court of law and a court of equity, must act in cases where there is no specific legislative provision in the statute law or the original texts of an ancient system of jurisprudence which we are bound to administer do not furnish an express authority in specific terms."

Commenting on this Sir Tej Bahadur wrote in the same article:—

That Mr. Justice Mahmood had high authority for thus interpreting the law would be obvious to those of us who have watched the course of English decisions in recent years. The enormous expansion of trade and the consequent competition in the market have led to a stage of economical progress where all attempts at interfering with open competition are strongly resented in England. The policy of *laissez faire* has so powerfully asserted itself in that country that even judicial tribunals have felt themselves called upon to adapt the theory of wrong to modern conditions of business life. In recent times the spirit of liberalism in law —a spirit certainly to be welcomed, considering that the law is pre-eminently conservative in its tendencies—began with the well-known decision in the case of the Moghul Steamship Company and has been working through a long series of decisions, though not always in an equally luminous manner. The growth in the powers of trade unions in England has also led the judges there to seriously consider the legal bounds of individual liberty and its relations to what may be called the collective pressure of trade arrangements. The rule may not have been explained with equal clearness in Allen *v.* Flood, Qunn *v.* Leatham and the Taff Vale case. But it is obvious that there is a strong tendency among Judges in England to recognize the current forces working upon the social and economic progress of their country. And indeed law and judges might be curses in the guise of blessings were they always to act as drags on the upward march of society. It must be said to the credit of Mr. Justice Mahmood that at least with respect to the Hindu law, he, like the late Mr. Justice Ranade of Bombay, always attempted to reconcile the wisdom of ancient sages to the mixed civilization of their descendants.

Justice Mahmood's conceptions of equity, justice and good conscience were in some respects materially different from those of many other Indian Judges; and it was perhaps because of these conceptions that he was enabled to grapple with the modern conditions of Indian life.

Equity with him was neither a roguish thing, nor a deceitful will of the wisp. On the contrary he could always trust to it for light'ing up some dark corners in our law. But he at the same time clearly realized that it was by no means desirable to import whole-sale those equitable maxims or rules which are the growth of ages in England and which are peculiarly suited to English life and English Courts. Perhaps he was not always successful in what may be called the process of adaptation; perhaps this very method led him to adopt views which did not always command universal assent. As instances of the inconsistencies in the results flowing from his methods, I may mention two of his most celebrated judgments, the one on a question of Mohammadan Law and the other on a question of Hindu Law. In Gobind Dayal *vs.* Inayatulla (7 All. p. 775), where his powers of reasoning display themselves at their best, it was this very doctrine of equity, justice and good conscience which led him to invest the right of pre-emption under the Muhammadan Law with the sanctity of a religious institution, a view to which exception was taken then and has been taken since. In Ganga Sahai *vs.* Lekhraj Kuar (9 All., p. 253), on the contrary, where the Mohammadan Judge traces back the history of the Hindu Law with all the avidity of an antiquarian, and discusses the subtle doctrines of the Hindu Law with a depth of reasoning which is truly astonishing, he relied upon equity, justice, and good conscience for prescribing the limits of the doctrine of *Factum valet* in its application to cases of adoption under the Hindu Law in a manner which may be said to have infused a spirit of liberalism into our law in so far as it secures the position of an adopted son against a claimant who may be disposed to question his status as such, because the adoptive father may have omitted to observe some of the rules and ceremonies prescribed by the ancient sages.

It is impossible to add anything to the above remarks of Sir Tej Bahadur as to how Syed Mahmood approached questions arising under the uncodified laws of Hindus and Mahomedans. How did he construe Codified Law? Here is what Sir Tej says:—

It is a matter of common experience that statute law is less flexible than that which has not been compressed in the form of codes, and indeed it would be more than questionable whether it is an advantage to have codes without having a system of their revision at regular intervals. In India where codification has been tried on such a large scale, much of the results of the Legislature's efforts is bound to depend upon the construction to be placed on Acts and Codes, 'The golden rule of construction' was very lucidly explained by Lord Herschell in the well-known English case, The Bank of England *v.* Vagliano. Mr. Justice Mahmood also not unoften acted upon this rule but inasmuch as the workmanship of our Acts and Codes hardly comes up to that degree of perfection which is generally the characteristic of English statutes, he seems to have felt himself justified in tempering the rigour of that rule by discovering the intention and policy of the Legislature and the mischief which it intended to cure. As an illustration of this statement, I may mention the case of Jadu Rai *v.* Kanizak Husain in which he upon a construction of section 191 of the Code of Civil Procedure, ruled that the successor in office of a Judge who had heard the evidence in the case, was competent to hear arguments and deliver judgment. In his exceedingly luminous judgment he first refers to the rule enunciated by Baron Parke in Becke *v.* Smith, which was in effect the same as that more recently laid down by Lord Herschell and then he delivers himself thus:—

"I have before now said, sitting as a Judge of this Court, that the general principles of Lord Coke's celebrated dictum in Heyden's case are applicable to the interpretation of our own Indian Enactments. and that in construing the rules of such departments of law as Civil Procedure, which has repeatedly been the object of repealing, amending, and consolidating legislation, it is important to consider the previous state of the law, the mischief and defect which that law did not provide for. the remedy which the Legislature adopted to remove the mischief, the true reason of the remedy, and (to use Lord Coke's own words) "then the office of all the Judges is always to make such construction as will suppress the mischief and advance the remedy, and suppress subtle inventions, and evasions for continuance of the mischief and *pro privato commodo*, and to add force and life to the cure and remedy, according to the true intent of the makers of the Act *pro bono publico*." ' Here again we find him calling to his aid the basal principle of equity which as Wooddesdon tells us is "a judicial interpretation of laws, which presupposing the legislator to have intended what is just and right, pursues and effectuates that intention." * This principle supplies us the keynote of his decisions on Indian Acts and the careful reader will hear its echoes in perhaps the largest of his judgments on the construction of some sections of an Indian Act. I refer of course to Matadin Kasodhan *v.* Kasim Husain (13 All. 432), in which he delivered a dissentient judgment. That the decision of the majority of the Allahabad Judges has made the litigation about mortgage transactions more complex than it used to be before, is, I believe the general experience of the profession, and that judicial opinion in the High Court itself seems now to be doubtful as to its soundness may be gathered from the occasional remarks of judges whose respect for it now would seem to rest mainly on the ground that it is a Full Bench ruling.

Syed Mahmood gave abundant proof, as a Judge, of his profound legal acumen and breadth of views. The following from Sir Tej Bahadur's critical observations on his work as a Judge will illustrate this aspect of his greatness :—

Who, for instance, in the profession has not read with admiration his judgment, in Chittor Mal *vs.* Shib Lal, in which he points out that a person, paying the revenue of a village on behalf of his co-sharer, acquires a lien on the latter's share in the village similar to what is created by salvage under the maritime law ? It is interesting to find that two other Indian Judges of great eminence, Sir Bhashyam Ayyangar and Sir Subramaniya Aiyar of Madras have recently adopted the same view. A common complaint against Mr. Justice Mahmood is that his judgments were prolix. It seems there is an element of truth in this charge, but at the same time it cannot be forgotten that he was appointed judge at a time when the Legislature had just passed two important measures, and when some other Acts, such as the Indian Limitation Act and the Specific Relief Act, not to mention others, had not been long in force. The Civil Procedure Code and the Transfer of Property Act were passed about the time that he was brought on the Bench at Allahabad and they had to be explained. A large number of

* It is noticeable that the Legislature itself removed all doubt on the question decided by Justice Mahmood, by a subsequent Act (VII of 1888, S. 18).

his earlier judgments relate to questions arising under these enactments, and it will require much hardihood to maintain that he has not done much to remove many doubts and elucidate many obscure questions which cropped up under them. If however to be copious is a fault in a judge, he requires no special apology as he shared it in common with other Indian Judges such as Sir Barnes Peacock, and Dwarka Nath Mitter, Muthuswami Aiyar, Holloway, and West, JJ., who have left permanent marks of their great talents upon our law. At all events, copiousness which is instructive and interesting may well be preferred to brevity which, so far from always being the soul of judicial wit, is very often a source of obscurity. In our own times who would not prefer spending three hours over a single decision of Sir Bashyam Ayyangar to spending one over half a dozen stunted products of judicial parentage which sometimes crowd the pages of the Law Reports.

AS HE APPEARED IN COURT.

How did he appear in the Court itself to practitioners before him, quite apart from how he appeared in the pages of the Law Reports? Happily we have picture of it in the following extract from Sir Tej Bahadur Sapru's reminiscenses of him in the *Hindustan Review* :—

> Tradition which is as much a part of all Bar Associations as the bulky volumes of Reports and text-books, tells us that he joined dignity to courtesy and abounded in patience with the confident 'leader' and the tremulous 'junior' alike. Thoroughness' was his watch-word as it is the watch-word of all scholarly minds. His mind was richly endowed by nature and assiduously cultivated by himself, and his judgments—exquisite pieces of legal composition—will live as long as the present system of our jurisprudence will continue to be a living factor in our polity.

RESIGNATION FROM THE BENCH.

The circumstances which led to his resignation of the post of Judge, in which he had shone with such great honor to himself and his country are too sad to narrate. Apart from an insidious—nay accursed—habit to which he had fallen early a prey to, it was whispered at the time that green-eyed jealousy as well had done its part. To whatever cause it was due to, his resignation (practically an enforced one) did irreparable injury not only to himself personally but proved a great loss to the High Court Bench. If the Allahabad High Court is famous to-day it was largely through the association with it of eminent Judges like Syed Mahmood. Though one of the latest High Courts to be created, it soon attained, because of its connection with Judges of the type of Syed Mahmood, a celebrity all over India equal to, if not greater than, that of any other older and longer established High Court in India. However it came about, Syed Mahmood's resignation was more than a public calamity. Personally it proved to him disastrous. He retired to Aligarh and lived under his paternal roof. He interested himself in College work. He traced out a financial fraud perpetrated by one of its clerks. He was nominated a Member of the N.W.P. Legislative Council and at it he worked, not as a modern member does, but rather in a manner becoming a retired Judge. But soon Syed Mahmood found the truth of the legal saying *Protectio trahit subjectionem, et subjectio protectionem* (*Protection involves dependence, and dependence protection.*) Ostensibly on legislative business at Allahabad, he once for all took leave of his father's home. He settled down at Lucknow, having joined the Bar there.

AT THE BAR.

His second innings at the Bar cannot be better described than in the words of the late Dr. Satish

Chunder Banerji, who was his 'devil' at the time at Lucknow. In an article in the *Hindustan Review*, published soon after the death of Syed Mahmood, he says:—

For sometime after his enrolment Mr. Mahmood no doubt had a very busy career as an advocate. I had to be constantly at his side and so I know that though his charges were very high, his hands were always full of work. But alas! Mr. Mahmood was then not what he once had been. We all know what lost him his judgeship. The same accursed habit lost him his practice too, and that pretty sharp. He had succeeded in removing himself from his father's restraining and beneficial influence, and he fell back to his old course. His habits became irregular, he became incapable of sustained work, and his clients fell off. Not only were his own habits irregular, but they were calculated to cause the greatest inconvenience to those who had to work with him. He would sometimes work day and night and at other times not work at all. I can recall many a day when he has positively refused to read the brief that I had prepared for him, and then on the following morning has called me up at 4 to explain to him the points in the case which he had to argue in Court that day. I can also recall days when owing to his erratic habits I could scarcely make time for my breakfast, and when he took hardly any solid food at all. Mr. Mahmood had inherited an iron constitution, so it did not much matter to him. But under the strain of these irregularities my health broke down and I left Lucknow finally in September, 1896. I was down then with an attack of high fever, but I still remember with loving gratitude how Mr. Mahmood who had his bed in another room would come 5 or 6 times in the night to feel my pulse and stroke my forehead.

AS A MAN.

The following is Mr. Banerji's general impression of Syed Mahmood as a man. It cannot be improved upon:—

The first thing that struck one about Mr. Mahmood was his culture. He was not only a well-read and well-informed man, but he was a thoroughly *cultured gentleman*. About his erudition as a lawyer it is not for me to speak. I may, however, note in passing that I have heard Mr. Mahmood observe that a judge of fact is greater than a judge of law, and imply that he had been more of a judge of law than of fact. He used to express the highest admiration for Dwaraka Nath Mitter and

Muthuswami Iyer, and once told some Muhammadan gentlemen in my presence that he was not worthy to untie the latchets of the shoes of those two eminent judges. He possibly ranked himself third in order of merit among Indian judges who have graced any High Court Bench. But I was referring here to his attainments generally and not merely as a lawyer. He was very fond of poetry and would pass whole evenings in the recitation and criticism of choice Persian and English poems. Among English poets he was particularly fond of Gray and Tennyson, and had himself composed some verses in the characteristic manner of these masters. He felt attracted by the *Sufi* doctrines, and was probably in sympathy with the Vedanta philosophy. He was at any rate prepared to appreciate the full greatness of Hindu thought and of Sanskrit literature, and when at Mr. Beck's suggestion the chair of Sanskrit in the Aligarh College was abolished it was principally through Mr. Mahmood's efforts that the old Pundit was reinstated. Mr. Mahmood wrote a bad hand and so preferred to dictate to an amanuensis. This probably accounts to some extent for his prolixity as a writer. Besides, he had a partiality for long rolling sentences and had an eye to 'style.'

HIS POLITICAL VIEWS AND SYMPATHIES.

The same writer's description of his political views and sympathies will be widely appreciated. He says:—

Mr. Mahmood was a man of liberal sympathies and a true friend of progress. He had the highest regard for Mr. A. M. Bose, (he would fondly refer to him as "my tutor when I was an undergraduate at Cambridge"), and his friends among the Hindus were, I believe, quite as numerous as among the Muhammadans. He certainly did not view the Indian National Congress with 'dread,' as some of his co-religionists who contribute to the *Aligarh Institute Gazette*, profess to; and I have reason to believe that, if Mr. Surendra Nath Banerjee and Mr. A. M. Bose had approached him properly, he might have presided over the annual deliberations of that national body. He once told me at Lucknow that he was seriously thinking about this matter, that he had sympathy with the movement, and that he was prepared to accept many of the resolutions adopted at meetings of the Indian National Congress. Unfortunately not having studied the science of politics with any thoroughness I do not care to dabble in politics, and so I did not push the matter any further. But that Mr. Mahmood was a much more clear-sighted man and had the true cause of his mother-country more deeply at heart than many self-styled politicians, both Hindu and Mussalman, who rush to print or clamber up the platform, I have not the least doubt. Mr. Mahmood was a proud man, he was a hot-tempered man, he had his fixed ideas (who has not ?) but he had no patience with hypocrisy, with pettiness, with servility and knee-truckling. I heard from father 18 years ago that Mr. Mahmood used to deplore the absence of a national leader in India and expressed a hope that Bengal might one day give to the country such a leader. True it is that distance lends enchantment to the view! There can be no doubt, however, that he would have liked to see perfect fellowship established between Hindus and Muhammadans, and he would often say to me, "You are a Brahman among Hindus, I am a Syed among Mussalmans; let us join hands together as of one kin."

HIS PERSONAL CHARACTERISTICS.

Syed Mahmood's liberality is well-known. He agreed with the saying "what you spend on a friend and comrade is gained." As Dr. Banerji says:—

> One word I must say here about Syed Mahmood's liberality and his generosity of heart. Nobody, I believe, ever approached him with a petition who did not get more than he wanted. Mr. Mahmood seems to have acted upon the theory that money was earned only with the object of being given away and his cheque-book was always at almost everybody's service. Another thing very characteristic about him was his hearty laughter. He was a very jovial man, whose heart was quite as large and as tender as his intellect was acute and bright. You could not have a better and kinder friend.

HIS WRITINGS.

A few words may be added about his literary remains. Syed Mahmood translated his father's *Life of Mahomed*, a book full of interest even now. The translation is a model of its kind. It is neither literal nor liberal; but well strikes the happy mean and is exceedingly readable. His *History of English Education in India* deserves to be reprinted, both for its views and for its brilliance. It deserves wider attention to-day more than ever. Syed Mahmood, in 1882, revised for Sir Frederick Pollock his "Indian

Civil Wrongs Bill" drawn up by him at the instance of the Government of India. He furnished Sir Frederick—as he gratefully acknowledges—with a careful memorandum, especially on the earlier parts of the draft and also gave him many "good suggestions" in regard to the Bill. The Bill of course, is not yet law, but it is still appreciated as a good working text, especially in the mofussal. When it is actually adopted, India will have owed it as much to Sir Frederick as to Syed Mahmood, as the former would be the first to acknowledge. Mahmood had also published his *Law of Evidence in British India,* in Hindustani: and edited Mahomedan law books in Arabic. It is said that he also began a *History of Islam.* His qualifications for this were indisputable, and the great attention he paid to studies in Islamic philosophy, law and education won him the esteem of his co-religionists to a degree not excelled by any save his illustrious father, Sir Syed Ahmed Khan. And when on May 8,1903, Mahmood breathed his last, his co-religionists and indeed the whole country fell into a profound grief. His fellow-countrymen felt that in him passed away a great scholar, reformer and judge, the illustrious son of an illustrious father. It is permissible to speak of Syed Mahmood in the words of Livy (as applied to Portius Cato) :—" In this man there was such force of mind and character that in whatever country he had been born, he would have been bound to have his fortune for himself."

P. 145.

THE RIGHT HON. SYED AMIR ALI

The Right Hon. Syed Amir Ali.

INTRODUCTION.

THE Right Hon'ble Syed Amir Ali, P. C. occupies a unique position not only in the British Empire but all over the Moslem World. As a leader and representative of Indian Mahomedans he is well-known in England and India ; as a Moslem jurist he has no equal ; as an interpreter of Islamic history and belief he is recognised, on all hands, as an authority ; as a reconciler of Islam with modern progress and enlightenment, he perhaps stands without a rival ; as a stout champion of pan-Islamic interests, he is known all the world over.

Mr. Amir Ali's life has been a continuous record of strenuous effort for the regeneration of Moslem India. He is closely associated with the late Sir Syed Ahmed Khan, the Founder of the Mahomedan Anglo-Oriental College and the School of Indian Mahomedan Liberalism, in all the reform movements which originated at Aligarh some forty years ago. Like Sir Syed, he figures as an apostle of English education and one of the earliest advocates of education for Indian Moslem women but, unlike Sir Syed, he is a social reformer of an advanced type and has even gone so far as to contract "mixed marriage" which the Aligarh sage pronounced to be detrimental to the interests of the conntry. Like Sir Syed, he stood aloof from the Indian National Congress from the conviction that the Moslem community "tied to the wheels of the Juggernaut of majority would be in the end crushed out of all semblance of nationality" but, unlike Sir Syed, he is an ardent politician, taking the lead in all political movements affecting the Moslem weal. Like Sir Syed, he forms a link between the East and the West, but unlike Sir Syed, he has purposely chosen the English language for communicating his thoughts and views to Moslems as well as to non-Moslems, for the reason that it is the language of culture and progress in the Modern World.

HIS FORBEARS

Mr. Amir Ali was born on April 6, 1849 at Chinsura—a quondam Dutch settlement—on the Hooghly in Bengal. He traces his descent, as all Syeds do, from Mahomed the Prophet through the Imam Ali-ar-Razza of Meshed. His forbears were in the employ of the Persian kings. One of them, Mahomed Sadiq Khan, held high office under Shah Abbas II. From him descended Ahmad Fazil, a soldier by profession, who, with a body of troops, joined the army of Nadir Shah when the latter invaded India in 1739. After the departure of the Persian monarch, Ahmad Fazil, however, chose to remain in India, taking service with his men under the Emperor of Delhi. When the Marathas sacked the Moghul capital, Ahmad Fazil's son fled from Delhi and took refuge in Oudh. Under the

Nawab Viziers of Oudh, his sons rose to distinction and one of them, Saadat Ali, removed to Bengal shortly before the annexation of Oudh. To Saadat Ali was born the subject of our biography.

STUDIES AT THE HOOGHLY COLLEGE

Mr. Amir Ali's father was a far-seeing man. His was an age quite different from ours. The Moslems of India were weltering in ignorance, superstition and bigotry. They turned a deaf ear to all things Western. They were so Mullah-ridden that they thought it a heresy to learn English. When such were the prevailing notions among "the faithful" in India, it argues a big heart for Saadat Ali Khan to depart from the stereotyped path and give his sons* an English education, facing the anathemas of myopic moulvies. Mr. Amir Ali was admitted into the Hooghly College which remained his *alma mater* throughout his academical career. He was a diligent student and was far ahead of his class-fellows. He soon passed the Matriculation Examination, securing a first class scholarship. By unremitting industry he worked his way up, graduating in 1867. A year after, he took the M. A. degree in History and Political Economy. He then prosecuted his studies in Law in the same college, passing the B. L. Examination with honours. Mr. Amir Ali is one of those who have, during their academical career received help

* Mr. Varis Ali, Mr. Amir Ali's elder brother, was also an *alumnus* of the Hooghly College where he was for some time Professor of Persian before joining the Revenue Department as a Deputy Collector.

from the "Moshin Fund" which has done so much to educate the Mahomedan youths of Bengal.

GOES TO ENGLAND TO STUDY FOR THE BAR

After passing the B. L. examination, Mr. Amir Ali practised for some time in the Calcutta High Court but very soon an opportunity was afforded him to give a finishing touch to his legal studies in England. He was elected as a State scholar by the Government of India. Mr. Amir Ali was one of the first Indian Mahomedans to study for the Bar. He joined the Inner Temple and was called to the Bar in 1873.

JOINS THE CALCUTTA BAR

Returning to India the same year, he again joined the Calcutta Bar and began to practise. He had, from the beginning, a large *clientele* and his fame as a lawyer grew. In 1874 he was elected a Fellow of the Calcutta University. The next year he was appointed Lecturer on Mahomedan Law at the Presidency College, Calcutta. He held the lectureship for five successive years. From about this time can be traced his deep solicitude for the Mohomedan community which has never flagged since. He became immensely interested in Mahomedan *Anjumans* and associations. He founded in 1876 the Central National Mahomedan Association and continued to be its Secretary for a quarter of a century. This association has done much for the amelioration of the Mahomedan community and as a proof thereof it may be remarked that, prior to Lord Minto's memorable reply to the Mahomedan deputation which waited on him at Simla on 1st October 1906, the most important declaration of policy emanating from the head of the Indian Government in regard to the Moslems, was the notable resolution issued by Lord Dufferin on the memorial of the Central National Mahomedan Association of Calcutta. Mr. Amir Ali was also President of the Committee of the Hooghly Imambara from 1876 to 1904.

HIS FIRST OFFICIAL CAREER

After five years of successful practice he was selected in 1878 to fill the post of Presidency Magistrate. So well did he discharge his duties that, in a very short time, he was appointed Officiating Chief Presidency Magistrate. He applied himself with zeal to the new work entrusted to him, winning alike the confidence of the public and the good-will of the Government. But Mr. Amir Ali could not remain long in Government service. It was difficult for a man who had lived in the bracing atmosphere of the Bar to be cooped up in the official crib. The spirit of independence was slowly working within him and he longed to be free. In 1881 when the air was thick with rumours of his being confirmed in the officiating incumbency, he resigned, in spite of the admonitions and friendly protests of his numerous friends and well-wishers. Although this action of his was then considered rash and short-sighted, it eventually bore good results.

AGAIN REVERTS TO THE BAR

Mr. Amir Ali after relinquishing the office of Chief Presidency Magistrate once again joined the Bar. This time he wielded an unusually large and lucrative practice. The sphere of his activities also became widened. He rose in public esteem and in the eyes of the Government. He was first made a member of the Bengal Legislative Council which he continued to be till 1883. Immediately after, Lord Ripon nominated him to the Imperial Legislative Council to represent the interests of the Moslems whose cause he pleaded with impassioned eloquence. He took a prominent part in the debates of the Council. Those were the stormy days of the ill-fated Ilbert Bill. His strength of character and sincerity of purpose left a deep impression even on those who differed from him in views. Lord Dufferin in one of his speeches spoke very highly of his services. In 1884 he was appointed Tagore Law Professor. In recognition of his many services he was awarded the title of C.I.E., in 1887.

BECOMES A HIGH COURT JUDGE

The year 1890 was a red-letter date in the life of Mr. Amir Ali. He was appointed to the then highest post in the gift of the Government open to natives of India, barring of course the oligarchical Civil Service which imposes so many restrictions. His elevation to the Bench was received with universal approbation and the Mahomedan community, in particular, felt themselves highly flattered at the nomination. Mr. Amir Ali was the second Mahomedan to be thus honoured, the first being Justice Syed Mahmood. For a man who possessed a sound legal knowledge, who had practised successfully in the Calcutta High Court, who had filled the posts of Presidency Magistrate and Chief Presidency Magistrate, who had sat in the Provincial and Imperial Legislative Councils, who had been Tagore Law Professor, it was not at all difficult to do full justice to the new responsibility entrusted to his care. Lord Lansdowne's selection was a happy one. Mr. Amir Ali possessed in a high degree all the qualifications and attributes that go to make a popular judge. Having passed through all the metamorphic stages of the Indian judiciary, he was in a position to sympathise both with the lawyer and the litigant. His keen sense of justice, his deep solicitude for the parties and his strict impartiality inspired confidence among the public. Even the worst political enemy of Mr. Amir Ali cannot but admit that, so far as judgments went, he was singularly free from bias and prejudice. His knowledge of Mahomedan Law is profound and of a rare order. His presence in the High Court helped to solve some of the knotty points of Mahomedan Law that confronted his brother judges. How deeply learned he is in Mahomedan Law may be gauged from the fact that, during the trial of an important case when the *Wakf* question was referred to in full bench, his sole judgment, as against the united and, therefore, weightier decision of the other judges, was upheld by the Privy Council. It may be said that the *Wakf* Bill, which was first introduced in the Imperial Legislative Council by the Hon'ble Mr. Jinnah in the winter session of 1911 and which in 1913 become law, owes its inception to Mr. Amir Ali.

Mr. Amir Ali's judgments give ample proof of his legal acumen, breadth of vision and close application. Even from a literary standpoint they occupy a high place. Chasteness of language, simplicity of style, lucidity and conciseness of expression, a rare command over the English idiom characterise his judgments and the lay literary reader, too, will find them interesting reading.

RETIRES AND SETTLES IN ENGLAND

After fourteen years of arduous service in the Bench of the Calcutta High Court, he retired in 1904. At the time of his retirement, it was thought that he would settle in India and give undivided attention to literary pursuits which it was not possible for him to do during his official career. But he rather chose to settle in England than in India. England had many attractions for him. It appealed to him as a land of liberty and the world's centre of learning and progress. It afforded him greater facilities and opportunities for his many-sided activities. It is puerile to suppose that he settled in England simply because it was the land of his "better half." Yet it strikes us that the peculiar social disabilities under which English wives of Indians smart in the

"Land of Regrets" must have weighed not a little with Mr. Amir Ali when the question of his future domicile was mooted. Nevertheless his love for India never waned. In fact it has grown with the distance. He is chiefly known in English society as an indefatigable fighter for the cause of Indian Mahomedans and Indian liberalism.

HIS ENGLISH HOME

Avoiding the bustle and turmoil of London life, he has settled in a secluded corner of Berkshire. He has made the "Lambdens" his home, "Lambdens" which was once the dower house of the lords of the manor of Ufton, one of whom, Francis Perkins, married Arabella Fermor, the Belinda of Pope's *Rape of the Lock*. This historic house lies half-way between Theale and Aldermaston. It is very picturesquely situated on a gentle slope. In the North are the Ufton hills and on either side lie the Beenham and Englefield Parks. The house with its trellised verandah in the old "Indian style" is approached by a charming avenue of lime-trees, while a small lake below lends additional charm to the scenery around. The "Lambdens" contains a choice collection of art treasures from India and Arabia which Mrs. Amir Ali so assiduously collected while in India. Here Mr. Amir Ali gives up much of his leisure to study and literary work.

MR. AMIR ALI AND THE MOSLEM LEAGUE

Of the many-sided activities which have engaged Mr. Amir Ali's attention since he made England his home, the work of the Moslem League claims the largest share. Ever since the inception of the London Branch of the Moslem League, of which he was President, he laboured week in and week out to emphasise the claims of the Indian Moslems on Lord Morley and the members of the India Council. The deference shown to the Moslem demands in the Reform scheme of 1909 is, in a large measure, due to the untiring and unceasing advocacy of Mr. Amir Ali. No single Mahomedan has done so much as he to get the Indian Moslems adequate representation in the Reformed Councils.

MR. AMIR ALI AND THE INDIA OFFICE MEMBERSHIP

When the question of appointing the first Mahomedan member of the India Council was on the *tapis*, there was a universal belief that the Secretary of State's choice would fall on Mr. Amir Ali than whom no one was more eminently fitted. There were of course other members of the Moslem community in India who had claims for consideration but Mr. Amir Ali stood head and shoulders above them. Besides being a conspicuous reformer and a learned exponent of present day Islamism, he had the hall-mark of a leader of proved capacity, while his choice of an English domicile and familiarity with London social and political life peculiarly fitted him to interpret India to England. Lord Morley himself had many opportunities of gauging Mr. Amir Ali's qualifications as a leading member of all the Moslem League deputations that interviewed him and as one who was privately consulted by him on the question of efficient representation of Mahomedans in the Reforms. In spite of all this Lord Morley's choice fell elsewhere, causing of course some disappointment among the Indian Moslem community.

IS SWORN IN AS A PRIVY COUNCILLOR

The feeling of disappointment at his not being appointed member of the India Council was changed into one of unbounded joy when on November 23, 1909, it was announced that Mr. Amir Ali was sworn into the Privy Council. Mr. Amir Ali is the first Indian to enter the precincts of His Majesty the King's Council. All India was highly gratified at the appointment. It was viewed in the light of a national honour and not as a case of "preferential treatment" accorded to a member of the Moslem community. This was the first occasion in the history of English polity when an Indian was invited by the King of England "to take his seat at the Board", and sworn "to advise the King according to the best of his cunning and discretion; to advise for the King's honour and the good of the public, without partiality; through affection, love, need, doubt or dread, to keep the King's counsel secret; to avoid corruption; to help and strengthen the execution of what shall be resolved; and generally to observe, keep and do all that a true counsellor should do to his Sovereign Lord." Mr. Amir Ali was sworn in with a view to his being appointed to the "Judicial Committee" which, according to the Statute of 3 and 4 William

IV C. 41, is the highest Court of Appeal for all the Over-seas Dominions of His Majesty. Indian legal knowledge and judicial experience have, from the first, been represented on the Privy Council but the appointments were exclusively from the *cadre* of retired English Judges of Indian High Courts. The need for direct Indian representation has been acknowledged by eminent English jurists. The inclusion of an Indian Judge of Mr. Amir Ali's judicial experience has already proved to be a tower of strength to the Judicial Committee, as is shown by the decisions of the Privy Council.

It is interesting to recall that in one of his judgments in an Indian appeal which came up before the Privy Council in March 1918 Mr. Amir Ali deprecated the practice of some Indian Courts of conforming largely to foreign decisions, which are often based on considerations and conditions totally different from those prevailing in India. He contended that this would only confuse the administration of justice.

MR. AMIR ALI'S VIEWS ON PUBLIC QUESTIONS

Although he did not support the Congress movement he was at no time a pronounced partisan. He has ever been a stout champion of liberalism. He has always advocated catholicity of views. His advocacy of Female Education in India dates from the time when many Indians themselves were backward educationally. He did much for the uplift of "the submerged half" of India. He believes that the regeneration of India rests with women and as such their education should in no case be neglected. He thinks that the Purdah system obtaining among the Indian Moslems is a drag and should be abolished. Whether every Moslem concurs with him or not, he is entitled to a hearing as he advances his views with an energy and persistence all his own. There is a freshness about his arguments which is always engaging.

Mr. Amir Ali is an Indian first and a Moslem afterwards. Who could have pleaded the cause of the Indians better or portrayed the inner sentiment of India in truer perspective? He wrote :—

Seventy years of English education and the gradual diffusion of Western knowledge have created among the more prosperous classes a perception of the responsibilities and obligations of Government and awakened in them a sense of their rights. However difficult this may make the work of administration, it is hardly possible even if it were expedient, to alter the current of progress. The great intellectual uprise among the educated sections due to the impact of West and East naturally rest on the masses. And the spirit of collectivism and organisation which has given birth to so many political and semi-political institutions exercises its legitimate influence. The whole continent, with the exception, perhaps, of tracts inhabited by backward communities is thus in a state of expectation eager for development.

He ridiculed the British conception of India as "an easy-going country, run on fixed, generally unalterable lines—the land of pageants and the home of durbars—the bulk of whose people, untouched by the changes in the conception of the thinking classes occasioned by the contact of two civilisations—one old and stationary, the other young, active and utilitarian—bow down before the British official as an *avatar* of progress and prosperity." He deplored the lack of sympathy between the rulers and the ruled.

The official atmosphere, he said, remained "charged with preconceived theories of racial inequality and the unwisdom of relaxing the bonds of tutelage, whilst the elder statesmen view with ill-concealed apprehension any change in the direction of liberalisation." The Indian masses, he warned, were no longer the apathetic people they once were, as they have given ample proof of discussing questions often with intelligence, always with acuteness.

As an educated Indian, Mr. Amir Ali advocates a wider application of the principles of local self-government, the employment of Indians in the higher posts of State service, and the admission of Indians to higher ranks of the Indian Army. He holds that Indians are not new to local self-government as is shown by the old village administration which, in a modified form, still largely governs the destinies of the rural classes. In regard to the official allegation that Indians bungle even at municipal government and have therefore no aptitude for local self-government, he observes:—

> Municipal government, even in England, is attended with mistakes, in India they are to be expected. A sympathetic, tactful and at the same time firm treatment would instead of making failure, have led to success. It would have made respectable sections understand the responsibilities of trust, imparted self-reliance and trained them to a large perception of duty as citizens of a great Empire.

Regarding the employment of Indians to the higher branches of State service, it might be said that since Mr. Amir Ali made these remarks, a new policy has dawned in India. The Minto-Morley regime saw the breaking up of the race barrier and Indians are now being slowly admitted into the sanctums of the Indian Executive Councils, both Imperial and Provincial, and the India Office, although it is patent that, for a very long time to come, the official element will be overwhelmingly Anglo-Indian.

As regards the admission of Indians to the higher ranks of the Indian army, Mr. Amir Ali is equally outspoken. He denounces the official view that they are unable to command obedience or exact deference. He urges that "in every country the amount of respect shown to an officer depends upon the consideration in which he is held by his superiors, for the people take him at Government valuation." He remarks that the closing of the Indian Army as a profession to the sons of respectable Indians has not only proved a source of considerable discontent but is slowly emasculating the virile races of India. The present policy, he adds, "instead of making their military predilections a source of strength, is driving them into unworthy and unhealthy, not to say, dangerous channels."

Speaking of the English Party system and the attitude of either party towards India and Indian questions, Mr. Amir Ali shrewdly observes:

> We in India often lose sight of the fact that generally speaking both the great English Parties treat Indian questions as outside the range of what are usually called party-politics; and although exceptions have recently appeared, on the whole it may be said the rule is faithfully observed. Both parties profess to have at heart the development of India on progressive lines and the training of her people in the work of self-govern-

ment, so that in the distant future when the growth of a true spirit of compromise and toleration among all classes and communities may make it possible to entrust them with the management of their own affairs, she may justly claim a release from her present (not irksome) tutelage. One party may be more inclined to hurry the pace, the other may feel it wiser to proceed more cautiously; whatever the difference in the method, both seem to have the same end in view.

THE MONTAGU REFORMS

Mr. Amir Ali was decisively enthusiastic over the Montagu scheme. When in July 1918 the Report of the Montagu-Chelmsford Scheme was published he warmly praised the Secretary of State and the Viceroy for their courage and statesmanship and commended the new Reforms to his countrymen for acceptance. Speaking at a luncheon given by the London Moslem League to the Indian representatives on July 17 of that year he said: "How soon the full position of the vast scheme framed by far-seeing statesmen would be realised depends upon the sobriety of judgment and spirit of toleration and compromise which the first pioneers brought to the task."

SEPARATE MOSLEM REPRESENTATION

Having outlined Mr. Amir Ali's views in general, we shall next set forth his plea for separate Moslem representation. Mr. Amir Ali's contention is that India not being a homogeneous country, every caste and creed has to watch over its own interests. The development of each community, he urges, must proceed on its own ideals and standards of thought and training. A community, "with great traditions," consisting of sixty two millions and forming one-fifth of the population of India, cannot be ignored in the governance of the country. Hitherto the Indian Moslems were suffering acutely from political inanition. The Moslem, while he was patted on the back for holding aloof from "political agitation" and told to apply himself like a good boy to his books, was relegated to the cold shade of neglect. To safeguard against further decline and disintegration, Mr. Amir Ali urged that there must be concerted action. He advanced that, in the absence of a recognised organisation capable of expressing freely and openly the sentiments and opinions of the Moslems as a body, the feelings of the masses are likely to take a wrong shape and find an outlet through unregulated channels. The system of representation obtaining in the various Councils was, until the passing of the Reform Act of 1909 very inadequate. This was due as much to the narrowness of vision on the part of the administrators as to their own individualism and lack of political training. Hence Mr. Amir Ali's solicitude for an organisation or league which would safeguard Moslem rights and interests in a form that would give them an assured position in the political institutions of the country. Asked as to why the Moslems should not join hands with the Hindus in the political evolution of the country and thus exonerate themselves from the charge of creating an Ulster in India, Mr. Amir Ali remarked that "any attempt at amalgamation at the present stage would mean the submergence of an ill-organised, badly equipped and badly trained minority under a majority vastly superior in numbers and immensely better organised. No one acquainted with the social, religious and moral conditions of the Moslems can view such a contingency without the gravest misgivings."

Yet Mr. Amir Ali is no "separatist." He believes that the development of India on modern lines depends upon the cordial co-operation of the two great Indian communities, Hindu and Moslem, in the work of national welfare. He exhorts his community to work in unity and harmony. He wrote:

> I trust that the two communities, whom the constitutional experiment (referring to the Reforms of 1909) mainly affects will work together in harmony and concord to make it a success. By bringing the representatives of the two peoples into the Council chambers and on the public platforms on fairly assured terms, it will, I venture to hope, lead to the growth of that spirit of compromise and mutual toleration on which depends the ultimate success of the reforms, and without which the welfare and progress of the country will be in jeopardy.

If such were his views in 1909 they suffered no change ten years hence. For in a letter to the *Times* in December 1918 he held that the success of the Montford Scheme would be seriously prejudiced if any attempt towards disturbance in principle of Mussalman communal representation was made. Such an action, he said, would create Mahomedan distrust both in the pledges of the Government and the Hindu leaders. "Unity of sentiment and consciousness of identity of interest which in due course will remove the necessity for special representation is clearly developing at the top and if details are rightly handled it should not take long before it reaches the bottom."

AS AN AUTHOR

No biographical sketch of Mr. Amir Ali would be complete without a reference to his works which are all in English. His maiden literary effort seems to have been a translation of an Urdu (?) pamphlet by Moulvi Syed Karamat Ali, the *mutavalli* (treasurer) of the Bengal Mohsin Fund whose patronage he enjoyed during his college career. Although written before he left college, it gives abundant proof of his early mastery over the English language. While still reading for the Bar in London, he wrote *A Critical Examination of the Life and Teachings of Mahomed* which was given a warm reception in England and introduced him into the literary circles of London. His most popular work is the "Spirit of Islam" which has passed through several and special editions. On this was built Mr. Amir Ali's fame as an author. Therein he has entered fully into the spirit of the religion of Mahomed. No better exposition of the teachings of the Arabian Prophet has yet appeared in the English language. It is a classic in its line. Mr. Amir Ali is also the author of "The Ethics of Islam" which deals, in his usual masterly way, with the precepts of Islam. For Constable's "Religions: Ancient and Modern" Series, Mr. Amir Ali has contributed a shilling volume entitled *Islam* which presents, in an admirably small compass, the salient features of Mahomed's Faith. His love for Islam further led him to fill a gap in Islamic history and write *A Short History of the Saracens* which has thrown a flood of light on the annals of a forgotten empire to which European savants, too, have done scant justice. The author has taken infinite pains to study, in minute detail, the inner life and the social, economic and intellectual development of the Sarcenic race and trace and show how much modern Europe is indebted to their civilisation. His historical analogies are bold, original and instructive. The comparison of the Saracenic administration with the British Rule in India is full of lessons for the Imperialist.

ISLAM

Mr. Amir Ali's expositions of the religion of Islam are characterised by a studied effort on his part to remove some of the misapprehensions and prejudices regarding the true aims and ideals of Islam and portray the religion of Mahomed in true perspective. He lifts the veil of formalism and ceremonialism and lets us see the "spirit" of Islam. Below are given a few extracts from his works which illustrate his method of elucidation.

Dwelling on the universality and rationalistic practicality of Islam Mr. Amir Ali remarks:

> In some religions the precepts which inculcated duties have been so utterly devoid of practicability, so completely wanting in a knowledge of human nature, and partaking so much of the dreamy vagueness of enthusiasts as to become in the real battles of life simply useless. The practical character of a religion, its abiding influence on the common relations of mankind, in the affairs of every day life, its power on the masses, are the true criteria for judging of its universality. We do not look to exceptional minds to recognise the nature of a religion. We search among the masses to understand its true character. Does it exercise deep power over them? Does it elevate them? Does it regulate their conception of rights and duties? Does it, if carried to the South Sea islander, or preached to the

Caffrarians, improve or degrade them?—are the questions we naturally ask. In Islam is joined a lofty idealism with the most rationalistic practicality. It did not ignore human nature; it never entangled itself in the tortuous pathways which lie outside the domains of the actual and the real. Its object, like that of other systems, was the elevation of humanity towards the absolute ideal of perfection; but it attained, or tries to attain, this object by grasping the truth that the nature of man is, in this existence, imperfect. If it did not say, "If thy brother smite thee on one cheek, turn thou the other also to him;" if it allowed the punishment of the wanton wrong-doer to the extent of the injury he had done, it also taught, in fervid words and varied strains, the practice of forgiveness and benevolence, and the return of good for evil.

It is not a mere creed, it is a life to be lived in the present —a religion of right-doing, right-thinking and right-speaking, founded on divine love, universal charity and equality of man in the sight of the Lord. However much the modern professors of Islam may have dimmed the glory of their master (and a volume might also be written on the defects of modern Mohamedanism), the religion which enshrines righteousness and justification by work deserves the recognition of the lovers of humanity.

Commenting on the absence of priesthood in Islam Mr. Amir Ali says:

The absence of a specially interested class to act as intermediaries between God and man differentiates Islam from all other creeds. In the Islamic system every man is his own priest and pleads for himself for forgiveness and mercy. No sacrifice, no ceremonial invented by vested interests is needed to bring the anxious heart nearer to its Comforter.

Essentially a democratic creed, it recognises no distinction of race or colour among its followers. High or low, rich or poor, white, yellow or black are on the same level in the sight of their Lord. The democratic character of its appeal, its repudiation of all adventitious barries of caste, explain the powerful fascination it exercises over diverse races of mankind.

Refuting the popular charge laid at the door of Islam that it is an aggressive religion and does not allow religious toleration to non-Moslems, Mr. Amir Ali pleads as follows:

By the laws of Islam, liberty of conscience and freedom of worship were allowed and guaranteed to the followers of every other creed under Moslem dominion. The passage in the Koran,

"Let there be no compulsion in religion" testifies to the principle of toleration and charity inculcated by Islam. "What, wilt thou force men to believe when belief can come only from God?" "Adhere to those who forsake you; speak truth to your own heart; do good to every one that does ill to you"—these are the precepts of a Teacher who has been accused of fanaticism and intolerance. Let it be remembered that these are the utterances not of a powerless enthusiast or philosophical dreamer paralysed by the weight of opposing forces. These are the utterances of a man in the plenitude of his power, of the head of a sufficiently strong and well-organised State, able to enforce his doctrines with the edge of his reputed sword.

The essence of the political character of Islam is to be found in the charter which was granted to the Jews by the Prophet after his arrival in Medina and the notable message sent to the Christians of Najran and the neighbouring territories after Islam had fully established itself in the Peninsula. This latter document has, for the most part, furnished the guiding principle to all Moslem rulers in their mode of dealing with their non-Moslem subjects, and if they have departed from it in any instance the cause is to be found in the character of the particular sovereign. If we separate the political necessity which has often spoken and acted in the name of religion, no faith is more tolerant than Islam to the followers of other creeds. "Reasons of State" have led a sovereign here and there to display a certain degree of intolerance or to insist upon a certain uniformity of faith; but the system itself has ever maintained the most complete tolerance. Christians and Jews, as a rule, have never been molested in the exercise of their religion, or constrained to change their faith. If they are required to pay a special tax, it is in lieu of military service, and it is but right that those who enjoy the protection of the State should contribute in some shape to the public burdens. Towards the idolators there was greater strictness in theory, but in practice the law was equally liberal. If at any time they were treated with harshness, the cause is to be found in the passions of the ruler or the population. The religious element was used only as a pretext.

Mr. Amir Ali's lucid exposition of the Moslem law of marriage and the Koranic provision for polygamy in certain conditions and stages of society is interesting, although he himself looks upon polygamy, in the present day, as an adulterous connection and contrary to the spirit of Islam. He proves by cogent reasoning that the status of women in Islam is as good as and, in some respects, better than that of many European women. He says:

A Moslem marriage is a civil act, needing no priest, requiring no ceremonial. The contract of marriage gives the man no power over the woman's person, beyond what the law defines, and none whatever upon her goods and property Her rights as a mother do not depend for their recognition upon the idiosyncracies of individual judges. Her earnings acquired by her own exertions cannot be wasted by a prodigal husband, nor can she be ill-treated with impunity by one who is brutal. She acts, if *sui juris*, in all matters which relate to herself and her property in her own individual right, without the intervention of husband or father She can sue her debtors in the open court, without the necessity of joining a next friend, or under cover of her husband's name. She continues to exercise, after she has passed from her father's house into her husband's home, all the rights which the law gives to men. All the privileges which belong to her as a Woman and a wife are secured to her, not by the courtesies which 'come and go' but by the actual text in the Book of Law, Taken as a whole, her status is not more unfavourable than that of many European women, whilst in many respects she occupies a decidedly better position.

CHARACTER OF MAHOMED

Lastly, we cannot refrain from quoting *in extenso* Mr. Amir Ali's impartial estimate of Mahomed's character:

The humble preacher had risen to be the ruler of Arabia, the equal of Chosroes and of Cæsar, the arbiter of the destinies of a nation. But the same humility of spirit, the same nobility of soul and purity of heart, austerity of conduct, refinement and delicacy of feeling, and stern devotion to duty which had won him the title' of *al-Amin*, combined with a severe sense of self-examination, are ever the distinguishing traits of his character. Once in his life, whilst engaged in a religious conversation with an influential citizen of Mecca, he had turned away from a humble blind seeker of the truth. He is always recurring to this incident with remorse and proclaiming God's disapprobation. A nature so pure, so tender and yet so heroic, inspires not only reverence, but love. And naturally the Arabian writers dwell with the proudest satisfaction on the graces and intellectual gifts of the son of Abdulla. His courteousness to the great, his affability to the humble and his dignified bearing to the presumptuous, procured him universal respect and admiration. His countenance reflected the benevolence of his heart. Profoundly read in the volume of nature, though ignorant of letters, with an expansive mind, elevated by deep communion with the soul of the universe, he was gifted with the power of influencing equally the learned and the unlearned Withal, there was a majesty in his face, an air of genius which inspired all who came in contact with him with a feeling of veneration and love.

His singular elevation of mind, his extreme delicacy and refinement of feeling, his purity and truth, form the constant theme of the traditions. He was most indulgent to his inferiors, and would never allow his awkward little page to be scolded whatever he did. "Ten years" said Anas, his servent. "was I about the Prophet, and he never said so much as "Uff' to me" He was very affectionate towards his family. One of his boys died on his breast in the smoky house of the nurse, a blacksmith's wife. He was very fond of children. He would stop them in the streets, and pat their little cheeks. He never struck any one in his life. The worst expression he ever made use of in conversation was, "What has come to him? May his forehead be darkened with mud!" When asked to curse some one, he replied, "I have not been sent to curse, but to be a mercy to mankind."

He visited the sick, followed every bier he met, accepted the invitation of a slave to dinner, mended his own clothes, milked his goats, and waited upon himself, relates summarily another tradition. He never first withdrew his hand out of another's palm, and turned not before the other had turned. His hand was the most generous, his breast the most courageous, his tongue the most truthful; he was the most faithful protector of those he protected; the sweetest and most agreeable in conversation; those who saw him were suddenly filled with reverence; those who came near him loved him, they who described him would say, "I have never seen his like, either before or after." He was of great taciturnity; and when he spoke, he spoke with emphasis and deliberation, and no one could ever forget what he said.

Mahomed was extremely simple in his habits. His mode of life, his dress and his furniture retained to the very last a character of patriarchal simplicity. Many a time, Abu Huraira reports, had the Prophet to go without a meal Dates and water frequently formed his only nourishment. Often, for months together, no fire could be lighted in his house from scantiness of means. God, say the Moslem historians, had indeed put before him the key to the treasures of this world, but he refused it!

HIS LEGAL WORKS

Mr. Amir Ali is also the author of several works on Law which combine in themselves the excellent features of a text-book and a book of reference containing up-to-date case-law, and as such they are indispensable to every legal practitioner in India. They are marked by sound scholarship, great ability, lucid exposition and careful arrangement. His "Student's Hand-book of Mahomedan Law" is a text book in almost all Indian Universities. His monumental work on "Mahomedan Law" (2 vols.) is a standard book of reference. He has also written "The Personal Law of the Mahomedans." He is the joint-author of "The Law of Evidence applicable to the British India." "A Commentary on the Bengal Tenancy Act" and "Civil Procedure in British India." He has also published an Indian Edition of "Ashburner's Mortgages" which illustrates, amplifies and explains the text from the Indian point of view.

AS A CONTRIBUTOR TO ENGLISH PERIODICALS

Mr. Amir Ali is a frequent contributor to English periodicals. His articles have, from time to time, appeared in the *Nineteenth Century and After* and other leading reviews. He is regarded in England as a sound authority on the varying phases of Indian life and sentiment. He is a thoughtful and outspoken writer and, if his trenchant remarks have sometimes evoked criticism in official and other circles, they have, nevertheless influenced the policy of Government. His writings have had a powerful effect in moulding

Indian as well as Anglo-Indian thought. He was engaged in recent years in writing a history of the development of Mahomedan civilisation in India.

HIS SERVICES TO ISLAM AND ISLAMIC COUNTRIES

Mr. Amir Ali's services are not confined to India. They extend to other Islamic countries. It may not be generally known that, while the Turkish Revolution of 1908 was brewing, Mr. Amir Ali convinced the Shaikh-ul-Islam by theological arguments, that the young Turk movement was not irreligious and opposed to Islam with the result that the highest ecclesiastical dignitary of Turkey gave the Revolution the sanction of the Faith, thus gagging the mouths of the fanatic Mullahs. But for the intervention of Mr. Amir Ali, the Shaikh-ul-Islam would not have been won over and the work of the Revolution would not have been accomplished so easily.* Mr. Amir Ali was also connected with Red Crescent work during the Turko-Italian and Turko-Balkan wars. He organised the British Red Crescent Society and sent field hospitals to the front for the relief of the sick and wounded. He sent weekly large sums of money to relieve the homeless and foodless refugees. He appealed for funds to the humanity of the people of Great Britain, India and the British Colonies and invoked the assistance of his co-religionists all over the world to start Red Crescent Societies of their own to alleviate the sufferings of the afflicted population of Turkey. Writing to the *Times*, he

---

* See Knight's "Awakening of Turkey" (p. 67).

deplored the use which was made of the symbol of Christianity by partisans in England to justify aggression and slaughter in the Balkans, pointing out the incalculable mischief done in England and India by ecclesiastical and newspeaper effusions against the Turkish Government. Mr. Amir Ali has also been a friend of Persia. When M. Sazonoff, the Russian Foreign Minister, visited London and there was a talk about the partition of Persia, Mr. Amir Ali came to its aid and wrote a strong letter of protest to the *Times*. In it he argued as follows:—

> In the matter of Persia's inability to govern herself, may I be permitted to ask the British public if a fair or honest chance has been allowed to that poor harried country, to recover from the effects of the grinding tyranny of her late ruler or to her distracted people to prove their capacity for government? I venture to affirm, without hesitation, that every effort on their part has been paralysed by outside action. The tribes do not know who governs them and the people themselves feel they are being crushed by a fate against which they cannot contend.
>
> The pressure for squeezing out the national life of Persia and preventing her regeneration has been relentless, unceasing and persistent. It is cruel, under these circumstances, to expect any country or any people to show any capacity for government. Had Persia been allowed even for five years a fair chance to govern herself, and had then failed, we would have been willing to accept the correctness, if not the justice of your (*The Times's*) argument.

THE WAR AND TURKEY

But it was Turkey's entanglement in the great war that has absorbed Mr. Amir Ali's whole time energy and service. Since the beginning of Armegeddon in the fateful August 1914, Mr. Amir Ali has thrown the weight of his commanding influence on the side of the Allies. His heart was touched at the plight of Belgium. The country devastated, her ancient seats of learning desolated, her people driven from their homes for refuge in distant lands,—these in his own words "made the heart throb with infinite sorrow and pain." His allegiance to England was not merely steadfast but joyous. But soon the failure of allied diplomacy in winning Turkey to their side, or even keeping her neutral, threw a baleful shadow over the whole Moslem world. Mr. Amir Ali, and H. H. the Aga Khân like other leading Indian Mahomedans endeavoured their best to prevent Turkey from committing what they deemed a wanton suicide. They reproached Turkey for her thoughtlessness alike to her own advantage and to her disregard of the sentiments of millions of Mahomedans owing allegiance to British or French rule, whose position their action was tending to compromise. Moslems in allied countries were loyal to their respective governments, but they were sorely tried as their heart could not be easily reconciled to the overthrow of Turkey and the destruction of the Khilafat which the allies were alleged to have contemplated. So during the war while they stood firm in their allegiance to the allies they were ceaselessly working to wean Turkey from the tragic consequences of her own miscalculation. Of those who served Turkey and the Islamic world in this great crisis a high place should be given to Mr. Amir Ali.

INDIAN MOSLEMS' MEMORIAL

For at the peace table British statesmen flushed with victory, seem to have forgotten their pledges to Indian Moslems. Mr. Lloyd George himself declared in a speech so often quoted against him: "Nor are we fighting to deprive Turkey of its capital or of the rich and renowned lands of Asia Minor and Thrace which are predominantly Turkish in race." And yet it was Mr. Lloyd George who, in spite of the efforts of Mr. Montagu, Lord Sinha and the Maharaja of Bikaner, stood up for vengeance against Turkey and for partitioning her rich and historic possession. On June 14, 1919 Indian Moslems in London under the lead of Mr. Amir Ali, H. H. The Aga Khan and Sir Abbas Ali Baig addressed a Memorial to the Prime Minister in which they pointed out:

> We venture to appeal to you for the sake of the fair name of Great Britain and the tranquil development of Asia, that Turkey proper and Thrace with Constantinople as its capital should be left intact and uninterfered with under the sovereignty of the Sultan, that his temporal power over the Turkish state should not be attempted to be reduced or diminished by any sort of mandate and that the principle of self determination which has been applied to the Christian peoples of Europe should be made applicable to the Moslem peoples, and that in the interests of the peaceful development of Western Asia the suzeranity of the Caliph over the non-Turkish provinces of the Ottoman Empire be left undisturbed.

Subsequently in a letter to the *Times* Mr. Amir Ali and H. H. The Aga Khan wrote of the attempted dismemberment of the Turkish home-lands thus;

> It would, in our opinion, be a cruel act of injustice to wrench any portion of this tract from Turkish sovereignty to satisfy the ambitions of any other people. Instead of bringing peace to Western Asia, such a settlement will sow the seeds of constant wars, the effect of which cannot be expected to remain confined to the country where they happen to be waged. * * *
>
> We submit that the maintenance of the Ottoman sovereign's spiritual suzerainty in those countries, whilst maintaining his prestige and thus conciliating Mussulman feeling, would be the means of making the position of the Mussulman rulers or governors of those countries unimpugnable. But so far as Thrace, Constantinople, and the home-lands of the Turkish race

concerned Mussalman feeling from top to bottom is absolutely opposed to any interference under any shape with the Sultan's sovereignty.

Thus through the efforts mainly of Mr. Amir Ali and his colleagues an agitation was kept up in England in favour of Turkey against which a compaign of hatred and calumny was not uncommon in the British press. It is true indeed that it was the strong arm of Mustapha Kemal that secured final victory to Turkey, but there is no doubt also that the propagandist work done in London on her behalf arrested an earlier and possibly tragic settlement of Turkish claims. Who will deny that if the settlement had been made earlier the Turks would not have had breathing time to equip themselves for the final fray? The victory of Mustapha and the reconquering of lost territories brought the balm to the bruised spirits of Mr. Amir Ali and his Moslem colleagues—as indeed to all interested in Turkey's welfare.

TURKEY AND THE KHILAFAT

But no sooner had victory been secured to Turkey than Angora began to look askance at the Khilafat itself which had inspired such a universal hegomony of hearts. It was the Khilafat which acted as the one unifying force of Islam. Moslems in East and West, in far away South Africa or Mongolia, looked to Constantinople as the centre of light. Indian Moslems, while owning loyalty to an English King, still looked to the Khalifa as their spiritual head and devoted themselves to save the Khilafat from fall. But the Young Turks of Angora, when they found themselves supreme in their State, lost no time in dismissing the gentle and noble Abdul Majid from his historic throne. The heart of the Muslim world was wrung with pity and remorse. Muslims in India, as elsewhere, who had exhibited such unbounded admiration for Kemal were dumbfounded. Their respectful and urgent pleadings to save the Khilafat were disregarded. Even their appeal for correct news was unheeded. Mr. Amir Ali wrote indignantly to the press :—

> The arrogation by a Muslim State to "abolish" any of the fundamental institutions of Islam is a grave tragedy—the gravest within the last seven centuries. It means the disruption of Islamic unity and the disintegration of the Faith as a moral force. It also means that the particular State, in its desire to bring itself into line with the new republics of Europe forfeits its primacy among Muslim nations and places itself on the same level as the Balkan States.
>
> The Caliphate is not a national institution, the property of any single State to be "abolished" at its free will. It is an integral part of the Sunni system. Any nation is free to abondon Islam cut no nation or State can arrogate to itself the power to alter or abolish its institutions so as to affect other Muslim communities.

Holding these views Mr. Amir Ali could not sleep over the catastrophic step that Angora had taken. Mr. Amir Ali and H. H. Aga Khan in a joint letter to Ismet Pasha

> invited the attention of the Grand National Assembly to a subject which is unquestionably of interest and concern to the whole Sunni communion. They affirmed that the present position of the Caliph Imam is disturbing the vast populations who belong to it and that the dimunition in the dignity and prestige of the Caliph are lessening the weight and influence of Islam. They disclaimed any intention to suggest that the powers of the Assembly should be lessened, but they urged that "the religious headship of the Sunni world should be maintained intact in accordance with the 'Shariyyet'" [the sacred law of Islam]. To them the Caliph-Imam symbolizes the unity of the Sunni

communion. The Vice-Gerent of the Prophet is the Imam of the Sunni congregations; he and the faithful are knit together by a mystical element which cannot be eradicated from the Moslem mind without creating discord in the world of Islam.

The publication of this joint letter in Constantinople before it reached Angora threw the Government into a rage and the three editors who published it were ordered to be arrested and tried for treason by an emergency tribunal. The writers were pained at the extra-ordinary attitude taken up by Angora and they explained their position in a letter to the *Times*:

We recognise the signal services which Kemal Pasha rendered to the country, but the uncertainty surrounding the position of the Caliph being likely to cause disintegration of Islam, we thought that we might bring the matter to the notice of the Turkish Assembly and urge that the Caliph's dignity might be placed on an assured position in order to maintain his prestige, and command the confidence and esteem of the Sunni World. We have not the slightest desire to hamper the established Government of Turkey. Such counsel coming from two consistent friends of Turkey should not have been so misconstrued. We personally greatly resent the imputations.

Mr. Amir Ali is an indefatigable advocate of Islam. Whenever the interests of an Islamic state are in jeopardy or any gross injustice is done to it, he is the first to uphold the cause of the wronged country. He uses both the Press and platform for the expression of his views and does it successfully. Mahomedan India is really proud to have in London, the world's news-disseminating centre, a son who is ever ready to champion the cause of Islam.

H. H. THE AGA KHAN

THE AGA KHAN

ANCESTRY

HIS Highness Sir Sultan Muhammad Shah, the present Aga Khan, was born at Karachi on the 2nd of November 1875. He comes of an illustrious Shiah family of Persia and as a Syed traces his descent from the Prophet of Arabia and claims blood relations with the Fatimite Caliphs of Egypt, to whose liberal culture and enlightenment, much of the glory and renown of that country and its University was due. We need not trouble ourselves with this distant past. Enough if we take a brief survey of the history of the Aga Khan's family from the dawn of the 19th century onward, as this has especial bearing on the status and position of the present Aga Khan in India.

GREAT-GRANDFATHER

We may begin with Aga Khalelullah Khan, the great-grandfather of the Aga Khan, the recognised religious head of the Ismàilees during the reign of King Fateh Ali Shah, of Persia. It is out of place to discuss here the religious beliefs and practices, of which the head of the Ismailia Shiahs was an embodiment. But this might be noted that Aga Khalelullah Shah occupied a distinguished place in Fateh Ali Shah's Court and was the Governor of

Kerman. His son, Aga Husain Ali Shah, who succeeded to the religious *masnad* after the murder of his father by a fanatic, is more known to us in India than the father who was more a religious recluse than a successful ruler or warrior.

GRANDFATHER

Aga Husain Ali Shah was recognised by Fateh Ali Shah, and was entrusted with the administration of the important District of Mehleti and Koom. He was a strong ruler and so long as Fateh Ali Shah reigned, the Aga was a power in the land. But his death in 1834 brought a change in his fortunes. The country was plunged in a fratricidal war of succession, and the Aga could not remain neutral. He threw in his lot with Mohamed Shah, a grandson of the deceased monarch, against the Zil-us-Sultan, his eldest son. The latter with other brothers was ousted, and Mohamed Shah was able to ascend the throne. The Aga had his own share of the power thus usurped. He was made Commander-in-Chief of the Army and was sent against one of the sons of Fateh Ali Shah, who was still holding the Governor-Generalship of Kerman, where the Aga's father was for some time at the head of the administration. The unfortunate Prince was taken as captive to the Court, where, after being subjected to much indignity, was finally deprived of his eyesight.

Matters went well with Aga Husain Ali Shah for a time. But complications soon arose in the political life of the country so much so that he was soon obliged to raise the standard of rebellion against the very king he had set up. But the odds were against him. He had to lay down his arms. He was imprisoned. But later on he was pardoned and set at liberty. But the political atmosphere was still very hot for him, and he had again to rebel against his master. He could not however effect much. Seeing that adverse powers were too strong for him, he left his native land in abject despair. Leaving his younger brother all alone to continue the struggle, he forced his way through Afghanistan to Sindh, where he received a hearty reception by his Ismailia followers.

Cowed down as he was in spirit, the old warrior still dreamed of going back to Persia and regaining his lost power there. His followers well financed his projects, but they all came to a sorry failure. His martial spirit, however, would not remain quiet. He gave vent to it in other directions. He assisted Sir Charles Napier in putting down the Amirs of Sindh and was much helpful to the East India Company in the Afghan War of 1839-40. As a reward for these services, the British Government granted him a decent pension, and the hereditary title of "His Highness" was conferred upon him. In 1845, he came to Bombay, where his Khoja followers gave him a warm welcome. He subsequently tried from there to establish himself in the outlying Persian Province of Bunpore; but at the instance of the Persian Government, he was obliged to go and reside in Calcutta.

His stay there was but a short one. His remaining days were spent either at Bangalore or at Bombay. He died in 1881, and was soon followed to the grave in 1885 by his eldest son Aga Ali Shah, the father of the present Aga Khan, Sultan Muhammad Shah.

THE PRESENT AGA KHAN

The boy Aga Khan was only 10 years of age when his father died, leaving his hereditary responsibilities on his young shoulders. "Happily, however," says the Aga Khan himself, "I had the inestimable, and, in the circumstances, essential advantage of receiving the fostering care of a gifted and far-seeing mother, the daughter of the famous Nizam-ud-Doulah, who renounced the life of the Persian Court to spend her days in religious retirement. She took care that I should continue the education commenced under my father's guidance.". He was already grounded in Arabic and Persian literature and history, and now under able English tutors he was able to receive a liberal education on Western lines. The physical side of education was also well attended to, and the boy grew to have a passion for outdoor games.

Even from his young age he began to take a keen interest in the welfare of his followers —the Khojas. These people were originally converts to Islam. They have come to regard themselves as followers of the Ismailia branch of Shiaism, of which the ancestors of the Aga Khan have claimed to be the religious heads. He holds practically the same position among them as does the Pope among the

Roman Catholics. Some of them even go beyond this and venerate him as the God incarnate. They pay him a certain share of their income called *Zakaat*. It is in this way that the Aga Khan makes a large amount of his income; and he is highly solicitous of their well-being. It is said that he spends away a large portion of his income in attending to the educational and other needs of his people. His religious authority and interest do not end with the Khojas. The Ismailians are dispersed in different parts of Asia and Africa. Though he has had no opportunity of personally meeting his followers in the interior of Asia, he has from time to time travelled amongst his followers not only in India but along the Persian Gulf, in Arabia, along the east coast of Africa and elsewhere. He has tried to take an active interest in their industrial and commercial advancement. His followers have from his very youth been much attached to him. His youthful commands were obeyed with as much willingness and zeal as his later ones. When, as early as 1893, the unfortunate Hindu-Muslim riots took place in Bombay, the Aga Khan kept his followers quite aloof from embroiling themselves in the muddle. He was of especial help to them in the troubled days of famine and plague which broke out in the Bombay Presidency about the year 1897. He was thus able to give at an young age positive proof of his practical sympathies towards his people.

His attention was not entirely confined to his Khoja followers. His charming personality and winning manners were a great asset in his favour, and he soon succeeded in impressing himself on the Mussalmans of Bombay at large. The influence he wielded among them was so great that on the occasion of the Diamond Jubilee of Queen Victoria, he was deputed by them to take their Address to Simla, where along with others, it was received in Durbar by Lord Elgin.

HIS FIRST VISIT TO EUROPE

Soon after, the Aga Khan paid his first visit to England. In the London society of learned men and politicians, quite new as it was to him, he did not find himself embarrassed in any manner. The training he had received at home stood him in good stead. Wherever he went, whether in England or on the Continent, he won golden opinions. Queen Victoria granted him several private audiences and also invited him to dine and sleep in the Windsor Castle. While he was still in England, the title of K. C. I. E. was conferred upon him for his valuable work in the days of plague in Bombay.

His first visit to Europe opened him a vista for much experience. The life and organisation of Western nations impressed him a great deal. To know more and more, and to move with people there, has since been the Aga Khan's chief hobby. His social position and status coupled with his affable and refined manners have enabled him to move in the highest circles of Europe. He has been intimately known to the several Royalties of Europe, and has received at their hands high distinctions, including one from the German Kaiser, which he flung back at him at the outbreak of the Great War in 1914.

MUSLIM UNIVERSITY

Because of this exceptional and growing influence he had with the powers that be, the Aga Khan was at a comparatively young age attracted to Nawab Mohsin-ul-Mulk and his compatriots of the Aligarh School. Mohsin-ul-Mulk was an extremely shrewd man. When he succeeded to Sir Syed Ahmed's place, the M. A. O. College was passing through a great financial crisis. The Aligarh ideal was almost in jeopardy. Mohsin-ul-Mulk was therefore straining every nerve to reorganise the College through all possible means. The Mohammedan Educational Conference was a great source of strength to him: it was his rallying point in all emergencies. When, therefore, the Conference was to assemble at the time of the Coronation Durbar of 1903 in the Imperial City of Delhi, Mohsin-ul-Mulk's eyes were rivetted on the young Aga, whom he invited to preside on the occasion.

The Conference of this year met under most auspicious circumstances. Owing to the Durbar, a great many princes and prominent men from all over India were able to attend. The late Lord Kitchener, Lord Northcote, the then Governor of Bombay, and many other influential European officers visited the Conference. The Presidential Address which the Aga Khan delivered on the occasion was a masterpiece of its kind. The young Aga rose to the full height of his eloquence, and from his presidential chair passsionately drew the attention of his co-religionists to the deplorable condition into which they had fallen. The descendants of those that carried the torch of learning into the heart of Europe and had founded Cordova and Baghdad were steeped in ignorance. He appealed to them to shake off their lethargy and indifference, and in order that they might live an honourable existence, carry out the sage of Aligarh's ideal to found a University of their own:

> to create for our people an intellectual and moral capital; a city which shall be the home of elevated ideas and pure ideals; a centre from which light and guidance shall be diffused among the Moslems of India, aye, and out of India, too, and which shall hold up to the world a noble standard of the justice and virtue and purity of our beloved faith.

They had sufficiently fallen down. Various causes were responsible for this downfall. 'The bad example and selfishness of the Abbaside's leading to political and religious differences, the fatal system of modern *purdah* with its restrictions on the intellectual development of the women, the constant and silent withdrawal of the most pious and moral Mussalmans into a life of private prayer and devotion, and the doctrine of necessity,' all operated together to bring the Moslem society down to the present low and degraded level of intellect and character. To arrest this downward tendency and to redeem Islam, he asked for a crore of rupees that with this amount a University might be started—

> a University where Moslem youths can get, in addition to modern sciences, a knowledge of their glorious past and religion,

and where the whole atmosphere of the place (it being a residential ' University) may, like Oxford, give more attention to character than mere examinations, such a University would restore the faded glories of our people. There is no doubt of the efficacy of the remedy, the element of doubt lies in the preparation of it. Will the Mussalmans of to-day exert themselves so much as to found such a University? Have we so wholly lost the noble disregard of self, the generous devotion to the good of Islam which characterised the early Moslems, as not to be able to set aside some of our wealth for this great cause? We are sure that by founding this University we can arrest the decadence of Islam, and if we are not willing to make sacrifices for such an end, must I not conclude that we do not really care whether the faith of Islam is dead or not?

In conclusion, he bitterly remarked :—

If our ideal is not realised, it will be because the ape within has swallowed the angel, it will be because though we profess veneration for the faith and for the Prophet, it is but a lip-loyalty that will not make this small sacrifice to revive in its purity the glorious faith of Islam.

This cry for a separate Muslim University was not appreciated by certain sections of the non-Muslim Indian population. It was pointed out that the Mussalmans were consciously and deliberately drifting away into a position of mischievous exclusiveness, which would assuredly in the long run prove most detrimental to the best interests of the country. The existing Universities, they thought, were quite capable of imparting to India's youth the best kind of education required; and the attempt to found a separate seat of learning on the basis of religion was not only unnecessary but was calculated to retard the progress of Indian unity. The Aga Khan, on behalf of the Muslim community, gave an effective answer to such a line of argument. In the course of his address as Chairman of the Reception Committee, at the Session of the All-India Mohammedan Educational

Conference held at Bombay, in December 1903, he was forced to say:—

> It would be the greatest of all our misfortunes if we now mistook instruction for education, and the mere power of passing examinations for learning. It is for this reason that the thoughtful welcome the reform of the Universities which the Government of India now contemplates. It is for this reason that the far-sighted amongst the Mussalmans of India desire a University where the standard of learning shall be the highest and where with scientific training there shall be that moral education—that indirect but constant reminder of the eternal difference between right and wrong which is the soul of education. It is a source of regret for many of us that in the Indian Universities there is that divorce between learning and religion which, especially in the case of Moslems, will, I fear, lead to disaster. Gentlemen, most Moslems, I think, would most gladly welcome a Hindu University at Benares, we would gladly welcome another at Poona, a third in Bengal and Madras. But because there is evidently no desire on their part to have a sectarian University with a Brahmanical atmosphere, it is absurd to deny us a University at Aligrah with affiliated colleges all over India. Another reason why we require a Central University where our individuality may not be lost for the sake of turning out a mechanical imitation of a European is this: we have a history in which noble and chivalrous characters abound; we have a glorious past so full of heroic figures that direct contact and communion with them could not but improve and give our youth early in life that sense of the necessity for self-sacrifice, for truthfulness, and for independence of character without which instruction and knowledge are, from the national point of view, worthless.

Though this passionate appeal for the establishment of a University at Aligarh did not bring any immediate fruits, still it was working in his mind and in the minds of others, and when, in 1910, an opportunity presented itself, he threw in it his heart and soul. Under his 'brilliant leadership' more than 30 lakhs were collected, and though even then the Mussalmans were not fortunate enough to achieve their object, this fund has nevertheless placed the Mussalmans nearer the goal than ever before.

IMPERIAL COUNCIL

The Presidentship of the Aga Khan over the Conference marked the beginning of the continuous All-India interest he took on behalf of his community and country. He was soon appointed a member of the Imperial Legislative Council where he acquitted himself creditably. There he advocated the cause of universal elementary education and suggested a scheme for co-ordinating the Imperial Service Troops employed by the various Indian States. His speeches were all frank utterances characterised by moderation and sobriety of judgment and were highly appreciated by the Government and the public.

THE ALL-INDIA MUSLIM LEAGUE

The Mussalmans were not politically well off. Sir Syed Ahmed's warning not to fall headlong into politics was still haunting their mind. So while the sister communities were advancing politically the Mussalmans were apethetic. But those among the community who were alive to the changing conditions of the time could well foresee what natural results would follow from their lifeless inaction. The Government under the sympathetic guidance of Lord Morley was contemplating the enlargement of the Indian Legislative Councils together with other constitutional organic changes in the administration of the country. Leaders of Muslim thought and public opinion became alive to the need of organising a political association with a view to safeguard their interests, and the Aga Khan had no small share in successfully launching out the scheme of establishing the All-India Muslim League.

The necessity for the immediate formation of a Moslem League impressed me on the occasion of my visit to Aligarh in 1906, and I communicated the idea to my late and most lamented friend, Nawab Mohsin-ul-Mulk, by whose death we have suffered a serious and irreparable loss. With characteristic foresight he accepted my suggestion, worked for its attainment, and brought about the deputation which waiting on H. E. Lord Minto in 1906, was the starting point of the recognition of the principle that the important Moslem minority in this country should have its fair and legitimate share in the administration of the country.

When after the Mohammedan Educational Conference assembled at Dacca, Nawab Khwaja Salimulla formally broached up the subject, the All-India Muslim League came into being. The following year its constitution was considered and adopted at its meeting held at Karachi, and H. H. the Aga Khan was elected its President, which office he resigned only very recently. His association with the League was of great help to the Mussalmans. From time to time he was pointing out to them the channels through which their national activities should run. The League was at first pooh-poohed in many quarters. It was condemned as a sectarian movement calculated to retard the progress of the Indian unity. But the Aga Khan and other Muslim leaders had faith in the value of a separate organisation like the League.

COMMUNAL REPRESENTATION

It was mainly due to its activities that the Mussalmans secured some sort of communal representation on the Councils. This was considered by certain classes of Indians as quite detrimental to the best interests of the country. But the President of the League was quite confident of contrary results. In his Inaugural Address delivered at the session of the League held at Delhi in January 1910, the Aga Khan frankly gave out his opinion on the Reform Scheme and warned the Indians not to make a mess of the whole thing.

> I am glad our just demand has been recognised. Now that the Reform Scheme has been finally settled and is actually in active operation, we must accept it as final in an appreciative spirit, worthy of our traditions, and try to make the best of it as loyal subjects of our beloved Sovereign, the King-Emperor and as citizens of India. May I venture also to say most emphatically that it is to the interests of Indians—Hindus and Moslems, Christians and Parsis alike—to accept the Reforms in a spirit of cordial appreciation, and that it now lies with us to do our utmost as enlightened citizens to co-operate with Government and our representatives in the Councils in working them for the common welfare of the people remembering that if we make a practical and beneficent use of this opportunity, we shall surley in time to come get a further advance towards Constitutional Government. In fact, I may say that Self-Government has come to our very doors. On the other hand, if we view the Reform Scheme and the Regulations under it in a spirit of obstructive particularism instead of using the wide powers placed in our hands for the conservation and development of those forces which are the dynamic factors in national progress all the world over, then as surely as night follows day we shall divert the slant of fair wind which ought to drive us far on towards the realisation of many of our cherished ambitions.

HINDU-MUSLIM UNITY

Though the Aga Khan has, as President of the League, championed the cause of Muslim representation and other exclusive needs of the community, he is by no means a sectarian in his views.

> While we hold fast, he observed, to our own religious, social, and ethical ideals, whilst we hold equally fast to the separate organisation and separate representation which are essential

for their maintenance and to secure for our Community its due influence in the body-politic, it must be the desire of our Rulers no less than of ourselves, to pursue these ideals, to work out our constructive programme, in harmonious co-operation with all other Indians who accept the cardinal principles of our political faith—*the ordered development of this country under the Imperial Crown.* Time, the opportunities for co-operation in stimulating the social and economic progress of this country, and the diffusion of education will also, I believe, remove the acerbities attaching to the religious difficulties and caste disabilities which sap the foundation of Indian society so that they will become, in the distant future, the minor forces that they are now in Western Europe and America. If we extend hearty and sincere co-operation in each other's transactions and interests and pursue higher ideals and act with moderation and judicious calm, then I have no apprehension for the future of India.

He has ever enjoined on his co-religionists in India to try their best to understand their Hindu brethren with whom their lot is inseparably cast. In his scheme of a Muslim University, he advocates that:

In order to enable us to come in touch with what is best in the ancient Hindu civilization and better to enable us to understand the origin and structure of Hindu thought and religion in its widest sense as well as to inculcate in us a feeling of respect and affection for our fellow-subjects and to teach us to consider their customs and prejudices, Sanskrit and other Oriental literature ought also to be given due prominence in the curricula.

Every one is well aware of his great move in the direction of a *modus operandi* between the Hindus and Mussalmans, by which the existing friction between them might vanish and joint action for the well-being of both might be made possible *viz*, the Hindu-Muslim Conference held at Allahabad on the New Year day of 1911, which was, besides the Aga Khan and Sir William Wedderburn, attended by such eminent representative members as Mr. Surendranath Banerjee, Pandit Malaviya, Sir Ibrahim Rahimtulla, Nawab Vikar-ul-Mulk, Messrs. Hasan Imam,

Mazar-ul-Haque and Jinnah. As a result of it, a Committee was appointed to consider all points of difference and suggest some satisfactory solution for minimising them.

The Aga Khan strongly believes that sooner or later the Hindus and Mussalmans will have to forget their differences and whole-heartedly work together for the common good. They are sailing in the same boat; they must sail together or sink together. There could be no other alternative. Attempts for reconciliation and rapprochement may not all at once be rewarded with success. The long sought-for end is, however, sure to come. It is to hasten this rapprochement, the Aga Khan contended that he had so staunchly advocated the need for special representation. He will have unity in India, not in name, not by hook or crook, but a real unity based on a sound and proper understanding of each other. In holding fast to this principle, he has certainly incurred the displeasure of many Hindu leaders. Even the late Mr. Gokhale more than once failed to see eye to eye with him on this question of Muslim demands. Some of the utterances of His Highness on this subject threw Mr. Gokhale into "considerable astonishment" and forced him to rub his eyes as he read them. But the Aga-Khan, in spite of his advocacy of vital Muslim interests with a rare tenacity and singleness of purpose, has been never known to be a stiff-necked one-sided politician. He sincerely believes that his com munity's demands are quite just, and he is confident that they will eventually succeed to appeal to their Hindu brethren. But this may not be achieved in a day; years and decades might pass before such a consummation might take place. But meanwhile, before the Hindus could understand the Mussalmans in the right perspective, the Aga Khan has ever exhorted his co-religionists not to do anything that might seriously injure the sentiments and susceptibilities of their countrymen. The Partition of Bengal, according to Lord Curzon, was aimed at restoring the Muslim population of the Eastern Bengal to their natural and legitimate place of importance in the administration of this part of India. But it was argued by the Bengalis, with all vehemence and passion, that this step of Lord Curzon had grievously injured the sentiment of the Bengali-Hindu population, and a strong well-organised agitation was set in motion. The result was that in spite of every possible assurances from Mr. Morley and in spite of his "settled facts," everything was unsettled and the Partition was annulled in 1912. Muslim sentiment was acute. Still there was no outburst. The Mussalmans observed a remarkable self-restraint in order not to hurl their Hindu brethren into any more agitation.

This commendable attitude on the part of the Mussalmans was due to the large-hearted toleration of Muslim leaders, who enjoined on their co-religionists to willingly acquiesce in the change that they might thereby show their practical sympathy with the

Hindu sentiment of Bengal. Said the Aga Khan:—

Then comes the undoing of the Partition. No doubt the Mussalmans were in a distinct majority in the province of Eastern Bengal and Assam, and this unique position is now lost. But looking at the position of Islam in India as a whole, I doubt if it will be found that it was a good thing to be in a clear majority in one province and in a minority in almost every other. The disadvantages of such a situation are obvious. Islam in India is one and indivisible. It is the duty of a Moslem to look not only to the immediate interest of his own locality but to those of his co-religionists as a whole. But if we look upon it from a still wider point of view as Indians, we shall find that the old Partition had deeply wounded, and not unnaturally, the sentiments of the great Bengali-speaking millions of India. Anything that permanently alienates and offends the sentiments or interests of millions of Indians, be they Moslem or Hindu, is undoubtedly in itself an undesirable thing and should not only be avoided by the Government but also opposed by all communities of India. Viewed in this light, the undoing of the Partition which has satisfied the great Bengali-speaking people, ought to be in itself a cause of congratulation for all Indians, whether Hindus or Mussalmans, and, I think, we should all be deeply grateful to His Excellency Lord Hardinge for this great act of statesmanship which has removed a grievance from one important section of His Majesty's Indian subjects.

The Aga Khan has often deplored the existence of strained relations between Hindus and Mussalmans in certain unfortunate parts of India and as a way towards a better state of things, he observes:—

It is eminently desirable that in the provinces and districts where goodwill and right feeling exist, missionaries should go forth to the less fortunate parts of the country in the effort to bring about good understanding. The Mussalmans have a great opportunity if they will only realise how far they can go in evoking and strengthening Hindu goodwill by voluntarily abandoning the public slaughter of cows for sacrifice. The question, as you are aware, is largely an economic one, and much could be done to solve it by committees of Mussalmans, and rich Hindus organising subscriptions for the purchase of other animals to be sacrificed in substitution of kine. Good work could also be done by local committees for bringing Hindus and Mussalmans together in social intercourse.

The Aga Khan has not only thus exerted himself to draw the two communities together in all possible ways but he has also given practical proof of his active interest in the welfare of the Hindu community. He is a regular subscriber to several Hindu Institutions and has contributed donations to the Deccan Education Society and the Hindu University. The Aga Khan is a strong advocate of denominational Universities. Without the development of those wholesome national traits and virtues which go to make a good Hindu and a good Mussalman, without that sense of national dignity and self-respect born of a true knowledge of what was best in their past, neither the Hindus nor the Mussalmans will be able to contribute anything substantial to the formation of a healthy Indian nationhood so essential for the future advancement of India.

SOUTH AFRICAN QUESTION

His interest in the welfare of his countrymen does not end with India. He is one of those who have championed the cause of the Indians in South Africa and other Colonies. The whole-hearted support he gave to Mr. Gandhi and his compatriots is too well-known for any special reference here. Both from the platform and through the Press, both here and in England, he has oftentimes pleaded for a better treatment of his countrymen in the Colonies. More than all, through his personal influence, through silent unobtrusive work, he has been able to achieve, perhaps, more than what he has actually done through public demonstrations. What exactly he has said or done for India and her sons in

South Africa and elsewhere it is not possible to trace in detail. But this can safely be hoped that throughout his untiring travels from one end of the year to the other, spending a large part of his time in England and the Colonies, he must have had a unique opportunity to enlighten British statesmen on the actual needs and aspirations of the people of India.

A CAUTIOUS POLITICIAN

His views on important political and other questions affecting the welfare of India, as a whole, have always been very moderate. He is of the school of thought to which Mr. Gokhale and Sir P. Mehta belonged, for both of whom he had the greatest regard and admiration.

> The sacred cause of Indian progress invariably has been served best by those who have shared with Mehta and Gokhale, the attitude of which I have spoken. The ideal of nationhood and the development of free institutions can only be retarded seriously by violent and intemperate advocacy on the one hand; or conversely a senseless and debasing demeanour of constant flattery of every official measure—a cringing attitude that makes superficial observers believe that Indians are incapable of anything except self-humiliation or violent vituperation.

It is this dignified attitude on political questions, he says, that should characterise every public worker as it did in the case of Sir Pherozeshah and Mr. Gokhale. This does not come in a day. It should be cultivated during years of hard toil and apprenticeship. While addressing a meeting held in London in memory of Sir Pherozeshah Mehta, he observed:

> Too often, I fear, Indian youths educated here return to the Motherland filled with ambition to shine in the political firmament, to quickly figure in the Legislature, to be known the country over as "leaders." But as necessarily only a few can reach the top, a large number gradually lose all connection

with public life, and devote themselves entirely to their personal and professional affairs. They wish to begin where the most successful men in public life gained footing only after years of apprenticeship in local affairs or other apparently undistinguished service of the people. Only in rare cases can these premature ambitions be realised, and even in them they are liable to engender an arrogant self-satisfaction standing in the way of true service of India. As to the disappointed majority, the opportunities that lie close at hand are despised and neglected. Hence much fine material for the advancement of India runs to waste, and progress in local self-government has been much less marked than would have been the case had it been more generally recognised that local patriotism and seemingly minor service are the seed of larger opportunities, besides being in themselves worthy objects of ambition for promoting communal good. This is constantly seen by those who look below the surface of English life, with its manifold local and unpaid civic activities. The lesson is writ large in the life of Gokhale as well as that of Mehta, for we can never forget the long years of professional drudgery on merely nominal pay, the former passed in the Fergusson College, nor the fact that he prized the later office or honour more than his helpful membership of the Poona Municipality. It is by attention to local affairs, by the exercise of local patriotism and effort, in the constructive spirit shown by these two great sons of India, that our country will advance most assuredly and most steadfastly to the realisation of her great destiny, and that our dreams of progress under the British Crown within the Empire will best be realised.

SELF-GOVERNMENT FOR INDIA

That India has a great future before her, a great destiny to fulfil, the Aga Khan does not for a moment doubt. In the fulness of time India will become a self-governing part of the great British Empire. But there is no swift and ready method by which this could be attained. The path of progress is by no means easy. Years of patient toil and preparation are necessary before anything substantial can be gained. Speaking at the fifth annual meeting of the London Branch of the All-India Muslim League, in July 1913, the Aga Khan draws pointed attention to the ideal of self-Government adopted by the parent League and says:—

> The ideal, whether on Colonial lines as has been suggested by so many of our compatriots, or in some form "suitable to India" the conditions of which we do not at present conceive and therefore do not attempt to define, must commend itself to thoughtful opinion, if it means, as I take it to mean, an ideal involving many decades of effort towards self-improvement, towards social reform, towards educational diffusion, and towards complete amity between various communities. Given personal and national self-sacrifice for generations to come, some form of self-Government worthy of the British Empire and worthy of the people of India will be evolved, and Indians will have won a proud place for their nation in the world under the British Throne. But if it means a mere hasty impulse to jump at the apple when only the blossoming stage is over, then the day that witnessed the formulation of the ideal will be a very unfortunate one in our country's annals. We have a long way to travel before the distant goal can be reached, and the voice of wisdom calls us to proceed step by step. The fact that the Central Committee confined itself to favouring some system "suitable to India" shows that at present it is difficult even to define the plan which may be evolved as Indian life develops and expands. Such development, I need hardly say, must be social, material and moral as well as political if a goal worthy of the self-sacrifice involved and of India's place in the Empire is to be reached.

HIS SERVICES DURING THE WAR

It is well-known that His Highness was in intimate relations with Gokhale. When in 1916 the Aga Khan published what was known as Gokhale's Testament on post-War Reforms, the event created a great sensation.

The Aga Khan has rendered signal services to the Empire, which services as offered in diverse capacities and at different times have all been highly appreciated by the King-Emperor, who graciously conferred on him many a title and distinction, the most notable of them being the recent conferment on him of "a Salute of 11 Guns and the rank and status of a first class Chief of the Bombay Presidency for life." Apart from his active work during the Great War in urging upon the Muslim world to hold fast to the Allies, the Aga Khan volunteered at the beginning of the War, as he did during the South African War, to go to the front as a private. Questioned by Reuter's representative if he had really offered to go as a private with the Indian troops, he forthwith replied:

> Yes, or in any capacity whatever. I have, alas! never had any military training, but if the War Office will accept my services, I shall be only too happy to go anywhere and do anything in order to equip myself for fighting. If they will only give me an opportunity, I will shed my last drop of blood for the British Empire.

So much was the Aga Khan desirous of going to the front and undergoing some real personal sacrifice that when addressing the Indian Field Ambulance Corps in England on the eve of its proceeding to the Front, he said magnanimously:

> One small and humble personal explanation: If I do not get anything of a more combatant nature, I hope to come with you as your interpreter, if I may. (Cheers.) I know English, French, German and Hindustani, and I do not think you will find many interpreters so useful; so that I will earn my bread, if I can, there. If I do not go, it will be because of some *force majure*, and not through any want of effort on my own part.

When the moment of the crisis came, Lord Hardinge, rightly trusting India's loyalty to the Empire and her indignant repudiation of German efforts to induce her to revolt, sent the flower of the Indian army to France and it arrived in time to share the glory of saving Calais. H. H. the Aga Khan in a long letter to the *Times* whole heartedly endorsed Lord Hardinge's courageous act of statesmanship.

FAITH IN ENGLAND

All this love for England, all this desire on his part to be of some use or other in her moments of stress and storm is due to his implicit belief and faith in the justice and righteousness of British connection with India. While speaking on the life-work of Sir Pherozeshah Mehta and his strong faith in the fertilizing principles of English culture and English civilization, as applied to Indian problems, the Aga Khan said:

> I can do no better than quote the words in which he declared his political faith in England, which I know was also the life-long faith of Gokhale, and which is mine also.
>
> When, in the inscrutable dispensation of Providence, India was assigned to the care of England, one can almost imagine that the choice was offered to her as to Israel of old: 'Behold, I have placed before you a blessing and a curse: a blessing if ye will obey the commandments of the Lord your God, a curse if ye will not obey the commandments of the Lord your God but go after other gods whom ye have not known' All the great forces of English life and society, moral, social, intellectual, political, are, if slowly, yet steadily and irresistibly, declaring themselves for the choice which will make the connection of England and India a blessing to themselves and to the whole world for countless generations.

That such is the belief of every Indian has been demonstrated in the most loyal and unanimous support India is actively giving to England in the hour of her need. While recognising that the relations between England and India have at times been not as one would desire, the Aga Khan has rightly demonstrated to the English public that India is too deeply attached to England to be influenced by any petty differences and that therefore she has risen as one man to assist the Empire during the War with Germany. Addressing a gathering in England, he said:—

> In this hour of India's and the Empire's difficulties, happily no differences of race and creed exist in India. They do not count. (Cheers.) And the Indian blood that will be shed on the fields of France and Belgium, and, I hope, Germany (loud cheers) will not have been shed in vain if it leads to a permanent disappearance of racial and religious antagonism, or any other suspicion in India. (Cheers.) We are absolutely united in the common purpose of taking our full share in the trials and sorrows of the Empire, and in contributing to the sacrifices entailed by the unconquerable determination of the British Empire and her Allies to win through.

INDIA IN TRANSITION

In the autumn of 1918 His Highness published a book detailing an elaborate Scheme of Reforms for India urging a federal constitution. In the foreword to the book the Aga Khan wrote:—

> Writing and thinking almost within hearing of the thunder of battle in Europe, I have been in a better position to apply to the Indian problem the widened outlook derived from a close and frequent contact with political systems and affairs outside, as well as within my own country. Further, thrown so fully on my own resources, I can at least claim that the work, whatever its demerits, is an original and strictly personal contribution to the Indian problem.

There are indeed some novel provisions in his scheme which should be noted. India is too vast and diversified for a successful unilateral form of free Government and therefore His Highness proposed autonomous Provinces in which official executive responsibility would be vested in a Governor as directly representing the Sovereign. The Governorships should be open to Indians confining the choice for some years hence to Ruling Princes who would leave their own territory for five years for this greater field. The Aga Khan recommends the adoption of the American principle of freedom of the executive from legislative control so far as tenure of office is concerned.

Provincial legislatures should be greatly enlarged, Bombay for example having 180 to 220 members in order to have a representative of every district, community and substantial interest. There should be a Senate or Upper House and the power of both Houses over the legislature and finance should be subject only to the veto of the Governor, but the Legislature might possess the right of removing by a three-fourths majority an unsuitable or incompetent departmental head. There should be a royal Viceroy with a Prime Minister presiding over a Cabinet, choosing his colleagues under the Viceroy's guidance as he thought best.

After due establishment of a federal constitution room for Imperial legislation as distinct from questions of policy would be so small that the Central Legislature should be a Senate for which each great Province would send eight or ten representatives and each Native State would have representatives, beginning with seven for Hyderabad. Once internal federation was complete it would sooner or later attract Persia, Afghanistan and all principalities from Africa and similar countries into a freewill membership of a great South Asiatic federation of which Delhi would be the centre.

Such is the scheme adumbrated in *India in Transition.*

THE MONTAGU REFORMS

Though His Highness had chalked out a distinct Scheme of reforms for India he was not slow to recognize the merits of the Montford Scheme. His Highness was indeed conscious of its limitations but he acknowledged that it was a great improvement in the direction of Responsible Government. At a Dinner given in honour of Mr. Montagu, the Aga Khan paid a well deserved tribute to his indefatigable labours in securing Parliamentary acceptance of the measure. India, said His Highness, was greatly indebted to the Joint Committee, particularly Lord Selborne and Earl Crewe. "I would gladly have seen the Reforms more liberal in some respects, but all rejoiced at the triumph which Mr. Montagu has won in making such an excellent compromise."

The Aga Khan was one of the principal witnesses at the sittings of the Joint Committee of the Government of India Bill. In the course of a memorandum which he presented to the Committee he said :—

> I accept the term "Responsible Government," though as an ideal my preference is for self-Government either on the American federal plan or on Swiss lines leaving ultimate power through the Initiative, the Referendum, and perhaps the Recall. But the facts of the situation have to be recognised. Our future is linked with Great Britain and not with the United States or Switzerland—and still less with an abstract perfect state conceived by the mind of a Plato. For a century and a half English institutions and sentiments have been moulding Indian political ideals. The very fact that this Bill is before the British Parliament shows that we must seek progress at this transitional stage in conformity with English views and English institutions. Under these circumstances "Responsible Government" must be our way towards evolving in the future some plan more suited to a congeries of great states, such as India will become, and I believe the way will be found in something akin to the American federal plan, plus the Initiative and the Referendum and possibly even the Recall. Meanwhile acceptance of the formula "Responsible Government" postulates the necessity for making the electorate as wide as possible, as well as the establishment in the Provincial Legislatures of a substantial elected majority.

In his oral evidence His Highness criticised some features of the Reform Bill and pointed the better way. The evidence is throughout marked by that clear grasp of realities which is a striking characteristic of His Highness' political work. The Aga Khan said in the course of his evidence that as an ideal he preferred self-Government on the American federal plan or Swiss lines, but he recognised that India's future was linked with Britain, and responsible government must be a way towards evolving some such plan more suited to the communities of great States such as India would become. He looked forward to the day when through the referendum and the initiative electors would fully supervise their representatives. Dualism could not be a permanent solution but it was difficult at present to imagine any other coherent scheme for the transitional period. A two-thirds' majority vote should be needed for the removal of a Minister. The Governor's power to disregard the opinion of Ministers was desirable at present as a safeguard from the British point of view, but he doubted the practical utility of such power. He was of opinion that the best guarantee against hasty, unfair, or partial legislation and the best protection for the Governor himself would be the referendum. He thought that the proposed restrictions on the financial and legislative powers of Legislatures were unnecessarily severe so far as Bombay and Bengal were concerned. The Legislature, he said, should certainly be empowered to vote supplies.

BRITAIN'S FAR EASTERN POLICY

Much has already been said in a previous sketch of the services H. H. the Aga Khan rendered to the cause of the Khilafat in company with the Rt. Hon. Syed Ameer Ali. Both in India and in England and indeed in all Muslim countries which he was constantly visiting he threw the weight of his influence on the side of peace and amity. He strongly protested however against Britain's Eastern Policy—particularly the imperialistic aims of British foreign policy in the East. The publication of the Esher Report caused him deep anxiety as to the fate of Mesopotamia and he wrote a remarkable protest in the English press:—

> All my life I have been a convinced and serious believer in the importance, not only to Great Britain and to India, but also to mankind and to civilization at large, of strengthening the true links which unite India to the British Empire. I believe in the development and growth of India into a vast self-governing and free Asiatic Dominion, attached to Great Britain and the other Dominions by the ties of a common Sovereignty and flag, and by a community of political, economic, and intellectual interests. I know that similar views are cherished by very large numbers of thoughtful Indians.
>
> But it would be idle to conceal the fact that ever since the Armistice most Indians who think as I do have had their faith and their hopes constantly and increasingly shocked. We have watched with growing apprehension the vague policy of Asiatic adventure pursued, apparently without coherence and without clear direction, by the Central Government to which we have been proud to render obedience. Our mis-givings have been deepened by the discovery that the views of the Government of India, still less Indian public opinion, count for little or nothing in the settlement of Imperial policy in the East. The Indian point of view, whether official or otherwise, appears to be almost entirely disregarded.
>
> The immediate results of the new habit of ignoring the Indian attitude towards external Imperial questions is unhappily plain to day. While the British Empire has drifted into difficulties and entanglements in the Near and Middle East, the political situation in India is causing natural alarm. For that situation the Imperial policy of the Home Government is, in my view, partly responsible.

THE TURKISH QUESTION

Though he strongly disapproved of British Eastern policy—and he was profoundly disturbed by Britain's part in the Treaty of Sevres—yet his influence was always on the side of moderation. At the time when India was torn with a tremendous agitation over the

Khilafat question His Highness, whose own views were not less pronounced, could still urge his countrymen to be patient. In an interview with the *Times of India,* he said that he was convinced that the majority of Englishmen who form the backbone of the British Empire desire fair and final settlement of the difficulties that have grown up during the last 40 years and that they realise the inequity of the dead Treaty of Sevres.

The difficulty was that the question of Holy Places was not properly understood by the man-in-the-street in England, and Englishmen, therefore, cannot make up their minds rapidly on the subject. But the number of people, desiring fair and final settlement of the Turkish question, was daily growing. Great efforts would be needed yet, before the just appreciation of real issues was secured.

His Highness hoped that if once public opinion in England realised how little Moslems' real desire and ambitions were, a satisfactory settlement would be possible which when once effected would relieve Indian Muslims from the burden of pre-occupation of non-Indian questions for many years to come. International difficulties especially after the bitter memories of the disasterous War would take long to settle. He therefore entreated the Muslims to remember that fact and not to become impatient of delays. He was a strong believer that a powerful Turkey would be a source of great strength to the British Government and their alliance would be an effective means of securing the world peace in future.

While he urged India to be patient and temperate in her agitation he did not suppress matters in his warnings to England. In May 1922 he told the Paris correspondent of the *Daily Express* that unless Great Britain revised her Mahommedan policy, a revolution in India was inevitable. He suggested that peace could be restored by relieving India of the burden of taxation for the upkeep of the army. He was also of opinion that the Turko-Greek situation could only be settled by giving the Turks Adrianople.

THE KHILAFAT AND TURKEY

The triumph of Kemal Pasha brought peace in its train. Ismet's firm stand at Lausanne brought the kind of peace for Turkey that was long sought in vain. But with the triumph of Turkey came the sad, shocking news that Angora had decided to dispense with the Khalifa. We have in a previous page given the story of how the Rt. Hon. Ameer Ali endeavoured to uphold the cause of the Khilafat. In all his efforts His Highness joined with characteristic energy. In a letter to Ismet which caused a great perturbation in Angora the Aga Khan suggested the integral maintenance of the Khilafat in conformity with the Sheriat Law, and pointed out that the restriction of the Khalifa's authority and his exclusion from all Turkish political organisations would result in the effective loss of the moral force which the Khilafat universally enjoys, and would weaken Islam. Therefore, he urged that the dignity and ascendency of the Khalifa should not be less than the Pope's. He concluded that all Sunnite Muslims, for fourteen centuries, have regarded the Khalifa as the representative of the Prophet and their Imam. This idea, he said, cannot be destroyed without causing grave dissension among them.

LABOUR AND INDIA

Early in 1924 His Highness returned to India after a long absence in England and gave his opinion as to what might be expected of the Labour Government in England. Always interested in the welfare of overseas Indians His Highness said that the problems of Kenya should come foremost in the list of our demands.

> Personally, I think, the immediate problem of India in England is the solving sympathetically of the problem of Kenya and if a Labour Government comes into power, that is the problem they may take up *first* very seriously, rather than the political questions of India. The political problems of India, they will judge after the Councils have set to work, I think, rather than before, as opinions will be crystallized later. If the new Councils work by reasoned arguments, by deep study of facts, we can make out such a case, as for instance, the reduction of military expenditure, as to be unanswerable on reasoned grounds. I personally think we can make out such a case. It must be remembered that the present military expenditure is very great, and I am sure if the Councils do as Mr. Gokhale did it will have a great influence in England.

Asked about the chances of India getting any advance from the Labour Government His Highness said:

> There is no Government either Labour, Liberal or Conservative which will reopen the question of a further extension o the Reforms at this moment. My honest opinion is that if you go to your Labour friends, they will say that this is the first normal Council after Reforms, as in the last Council the majority kept away. "Let us see what the Nationalists and Moderates combined will produce. Let us see the combination of wisdom, which these two elements will bring forth and then we shall act" will be the reply India will receive.

Much has happened since these words were uttered. Dyarchy has failed in Bengal and the Council, prorogued. It is so in the Central Provinces. Its success has been questioned in other provinces also. The bulk of evidence before the Reforms Enquiry Committee presided over by Sir Alexander Muddiman go to show how completely Dyarchy has broken down. And the country is in no mood to work the Reforms without drastic changes. Already the Government of Bengal with the sanction of the Viceroy have embarked on a repressive campaign in order to punish the anarchists. In their enthusiasm to bring the culprits to book, innocent people also suffer. The return of the Conservatives to power in England leaves the prospects gloomy. What will be the outcome of the present discontents and of the policy pursued by the Government of India and the Cabinet at home, it is yet too early to speculate.

P. 209.

MIAN SIR MUHAMMAD SHAFI

Sir Muhammad Shafi

FAMILY HISTORY

MIAN Sir Muhammad Shafi belongs to the well-known Mian family of Baghbanpura in the District of Lahore, members of which own extensive landed and house property in the Districts of Lahore, Montgomery, Sheikhupura, Lyallpur, Muzaffargarh, Mianwali, Dera Ismail Khan, Simla and Delhi, as well as in the Bahawalpur State.

EARLY LIFE

Mian Muhammad Shafi, who is the only surviving son of the late Mian Din Muhammad, was born on 10th March 1869. As is the custom in most respectable Muslim families, he was first placed in a local Mosque under one Maulvi Allah Din, a strict disciplinarian, in order to learn the Quran and the rudiments of Muslim Theology. Thereafter, he entered the village school, from which he passed the Vernacular Middle School Examination. Proceeding thence to Lahore, he joined the Central Model School. In 1886, having passed the Matriculation Examination of the Punjab University, he joined the Government College at Lahore; and two years later, being attracted by the magnetic personality of Dr. J. C. R. Ewing, Principal of the Forman Christian College and Vice-Chancellor of the Punjab University, he transferred himself to the latter Institution, where he received instruction under that great educationist for a period of 18 months. In August 1889, he left for England in order to study for the Bar, a profession for which he had a great natural aptitude. Even during his college career at Lahore, he began to take a keen interest in the public affairs of India and contributed articles and letters to THE PIONEER, THE CIVIL AND MILITARY GAZETTE, THE TRIBUNE, THE PUNJAB PATRIOT and THE MUSLIM HERALD of Madras.

CAREER IN ENGLAND

Two years before his arrival in London, he had been preceded to England by his cousin Mian Muhammad Shah Din (subsequently the Hon'ble Mr. Justice Shah Din of the Punjab Chief Court), who was at the time reading for the Bar at the Hon'ble Society of the Middle Temple. Mian Muhammad Shafi, in consequence, very naturally joined the same Inn of Court. Two months after his arrival, partly on his initiative, a consultation took place in the Temple Gardens on the occasion of Lord Mayor's Show on 10th November 1889, as a result of which the principal Muslim residents in London met at the house of Mr. (now Sir) Abdur Rahim, when the Anjuman-i-Islamia, London, was founded with Mr. Abdur Rahim as its President, Mr. Shah Din and Syed (now Sir) Ali Imam as Vice-Presidents, Maulvi Rafiuddin Ahmed (now a member of the Bombay Legislative Council) as Secretary, and among others

Mr. Hasan Imam and himself as Members of the Executive Committee. At that preliminary meeting, Mian Muhammad Shafi was asked to deliver the first Address at the first General meeting of the Anjuman when he selected "The Past, Present and Future of Islam" as the subject-matter of his Address. During the following year, on return to India of Messrs. Abdur Rahim, Shah Din and Ali Imam, he was elected President of the Anjuman. In February 1890, he had the honour of being presented at the Royal Levee held in St. James' Palace and during that year successfully competed for a Scholarship in International and Constitutional Law and Constitutional History at the Middle Temple. During his stay in England, he took a prominent part in various Institutions that had the welfare of Indian students in England, as their object. He was a member of the House Committee of the Northbrooke Indian Club and spoke at the meetings of the Indian Section of the Royal Society of Arts, the National Indian Association, the Society for the Encouragement and Protection of Indian Arts and the Indian Temperance Association, of which last the late Mr. W. S. Caine, M. P., was the Honorary Secretary His study of the British Constitution and British political life was not confined merely to text-books. He constantly attended the sittings of the House of Commons as well as political meetings held in various parts of London. Soon after his arrival in London, he joined the Paddington

Parliament, a high class political Society, of which some Members of Parliament, Barristers, Solicitors, merchants and householders were members. For over a year he was a Member of the Unionist Cabinet in that Parliament. In the General Elections held in July 1892, he addressed several meetings in London. Having been called to the Bar in June 1892, he returned to India in August of that year.

INDIAN CAREER

Mian Muhammad Shafi's training in England and successful career at the Bar have, as a matter of course, endowed him with powers of effective debate and impressive speech. His activities, inside and outside the Legislative Councils, have been many and varied. His profession as well as the Muslim Community have, very naturally, had the benefit of a considerable portion of his attention and energies. But he is one of those public workers with whom a genuine zeal for communal welfare is only a part of that larger spirit of Indian patriotism which sincerely believes in inter-communal co-operation and good-will as an essential element in the future constitutional, material, and moral progress of the country. He has helped many a non-Muslim young man to start in respectable careers of service and has also rendered material help to a number of non-Muslim Institutions.

LEGAL

Having been enrolled as an Advocate of the High Court at Allahabad and of the Punjab Chief Court at Lahore, he started practice on 1st October

1892, at Hoshiarpur, with a view to acquiring practical experience of Original Court work before commencing practice in the Chief Court at Lahore. During his stay at Hoshiarpur, he published a Commentary on the "Punjab Tenancy Act, 1887," and by the end of 1894 acquired a leading position in the District Bar. On 1st May 1895, he shifted to Lahore and began practice in the Chief Court. He was soon marked out as a junior who would some day rise to a prominent position in the profession. In 1896, the late Mr. Justice Rivaz, before proceeding on leave to England, suggested to him the desirability of publishing an annotated edition of the "Provincial Small Causes Courts Act," on which no commentary had been published up to that time and left his own private notes with him for that purpose. That work was published by Mian Muhammad Shafi in the following year. In 1898, he was elected as Secretary of the Punjab Chief Court Bar Association and, thereafter, was a member of the Executive Committee of that Association for a number of years. Some four years after the publication of his "Commentary on the Provincial Small Causes Courts Act," he compiled and published an original work on "The Law of Compensation for Improvements in British India." By that time his practice had become extensive and went on increasing rapidly so that, together with his other public engagements, it became impossible for him to continue the work of authorship. By the year 1907, he had become one of the leading practitioners in the Punjab Chief Court and, in recognition of his position, the Judges recommended him for the title of Khan Bahadur which he received on 1st January 1908. His extensive practice covered both the civil and criminal fields of litigation and he came to be looked upon as an authority on the Punjab Customary Law. On the appointment of Mr. Justice Abdur Rahim of the Madras High Court as a member of the Royal Commission on Public Services, he was offered the officiating appointment in his place as a Judge of that High Court in September 1912. But his love of his profession as well as of public life and the position he had come to acquire in both prevented his accepting that offer. When examined as a witness before that Commission, he strongly pressed the claims of the Bar for an adequate share in the Judicial Service of the country. On the appointment of the late Mr. Lal Chand as a Judge of the Punjab Chief Court, he was elected Vice-President of the Punjab Chief Court Bar Association and was, about that time, also appointed by the Judges as a member of the Punjab Bar Council and of the Civil Procedure Code Committee. By 1916 he had risen to the position of the acknowledged leader of the Punjab Bar and in the beginning of 1917 was elected President of the Chief Court Bar Association and, as such, became the *ex-officio* President of the Punjab Bar Council,—a position which he continued to occupy after the Chief Court was raised to the status of a High Court and until his appointment as a Member of the Executive Council. He was the first Indian Member of the Punjab Bar to be elected to that position. as, hitherto, ever since the foundation of the Association, the President had always been a European Member of the Bar. On the death of his cousin, the late Mr. Justice Shah Din, at that time the senior Puisne Judge of the Punjab Chief Court, in the summer of 1918, he was offered the consequent vacancy on the Chief Court Bench. But the reasons which had prevented his accepting the Madras High Court Judgeship again stood in the way of his accepting the Judgeship of his own Court.

About that time the idea of organising the Provincial Bar for the purpose of safeguarding the interests of the profession had gained ground in certain sections of the legal practitioners at Lahore. Into the causes of the existence of this feeling of dissatisfaction with the then existing state of things, it is unnecessary here to enter. On a requisition signed by twenty leading members of the Chief Court Bar Association, steps were taken to convene a Provincial Bar Conference which took place on the 29th and 30th March 1919 at Lahore. Mian Muhammad Shafi was unanimously elected its President and the Address which he delivered on that occasion is characterised by a high tone of professional morality and zeal for upholding the privileges and dignity of the profession.

In the July of that year, Mian Muhammad Shafi's professional career was suddenly cut short by

Sir Sankaran Nair's resignation of his office of Education Member in the Government of India and the acceptance of that post by the subject of this sketch which has removed him temporarily from one sphere of usefulness to another sphere of equal usefulness and of greater responsibility. After holding the office of Member for Education and Public Health until the end of 1922, he was appointed to the office of Law Member of the Government of India, of which he assumed charge on 2nd January 1923, and thus attained the highest rung of the legal ladder open to a member of the profession in this country.

POLITICAL

The educational backwardness of Indian Mussalmans, due to causes into which it is unnecessary to enter for our purposes, inevitably led to their political backwardness. Individual leading gentlemen in the community here and there might have taken part in one or other political movement in the country. But, as a community, the Indian Mussalmans remained, for a long time, apathetic in so far as politics were concerned. Indeed, realising that they must, first, make leeway in education before participation in political activities, their great leader, the late Sir Syed Ahmad Khan for a long time insisted on concentration of communal efforts upon educational advance and discouraged participation in political agitation that was going on in the country in the Eighties of the last century. When Mian Muhammad Shafi returned from England in 1892, there was no organized political movement in existence among the Indian Mussalmans, although local Anjumans here and there occasionally made spasmodic efforts to safeguard and promote local Muslim interests. During the Christmas of 1892, after the retirement of the late Mr. Justice Mahmud from the Allahabad High Court, leading Muhammadan gentlemen, assembled at Aligarh, induced the late Sir Syed Ahmad Khan to agree to the starting of a Muslim Association which, owing to his insistence, consisted merely of selected representative Mussalmans from the various Provinces, adopted as its *modus operandi* the promotion and defence of Muslim interests by means of representations to Government, and scrupulously avoided public agitation. The Association was given the name of the Anglo-Muhammadan Defence Association of Upper India and had Mr. Syed Mahmud and Mr. Theodore Beck, the then Principal of the Aligarh College, as its Joint Secretaries. Mian Muhammad Shafi was selected as one of a small group of Muhammedans from the Punjab to represent that Province on the Council of this Association. While practising at Hoshiarpur he founded the local Anjuman-i-Islamia of which he continued to be the Honorary General Secretary until his departure from that District for Lahore. Soon after his arrival at Lahore, he was elected Vice-President of the Young Men's Muhammadan Association, of which his cousin Mr. Shah Din was the President, as well as a member of the Executive Committee of the Anjuman-i-Islamia.

Punjab, at that time the only representative body which included political work among its other activities. There was at that time no Muslim newspaper in Northern India. This paramount need in the interests of the Muslim community was satisfied by the formation in 1895, of a Committee at Lahore which started, and for a number of years managed the "OBSERVER", a newspaper which played an important part in the political awakening of the Indian Mussalmans. Of that Committee Mian Muhammad Shafi was the Secretary. In 1897 when Lord Elgin, the then Viceroy of India, held a Durbar at Simla in celebration of the late Queen Victoria's Diamond Jubilee and Deputations representing all communities and interests presented congratulatory addresses on that auspicious occasion, Mian Muhammad Shafi was elected as a member of the Punjab Muslim Deputation for presentation of their Address to the Viceroy.

After the death of the late Sir Syed Ahmad Khan, the younger generation of educated Indian Mussalmans were becoming restive of the political inaction which was a noticeable feature of Muslim life in India. In September 1901, Mian Muhammad Shafi wrote a series of leading articles in the "OBSERVER" in which he advocated the formation of a political organization among the Indian Mussalmans for the safeguarding of the community's interests, sketched its constitution and suggested that it should be called the "Indian Muslim League." The events which took place between that date and the ultimate formation of the All-India Muslim League are wellknown to all leading Mussalmans.

There were whispers in the air of an intention, on the part of His Excellency Lord Minto's Government, of introducing important changes in the legislative and administrative machinery. Time had now arrived for a clear and definite pronouncement of Muhammadan demands and for organized action on the part of the Muslim leaders in defence of the community's rights and interests.

At this critical moment the late Nawab Mohsin-ul-Mulk, Sir Syed's worthy successor in the leadership of the community, came forward to champion his community's cause. He obtained permission, on behalf of Indian Mussalmans, from His Excellency the Viceroy, to present an address, embodying their just claims through a Deputation representative of the whole community.

As an integral portion of the larger scheme, the Provincial Branch of the All-India Muslim League in the Punjab was inaugurated at a Conference of the leading Muhammedans of the Province held at Lahore on 30th November and 1st December 1907, at which Mian Muhammad Shafi was elected as the Honorary General Secretary of the Provincial League, which office he continued to fill until the end of 1916, in addition to holding the office of a Vice-President of the All-India Muslim League. It was owing to his great organizing capacity that within the short period of one year, District Muslim Leagues were established in almost every District of the Punjab.

When presiding over the Lucknow anniversary of the All-India Muslim League in March 1913, Mian Muhammad Shafi said:

Now the Indian Mussalmans consist of two sections. Firstly those who, themselves being descendants of the pre-Aryan aborigines and of Aryan settlers in India, were converted to

Islam during the long centuries of Muslim ascendancy in this country and, Secondly, those who are descendants of the Muslim conquerors from the West. It is obvious that the former are as much Indians as our Hindu brethren, and the latter, having settled in India centuries ago and having made it their permanent home, have as vital a stake in the material prosperity and political progress of their Motherland as any other section of the Indian population. But there is, in this connection, a fact of great political importance which must not be lost sight of. The majority of Indian Mussalmans belong to agricultural or quasi-agricultural classes and are, therefore, relatively more identified with the permanent Indian interests than the other classes of our population. Under these undeniable circumstances, it is but natural that the warm blood of Indian patriotism courses through the veins of Indian Mussalmans with the same vitality as is the case with those articulate classes whose patriotic spirit finds loud expression from the public platform and in the press.

But the very fact that they are Indians is naturally, in their case, productive of an ardent desire to play, on the Indian political stage, a *role* to which they are, by reason of their important position, legitimately entitled. And so long as the evolution of a common Indian nationality, which all genuine well-wishers of the country must sincerely long for, does not become an accomplished fact, it is obviously natural, on the part of the Indian Mussalmans, to seek to protect their communal interests by securing their due share in the administrative and legislative machinery of the country. Why should anybody grudge us that share, I have never been able to understand. Why should we be looked upon as separatists because we claim but what is our due, passes my comprehension. A joint family system in which the junior member must be content to sink his individuality and to remain under the permanent tutelage of the *Karta* is foreign to our religious, political and social traditions. Our Hindu brethren ought to realise that a discontented member, smarting under a conviction that he is being deprived of his natural rights, is but a source of weakness to the family as a whole.

Mian Muhammad Shafi abstained from taking part in the activities of the Indian National Congress. But when on the publication of the Montagu-Chelmsford Report on Indian Constitutional Reforms that organization split into two, the Liberal and Moderate element in it accepting the Reforms as a step towards the ultimate realization of Responsible Government in India, and the Extremist section rejecting it as absolutely unacceptable. Mian Muhammad Shafi telegraphed his warm support to the first Moderate Conference held in Bombay under the presidency of that " Hero of a Hundred Battles " Mr. (now Sir) Surendra Nath Bannerji, and was elected a member of the Council of the National Liberal Federation. Since then he has worked in close harmony and co-operation with the Liberal Party in the service of the country. He reviewed the Montford Report in a series of 14 articles published in the columns of the CIVIL AND MILITARY GAZETTE (Lahore), in the concluding portion of which he appealed to the Europeans—official and non-official—in this country as well as to his own countrymen to co-operate whole-heartedly in making the Reforms a success.

That appeal is, in view even of the existing political conditions, worthy of being reproduced here :—

To those of my British fellow-subjects, in India as well as in England, who would grudge India this measure of constitutional reform, I earnestly appeal for more generosity than they seem to be inclined to show towards ' the brightest jewel in the British Crown.' I appeal to them to cast aside all suspicion, to disabuse their minds of even the slightest misgiving about India's fidelity to the Empire of which she is proud to be an integral part. The British and Indian blood has flowed freely together in its defence on the battlefields of three continents in this devastating war, the union of England and India has thereby been consecrated afresh. The Empire is henceforward our common heritage, and in the increasing strength of India the British race will find the ever-increasing might of the mightiest Empire known to history. Let us then sink our racial prejudices and, inspired with the high pride of a common citizenship, join hands and hearts together in a spirit of genuine co-operation and good-will in raising India to her proper place within the Empire.

To my own countrymen I appeal with equal earnestness to recognize that our British fellow-subjects in India have as permanent an interest in her future well-being as ourselves, and are entitled to play a leading part in her constitutional development. Let us realize that in their co-operation and good-will for India's regeneration lies our sure and certain success along the path of constitutional development. We too, should cast aside all distrust and, imbued with a feeling of mutual confidence, meet the British elements in this country more than half way. In union lies strength and with Indo-British union there is no height to which India may not rise. Let us then sink our differences, unite in welcoming the Chelmsford-Montagu Scheme of Reforms and, ...extend our fullest measure of co-operation to its successful working. Thus alone shall we deserve the confidence which the British Parliament is about to place in us; thus along shall we strengthen our country's claim to full Responsible Government.

When the two Committees on Franchise and Subjects presided over by Lord Southborough came to Delhi, Mian Muhammad Shafi was one of the two members co-opted to the Subjects Committee on behalf of the Government of India.

LEGISLATIVE

When still a comparative junior at the Bar, Mian Muhammad Shafi began to take a keen interest in the work of legislation. His series of articles on the Punjab Courts Bill, the Punjab Alienation of Land Bill and the Punjab Pre-emtion Bill, published in the columns of the "OBSERVER," marked him out for a career of usefulness in the Legislative Councils. Towards the commencement of 1909, he was nominated to represent the Punjab Muhammadans on the Provincial Legislative Council. In those days, there were only three Indian non-official members on that

Council, all nominated, to represent the three great Indian communities in the Punjab. On the 1st of January 1910 was introduced the Minto-Morley Scheme of Reforms, of which the expansion of the Indian element in the Provincial and Imperial Legislative Councils was a prominent figure. The Punjab was given three non-official Indian representatives on the Imperial Legislative Council, two representing the Muslim Community and the landholders of the Province, to be nominated by Government, and one to represent the Province to be elected by the non-official members of the Provincial Legislative Council. Sir Louis Dane, the then Lieutenant-Governor of the Punjab, wanted Mian Muhammad Shafi to accept a nomination on the Imperial Legislative Council as representative of the Punjab Muslim Community, but owing to his heavy professional engagements and to the Capital of India being still in Calcutta he was unable to accept the nomination. He was, however, re-nominated to the Punjab Legislative Council. In December 1911 about the time of the announcement of the Durbar administrative changes, including the transfer of the Capital of India from Calcutta to Delhi, the late Sardar Pratab Singh, who was the elected representative from the Punjab on the Imperial Legislative Council, died. A meeting of the Punjab Legislative Council was held in the Durbar Camp at Delhi and Mian Muhammad Shafi was elected to represent the Province on the Imperial Legislative Council. On the 10th January 1912, he took his oath of office in the last Session of that Council held in Calcutta. And at its very next meeting, held on the 23rd February following, he took part in the Debate on Mr. (now Sir) Maneckji Dadabhoy's Resolution on Income Tax, when the Hon'ble Mr. N. Subba Rao, the Hon'ble Mr. G. K. Gokhale and himself were constrained to oppose that Resolution. Sir Guy Fleetwood Wilson, the then Finance Member in the Government of India, when speaking on behalf of the Government, commenced his speech with the following significant words:—

> My Lord, my Hon'ble friends Mr. Subba Rao and Mr. Gokhale and others—and I should like for a moment to pay a tribute to the remarkably able exposition of a new Member, Mr. Muhammad Shafi—have, I think, dealt so successfully with the Resolution of my Hon'ble friend Mr. Dadabhoy that there is not really very much for me to say.

At the next sitting of the Council, held on the 27th February, he again took part in the Debate on the late lamented Mr. Bhupendra Nath Basu's Civil Marriage Bill, and opposed the measure from the point of view of Muhammadan Law. Mr. Bhupendra Nath Basu, when winding up the debate, referred to Mr. Shafi in the following words:—

> Now, I shall deal with a few observations of my friend the Hon'ble Mr. Shafi. I hope he will not take it as an impertinence in me to congratulate him upon the effect that he has already produced in this Council. I wish I had his powerful support on my side.

At the conclusion of his term of office towards the end of 1912, he was again re-nominated as a Member of the Punjab Legislative Council and two years later, on the appointment of Sardar (now Raja

Sir) Daljit Singh, who then represented the Punjab on the Imperial Council, as a member of the Secretary of State's Council, he was again elected by the non-official members of the Provincial Council to represent the Province on the Imperial Council. It will be remembered that the life of that Council was extended by one year on account of the Great War; and, thereafter, in the beginning of 1917, Mian Muhammàd Shafi was again re-nominated a member of the Imperial Legislative Council as representative of the Muslim community in the Punjab. This brief statement of facts will show that he had been a non-official member either of the Punjab or of the Imperial Legislative Council continuously for over ten years when he was appointed a Member of the Viceroy's Executive Council in July 1919. And this long experience gained by him as a non-official member of Council has been of great service to him in the discharge of his responsible duties as a member of the Government of India.

By his contributions in debate as well as his work on Select Committees, Mian Muhammad Shafi won a prominent position in the Provincial and Imperial Legislative Councils. His greatest achievement in this legislative career was his successful advocacy of India's claims for representation on the Imperial Conference. On the 22nd September 1915, he moved the following Resolution in the Imperial Legislative Council: "This Council recommends to the Governor-General-in-Council that a representation be sent, through the Right Hon'ble the Secretary of State, to His Majesty's Government urging that India should, in future, be officially represented in the Imperial Conference." In his speech delivered on that occasion, having referred to the world-wide nature of the British Empire he emphasized the proposition that "the gradual evolution, in a world-Empire like this, of a constitutional system of Government which, while conceding to its component parts varying degrees of internal autonomy suited to their local circumstances, should, at the same time, enable them to play their legitimate part in Imperial affairs is undoubtedly the ultimate guarantee of its permanence and stability."

Having referred to India's prominent position within the Empire, he proceeded to observe:—

My Lord, is there a single problem of Imperial or even international interest in which India, as an integral and an important part of the British Empire, is not directly concerned? Is there a single Imperial question in relation to which the interests of Great Britain, of the self-governing Colonies and of India are, under the existing conditions, not indissolubly bound together? Can any scheme of Imperial defence be regarded as complete without taking into account India's defensive requirements and her offensive capacity not only in relation to her own frontiers, but as recent events have made it abundantly clear, also in connection with the military needs of the Empire in every portion of the globe? Is it possible to evolve any scheme of Imperial Preference, or to introduce any workable Imperial fiscal reform without taking into consideration what may be called India's inter-Imperial interests? To these and other cognate questions there can be but one answer. India is directly and materially interested in all important problems of the Empire, of which she is proud to form an integral part, to the same extent and in the same degree as any other portion of His Imperial Majesty's vast dominions. Moreover, are there not a number of domestic problems of the nature of family complications, such as, immigration, tariffs, etc., which can only be satisfactorily solved by the representatives of the Imperial, Colonial and Indian Governments meeting together in periodical Conferences? And is not their solution indispensable to the smooth-working of the Imperial machinery and to the happiness and contentment of His Majesty's subjects in all parts of the world? The more or less satisfactory settlement of the South African Indian troubles—due mainly to the firm stand made by your Excellency on behalf of this country—was, in part, brought about by the timely deputation of the Hon'ble Sir Benjamin Robertson as the representative of our Government, and by the visit of that devoted Indian patriot, the late Hon'ble Mr. G. K. Gokhale, to the scene of that unfortunate conflict. The presence, in the Imperial Conference, of one or more representatives of the Government of this country, with intimate knowledge and experience of the East generally, and of India particularly, would not only satisfy Indian sentiment, but also prove of immense benefit to the Empire, and would help to solve smoothly and expeditiously, many difficult problems which have, in the past, imposed a tremendous strain on British statesmanship.

Having then proceeded to take a bird's-eye-view of India's services in China, South Africa, Somaliland, Egypt, Persian Gulf and at other places of vital importance outside her statutory boundaries and more particularly of her great services during the World War then in progress, he added :—

My Lord, India is not content with the occasional presence of the Secretary of State at the Imperial Conference : what she wants is her own direct representation like that of the British Colonies. And just as the glimmer of the early dawn heralds the coming of the Fountain of Light, so is the gracious permission granted me to-day the harbinger of the happy period when, this her just claim being duly recognised, India will take her proper place in the Councils of the Empire. Fortunately for her, the affairs of the Empire are at this moment presided over not by this party or that, but by a truly National Cabinet representative of the entire British nation. And the glorious example of South Africa has already furnished an object-lesson to those who may have entertained any doubts regarding the absolute efficacy of a policy of sympathy and trust. On behalf of 313 millions of my countrymen, representing over 75 per cent of the entire population of the Empire, I appeal, through Your Excellency, to His Majesty's Government and, through them, to the enlightened conscience of our British fellow-subjects in

Great Britain and her Colonies for India's admission in the Imperial Federation which, with the resulting contentment in all parts of the Empire, will constitute the best guarantee not only of the happiness of His Majesty's subjects, belonging to all races and creeds, but also of the peace of the world.

His Excellency Lord Hardinge, who immediately followed the delivery of this speech, while accepting the Resolution on behalf of his Government, said :—

It has been a source of profound satisfaction to me that it has been within my power to accept for discussion the very moderate and statesmanlike Resolution, happily devoid of all controversial character, that has been proposed by the Hon'ble Mr. Muhammad Shafi, and it is a matter of still greater satisfaction and pleasure to me to be able to announce that the Government of India gladly accept this important Resolution, which has their warmest sympathy, and, if it is accepted by Council as a whole, the Government will readily comply with the recommendation contained therein.

We have all listened with deep interest to Mr. Muhammad Shafi's eloquent speech, and it is a real pleasure to the Government of India to be able to associate themselves with his Resolution.

The Resolution having accordingly been forwarded by the Government of India to His Majesty's Government was ultimately accepted by them and by all the Colonial Governments and India thus found admission as an equal partner into the Councils of the Empire.

Mian Muhammad Shafi's last contribution to the Imperial Legislative Council debates before his appointment as a Member of the Executive Council was in the Spring Session of, 1919 when, in common with Indian representatives like Mr. (now Sir) Surendra Nath Bannerji, Mr. (now Right Hon'ble) Srinivasa Shastri and others, he strongly appealed to the Government of India to refrain from passing the Rowlatt Bill. The country was then ardently longing for the fulfilment of the solemn pledge made by His Majesty's Government on 20th August 1917, the proposed enactment was entirely unnecessary and inadvisable and the consequences of passing a measure like that in the circumstances then existing in the country would be disastrous. Had the earnest advice of sincere well-wishers of the British connection and of the country been listened to on that occasion, India would undoubtedly have been spared the painful experiences through which she has had to pass during the last 5 years of what cannot but be looked upon as the most critical period in her history.

EDUCATIONAL

From the very commencement of his public career, Mian Muhammad Shafi began to take active interest in educational matters. One of the main objects with which he founded the Anjuman-i-Islamia, Hoshiarpur, was the establishment of a Muslim High School in that District and during his stay at that place he collected the nucleus of a fund which ultimately, owing to the zealous efforts of Mian Abdul Aziz, Barrister-at-Law, who succeeded him in the office of General Secretary, resulted in the foundation of the very flourishing Muslim High School which caters to the needs of the District in that place. He was specially invited from Lahore to be present at the laying of the foundation-stone of that School by the late Nawab Vikar-ul-Mulk.

In 1897 he was nominated by Sir Thomas Gordon Walker, the then officiating Lieut. Governor of the Punjab, as a Fellow of the Punjab University and when Lord Curzon's University Act came into operation, he was elected as a Fellow, securing the largest number of votes in the elections held on that occasion. He continued to be a Fellow of that University throughout his non-official career and even after his appointment as Member of the Executive Council. During this long period of his close and intimate experience of University administration, he was a member of the Arts, Oriental and Law Faculties, occupied at various times the positions of a member of College Inspection Committees, Secretary of the Law Faculty, Secretary of the Law College Committee and Syndic of the University. And the intimate knowledge of the working of the University system thus acquired by him was of great help to him in the discharge of his responsible duties as Education Member in the Government of India.

In view of the conditions prevalent in this country, Mian Muhammad Shafi has always believed in the potency of Urdu as the *lingua franca* of India and has, therefore, when in public life, contributed towards the promotion of Urdu as the common language of India. For his services in that direction he was elected President of the All-India Urdu Conference held at Poona in July 1911. Dealing with the main problem and referring to the anti-Urdu agitation in certain parts of India, he observed :—

The attitude of some of our brethren in regard to the language question appears to me, to be absolutely paradoxical. The abandonment of a neutral ground perfectly..................

congenial to the Christian, Hindu and Muhammadan races and calculated to bind them close together constitutes a course of action diametrically opposed to this political creed. The professed motive of and the line of action adopted by some of the Nationalist leaders are utterly inconsistent with each other. Instead of welding together the various classes of His Majesty's Indian subjects into one comparatively homogeneous whole, insistence on this line of policy is calculated to widen the rift and to create antagonism of sentiment and interest, the baneful effects of which upon peaceful progress and on the future of India cannot now be foreseen. The course adopted by our friends is opposed to the best interests of both and will lead to an amount of chaos and confusion highly prejudicial to inter-racial unity.

Under these circumstances I venture, on behalf of the Muhammadan community and as a sincere well-wisher of the country, to address an earnest appeal to my Hindu brethren to abandon the anti-Urdu propaganda which has of late been started in various parts of India. The attitude of the Muhammadan community in regard to this question is entirely non-sectarian, else they would have met this by a counter- movement in favour of Persian and Arabic.

In conclusion, he earnestly pointed out that

the encouragement and extension of Urdu as the common vernacular of the country side by side with the cultivation, in a spirit of mutal harmony and good will, of Sanskrit and Hindi by the Hindus and of Persian and Arabic by the Muslim community constitute a programme which ought to be adopted as a universal policy by all leaders of public opinion, without distinction of caste and creed.

Soon after his return from England in 1892, he also began to take keen interest in the Aligarh educational movement founded by the late Sir Syed Ahmad Khan. From 1892 onwards, he almost regularly attended the annual gatherings of the All-India Muhammadan Educational Conference held in different places in India and on various occasions presided over the Female Education and other sections of that Conference. Of the Muhammadan Anglo-Oriental College at Aligarh, the great seat of Muslim learning in this country, he was elected a Trustee in 1898 and was a member of the first Syndicate of the College. That Institution had, of course, been founded by the late Sir Syed Ahmad Khan with the ultimate object of its being raised to the status of a Muslim University. And when, after the death of its venerable founder, the College having reached the acknowledged position of the best Residential Institution in India, the movement for its elevation to the status of a University assumed an active form under the leadership of His Highness the Aga Khan and the late Nawab Vikar-ul-Mulk, the then Secretary of the College, Mian Muhammad Shafi was elected a Vice-President of the All-India Muslim University Association as well as Honorary General Secretary of its Provincial Branch in the Punjab. By his indefatigable efforts, extending over nearly two years, he collected a sum exceeding three lakhs in his Province, himself contributing Rs. 5,000 to the University Fund. He was a member of the Deputation which waited on Sir Harcourt Butler, the then Education Member in the Government of India, with a view to a discussion of the scheme with him and was one of the three spokesmen who were then elected to address the Hon'ble Member on behalf of the Deputation. Who could have foreseen at that time that he himself should ultimately frame the Muslim University Bill and pilot it through the Imperial Legislative Council as Education Member? In recognition of his long and valuable services to the cause of Muhammadan education, Mian Muhammad

Shafi was elected as President of the All-India Muhammadan Educational Conference held at Aligarh during the Christmas of 1916 and thus gained the unique distinction of being the only Muhammadan public worker in India who has had the honour of presiding over all the three All-India Movements, *i. e.* the All-India Urdu Conference, the All-India Muslim League and the All-India Muhammadan Educational Conference In his admirable Presidential Address delivered on that occasion, he reviewed the history of the educational policy of the Government of India ever since the time of Lord Macaulay in relation to Primary, Secondary and University Education; and after dealing with such questions as Muslim representation on the Senates of the Indian Universities, the need for the establishment of a scholarship fund and the necessity of renewed efforts towards the establishment of a Muslim University, he emphasised the urgent necessity of Indian Mussalmans turning their attention to technical and industrial education.

It was in the fitness of things that, on the resignation of Sir Sankaran Nair in June 1919, a public man of Mian Muhammad Shafi's long and intimate acquaintance with and experience of educational institutions and movements in this country should have been called upon to assume office in the Government of India as its Education Member.

OFFICIAL CAREER

Mian Muhammad Shafi assumed charge of the office of Education Member at Simla on the morning of the 28th July 1919. At that time, the particular portfolio, of which he was appointed the head, consisted of business connected with the administration of Education, Local Self-Government, Archaeology, Epigraphy, Census, Records Office, Imperial Library, Copyright and certain other subjects. Towards the beginning of April, 1920, the Department of Public Health which had till then been in charge of the Home Member was also transferred to him. When subsequently Sir Thomas Holland resigned his office as Member of Commerce & Industry, Mian Muhammad Shafi was, for a short time, placed in charge of that portfolio in addition to his own. And on the retirement, owing to ill-health, of Sir Tej Bahadur Sapru from the Law Membership, His Excellency the Viceroy appointed Sir Muhammad Shafi as Law Member. He had, thus, during the tenure of his office as Member of the Viceroy's Executive Council, been in charge at one time or another of three portfolios—a fact unprecedented in the history of the Government of India. On the retirement of Sir William Vincent towards the end of November 1922, Sir Muhammad Shafi was appointed Vice-President of the Viceroy's Executive Council and occupied the same position till he retired in January 1925. He was in addition, the Chairman of the Employment (Demobilised Soldiers) Board, Chairman of the General Committee of the Lady Reading Fund, and was President of the Indian Soldiers' Board. Moreover, he was a member of the Military Requirements

Committee, was an ex-officio member of the Standing Commitee of the Princes Chamber and was also a member of the Reforms Inquiry Committee presided over by Sir Alexander Muddiman. He was also a member of various Sub-Committees of the Executive Council and had worked on a number of Select Committees of the Legislature. In November 1922 he was appointed Leader of the Council of State, which position he occupied with distinction until the termination of his period of office. In the winter of 1922, he was, along with Sir William Vincent, deputed to hold a confidential enquiry along the North-West Frontier Province and Waziristan, the nature of which has never been divulged to the public.

The responsible work done by a Member of the Viceroy's Executive Council is, in the existing constitutional position in India, performed mostly in *purdah*, only a relatively small portion of which comes to the knowledge of the public or even of the contemporary historian. Some of the knowledge of that work is confined to the members of the Departments of which he may be in charge, a portion of it is known only to his colleagues in Council and the rest to His Excellency the Viceroy who, as the head of the Government of India, has constant opportunities of consulting him on various matters of public importance. In this connection, Sir Muhammad Shafi said during the speech delivered by him at the Farewell Banquet given in his honour by the members of the

Council of State and the Legislative Assembly at Simla on 22nd Sept. 1924:

> As my Hon'ble friend Sir Sivaswamy Aiyer remarked, the office of a Member of the Executive Council is not a bed of roses. The responsibility resting on the shoulders of a member of the Central Cabinet of India is indeed very heavy and, if I may venture to say so, the responsibility on the shoulders of the Indian Member of that Cabinet is still heavier. ....He occupies within the Cabinet of India not only the position of a Member in charge of a portfolio and, therefore, the responsibility of administering it rests on his shoulders, not only as a Member of the Government there is a cumulative responsibility along with his colleagues resting on his shoulders, but he, as the Indian Member of the Government, is the Indian adviser to the representative of His Majesty the King-Emperor. He has to represent the wishes and the feelings of the Indian people truthfully and scrupulously before his Chief and has to keep him from time to time acquainted with the true state of things in the country.

As Education Member it fell to his lot to carry out the recommendations of the Sadler Commission and, as a result Teaching and Residential Universities were established at Dacca, Rangoon, Lucknow, Aligarh, Delhi and Nagpur, and legislation for the reform of Allahabad and Madras Universities was sanctioned by the Government of India. In recognition of his valuable services to the cause of education, the Aligarh University conferred the Honorary Degree of Doctor of Literature and the Delhi University that of Doctor of Laws and H. E. the Viceroy appointed him Pro-Chancellor of the latter University in his own personal capacity. In the matter of Indianization of the Indian Educational Service, the results achieved during the short period of 3½ years of his Education Membership must be gratifying to all advocates of Indianization of our Services. There were only 29 Indians in that Service when he assumed charge of his office; the number rose to 120 by the time he transferred his activities to the Legislative Department, 36% Indianization having thus been achieved in 3½ years. Equally satisfactory were the results obtained during the 2 years and 9 months he was in charge of the Department of Public Health. For the first time in the history of the Government of India Secretariat an Indian was appointed to the Medical Headquarters in the Government of India as Asst. Director-General, in the Indian Medical Service. And, similarly, for the first time an Indian was appointed as permanent Chemical Examiner in the U. P. as well as to the post of Principal, Medical School, Agra. In the Department of Records an Indian was for the first time appointed as Keeper.

In their letter dated the 9th March 1921, addressed to the Secretary of State, the General Council of Medical Education and Registration of the United Kingdom, dealing with the subject of the recognition of medical diplomas of the Indian Universities, threatened to withhold recognition of the medical degrees and diplomas of the Indian Universities owing to the alleged deficiency in midwifery training in India. The action taken by Sir Muhammad Shafi in that connection gave entire satisfaction to the members of the Central Legislature. It was, as a result of his prompt as well as strong action, that ultimately the General Medical Council postponed the execution of the threat given by them, sent out a representative of their own to India for investigation of the problem, and finally a satisfactory solution of the problem was arrived at between the Government of India and the Medical Council.

Mian Muhammad Shafi has always realised the urgent need for the spread of primary education among the masses. Speaking in the Imperial Legislative Council on 23rd February 1912, he gave expression to his views regarding this important problem in the following words:—

> The remarkable educational activity observable on all sides is one of those gratifying features of the existing situation which mark the turning of a new leaf in the history of India, and will prove a source of incalculable good to the country. The establishment of an increasing net work of elementary schools throughout the length and breadth of the Indian continent and the gradual adoption, as the financial conditions of the country permit, of steps towards making elementary education free so as to bring it within easy reach of the masses.........constitute the foremost need of the time.

At that period he was not in favour of the use of compulsion as an instrument in the propagation of elementary education. Five years afterwards, speaking as President of the All-India Muhammadan Educational Conference, he strongly advocated the grant to the Indian people of the boon of free primary education and urged upon the Government and the various Municipal and other Local Bodies to co-operate in bringing the means for the acquisition of free elementary education within easy reach of the people in all urban and rural areas. "If this is done", said he, "the progress of mass education will be found to have been so vastly accelerated as to bring about a speedy realization of the aims which the most ardent lovers of education in India have in view." Partial responsibility in the Provinces having been made an element in the Reformed Constitution of India and franchise having been conferred on a section of the people, Mian Muhammad Shafi realised that time had arrived when the educational policy of the Government of India ought to be revised in order to enable the Provinces to introduce compulsory primary education. This reform became essential in view of the conferment of franchise on Indian electors and its probable extension in future. As Education Member, therefore, he took steps towards the revision of the policy of the Government of India in regard to compulsory education, and Provincial Governments were given full liberty to introduce in their Provincial Legislative Councils such legislation as the conditions in the Provinces justified. The various enabling Acts passed in the Provinces authorising Municipal and District Boards to introduce compulsory primary education within their respective areas, should they so think fit, are the results of the action taken by Sir Muhammad Shafi.

Mian Muhammad Shafi had, as a result of his close study of the eductional system obtaining in the country, come to the conclusion that a system of purely secular education divorced from all religious and moral instruction had been the source of grave injury to the people of this country. Soon after his appointment as Education Member, he turned his attention to this problem of vital importance to the welfare of his countrymen. The result was that the Government of India revised their policy in regard to this important matter and the embargo upon the introduction of religious and moral instruction in our public schools was removed, leaving it to the Provincial Governments to take such steps as, consistently with local conditions, they considered advisable in this direction.

It will be within the recollection of our readers that the passing of what was known as the Rowlatt Act, against which Mian Muhammad Shafi voted as a non-official member of the Imperial Legislative Council, led to Mr. Gandhi's adoption of the *Satyagraha* movement. The action taken by Sir Micheal O'Dwyer's Government against Messrs. Gandhi, Kitchlew and Satyapal led to a violent riot in Amritsar and to *hartal* in the principal towns including Lahore. The evidence recently recorded in the case of Sir Michael O'Dwyer *vs.* Sir Sankaran Nair has disclosed the fact that when, on the morning of 11th April 1919, Sir Michael O'Dwyer summoned a meeting of the leading Hindu, Muhammedan and Sikh representatives present in Lahore on that occasion, Mian Muhammad Shafi advised against the adoption of a strong policy and advocated the adoption of measures calculated to bring about co-operation between the Government and the popular leaders. Subsequently, having been summoned as a witness during the main conspiracy trial before one of the Martial Law

Special Tribunals, in which Messrs. Harkishen Lal, Dhuni Chand, and others were accused of conspiracy to subvert British Rule, he gave straight and fearless evidence. Lord Chelmsford's statement in the O'Dwyer—Nair suit has now made it clear that, according to His Lordship, all the facts relating to the happenings in Lahore and other places were not known to the Government of India until after July 1919. It is a fact full of significance that Mian Muhammad Shafi assumed charge of his office as a Member of the Viceroy's Executive Council towards the end of that month. It is further significant that it was some five months after his coming into the Government of India that the vast majority of those convicted of various offences in connection with the Punjab troubles, including political leaders of the position of Harkishen Lal, Dhuni Chand and others, were released as an act of amnesty. And finally when the Hunter Committee inquired into the unfortunate occurrences in the Punjab and submitted their Report, Mian Muhammad Shafi, who at that time was the only Indian Member in the Viceroy's Executive Council, gave signal proof of his independence by dissenting from the rest of the Government in regard to the main findings of the Hunter Committee and of the Government of India regarding the existence of rebellion in the Punjab. The evidence given by him in the O'Dwyer—Nair case again shows how deeply he feels the wrong done to the Punjab in the unwarranted charge of rebellion brought against a

Province which has, from the time of the Mutiny of 1857 onwards, on all occasions both inside and outside India, given signal proof of its loyalty to the British connection.

The passing of the Rowlatt Act and the unhappy occurrences in the Punjab immediately preceding and following the declaration of Martial Law in certain districts of that Province had created a widespread stir throughout the length and breadth of India and had deeply wounded the Indian sense of self-respect to an extent which, we fear, is not even now fully realised in certain quarters. Even the passing of the Government of India Act, 1919, did not succeed in healing that wound and, indeed, a great many of the politically-minded Indians who might have accepted the Chelmsford-Montagu Reforms and co-operated in making them a success, had these been introduced in normal times, declared them as inadequate and unacceptable simply because they still left real power in the hands of the Executive and did not prevent the recurrence of similar events in the future. And when, following in quick succession, came the Treaty of Sevres, with all its over-stringent Turkish Peace Terms, the resentment as well as sorrow among the ranks of His Majesty's Indian Muslim subjects was profound and sent a large section of them into the arms of Mahatma Gandhi. In addition to these, certain leading figures in the Indian Muslim world who had joined Mr. Gandhi's Non-Co-operation Movement preached that India was a *Darul-harb*, no longer fit for any Mussalman to live in. And this preaching gave rise to the *Hijrat* movement, as a result of which thousands of uneducated and illiterate Muhammedans sold their houses and lands and migrated to Afghanistan. Had any untoward step been taken by Government during this crisis, the results would have been disastrous. But the Government very wisely adopted the policy of non-interference in respect of all these activities of the Non-Co-operators. Indeed, they went further. When the vast majority of *Muhajarins*, after suffering untold hardships in Afghanistan, returned to this country, the authorities gave every possible help in restoring their property to them and in seeing them peacefully re-settled in their homes. His Excellency Lord Chelmsford and, subsequently, His Excellency the Earl of Reading, adopted in relation to the near-Eastern problem a far-sighted policy which had a profound effect in this country. And finally, the action taken by Lord Reading in February 1922 in respect of the lines on which the Treaty of Sevres should be revised, the publication of the telegram embodying those views and the subsequent resignation of Mr. Montagu as a result of that publication had a profound effect in soothing the disturbed feelings of His Majesty's Indian Mussalman subjects.

That Sir Muhammad Shafi had a considerable share in the adoption by the Government of India of this wise and far-sighted policy is now conclusively established by what His Excellency

Lord Reading said in this connection in his speech proposing his Health at the Farewell Banquet given by His Excellency in the Viceregal Lodge at Delhi on Friday the 14th November, 1924. "There is one aspect of this association," said His Excellency, "to which I desire to make special reference. During the time when there was considerable agitation among the Mussalmans in India regarding the affairs in the Near East, I was fortunate in having as my adviser Sir Muhammad, who was specially equipped to keep me informed of the feelings and views of his co-religionists. I refer to the period when there were doubts and difficulties in the minds of Indian Mussalmans regarding the situation with Turkey and the Treaty of Sevres. Sir Muhammad was of the greatest and most valuable assistance to me during that difficult period and, I may also say, to the community of which he is so distinguished a member."

As has been mentioned in the earlier portion of this sketch, Sir Muhammad has, during his tenure of office, sat on many Sub-Committees appointed to inquire into military expenditure and military affairs generally. Moreover, he was, along with Sir William Vincent, deputed to make inquiries into Frontier affairs, and more particularly in Waziristan, the nature of which has never been disclosed. He was also appointed President of the Indian Soldiers Board in succession to Sir Malcolm Hailey on the latter's elevation to the Governorship of the Punjab. He took a leading part in bringing about the reduction of the military expenditure from 72½ crores in 1920-21 to 63 crores gross and 60'25 crores net in 1924. From what Sir P. S. Sivaswamy Aiyer, who himself was a Member of the Military Requirements Committee, said at the Fare-well Banquet given to Sir Muhammad by the Members of the Council of State and the Legislative Assembly at Simla on the 22nd September 1924, one may legitimately conclude that Sir Shafi must have played an important part in bringing about this reduction. "Shortly after my entry into the Assembly," said Sir Sivaswamy, "it so happened that we were both members of a very important Committee about three years ago, the details of which I am not at liberty to go into, but in which our close association for a period of three months, almost day by day, impressed me with a high sense of his merits. I found that his heart was in the right place; that he was a true Indian and a true patriot. The impression that I formed during those months of close intimacy has been deepened by my experience of him during the years that have passed since."

As a Leader of the Council of State, he won a well deserved popularity by his tact and broadminded statesmanship in that House. It may not be quite out of place here to point out that on the last day of the September Session of 1924, when the House bade him farewell, member after member, belonging to European, Hindu, Muhammadan, Sikh and Parsi communities, bore eloquent testimony to his patriotism, ability and tact. We will recall only what the President of the

House, Sir Montagu Butler, (now Governor of the C. P.) said on that occasion :—

The Hon'ble Sir Muhammad Shafi. has been the Leader of this House almost from its beginning, and the traditions of leadership which have been created here are the work of his hands. A smaller man might have been content to be the leader of the Government forces. The Hon'ble Sir Muhammad Shafi has never faltered in presenting the Government case. but as Leader of the House he has formed a higher conception of his duty, and has made it his business to represent the interests of the House as a whole, and no one knows that better than the President of the Council. Much of the smooth working of the Council is due, I think, to the fact—and I know my distinguished predecessor would say the same—that the Hon'ble Sir Muhammad Shafi has always kept the chair in touch, not only with the feeling of Government, but with that of the House as a whole ; and that tradition is a very valuable one, and one which will, I know, bear fruit after he is gone. Therefore, in a very special sense, the Chair is grateful to the Hon'ble Sir Muhammad Shafi.

As Member of Council, Sir Muhammad Shafi was closely associated with the Reforms Inquiry Committee. What part he played in initiating within the Government the movement which led to this inquiry cannot obviously be known now. But he was, as Law Member, the leading figure in the first stage of the Inquiry. And when the further development of association of non-officials with the Inquiry took place, his term of office was extended by nearly six months and he was appointed a member of the expanded Committee. On the publication of the Report it was found that Sir Muhammad had signed with the majority; but he subsquently (when freed from the trammels of office) expressed himself in favour of the Minority Report. We may conclude this sketch with the words His Excellency the Viceroy said during his speech at the Farewell Banquet. The

Viceroy concluded his appreciation of Sir Muhammad's services by saying :—

> He gave proof, during that period, of special qualities. Among his many qualifications for membership of my Council, his judgments were characterised by shrewd intelligence, keen political insight, a deep sense of loyalty to the causes he espoused, a high idealism tempered by practical considerations, devotion to the interests of India and an all-abiding belief in the higher destiny of India within the Empire. * * * * Sir Muhammad never failed to represent the Indian aspect to us, to portray the Indian sentiment with all the force at his command.

Sir Muhammad has retired from office after 5½ years and the number of farewell banquets and parties given in his honour at Simla, in Delhi and in Calcutta, and the welcome entertainments given in his honour at Lahore and Amritsar on his return home, furnish conclusive proof of the high regard in which he is held by officials as well as by non-officials irrespective of caste, creed or colour.

He was created a C.I.E. in June 1916 and a K.C.S.I. on 1st January 1922.

Sir Ali Imam

HIS ANCESTORS

SIR ALI IMAM, who succeeded Mr. (now Lord) Sinha as Legal Member of the Governor-General's Executive Council and was later appointed by H. E. H. the Nizam of Hyderabad as the first President of his Executive Council, was born at the village of Neora, a small station on the East Indian Railway, near Patna, on the 11th of February 1869. He comes of a distinguished Syed family, who justly take pride in the purity of their blood, his ancestors having come to India before the Moghul Empire was founded. In fact one of his ancestors Mallah Saad was tutor to the Emperor Aurangazeb. Mallah Saad's son, Nawab Syed Khan, rose to be a Wazir of the Empire. One of the forefathers of the subject of our sketch, Nawab Mir Askari, was Commander-in-Chief under the Nawab of Bengal in the time of Lord Clive; Sir Ali Imam's great-grandfather, Khan Bahadur Syed Imdad Ali, retired as a Subordinate Judge of Patna, while his son, Khan Bahadur Shams-ul-ulama Syed Wahid-ud din was the first Indian to be made a District Magistrate and a District and Sessions Judge. From 1854 to 1858, Mr. Wahid-ud din was the District Magistrate of Monghyr (Bihar), and towards the end of his service he became the District an

Sessions Judge of Shahabad. Sir Ali Imam's father, Shams-ul-ulama Nawab Syed Imdad Imam, was for some time Professor of History and Arabic in the Patna College and well-known all over Bihar for his great facility in writing Urdu poetry and his vast and varied scholarship. The Shams-ul-ulma is known throughout as a brilliant poet, a versatile scholar and a voluminous writer, alike upon literary, scientific and agricultural subjects. One of his philosophical treatises, called "Mirat-ul-Hukama," has been translated into Swedish and the learned author received some years back a letter from the late King Oscar of Sweden in appreciation of his work. Mr. Syed Sharf-ud-din, late Judge of the Calcutta and Patna High Courts and ex-Member of the Bihar Executive Council, is the maternal uncle of Sir Ali Imam, and another of his uncles Khan Bahadur Syed Nasir ud-din, was the Finance Minister of Bhopal. Sir Ali Imam's younger brother is the well known Mr. Hasan Imam of Patna who was for some time Judge of the High Court of Calcutta and subsequently President of the Special Congress of 1918.

Mr. Hasan Imam, whose sketch appears in the subsequent pages, it may be remembered, represented India at the League of Nations in 1923.

EARLY CAREER

Ali Imam received his early education in the Arrah *Zilla* school and afterwards in the Patna College. With a view to complete his education he went to England in September 1887, and was called to the bar by the Middle Temple in June 1890, in which year he returned to India. In the same term and by the same Inn of Court were called Sir Abdur Rahim (who is married to a cousin of Sir Ali Imam's) and Mr. Justice Shah Din of the Punjab Chief Court. While in England, he was of great service to the Indian delegates, who were sent to England in 1890 by the National Congress. That delegation, it will be recollected, consisted of the late Sir Ganesh Narayan Chandavarkar, Mr. Salem Ramaswami Mudaliar and Mr. (now Sir) Surendranath Banerjea. Mr. Ali Imam went with the delegates to several of the more important places in England and Wales and did much good work for India with them.

CAREER AT THE BAR

Returning to India, Mr. Ali Imam devoted himself almost exclusively to the practice of his profession. His whole hearted devotion was attended with early success. He had not to wait and watch and hope as most juniors have to do. He was engaged in almost all the celebrated cases, civil and criminal. During his later years, Mr. Ali Imam acquired such a fame as a "case-winner," that suitors came to regard their case half won when the services of Mr. Ali Imam had been secured. At the time he left Bihar he had been frequently entertained by the Crown, and Government retained him to conduct on behalf of the Court of Wards the case for the defence in the now well-known Dumraon Raj adoption case before the special Judge at Arrah. During the last years of his professional career his practice was so large that even a seat on the bench of the High Court did not offer him sufficient temptation to make him think of changing the Counsel's gown for the robes of a Judge. His appointment as Standing Counsel in 1909, therefore, was but a mere recognition of his legal abilities. His success as a lawyer has helped him in becoming conspicuous in other walks of life also.

PUBLIC WORK

He was for six years a member of the Patna District Board and of the Patna Municipality and for about six months he acted as the Vice-Chairman of the Municipality in place of his uncle, the late Khan Bahadur Syed Fazal Imam. He was elected a Trustee of the Aligarh College in 1903 and his interest in the education of his co-religionists has always been an abiding one. Besides donating handsomely to the Funds of the Aligarh College he has taken a keen and an active interest in the affairs of the Mahomedan Educational Conference. His nomination as a Fellow of the Calcutta University, in 1909, recognised the good work he had done in this direction. In April 1908, he was unanimously elected President of the first session of the Behar Provincial Conference. In the Commissioner's Conference to which the Bengal Government invited him during the latter part of his professional career, as a non-official member, he proved a staunch and undaunted people's advocate, while his notes on the separation of the executive and judicial functions, prepared about the same time, gladdened the hearts of all, including the Congressmen.

PRESIDENT, MUSLIM LEAGUE.

His co-religionists recognised his talents by nominating him, in 1910, to the Presidentship of the Amritsar Session of the All-India Muslim League. It is unnecessary to write more of his Presidential address than to remark that it brought him at once into the front rank of Indian public men. The Indian Press deservedly characterised it as a highly meritorious performance, though the appreciation was naturally qualified by disapproval of some of the opinions contained therein.

GOKHALE AND MR. IMAM

Mr. Ali Imam attended the second session of the Bihar Provincial Conference, held at Bhagalpur during the Easter of 1909, and it was there that the memorable 'Conference' between Mr. Imam and the late Mr. Gokhale took place. The many long interviews which took place between these two gentlemen resulted in a resolution, which was unanimously accepted by the Conference, supporting the Government's scheme of mixed electorates open to all classes, with some special electorates open to Mussalmans only. Mr. Ali Imam seconded the resolution, which was proposed by Mr. Deep Narayan Singh. Mr. Gokhale formed a very high opinion of Mr. Ali Imam's abilities. Mr. Gokhale and Mr. Imam parted as the best of friends; their so-called "compromise" at Bhagalpore was for weeks the subject of acrimonious discussion in the Press, principally in the section conducted by Mussalmans. Lord Morley was apparently favourably impressed with his personality. And no wonder, when Mr. Sinha resigned he was nominated to the high place of Legal Member of the Viceroy's Council.

A STURDY LIBERAL

In politics, Mr. Ali Imam may be described as a sturdy Liberal. In his address at Cambridge, he declared that Indians had realised that "Government of the people, by the people, for the people, was a very natural adjunct to Government by the British." He said:—

> English education has given Indians a common language, common aspirations and a common patriotism, and it was possible for the Muhammedans and the Hindus to work together for the development of India united among themselves and united to Britain.

His ideal for India is "Self-Government within the British Empire." His utterances at the Indian Union were still more outspoken. Introduced by the President, Mr. D. C. Ghose, as an "Indian first and Mahomedan afterwards," and as one whom "the Hindus also claimed as a leader," Mr. Imam declared that he "was pleased to be described as first and foremost an Indian." He then proceeded:—

> The sectarian aggressiveness which was rampant in the land was the great danger to the country, and all thoughtful Indians ought to put their foot down upon it, for the danger was not so much from without as from within. Mahomedans ought to recognize that they should be Indians first and Mahomedans afterwards, and Hindus that they should be Indians first and Hindus afterwards.

MEMBER OF THE VICEROY'S COUNCIL

He spoke in a similar spirit at the banquet given

him on his appointment to the Viceroy's Executive Council in October, 1910.

> In the faithful discharge of my duties. I cannot lend myself to partnership, sectarian prejudices or denominational bias. My placement of the Indian view has to be an honest portrature of the true and existing conditions of the political and social life of the country. My treatment of the subject has to be from the standpoint that subserves the greatest good and contributes to the happiness of the largest number of my fellow-countrymen.

Sir Ali Imam's work on the Viceroy's Council was greatly appreciated and H. E. Lord Hardinge gave public recognition of his great services in the speech he delivered at the Council Chamber at Delhi in March 1915 previous to Sir Ali Imam's retirement. Sir Ali Imam in his parting speech at Simla in October of that year made touching reference to the Viceroy's appreciation and added: "I am proud to have received such notice from the King's Representative, but I am prouder still in that I may without any vanity, regard these words as the title of my country to the inclusion of her sons in the Indian Cabinet." The position of an Indian Member of the Viceroy's Council, he said, is not without its difficulties.

> It is true that he has to be grateful for many things without which his position might have been harder, yet it would be an affectation to hold that his path is strewn with roses. There are inherent causes that sometimes leave him isolated in the discharge of his official duties. This is in no way attributable to any unkindness on the part of any one. As a minister of the Crown, the first and foremost duty of the Indian Member is to do all in his power to strengthen the foundations of British Rule in India. But his difficulties do not begin here for a little reflection will satisfy him that the foundations of that rule can rest secure only in the increasing prosperity and contentment of the people of India and that whatever he can do in the direc-

tion of securing this object is the very essence of real and true loyalty to the Sovereign whose confidence he has the privilege to enjoy. The ready willing acceptance of this principle by his colleagues is a source of great inspiration and strength to him, for it is an agreement on the very first principles of the relations of England and India. To me, personally, the conviction that duty to my Sovereign is in absolute and complete keeping with my duty to my country, has been a great support and a sustaining force of incalculable value.

And he concluded with a fervent appeal to all classes and communities irrespective of their religious denominations, to unite in the name of India and serve the cause of their common country.

As Indians, it is the duty of all of us, in whatever station of life we may be, to take out full share in the building up of the national life. We have to set ourselves a programme of work in which true and unadulterated nationalism should be the mainspring of action. Nationalism is a much misunderstood word in India. I have come across people who are scared at the very mention of it as if it were a bogey. What I understand by Indian nationalism is the supersession of all sectarian and communal bias in the growth of the political life of the country by territorial patriotism based on loyalty to the Sovereign, pride in the Empire and love of the country. Gentlemen, this is a political creed which is catholic enough to embrace within its fold all those that love India. Here is work for all the numerous communities that inhabit our country. The Hindu, the Mahomedan, the Parsi, the Indian Christian, the Anglo-Indian, and all unite to raise India and secure for her a seat of honour in the assemblage of nations.

JUDGE OF THE PATNA HIGH COURT

In November 1917, Sir Ali Imam joined the Patna High Court Bench in succession to Mr. Justice Sharf-ud-din who retired in the previous September. So far as the Patna High Court was concerned, his was the first appointment to the Bench from the Members of the High Court Bar. Commenting on the appointment the PATNA LAW WEEKLY observed that he would be an acquisition to the Bench.

We disfavour, as a rule, the practice of translation from the Bench to the Executive Council and *vice versa*. But we think Sir Ali Imam's experience at the Bar, especially during the few months before his elevation, will stand him in good stead in discharging the onerous duties of his office.

PRESIDENT, NIZAM'S EXECUTIVE COUNCIL.

In June 1919, H. E. H. the Nizam of Hyderabad decided upon establishing an Executive Council and whom could he choose but Sir Ali Imam for the first Presidentship of his Council? Sir Ali Imam brought to the conduct of the Nizam's new Council all the varied experiences of his high offices in British India. But in October of the next year Sir Ali Imam was selected by H. E. the Viceroy to represent British India in the League of Nations. He was thus the first Indian representative to sit at the first meeting of the League of Nations. His Exalted Highness concurred with the Viceroy in his choice and Sir Ali Imam's absence from the Nizam's Dominion was treated not as on leave but on deputation. On his return to Hyderabad he took over charge of his office. But suddenly in the first week of September 1922 a *firman* was published announcing Sir Ali Imam's resignation of his high office and the Nizam's acceptance of the same. No reason was given but the *firman* added that Sir Ali Imam was to be paid the honorarium for the rest of the period contracted for. The resignation, whatever might be the cause, was much regretted by the public; and Sir Ali Imam commenced practice at once at Patna.

SIR ALI IMAM

THE BERAR QUESTION

It was not long before H. E. H. the Nizam requisitioned the services of Sir Ali Imam again. This time it was in connection with the Nizam's efforts to regain his sovereignty over the Districts of Berar. These districts had been administered by the British Government on behalf of the Nizam since 1853.

Under the treaties of 1853 and 1860, they were "assigned," without limit of time to the British Government to provide for the maintenance of the Hyderabad contingent, a body of troops kept by the British Government for the Nizam's use, the surplus revenue, if any, being payable to the Nizam. In course of time it had become apparent that the maintenance of the Hyderabad contingent on its old footing as a separate force was inexpedient and unnecessary and that similarly the administration of Berar as a separate unit was very costly while from the point of view of the Nizam the precarious and fluctuating nature of the surplus was financially inconvenient. The agreement of 1902 re-affirmed His Highness's sovereignty over Berar, which instead of being indefinitely "assigned" to the Government of India, was leased in perpetuity to an annual rental of 25 lakhs, the rental is for the present charged with an annual debit towards the repayment of loans made by the Government of India. The Government of India were at the same time authorised to administer Berar in such manner as they might think desirable, and to redistribute, reduce, re-organise and control the Hyderabad Contingent, due provision being made as stipulated in the Treaty of 1853, for the protection of His Highness's Dominions. In accordance with this agreement the Contingent ceased in March 1903, to be a separate force and was re-organised and re-distributed as an integral part of the Indian Army, and in October 1903 Berar was transferred to the administration of the Chief Commissioner of the Central Provinces.*

The present Nizam has been making strenuous efforts towards the recovery of these Districts and Sir Ali Imam was sent in the middle of 1923 to England to pave the way for an understanding with the Home Government. Sir Ali Imam, besides

* The Indian Year Book, 1925.

interviewing influential members of Government, on this subject, did splendid propaganda work by interesting British journalists in the Nizam's claims over Berar and it was mainly through his efforts that several English Magazines and newspapers became interested in the question.

RECEPTION TO KENYA DEPUTATION

Sir Ali Imam also took advantage of his stay in England to participate in all functions calculated to promote the interests of his countrymen in British India. Thus when the Rt. Hon. Sastri returned to England from Kenya, Sir Ali Imam gave a reception to the Indian Delegation at the Hotel Cecil in August 1923 and expressed himself in complete agreement with Mr. Sastri in regard to the Cabinet's decision.

> The Kenya decision has given a rude shock to that ideal. It has plainly told us that the present British Cabinet does not recognise equal political rights between Europeans and Asiatics within the Empire. • • •
>
> As an Indian who has gathered some knowledge of his country, both as an official and a non-official, I have to say in sorrow that the Kenya decision forebodes a political development in India of which it is impossible to think without the gravest misgiving regarding the future
>
> It has been said that there was threat of White Rebellion in Kenya. If that be so, it was an evil example to set. It has also been said that His Majesty's Government sacrificed justice to fear. If so, a bad precedent has been established. The political psychology in India is of sufficient keenness to draw its own conclusions. I much fear the Kenya decision will give a turn to political thought in India that is bound to overrun the bounds of moderation, unless side by side with that decision immediate steps are taken to give India Self-Government.

THE REFORMS

Sir Ali Imam, during his stay in England, took the opportunity to instruct the British public on the real nature of the situation in India. In March 1924, he addressed the Indian Parliamentary Committee, defending the Swaraj leaders against the charge of irresponsibility and childishness hurled at them by the greater part of the British Press because of their rejection of the Budget. He pointed out that the Indian leaders, whether they were right or wrong in taking this action, could not possibly embarrass the administration of the country, since the Budget, they were well aware, could and would be certified by the Viceroy. On the question of the Reforms, he said that the firm government that was recommended in certain quarters meant simply standing still. But it was too late for that. He said :—

> Unless something were done within the next two years, the Independants would receive tremendous encouragement, and it might then be too late for moderate counsels to prevail. The time was ripe for complete autonomy in the Provinces and the transfer of all the functions of the Central Government to responsible Ministers, save the Army, Foreign Affairs and the Political Department, pending the gradual Indianisation of these last departments.

Sir Ali Imam returned to India about the end of 1924 and in an interview with the Associated Press at Bombay, urged "a moderate measure of constitutional reform, within the bounds of safety." He emphasised the urgent need for reforming the Indian constitution, in view of Dyarchy having been wrecked in two Provinces and in view of the unyielding obstruction in the Assembly.

> The last general election was fought on the Swaraj cry and it returned to the Provincial and Central Legislatures the protagonists of immediate Self-Government in overwhelming numbers. Obstruction in the Councils signified a united

demand for a more satisfactory constitution. In his opinion it would be folly not to recognise the robust assertiveness of the new movement. A moderate measure of reform, within the bounds of safety, could impair neither the British overlordship of India, nor damage the individual classes.

He made certain proposals for reform, which he said were only sketches dealing with principles, requiring elaboration at the hands of constitutional experts.

Amongst the proposals made by Sir Ali are those advocating complete Provincial Autonomy, responsibility in the Central Government in all subjects save the Navy, Army and Political Departments, administration of the Army, Navy, etc., being left to an Executive composed of the Governor-General, the Commander-in-Chief and the Prime Minister, the last of whom will serve as a useful link between his Government and the Governor-General-in-Council. Sir Ali would also provide for the taking over of provincial administrations by the Governor-General in the event of a fourth of the members of the legislature concerned desiring it for the protection of minorities.

In Sir Ali Imam's view these Reforms should not be deferred. For, the breakdown of the democratic machinery set up by the Government of India Act of 1919 "has created a situation of serious political gravity." In a communication to the Press in the first week of June 1925 Sir Ali Imam pointed out how imperative it was that the next step in the Reforms should be taken at once, without further delay:

The urgency of a further Constitutional advance should not be judged by the text of a Parliamentary Statute nor by the

argument that a period of five years is negligible in the life of a Nation. It is very doubtful whether the language of the Act of 1919 is a bar, but even if so, it should be subordinated to the urgent and insistent dictates of public policy and, in consequence duly amended. The plea of time is equally inapplicable. Moments make eras as much in the life of an individual as of a country. A slumber of centuries may not call for any action, but inaction during the awakened hours of a people may cause disaster. A political crisis brooks neither Parliamentary Statutes nor measured march of time. The real issue is: Is India on the verge of a political crisis? If she is, an ostrich policy will be a crime against civilization and a blow to Imperial unity.

Sir Ali Imam also warned the rulers of the futility of mere "bogus expressions" of generous sentiment towards the aspirations of Indian people, as in the past. They might have served their purpose at one time: but they can no longer hold good. Political and social thought has advanced too far in the country to tolerate camouflages of the kind indulged in by men of mawkish sentimentality. Extraneous world events like the Russo-Japanese War and the recent armageddon in Europe and the story of the American Independence, the South African Self-government, the struggle for freedom in Ireland and Egypt and the Emancipation of Turkey have produced far reaching consequences in India. The lesson of these efforts is not lost on India. Add to it the momentum created by recent political awakening in the country.

During the progress of the great War sentiments conceived in terms of Empire gave currency to such expressions as "Comradeship," "Imperial Citizenship" but on the conclusion of that great struggle appeared, as an antithesis to India's loyalty, the Rowlatt Act, proclamation of Martial-Law, the Amritsar Massacre, the unjust and invidious Kenya decision, the drastic dispersion of bands of passive Akali dissenters and the repeated

exercise of the power of certification in opposition to the popular will. It is only human that confidence has been shaken and a great distrust has taken its place. There is no political party in India that does not entertain serious doubts and suspicions regarding the bona fides and sincerity of England towards her. This is a malaise of evil potentiality and must be removed in the best interests of the British Commonwealth by deeds and not mere repetition of assurances couched in high-sounding and generous phraseology. Political conjuring with words has ceased to have any meaning, and the only rational solution of the difficulty is a further and immediate Constitutional advance if there be a genuine desire to restore that spirit of confidence that governed India's conduct during the last World War.

Wise words by a wise Indian—rich in practical statesmanship!

Syed Hasan Imam

EARLY YEARS

MR. Hasan Imam brother of Sir Ali Imam comes, as we have seen, of a highly respected Syed family, the members of which obtained great distinction during the Moghul period. He was born on the 31st August 1871 at Neora, a little village in the District of Patna. Owing to his delicate health young Imam was sent to school only about the close of his ninth year, when he was first admitted into the T. K. Ghosal's Academy, but subsequently after a year he was transferred to the Patna Collegiate School. He was not three years at school, when his studious habits made him ill again and he had to be sent to Arrah, a district in Bihar, for a change, where he joined the Government School and studied for two years. While here he met Mr. S. Sinha—now member of the Executive Council in Bihar and formerly well-known as Editor of *The Hindustan Review*—for the first time and a close intimacy soon sprang up between the two—their fathers being great friends. Mr. Hasan Imam's elder brother passed the Entrance Examination in 1887 and had to come to Patna to prosecute his studies further ; young Imam also went with him and joined the Collegiate School again. In the September of the same year Mr. Ali

Imam sailed for England. At school Mr. Hasan Imam was far more ahead in English literature than in other subjects. English Poetry and English History were, as they are even now, his favourite subjects and while yet in his fourteenth year he was believed to have read most of the English poets, Shakespeare, Milton, Wordsworth, Cowper and even some of the poems of the then Poet-Laureate, Lord Alfred Tennyson. His style and command of the English language elicited admiration from his Head Master, Mr. Phillips, who used to read out his essays to the class as models of composition. Though a school boy he was allowed to join the Patna College Debating Society, and take part in the discussion.

IN ENGLAND

The idea that he too should go to England first emanated from his mother and on the 24th of July, 1889, he sailed for England. Mr. Hasan Imam had a very busy time in England spending the day in the Middle Temple Library. At night he used to take lessons on Elocution. Six months after he was in England he was joined there by his friend Mr. S. Sinha, and the two thenceforward lived together and had practically a common purse between them. Scmetime after this the two began attending regularly for one year the History lectures of Professor Henry at the London University College. Mr. Imam regularly attended the debates in the Paddington Parliament in London of which he was a recognised leader. His speeches in that Parliament were generally the best of the session and used to be frequently noticed by the Press. But while Mr. Hasan Imam was doing so much for his own improvement he was not in the least forgetful of the interests of his country or community. He was the Secretary of the Indian Society, which had the honour of having Dadabhoy Naoroji as its President. He was the Secretary also of the Anjuman Islamia of London. But the unique honour of which any Indian student in England may well be proud, was the great privilege he had, of living with Mr. William Digby for 4 months and of acting as his Private Secretary during the time Mr. Digby was touring in Wales. The late Mr. Digby and his family had a great admiration for him and in his magnificent library at Hasan Manzil could be seen to-day all the works of the great friend of India with the words "with the author's esteem" written on the first page of each of them by the author himself.

Mr. Imam was one of the principal convassers for Mr. Naoroji in the General Election of 1891 for Central Finsbury and the tact with which he spoke to the voters, how he went directly into the English homes, freely conversed with the prominent members of each of them and finally brought round the voter to his opinion—all redound to his credit as a practical politician. Mr. Naoroji got into Parliament that time. Having thoroughly equipped himself for the battle of life, Mr. Hasan Imam left England in 1892 after having been called to the Bar.

AT THE BAR

Mr. Hasan Imam began to get good practice as soon as he joined the Bar. It was not long before acquired the reputation of being a powerful speaker, a successful debater and a man of vast and varied studies and began to be appreciated for his work and worth by the Senior Counsel of Bihar and elicited the confidence of a rapidly growing clientele. It would be idle to narrate here the many *cause celebre* in which he has figured prominently. Suffice it to say that he, along with his elder brother, is one of those fortunate few who have amassed a very large fortune by their practice. For sometime past Mr. Imam has been the undisputed leader of the Patna Bar and there has been hardly any important civil or criminal case in any part of Bihar in which his services have not been requisitioned by one side or the other.

JUDGE AT CALCUTTA

In November 1910 Mr. Hasan Imam transferred himself to Calcutta. There also his large Bihar clientele followed him and he very soon acquired considerable practice on the appellate side. His forensic ability and his legal acumen were very soon recognised by his compeers at the Bar and the Judges. Sir Lawrence Jenkins, the late Chief Justice of Bengal, was one of those who quickly recognized his ability and persuaded him to accept a seat on the bench which he did in April 1911. On the bench Mr. Hasan Imam was soon able to distinguish himself as a fearless and upright judge whose legal ability was only equalled by his desire to do justice. He was a judge always jealous of encroachment by the Executive on the province of the judiciary, ever keen to dispense justice tempered with mercy, vigilant and watchful of the people's rights.

When the proposal for the establishment of the Patna High Court received the sanction of the Secretary of State for India, the people of Bihar and Orissa passed resolutions almost in every district praying the Government to transfer Mr. Imam from the Bench of the Calcutta High Court to that of Patna. It was the highest compliment that could be paid to a judge and even now when Mr. Imam comes to think of it, a thrill of grateful pride runs through his nerves. But it is said that the then Lieutenant-Governor Sir Charles Bayley threatened to resign, should Justice Hasan Imam be transferred to the new Patna High Court. This is neither the place nor the occasion to dilate at length on the contribution which he has made to the legal literature of this country in the shape of judicial pronouncements. On the subject of Criminal Law his decisions are unanimously regarded as having crystallised the irrevocable principles of British jurisprudence from a mass of overgrown literature which instead of defining and clarifying the principles only clouded and mystified them. In the matter of Civil Law his pronouncements are as clear as any to be found in the vast mass of legal literature in India. Always concise, with an aptitude for direct and penetrating style, consistently attached to the leading points of a case rather than to superfluous details his judgments are now generally regarded as lucid expositions of legal principles. Such exacting critics as Mr. Jackson and Mr. Earldley Norton and reputed Indian lawyers like Lord Sinha, Sir P. C. Mitter and Mr. C. R. Das were ungrudging in their tribute to him.

But the damp climate of Calcutta began to have its effects on Mr. Imam and by the year 1913, his health had become so bad that he once fainted on the steps of the High Court of Calcutta. Although he betook himself to England in quest of health and never failed to run up to the hills when opportunity offered, Mr. Imam's health was shattered almost beyond redemption. The doctors advised him to leave Bengal and go to a drier climate. He therefore came to Patna and joined the Patna Bar. For a man of his ability and for one who already occupied the position of the leader of the Bar, it was not difficult to immediately take up the threads of the profession and win back his old position. He is to-day the acknowledged leader of the Patna Bar. He was soon after offered a seat on the Bench but he had so much identified himself with politics and had entertained so many public claims upon his time that he regarded his translation to the Bench as the betrayal of national trust. He, therefore, refused the offer once again contenting himself with the practice of his profession.

PUBLIC WORK

Mr. Hasan Imam's public activities are on a par with his success in the practice of his profession. As in the profession he reached the highest rungs of the ladder so in politics he attained the highest eminence permitted to an Indian under the present circumstances. He was elected President of the Special Congress at Calcutta. The interest of the country has ever been nearest his heart. He served his apprenticeship in Indian public life as a member of the Municipality and the District Board of Patna. And it is no exaggeration to say that his subsequent activities have justified the high hopes entertained by his friends. "No observer of incidents in this country, harsh and agonising as are the jarring elements that make our nation, will hide from you the fact that till we establish harmony amongst ourselves a foreign hand must guide our destiny," said Mr. Imam, on a memorable occasion "Let the motherland be the first in your affections, your province the second, and your community wherever thereafter you choose to put it." And he asks everyone he comes across to do the same, to remember that he is an "Indian first and anything else afterwards." Consistently with his political creed Mr. Imam has been in principle opposed to the granting of special electorates to the Mahommedans. A still clearer and stronger declaration of his principle was given in one of his speeches in the Indian National Congress. In supporting the resolution which strongly deprecated "the extention or application of the principle of separate communal electorates to Municipalities, District Boards or other Local Bodies," Mr. Imam made a speech in the Allahabad Congress of 1910, that deserves to be well remembered as the words of a great patriot strong in his principles. Said Mr. Imam:—

> It is quite apparent that when a few thoughtful men of this country at the time that the Reforms were inaugurated raised their voice of protest against any scheme of separate electorates, they fully realized the consequent effect of such scheme . . . . every thoughtful man in the land realised, and justly realised, that this pernicious scheme would travel down from the Chamber of the Viceroy's Council to the chambers of the District and Taluk Boards. It was then that we considered that our voice ought to be raised against all institutions that might create a division between the various classes that inhabit this land.

PUBLIC BENEFACTIONS

According to Mr. Imam "we have no Hindu, we have no Mahomedan, we are Indians and we are Beharees." He keeps his religious beliefs all to himself as rules for his private guidance and he does not let his judgment on any matter of public character be in the least influenced by them.

Like other leaders of Bihar public opinion Mr. Hasan Imam has been proud of the historic past of his Province. His public generosity raises him above the level of ordinary publicists, in that he gave equal donations to the two great Indian Universities of Aligarh and Benares. There could be no hesitation in saying that this particular act of discerning munificence could have been possible only from a man of the type of Mr. Imam.

In fact Mr. Imam has devoted a considerable portion of his time and a large amount of his money to the education of both Biharees and outsiders. The Bihar National College has received substantial support from him and it is an open secret that once when the College stood in fear of disaffiliation owing to its inability to deposit a certain amount within a specified time, Mr. Imam generously came forward and placed the necessary sum at the disposal of the Committee. He used to give Rs. 1,000 to the B. N. College every year before its absorption by the Government and its welfare has always been a matter of Mr. Imam's greatest concern. He spends a very considerable amount of money in educating a number of Hindu and Moslem young men at his expense and he is well-known as a liberal patron of needy students.

He has always evinced deep sympathy with the aspirations of the young men of his Province and he presided in 1909 at the fourth session of the Bihari Students' Conference at Gaya. His inspiring message to the student community was in the words of the famous Frenchman Mirabeau, that India wanted her sons to acquire three and only three virtues, *viz* "first, courage; second, courage; third, courage." It rang in all the intensity of its original fervour in the ears of his youthful hearers. The student movement in Bihar has one of its warmest supporters in Mr. Imam who has guided the young men along the paths of disciplined citizenship. In August 1917 Mr. Imam presided over the Bihar Provincial Conference held for the purpose of protesting against the internment of Mrs. Besant and the policy of antagonism to the Home Rule agitation on the part of the Government which was then in evidence. He said :—

These are the three problems you have got to consider, discuss and resolve upon at to-day's meeting—(a) the irreducible minimum of Reforms that will for the time being satisfy the legitimate aspirations of the people as marking a definite step towards the goal of our attaining self-Government within the Empire in the near future, (b) the policy of repression which is being systematically pursued in various Provinces with a view to stifle the active and earnest propaganda for Home-Rule and (c) the steps necessary to be taken by us, if the Government persist in their present policy of repression, with a view to make an effective and telling protest against the same.

He then spoke of the bureaucracy's attempts to stifle constitutional agitation, showed how the bureaucracy had failed to retain its vaunted reputation for efficiency and indicated the lines on which the proposed reforms should be framed. He concluded :—

Whether we shall get at present all that we want is not known to us, since the future is on the knees of the gods. But about one thing we shou'd be under no delusion and that is that whether we get it now or later, to-day or to-morrow, we *shall* come into our birth-right and nothing—nay, no power on earth—can keep us out of our inheritance, if only we ourselves are not slack in pressing our demands earnestly, forcefully and constitutionally on the attention of the great British democracy who are the real sovereign power in the State. For though the King-in-Parliament is the supreme power in the British State from the legal point of view, it is the democracy of Great Britain that is for all political purposes the master of even the Parliament. What is, therefore, essential to our success is an agitation on a gigantic scale to convince the British democracy of the justice of our claims to Self-Government and the moment their leaders are satisfied of it, they will unhesitatingly bring to bear upon the House of Commons the force at their disposal.

P. 273.

SYED HASSAN IMAM

AS A SOCIAL REFORMER

Mr. Imam does not, however, forget our shortcomings. He realises, more than any one else, the limitations under which we have to work as also the many defects in our social organisation which make our difficulties so perplexing. He is of the opinion that " much of our troubles is due to our social condition " and that the reform of social institutions must go side by side with, if not precede, political advancement. " With the depressed classes in a state of eternal servitude and the women in a state of hopeless neglect and unreasonable subjection, your wheel of progress will more likely run backward than forward " passionately exclaimed Mr. Imam at the Gaya Students' Conference. He is convinced that unless we emancipate our *Zenana* " our claims to equality of treatment with the more advanced peoples of the world has to be examined before it can be decreed " and that the foundations of the world's great successes were always laid by the fireside of the home. In this direction the work of his father's sister in founding the Patna City Zenana School deserves special mention. The school was for years maintained out of the family purse and was directly under her control. In 1903 there were some 60 to 70 students in the school, which subsequently ceased to exist after the foundation of the Padshah Nawab School, with Mr. Imam as its Secretary. As one who is more anxious to practise his principles before he preaches them to others, Mr. Hasan Imam overcame the tenacious opposition of near relations and brought his two daughters out of *purdah,* and gave them the best education that was possible in the culture of the East and the West. When in 1915, he visited England, he took his daughters with him; for in his opinion it meant a denial of justice to his daughters if his son alone was to have the benefit of an education in England. The result of such an example of courage and much needed social reform was that his enthusiasm for the emancipation of women spread among his people in the Province. It was his courageous example that inspired the Maharaja of Tikari to endow his whole estate worth about 3 crores—the largest endowment made in India within living memory—for the education of Indian women. Mr. Imam is the most influential member on the Tikari Board of Trust.

HIS MANY-SIDED ACTIVITIES

Mr. Hasan Imam succeeded his elder brother as a trustee of the Aligarh College in 1911. He was made the President of the Bihar Committee formed for collecting funds for the Aligarh University and he along with his other friends made it a point to set apart all Sundays for visiting other towns of Bihar for the great national movement. Mr. Imam has been a staunch Congressman and when the first meeting of the All-India Moslem League was held at Dacca, Mr. Imam in company with Mr. Mazar-ul-Haque, a staunch nationalist, travelled all the way to Dacca and it was due greatly to them that the League was stripped of much of its militant sectarian attitude. When in the year 1903 a mass meeting of Patna Moslems was held to undo the effect of Mr. (now Sir) Surendranath Banerjee's visit to carry on the Congress propaganda, Mr. Imam went there as a spectator and inspite of the entreaties of many of his friends and relations, stood out of the pandal as a protest against the meeting.

The *Beharee*, the organ of the educated community of Bihar was conducted by a Board of Directors with Mr. Imam as its President. On his translation to the Bench the *Beharee* passed into the hands of Benaily Raj. Mr. Maheshwar Prasad who conducted the paper with great independence and ability fell under the disfavour of Sir Charles Bayley, the then Lieutenant-Governor of Bihar. It has recently come out that it was due to Sir Bayley's interference that Mr. Maheswar Prasad's connection with the paper was cut off and it passed into the hands of one Mr. Alfred Cunningham and subsequently came to an ignoble end.

When Mr. Imam reverted to his profession, he realised that the interest of his Province greatly suffered on account of the lack of an independent organ of public opinion. He along with his old co-worker Mr. S. Sinha, the veteran journalist, immediately set to work and it was due to their collaboration that the *Searchlight* came into existence on the 15th June 1919. It must be mentioned, however, that had it not been for the princely donation of Mr. Hasan

Imam and his standing surety for all its liabilities that paper would yet have been in the land of dreams. The *Searchlight*, however, came into existence and is to-day, the most powerful and influential organ of public opinion in Bihar.

PRESIDENT, SPECIAL CONGRESS

A man of such sterling character and superb abilities, an undaunted champion of the people's rights—could not long remain without recognition at the hands of his countrymen. His name for several years past had been proposed for election to the Presidentship of the Indian National Congress; and in July 1918 he was with the unanimous approval of Congressmen elected to preside over the Special session of the Congress held at Bombay. The Montagu-Chelmsford Reform Scheme had been promulgated and was the subject of much bitter and acrimonious controversy. In India, politicians who had years ago divided into extremist and moderate sections had by the exercise of mutual forbearence and mutual accomodation attained some measure of solidarity at the Lucknow Session of the Congress in 1917. But the Reform Scheme revived the old division, and political life in India was once again full of mutual distrust and mutual recriminations. One section was avowedly in favour of the rejection of the Scheme; while another section desired drastic changes to make it acceptable to Indians; yet another was willing to accept the scheme such as it was and only pressed for improvements. Thus it was no ordinary responsibility that Mr. Imam took upon himself in responding to the call to preside over the Special Congress. As a practical worker he fully realised that nothing was so important to win the country's fight as union. He perceived that in the disagreement between the different schools of politicians the difference on fundamentals was much less than those on mere negligible details. He, therefore, pitched his Presidential Address in a key of sobriety, yet of firmness. It was due primarily to the conciliatory tone of his previous public pronouncements and his general reputation as a practical politician that, despite the declared opposition of the Moderates under the leadership of Mr. (now Sir) Surendranath Banerjee and Sir Dinsha Wacha, such prominent Moderates as Sir Dinsha Petit, Mr. Lalubhai Samaldas, Sir Fazulbhoy Currimbhoy, Mr. Abbas Tyabji, Dr. Besant, Dewan Bahadur Govindaraghava Aiyer, Mr. G. A. Natesan, Mr. Muhammad Ali Jinnah, Dewan Bahadur Ramachandra Rao and others joined the Congress and took part in its deliberations. Mr. Hasan Imam said :—

If you will permit me to point out, there seems to me no material difference between those that advocate rejection and those that advise acceptance, for the common feature of both is to continue the struggle till our rights are won. In politics as in war, not combat but victory is the object to be pursued and where ground is yielded, not to take it would be to abandon what you have won. The Secretary of State and the Viceroy in their Report have earnestly exhorted us to put our heads together in constructive statesmanship and I have no doubt that at this crucial juncture in our political history we shall preserve that deliberative calm which is necessary for the building of a great project.

He thus sketched, the problem facing great Britain and India:—

Leaving aside historical survey of the past, facts have to be faced whether by British statesmen or by us. Macaualy has said: "Of all forms of tyranny I believe the worst is that of a nation over a nation" and "the heaviest of all yokes is the yoke of the stranger." That is as true now as in the days of Macaulay and his observation applies as much to India as to any other country. To deny that India feels the yoke of the stranger is to shut one's eyes to fundamental facts. The apologists of British rule in India have asserted that the presence of the British in this land has been due to humane motives; that British object has been to save the people from themselves, to raise their moral standard, to bring them material prosperity, to confer on them the civilising influences of Europe, and so forth and so on. These are hypocricies common to most apologists. The fact is that the East India Company was not conceived for the benefit of India but to take away her wealth for the benefit of Britain. The greed of wealth that characterized its doings was accompanied by greed for territorial possession and when the transference of rule from the Company to the Crown took place, the greed of wealth and lust of power abated not one jot in the inheritors, the only difference being that tyranny became systematized and plunder become scientific. The people know it, they feel it, and they are asking for a reparation for the incidents of the past. If, in the language of Mr. Asquith, the Empire is to be for us worth living in, as well as worth dying for, that reparation must be made. The plea, to resist our demand, is put forward by short-sighted people that India is not yet educationally fit. They ignore the fact that it is not in literacy that the knowledge of one's rights lies but in that intuitive capacity which is God's gift to all races. We are told that the educated Indian is removed from the masses and between them there is no bond of sympathy to unite them to a common purpose; that the educated Indian is not capable of representing his less fortunate brethern; that the interests of the uneducated classes can be best administered by the British officials. The charges against us are unjust calumnies and the claims of the bureaucrat to represent the masses are arrogant assumptions. After more than a hundred years of uncontrolled sway over India the British administration in this country is not able to show a greater result in the spread of literacy than about six per cent. of the population. Those that have kept the people in the darkness of ignorance are the very people who lay claim to the entrustment of the people's interest to them. It is we who have been crying for more education and it is they that have been trying to retard mass education. It was our representative Gopal Krishna Gokhale that introduced the Primary Education Bill and it was the bureaucrat that threw it out. It is we who have been trying to broaden the political basis and it is they who are trying to narrow it down. The interests of the rulers and the ruled have been not only apart but widely divergent. To the advocates of the patriarchal system of sheltered existence we raise our warning finger to point out the importance of facing facts. For India to remain within the Empire she must be freed from an unwholesome tutelage and unless she is accorded a place of honor and of dignity alongside the self-governing units of the Empire, what is now a source of profit will assuredly turn into a source of peril. The present War has revealed the importance of cohesion, and unless that cohesion means to India her uplift, it is idle to expect her to work for an Empire in which her position is base and degrading. The sense of the unity of sentiment and consciousness of the identity of interest that now pervade all classes can not now be checked and Indian progress can not any more be resisted and wise statesmanship dictates that in dealing with India Great Britain should adopt the noble policy of helping India to rise to the full stature and dignity of a Self-governing member of the British Empire.

He then passed on to discuss the proposals from the standpoint of the Congress-League Scheme and concluded with an appeal for calm and dispassionate consideration.

The subject itself is vast, the atmosphere in which it has to be discussed has to be calm, heat has to be avoided, rhetoric has to give place to sound reasoning. To my countrymen I say, "Press your demands forcefully and insistently and if you are not heard now, your cause being righteous you will prevail in the end." And to the great British nation I commend the warning words of their great liberal statesman, Lord Morley: "If Imperialism means your own demoralization, if it means lowering your own standard of Civilization and humanity then in the name of all you hold precious, beware of it."

THE SATYAGRAHA MOVEMENT

When Mr. Gandhi inaugurated his Satyagraha movement against the Rowlatt Legislation, Mr. Hasan Imam was one of the very first of the Congress leaders to extend his moral support to it. We are not concerned here with the efficacy or the expediency of Satyagraha as a political weapon in India. That would take us far afield and we shall only indicate Mr. Hasan Imam's position in this respect. He was convinced that 'the principles underlying the Rowlatt Legislation were not only unjust and inexpedient but also pernicious in as much as they tended to dwarf the growth of Indian Nationhood. He felt that the whole country was with him on the question of the Black Legislation, the voice of protest against the Rowlatt Bills being raised from every corner of the country. He realised that the official attitude was one of obduracy. The problem that the situation had raised for an Indian was whether he should rest content and solace his conscience with such gutteral performances as had already been indulged in by public men all over the country or to take some step that will give an effective demonstration of the people's resentment against an unrighteous and unprincipled piece of legislation. . The situation to Mr. Imam was one of agonising despair. To one of his mentality to yield to counsels of moderation was tantamount not only to a weakening of his faith in the ultimate destiny of the Motherland but also the betrayal of her honour and her rights. Thus Satyagraha came to Mr. Imam as the call of duty. Success or, failure was to him a matter of very secondary importance. He signed the pledge in a spirit of service. At a mass meeting held at the Patna city he spoke of the intellectual as well as the practical side of the Satyagraha Movement:—

> Their leader Mahatma Gandhi, had inaugurated the same movement to make our protest effective which had succeeded so remarkably well in South Africa. He considered it their duty to follow him. There were times when a common misfortune brought them together so that they may derive strength in each other's company. The present was a time for sorrow when they remembered not only their past misfortunes and calamities but also those to come. It was an occasion when a common danger had steeled them to declare in one voice that though others had the sword in their hands, no one could conquer their souls. A Satyagrahi declined to be subjugated and conquered. He might be lodged in a jail, but the very prison walls yielded before the strength of his soul force. Though their misfortune was great and terrible and though the consciousness of their fallen condition was poignant, they need not look up to their arms. They must declare that though others may rule their country and their people no one could rule their soul. They would be their own masters as God had given them the right to be. Whoever may possess the political power, whoever be their master, the Satyagrahi declared that he would be his own master, he would be free, aye, as an Englishman was in England, or a Frenchman in France. That was the vision of the Satyagrahi—the development of the soul force.

We have said that Mr. Hasan Imam is essentially a man of action. When the time came for urging the Reforms in England, he led the Home Rule League Deputation and served the cause of India with his accustomed zeal. He made several speeches and interviewed many leading men and journalists and thus he utilised this opportunity to press the cause of Indian Reforms on the British public. He also represented the Indian feeling against the proposed dismemberment of the Ottoman Empire. When in November 1919, he returned to India he gave the following opinion on the recommendations of the Joint Committee of the Houses of Parliament on the

Reform Bill and also on the Punjab troubles and the Khilafat wrongs:—

The Joint Committee's proposals, seem to be an advance upon the proposals of the Government of India as also upon the original Bill itself. I believe the Bill will now be amended and passed in the form recommended by the Joint Committee and we have to see that we make the best of what is being given to us. To my mind there is no question of our accepting or neglecting the measure. India's right to Home Rule, without necessary backing, leaves that right to the pleasure of England.

* * * * * *

The value of these Reforms will be underestimated at the present moment by reason of the existing unsympathetic rule, as evidenced by the Punjab incident and the policy of exploitation of the non-Christian people as evidenced by the attitude of Great Britain towards the Islamic countries. There is no doubt that our faith in the honesty of the utterances of the British Cabinet has been greatly shaken by the First Minister of the Crown having belied, by his present conduct and attitude, all his previous professions of goodwill towards Turkey and the question of the Khalifate. The feeling of mistrust that is growing in India is due to many circumstances and not the least amongst the contributory causes is the attitude of Mr. Lloyd George towards the Ottoman Empire. The dismemberment of the Turkish Empire and the expulsion of the Turks from Europe may afford to the fanatics of Europe the satisfaction that the Muslim is no more on the European soil, but I have no doubt that if such an event takes place, the Muslim population, living within the British Empire, will retain in bitter memory this act of injustice. Whether such memory will be conducive to cordial relations between the Muslim population and Great Britain is a matter that does not require to be discussed, but it certainly is deserving of notice.

THE MOSLEM DELEGATION

But not long after, Mr. Hasan Imam had an opportunity to present the case for the Turks on behalf of the Indian Muslims. He joined the Indian Moslem Delegation in London consisting of H. H. the Aga Khan, Mr. Chotani and Dr. Ansari. The Delegation was enabled to meet Mr. Montagu, the Secretary of State for India, who took a warm interest in the cause of Turkey. Mr. Montagu also arranged for the Delegation to meet Mr. Lloyd George, the Prime Minister and other Members of the Cabinet.

On these and other occasions Mr. Hasan Imam pressed the claims of Turkey with his characteristic lucidity, so that if the Government did not profit by the counsels of the Delegation it could not at least plead ignorance of the Indian view point. In an interview with the Associated Press soon after his arrival in Bombay in April 1921 Mr. Hasan Imam spoke with the caution of a statesman dealing with delicate negotiations. "The Premier" he said, "viewed the Moslem representation with sympathy, and if he is unable to fulfil the hopes of Indian Moslems it will not be for want of inclination, though it may be by reason of his limitations."

In fact, inspite of strong feelings on the Khilafat Question, Mr. Hasan Imam showed throughout marked self-restraint. He never spoke without a sense of responsibility. On the 1st June he again expressed his views with the same caution. He acknowledged that Lord Chelmsford's Government stood by the Indian Moslems' cause faithfully and said that Mr. Montagu fought for the cause as few would have fought. Lord Reading and his Government were also doing their best, and, if the Muslim demands were not conceded in any measure, it would not be the fault of the Indian Government or the Secretary of State.

During his stay in London he gathered that the Turkish Delegates were not anxious to get back Palestine, Mesopotamia, Syria and the Hedjaz. All that they wanted was to be left to

develop themselves, free from outside control in their homelands of Asia Minor, Constantinople and Thrace. He believed the Indian Muslims also did not now insist on the restoration of the pre-War Ottoman Empire, provided the Arab races were allowed to remain as separate States, without non-Muslim domination.

Mr. Hasan Imam referred to the Prime Minister's pledges on the subject and said that

> he did not know what influenced him to change his earlier attitude towards Turkey and the Arab Provinces, when the Sevres Treaty was framed, and added that he was convinced that the Premier had realised the mistake of that Treaty, which he would be only too willing to rectify if the other executants of the Treaty were agreeable.

EVIDENCE BEFORE THE LEE COMMISSION

We have seen that Mr. Hasan Imam is a pronounced nationalist and that he never hesitated to express himself with vigour. This sketch would be incomplete without some extracts from his characteristic evidence before the Lee Commission. At its Patna sittings in February 1924 Mr. Hasan Imam gave his views, both written and oral, with telling frankness. In reply to the Commission's questionaire he pointed out that

> Responsible administration with the aid of a preponderating foreign element in the various services suggested a system that did not consort with one's accepted notions of popular control over the executive and even this aspect was not clearly appreciated by the framers of the Government of India Act of 1919, with the result that though in theory and also to some extent in actual practice the Provincial Governments were rendered mainly responsible to the legislatures in the administration of the transferred departments, the members of the various services remained practically outside the control of Ministers and Legislatures and continued to be under the immediate control of the Secretary of State in all matters.

As in his opinion, the position of the services as laid down in the Act was grossly inconsistent with the spirit and essence of even the little modicum of Responsible Government introduced into Provincial administrations, he suggested that the departments under the control of Ministers must be provincialised and the Ministers should have full control over such services. He then emphasised the fact that Indians had been fed long on promises that had been broken directly they had been made.

The problem of Indianisation must now be properly grasped and appreciated. Recruitment in England on the present basis must cease altogether and efficiency must not be interpreted in a narrow and misleading sense in which it had so far been utilized to retard all progress and reform. From a calculation of the present position it would appear that Indians did not form to-day more than 12 per cent. of the total strength of the Civil Service and on that basis for 20 years to come there would be a dominating British element in the administration. The stoppage of recruitment in England was necessary on both political and economic grounds. India had obviously reached the stage of diminishing returns and she could not perpetuate a system of civil administration which was beyond her paying capacity.

He recommended the retention of the Civil Service and the Police Service as at present on an all-India basis but he suggested a material reduction of the cadre of the former by throwing open many of the posts now held by members of the Civil Service to men picked up by reason of their merit and capacity from the Provincial services.

In regard to the judicial branch of the Civil Service he had not the slightest doubt speaking from his personal experience at the Bar that the judicial administration would be all the better for the abolition of a system under which at present civilians were appointed as Judges.

Continuing, he said, that the principle of appointment and control had nothing to do with any question of nationality and race and any attempt to introduce this principle in matters of appointment and control would be inconsistent with the position of India as a self-governing unit in the comity of nations.

Indian opinion was unanimously opposed to the Secretary of State continuing to appoint and control the superior services in this country. As long as this practice continued members of such services would be apt to regard themselves as beyond the authority and control of the Governments under which they had actually to serve. Feelings of bitterness and rancour would continue to brew in the hearts of Indians who would naturally feel that while in theory the members of the services were servants of the people, they were for all practical purposes their masters. In any case the control of the Secretary of State must cease as also his authority to involve Indians in commitments which they could not reasonably be expected to accept.

Hakim Ajmal Khan*

FOR more than twenty-one years a friendship, which has grown stronger year by year, has bound me to Hakim Ajmal Khan Sahib, in Delhi. The history and tradition of his family is one of great interest in modern India, and the Hakim Sahib holds a place as one of the chief leaders of the popular movement in India, which is a sure token of the respect of Hindus and Mussalmans alike.

HAKIM SAHIB'S ANCESTORS

The chief ancestors of the family, to which Hakim Ajmal Khan belongs, and from whom he derives his origin, were residents of Kashgar, the famous city of Turkistan in Central Asia. The ancestor, who came to India held a leading place in the service of the Emperor Babar. When the King invaded India, this ancestor was given the command of one thousand horsemen, and was a close companion in all the Emperor's adventures.

Among the descendants of this cavalry leader under Babar, were the two famous brothers, Khawajah Hashim and Khawajah Qasim, who lived their saintly lives at Hyderabad, Sindh, and also died there. Both of these brothers were honoured as great saints, and

* **We are indebted to Mr. C. F. Andrews for permission to include this sketch in the "Biographies of Eminent Indians" Series.**

they had many disciples among the people of Sindh. The reverence for their saintliness extended among the Hindu population, and was not confined to Mussalmans only. This has always been a feature of the religious life of Sindh, where the Hindu and Mussalman religious ideals have approximated more nearly than in any other part of India.

A FAMILY OF PHYSICIANS

The art of medicine began to be practised as a profession in this family, to which Hakim Ajmal Khan belongs, in the time of Hakim Fazal Khan, who was the grandson of Mulla Ali Quari.

After him, followed a long line of physicians in this house, who were not only skilled physicians, advancing the art of Unani medicine in India and keeping in close touch with Central Asia, but also men of great learning in their own days, keeping up the traditions of nobility, and culture which they had inherited from the Emperor Babar's Court.

The reputation of the family for medicine reached its highest point under Hakim Sharif Khan, who was the honoured grandfather of Hakim Ajmal Khan himself. Hakim Sharif Khan had written before his death a large number of treatises on medicine. He was greatly trusted by the physicians of his day, and his advice was frequently sought. His times coincided with the reign of Mahammad Shah.

In return for services rendered to the Mughal Emperors in Delhi, the family received, three times over, jagirs. The last of these was confiscated by

P. 289.

HAKIM AJMAL KHAN

the British Government, at the time of the Mutiny, in 1857.

BIRTH AND PARENTAGE

Hakim Mahmud Khan was the father of Hakim Ajmal Khan. He lived to a great age and died in his 74th year. As in the case of Hakim Sharif Khan, he had a very large medical practice in Delhi itself and in the whole of the North of India. People came to consult him from all parts. His house in Delhi was famous for its open-hearted hospitality. During his days, the School of Unani Medicine at Delhi became celebrated, not merely in Delhi itself, but in all the Middle East and Near East,—as far as Constantinople and Cairo in one direction and as far as Bokhara in another.

The reputation of Hakim Mahmud Khan was well sustained by his successor, Hakim Abdul Majid Khan, who tendered great and valued service to his countrymen by his profound knowledge of medicine and by his training and education of a school of physicians, practising indigenous methods. He received the title of Haziq-ul-Mulk, which was well merited on account of the great width of his experience and practice. He left a living monument in the shape of the Tibbiya School which was developed into a famous institution in his time. Physicians who have been educated in the Tibbiya, are now to be found in every part of India and in many parts of Asia.

Hakim Abdul Majid Khan died in his fifty-third year. He was followed by Hakim Wasal Khan, his younger brother, who carried on his elder brother's work at the Tibbiya after his death with the same diligence and care as before. His devoted service was very deeply appreciated in the Punjab and United Provinces and the whole city of Delhi was thrown into mourning by the news of his early death, at the age of forty-three. On the death of Hakim Wasal Khan, the succession to the Tibbiya and the medical position in Delhi came to Hakim Ajmal Khan himself. He was born on the 17th Shawwal, 1284 Hijra, and was thus in the prime of his life, when he took up the work as leading Unani physician in Delhi.

It was at this period, when his fame was beginning to show signs of still wider recognition than that of his predecessors that I first became acquainted with the Hakim Sahib. At the Tibbiya I found present, as students, not merely Indians, but those who had come from countries as far distant as Turkistan and Macedonia. One specially I remember who had the features of a European. When I asked his nationality I was told he was an Albanian.

FIRST VISIT TO HAKIM SAHIB

The first visit I paid to the Hakim Sahib, was to me a memorable occasion. It threw entirely new light upon India and Indian affairs. I had been brought up in the old school of Anglo-Indian thought, and imagined that there was an almost impassable gulf between Hindus and Mussalmans due to caste on the one hand, and religious prejudice on the other.

I had been told, that it was no more possible for Hindus and Mussalmans to mix than oil and water. This opinion, which I had carried with me direct from England, had already received a good many shocks on my arrival at Delhi. But the sight which shattered it and made me revise it altogether, was the evidence before my eyes of the Hakim Sahib's hospital waiting-room where the sick people had gathered together. It was pointed out to me by the person, who introduced me, that every type and religion were represented, and when Hakimji came in, he made no difference whatever between rich and poor, Hindu and Mussalman: all were treated alike, and I noted especially the number of the Hindu poor who received free treatment. After that first visit, my acquaintance with the Hakim Sahib ripened into a close friendship.

EARLY EDUCATION

But to return to Hakim Ajmal Khan's own life story, he was educated in his youth in all the Islamic branches of learning. His literary education was completed under different teachers. It consisted of Persian and Arabic Grammar, the study of the Quran, Logic, Physics, Literature, Astronomy, Mathematics, Islamic traditions. He was not taught English. He still speaks English with some hesitation, though he has picked up a good working knowledge of the language from his journeyings abroad. His knowledge of Urdu literature is extensive, and it is always a pleasure to hear him speak in the Urdu language.

His knowledge of medicine began from a very early age under his father. But the chief store of his medical knowledge he received from his elder-brothers, especially his elder brother Hakim Abdul Majid Khan. It is probably true to say, that his own medical reputation has exceeded that of any of his predecessors. The fame of the Tibbiya never stood so high in the estimation of countries abroad as in the days of Hakim Ajmal Khan.

TRAVELS ABROAD

When I arrived in Delhi from England in March, 1904, the Hakim Sahib was absent in Mesopotamia. This was the first of his travels abroad, and his tour was an extensive one. He visited Basra, Osair, Kat-ul-Amara, Baghdad, Zulkifi, Kufa Najaf-i-Ashraf and Karbala-i-Mulia. In addition to many visits to pilgrim shrines, he consulted libraries in those cities and met and conversed with experts of every science, especially that of medicine. His whole journey lasted three months. He was greatly interested in the indigenous schools where education was given to the children. The new type of school which was introduced by the late Sultan, Abdul Hamid Khan, gave him many suggestions, some of which he utilized later.

When he returned to Delhi in May, 1904, I was in the Hills, on language study as a missionary. My first visit to the Hakim Sahib, which I have already mentioned, took place later in that year. From that time forward until his visit to Europe in May, 1911,

I constantly went to see him at his house and dined with him frequently and met him at public functions where we would often get apart from the crowd and talk together about different public affairs. It is strange now to think of those days when it was regarded as the special duty of every gentleman in Delhi to attend each tea-party or entertainment given by the Deputy Commissioner, and when the absence of anyone would be looked upon as a slight. What long weary hours were wasted! What empty formalities! It was easy to find the Hakim Sahib on such occasions, for he would sit apart and would do nothing to court favour or to gain recognition. I could well imagine how irksome they were to him, and how he must have looked back to the old Mughal days when his ancestors were truly honoured guests at the great Mughal Court. There was a humiliation under the new regime, which was never far distant and sometimes came acutely near. I greatly admired the dignity and courtesy of the Hakim Sahib, which was always united with a gesture of independence. No one could mistake that gesture. It was inherited from generations of ancestors. It was a birth-right, not something acquired.

An event of great importance happened in his own life, when Hakim Ajmal Khan visited Europe in the year 1911. The journey in Europe lasted three months, and he returned to India in the autumn of the same year. He reached London on June 7th, and through the intervention of Sir Theodore Morison, who had been Principal of the M.A.O. College, Aligarh, in earlier days, he was able to visit all the leading hospitals and medical colleges of London. He also spent many hours in the Libraries of the Indian Office and the British Museum. From London he went to Oxford and Cambridge. At the latter University, he met Professor E. G. Browne. Then he returned to London and took part in the Coronation ceremony of H. M. the King on July 7.

On his way back, to India, Hakim Ajmal Khan made a tour of the Continent. In Paris, owing to the good offices of certain friends he was able to see thoroughly the famous State Hospital and also to visit historical places. He felt greatly drawn towards the French people. From Paris he went on to Berlin, where he again made every enquiry into hospital arrangements with a view to his own proposed College in Delhi. The Oriental Library was also open to him for cousultation. At Vienna he followed the same course of enquiry.

It was naturally at Constantinople that he made his longest stay. There he was entertained and given permission to see all that would help him in his great object of founding a Medical College at Delhi. The visit to Constantinople made a lasting impression upon him and I can well remember his speaking to me about it with eagerness and enthusiasm. It was probably from this visit to Constantinople that his deeper interest in Turkish questions began. At Cairo also he stayed many days and visited El Azhar. He found many of his old pupils both in Turkey and in Egypt. They gave him the warmest welcome.

HAKIMJI AT DELHI

After Delhi had been made the capital of India, Lady Hardinge took great pains to study the condition of the poor and to seek in every way to increase the medical arrangements for their help and comfort in times of sickness. She came into touch with Hakim Ajmal Khan in this work of charity and human kindness. At the critical time when Lord Hardinge was lying almost fatally wounded by the bomb, which had been thrown, and when Lady Hardinge herself so narrowly escaped, his warm heart went out to them both in a manner which went far beyond the bounds of formal sympathy. He was very deeply moved by the dignity and magnanimity with which Lord Hardinge and Lady Hardinge acted, and a personal friendship sprang up which had important results. For, when the Hakim Sahib at last had finished the plans of his new hospital, it was named after Lord and Lady Hardinge. A very beautiful act was performed in the midst of the political controversy, a little more than a year ago. Mahatma Gandhi was asked by Hakim Ajmal Khan to unveil a portrait of Lord and Lady Hardinge in the Hospital buildings. In doing so, Mahatma Gandhi expressed the greatest pleasure. He indicated by the act that his political movement was not directed against Englishmen as a people. He admired them greatly, he said, as a people, and Lord and Lady Hardinge in a special manner for their noble character and their love for the Indian poor, which was genuine and sincere. But he was opposed to the system of administration and was fighting against the system.

Hakim Ajmal Khan is not merely famous for his medical skill, but also for his writings on medicine. He has written many treatises which have become popular among which the best known are an 'Introduction to Medical Terms,' and 'A Taun' or 'The Plague.'

INTEREST IN PUBLIC AFFAIRS

For very many years Hakim Ajmal Khan, following the tradition of his family, had been taking interest in public affairs. But, up to the time of his visit to Europe his interests were almost entirely confined to his own community though all the while he had been on friendly terms with others, as I have shown. On his return from Europe a new idea came into prominence. He saw that the question of Hindu-Muslim unity was of supreme importance and he became its ardent upholder, up to the year 1918, however, he had taken but little part in the active political life of the country. He had worked patiently and quietly for the M. A. O. College, Aligarh, and for the formation of a Muslim University. He had also been a member of the Muslim League and had been elected a Vice-President. He had warmly welcomed what might be called the Hindu-

Muslim Entente and had done his utmost to bring it about. But it was not till the year 1918 that he became actually prominent in politics. In December of that year a memorable Congress was held at Delhi, and Hakim Ajmal Khan accepted the responsible post of Chairman of the Reception Committee. The Congress at Delhi, was exceptionally large in its numbers, and the work of the Chairman of the Reception Committee was extremely arduous.

After the Congress was over, Hakim Ajmal Khan had settled down to his regular work of healing the sick and looking after the hospital patients and the medical students, and encouraging the growth of medical knowledge among Indian women by his Tibbiya Medical School. Suddenly, into the midst of these quiet activities came the out-break in the Punjab, in April, 1919. It was then that I saw the Hakim Sahib in all the true greatness of his character. Night and day he laboured for peace among the common people ; and it was only through his intervention, along with Swami Shraddhananda, that peace was maintained, and the city of Delhi, which he loved so well, was saved from Martial Law. Then came later the disclosure of the terrible things that had actually been done in Amritsar and Lahore and other places under the stress of Martial Law. The Hakim Sahib had written to me quite simply : " My political ideas were wholly changed by the iniquitous deeds of the present bureaucracy in India during the Martial Law days in the Punjab, in the year 1919." This sentence is literally true.

A SUPPORTER OF MAHATMA GANDHI

Later, in the year 1920, came the further knowledge of broken pledges, when the Treaty of Sevres was signed on behalf of the Indian Government and with the Indian Government's consent. From that time forward the Hakim Sahib became a staunch supporter of Mahatma Gandhi; and when Mr. C. R. Das was arrested on the eve of the Ahmedabad Congress in 1921, he accepted the post of President, which was unanimously offered to him and thus crowned the whole work of his own life in the cause of Hindu-Muslim Unity. Since the arrest of Mahatma Gandhi and his imprisonment, the leadership of the whole movement, for the time being, has practically devolved upon him, and in spite of failing health and a weakened physical constitution he has done his very utmost to fulfil the work. In all this arduous undertaking, he has had the devoted sympathy and support of Dr. A. M. Ansari who has been, all through, his translator into English as well as active helper in organisation. The friendship between Dr. Ansari and the Hakim Sahib has been very close indeed, and it has become closer than ever during the past year. The spirit of Hakim Ajmal Khan is seen most simply expressed in his letter to Mahatma Gandhi when the Mahatmaji was arrested and placed in Sabarmati Jail in March, 1922.

"I can feel happy" he writes, "at your arrest only when I find that as a mark of the profound respect, which it has for you, the country takes still greater interest in the national movement than it did when you were free. It gives me infinite pleasure to see that the country observed perfect peace. This is a clear sign of the spread of the spirit of non-violence in the country, which is as essential for our success as pure air is necessary for life. I have no doubt that the secret of the progress of our country lies in the unity of the Hindus, the Mussalmans and other races of India. Such a unity should not be based on policy, for that in my opinion would be only a kind of an armistice. But I clearly see that the two great communities are coming closer together every day, and although the number of men, whose hearts are absolutely free from any sectarian prejudices, may not be very great, I feel convinced that the country has found the road to real unity and will advance on it with steady steps towards its goal. So highly do I prize this unity, that if the country gave up all other activities and achieved that alone, I would consider the Khilafat and Swaraj questions automatically solved to our satisfaction. For the achievement of our objects is so intimately connected with this unity, that to me the two appear identical. The question, then, naturally arises, how are we to achieve this living and lasting unity? We can achieve it only by the sincerity and purity of our hearts. Not until everyone of us has driven selfishness out of his mind, will our country succeed in achieving its objects."

The ending of this letter shows, along with this passage which I have quoted, the true spirit of the Hakim Sahib:—

"In the end," he writes, "I join you in your prayers and wish to assure you that though my failing health will not enable me to be of very great service to my country, it will be my earnest endeavour to discharge my duties until Mr. C. R. Das is once more among us. May God help us in the sacred work, which you and the country have undertaken for truth and justice."

CHARACTERISTICS

I feel that any estimate of the character of Hakim Ajmal Khan, given in my own words is unnecessary after quoting such self-revealing passages as these from his own writings. Quiet, humble, modest, with all the dignity of a man of character, learning and religious sincerity, he stands out to-day in the city of Delhi as the one recognised head, whom all alike acknowledge to be their moral leader, for his character and his character alone. In times of trouble and in times of rejoicing alike, the poor people of Delhi flock to his house to share their sorrows and their joys with the Hakim Sahib. When at the beginning of the year 1922 the rumour was spread abroad that he was to be arrested, the crowds of the city of Delhi became excited almost beyond the limits of endurance, but the Hakim Sahib went about his daily work of healing the sick and ministering to the poor, quiet, silent, calm and fearless ; sustained in his inner spirit by his trust in God and his belief in the victory of righteousness.

It has been difficult to write calmly and dispassionately concerning one whom I have learnt during all these years to love as an intimate friend; but I have tried to do so knowing what would be his own wishes in such a matter. It is no slight thing, that the country should have found a character, so pure and sincere for its leader, during the months that immediately followed the arrest of Mahatma Gandhi. No one could have better represented, at the time, Mahatma Gandhi's spirit.

THE MAHATMA AND HAKIM SAHIB

All that I have written above was printed nearly three years ago. Yet so consistently and unswervingly sincere and truthful is his character, that I have found no necessity to modify a single word that I have written about those earlier days. I can only add that these three eventful years have found him as steadfast as ever in upholding the honour of his country and his religion. On many occasions, I have been with him in company with Mahatma Gandhi,—especially during Mahatmaji's serious illness at Poona and Juhu after his operation and also during the Fast of twenty-one days in September 1924. The friendship between these two has ripened and deepened as the years have gone by. It is a thing which one hardly dares to write about, so sacred is it and so profound. But I may, perhaps, be permitted to speak of one day, when our hearts were filled with a very deep gloom because the hand of death seemed to have come very near to Mahatmaji himself. His two daily attendant doctors, Dr. Ansari and Dr. Abdur Rahman, had both implored him to give up the Fast, because it had appeared by unmistakable signs, that to continue it any longer would prove fatal. But Mahatma Gandhi on his day of silence simply wrote upon his slate—'Have faith in God' and again 'you have forgotten the power of prayer.'

I had gone with them, to join in their beseeching, and had been equally rebuked by his spiritual strength of endurance. Then later in the day, Hakim Ajmal Khan also came. He went upstairs alone to see Mahatmaji. By this time the day of silence was over and the two friends communed in spirit together. When the Hakim Sahib came down-stairs, his face was calm and peaceful. He had won from Mahatmaji himself complete confidence that he would survive, and he had not pressed him to take food. I felt, as I saw the Hakim Sahib that evening, how much deeper his faith in God was than my own; and when he urged that no further attempt should be made to induce Mahatmaji to break his vow of fasting, I felt that he was right and that all would be well. Indeed, from that time my own confidence returned, and it was more easy to be quiet and collected.

A PILLAR OF HINDU-MUSLIM UNITY

There is one other thing to note. It is this. For all those days at Delhi, when Hindu-Muslim Unity was strained almost to breaking point, it was Hakim Ajmal Khan more perhaps than any other prominent leader, who by his supreme moral determination preserved it. With him, as I have pointed out, earlier in this article, it was an age-long family tradition. It was a part of his very nature. It ran in his blood. Therefore when the straining point came, he could bear the whole of the strain. Upon him, more than upon any one else, came the heavy burden of the peace-maker between two contending parties, when passions were running very high and angry voices were being raised on every side.

To-day, the Hakim Sahib's health is gone.* The strain, which his spirit was able to bear, has been too much for his tired body, Only by complete

* For the sake of his health the Hakim Sahib left for Europe on April 10, 1925 reaching Marseilles on the 22nd. From there he wrote a letter to Mahatma Gandhi which he published in *Young Ind a.* Hakimji writes :—

"I was sorry not to have been able to meet you before I sailed. God willing, I shall give myself the pleasure on my return. I shall feel deeply ashamed when any one asks me about the condition of India. For what shall I be able to say except that it is wretched,—that its two great but unfortunate communities are fighting to their hearts' content among themselves. How I wish that those who are engaged in widening the gulf would have pity on India, on Asia, indeed on their own respective communities, and would turn their faces towards the true path and would put life into the lifeless Congress."

Those who know the good soul, comments the Mahatma, will readily appreciate and share his great grief over our dissensions.

cessation from active public work, will his physical strength return. For the sake of India, the Mother-land which he has loved so well, our prayers will go up to God, the Source of all Life and Strength, that he may be preserved to us for many years to come. For the love and devotion which bind all who know him to himself in answering affection, are so deep and true that their healing power will be felt in every part of India at this time of communal tension. He is one of the greatest links binding Hindu and Mussalman together.

P. 305.

SIR IBRAHIM RAHIMTOOLA

Sir Ibrahim Rahimtoola

INTRODUCTORY

BORN in a family with no political traditions, Sir Ibrahim Rahimtoola has slowly but steadily pushed his way to the front until he has had the honour to be described by so high an authority as His Highness the Aga Khan as "the most distinguished member our community has produced in Western India." Mussalman by birth and by faith, he has secured the confidence of the other communities in India without neglecting the claims of his own community on his leadership; without the initial advantage of collegiate education he has by sheer dint of effort and perseverance cultivated a style of lucid and terse English both in speaking and writing which extorts the admiration of all; at a time when popularity rarely falls to the lot of a Government nominee for an office, he has held the highest executive office in a province and easily retained the confidence of the people without losing the approbation of Government.

EARLY YEARS

Sir Ibrahim Rahimtoola was born in 1862 as the second son of Mr. Rahimtoola Kaderbhoy, a merchant in Bombay. As soon as he attained school-going age young Ibrahim was duly put to school. He was a diligent student and showed particular aptitude for arithmetic, algebra and geometry. He always secured high marks in these subjects in the class examinations. In the field of sports, he won early reputation as a cricketeer, and later became captain of the Islam Gymkhana. It was in the cricket field and in the tennis court that he acquired those sportsmanlike qualities which have stood him in good stead in his political career.

His failure in the Matriculation Examination in 1879 marked the end of his scholastic career, and he joined his elder brother, Mr. Mahomedbhoy Rahimtoola, in business. The death of his father Mr. Rahimtoola Kaderbhoy, in 1880 was a great calamity for the young brothers who were left without his ripe experience in business. It was inevitable that the combined qualities of shrewdness and courage which have characterised Sir Ibrahim in his political career should have helped him in business. Without following, however, the example of the ordinary Bombay merchant who loses himself in the work of money-making, oblivious of the larger life of the country, Mr. Ibrahim chalked out a different path for himself. It was the beginning of a busy and changing age in India; and there was enough animation in the city life of Bombay. Giants like Sir Pherozeshah Mehta were already astir and the newspapers were not idle in creating a public spirit in their readers by publishing the debates of the City Corporation. By 1884 the still waters of Indian political life began to be stirred into gentle ripples by the breath of freedom and reform, and the Indian National Congress came into being in 1885. Thus Sir Ibrahim's youthful days were cast in auspicious times; and as a steady reader of newspapers he caught the spirit of the new age and aspired for the civic honours of a city father. His was not the temper to sit quiet when he set his heart on a thing. He availed himself of every opportunity to practise the art of speaking, taking to heart the Roman orator's advice "an orator is not made by the tongue alone, as if it were a sword sharpened on a whetstone or hammered on an anvil, but by having a mind well-filled with a free supply of high and various matter."

AS A CITY FATHER

In January 1892, he stood for election to the Municipal Corporation of Bombay and succeeded, thus realising the ambition of his youthful days. In 1894 he was made a Justice of the Peace. His ability and perspicacity were brought into evidence in his dealing with the problems that sought for solution at the hands of the city fathers; and his colleagues elected him to the Standing Committee in 1895 and elevated him to its chairmanship in 1898. In 1899, within seven years of his membership, he occupied the honored post of President of the Corporation. Endowed with qualities of leadership he could hardly confine himself to the activities of the city. However, his membership of the Corporation did not cease with his participation in other spheres of political life, but continued till his appointment as Member of the Governor's Executive Council in 1918. His connection with the Corporation therefore covers an uninterrupted period of 26 years of strenuous work.

His services for his city were various and manifold: there was hardly a single subject of civic importance which he did not deal with in a spirit of broad statesmanship. He served the Improvement Trust for a period of 20 years, from 1898 to 1918. He was a member of the Schools Committee for many years, where he rendered enduring service to the cause of primary education in the city. He was one of those early political workers who realised that unless rapid strides were made in the direction of mass education any substantial political progress in the country was impossible. As an enthusiast for mass education he was greatly concerned to see that the efforts of the Schools Committee to promote education among Mahomedan boys, which was then in a very backward state, proved largely futile. A large number of municipal Urdu schools had been opened in the city, but owing to the fact that the Koran was not taught in those schools the Mahomedan parents preferred to send their boys to *muktabs.* In order to make those schools more attractive to Mahomedan parents he wanted the introduction in them of Koran teaching. This proposal encountered sturdy opposition in the Corporation, but Sir Ibrahim was able to win a majority in his favour. The result justified his stand: and after the introduction of Koran teaching in Urdu schools, the number of Mahomedan boys attending those schools rapidly increased to large proportions, and thus the benefits of primary education were extended to a conservative section of the city population.

The esteem in which he was held by the public was recognised by the Government, who appointed him as the Sheriff of Bombay in 1904, and also nominated him as a Fellow of the Bombay University in the same year.

In such a short sketch as this it is impossible to review at length his activities in the Corporation. As an evidence of his great and valuable service for the city and his ability as a leader of men it may be mentioned that after the death of Sir Pherozeshah Mehta the mantle of that noble and fearless tribune of the people may well be said to have fallen upon Sir Ibrahim's worthy shoulders, as far as the city Corporation was concerned.

AS PROVINCIAL LEGISLATOR (1899-1910.)

When he was President of the Corporation Sir Ibrahim was nominated a member of the Bombay Legislative Council in 1899, and his connection with that body as a nominated member continued till 1909. In this sphere of his work, as in his work as a city father, Sir Ibrahim received a great deal of encouragement from Sir Pherozeshah Mehta as he had received in his civic career from him and from that great leader of the Mahomedan community in Bombay, Mr. Abdulla Meherally Dharamsey.

The Indians' place in the constitution of those days was, as picturesquely described by Sir Pherozeshah, "generally to trot along the governmental triumphal car for such largess as might be generously thrown out." The few Indians who had been fortunate to get into the Councils found themselves lost in the array of officials. In such chilling atmosphere the Indians worked under many difficulties. The saying of Turgot, "the greatest geniuses are themselves drawn along by their age" proved true in the case of such stalwarts of the national cause as Sir Pherozeshah and Mr. Gokhale, who were Sir Ibrahim's co-workers in the Council. The power of initiating Bills being confined to Government members, the private member could only exercise his knowledge and experience simply as a critic. This Sir Ibrahim did to the full measure. As an accomplished sportsman he knew how to play within the rules of the game. Unlike others he mastered the rules of the legislature. His practical wisdom and wide knowledge and experience as a businessman and city father were given to the shaping of many a piece of legislation enacted in those days. There was hardly any Select Committee for the consideration of any important Bill, on which he was not invited to serve, but it was particularly in connection with legislation relating to local self-government and land revenue that his advice was frequently sought. He was no mere ornamental figurehead for the Committees he joined, for he studied every aspect of the problem he approached. Even legal problems gave way to his keen power of analysis.

FIGHT FOR COMMUNAL REPRESENTATION

The spread of education, the dramatic victory of Japan over a first class European Power like Russia, and last but not least, the reactionary regime of Lord Curzon gave rise to a tremendous upheaval of national feeling in India in 1906. With a view to quieten the unrest, Lord Minto, the Viceroy, with the approval of Lord Morley, the Secretary of State, set about to introduce reforms in the Government of India and in the Provincial Governments. During the discussion stages of those reforms the principle of election to the councils, which had till then been disguised as recommendations, was formally accepted by the authorities; and this raised the question of the form of constituencies. The question of communal representation thus became a live issue. It was easy enough to argue against communal representation on doctrinaire grounds, but it was not so easy to quieten the fears of a community who imagined that their interests would not be safe under joint electorates. When such fears were openly expressed by the Mahomedan community, the path of wisdom and discretion should have led the Hindu leaders gracefully to compromise with their Mahomedan brothers and take the wind from the sail of official spokesmen as the friends of minorities in India. In connection with this controversy Sir Ibrahim championed the cause of communal representation for Mahomedans. To him, however, it was not a question of Hindu *versus* Mahomedan, but a principle involving national uplift. Under the stress of competition it was feared that the backward community of Mahomedans might sink still further into ignorance and inaction weakening the strength of the nation as a whole. He appealed to the Hindu leaders that they should themselves yield this concession to Mahomedans in the interest of creating a united demand for constitutional advance; and he pointed out to them the folly of dividing on a minor issue like this when the interests of the nation as a whole were in jeopardy. In May 1908 he went to England for reasons of health; and while there he exerted a great deal to get the principle of communal representation for Mahomedans recognised by the authorities. He returned to India in October of the same year and undeterred by opposition threw all his weight and popularity in furtherance of the same cause. When Muslim agitation in this respect proved effective and Government declared it to be their policy to give respresentation to Mahomedans in excess of their numerical strength, the extreme section of Mahomedans claimed that this policy should be carried out by the reservation of all seats for Mahomedans in separate electorates, thus dividing the two communities into water-tight compartments. Sir Ibrahim realised the undesirability of such a division, and when he was invited as a representative Mahomedan to meet the Council Committee at Simla, he advocated as an alternative that the Mahomedans while having a minimum number of seats based on their numerical strength by separate electorates, should participate in elections by mixed electorates and take their chance of securing such additional seats as they may be able to win as candidates in constituencies which were largely composed of non-Moslems. This view which met the Hindu objection to water-tight compartments ultimately prevailed with the Government of India and the Morley-Minto Reforms were based on this principle.

IN MORLEY-MINTO COUNCILS (1910-1916)

With the advent of the Morley-Minto Reforms he widened his activities to take full advantage of the added privileges. As the principle of direct election was recognised under the Reforms he at once sought for, and obtained, the suffrage of his community. He was the first, at any rate in the Bombay Council, to use the right of introducing private Bills. His Bill for the registration of charities, introduced in 1910, was no wild cat measure. It required that every trustee possessed of property in trust for a charitable purpose should register it with the Registrar of Charitable Trusts, together with a statement of the conditions in which the trust was held, and also file with him an annual audited statement of the sums of money received and expended and the matters in respect of which such receipts and expenditure took place. This register of trusts and the file of audited accounts were to be open to the inspection of any person on payment of a fee of one rupee. Sir Ibrahim argued that one of the most potent causes of maladministration of charitable endowments was the serious difficulties which the ordinary law placed in the way of bringing the trustees to account: the trouble, worry and expense of a prolonged litigation were more than enough to discourage people ftom instituting a suit. A regular annual submission of audited accounts would be an effective check on such malpractices that existed and would stir up to an efficient discharge of their duties those trustees who through indifference or carelessness allowed the charities to remain dormant. In order to escape from the cry of 'religion in danger' he shrewdly excluded religious charities even preferring to incur the criticism of friends of the measure that it was only partial. The Bill was supported by the Government of Bombay, a very large majority of the officers consulted by them, the Chief Justice of the Bombay High Court, the Press, both English and vernacular, and the general public. Lord Sydenham, the then Governor, gave wholehearted support to it. It passed the first reading in the local Council and was referred to a Select Committee. As the Government of India were contemplating an all-India enactment, they advised the postponement of the local Bill. The War and the Government of India's vacillation dragged on the measure for full five years, and when he felt that the delay was unreasonable, Sir Ibrahim gave notice of his determination to press the Bill, through the local Council.

The ultimate fate of this Bill did not reflect much credit on the Government of India's regard for the intentions of Parliament. The Indian Councils Act of 1861 had conceded to Provincial Governments full powers of legislation, except those which were expressly barred under Section 45 of that Act. In spite of this Act of Parliament, the Government of India claimed that they had the right under the Parliamentary Act of 1833 to issue instructions to local Governments requiring them to oppose any measure introduced in a Provincial legislature irrespective of their own convictions. Though the exercise of such powers could not affect the legislature, the Government of India issued instructions to the Bombay Government to oppose the Bill if it was placed before the Council. When Sir Ibrahim was made aware of this, he had to drop his Bill, as under the then constitution, it was impossible to get a majority against Government opposition.

The principles of his measure have, however, now found enactment in a wider measure, the Muhammadan Waqf Act of 1923, covering even religious charities, piloted through the Legislative Assembly by Mr. Abul Kasem of Dacca; and Sir Hari Singh Gour has already introduced in the Assembly a similar measure covering the charities of communities other than Muhammadan.

The question of Haj pilgrims had come to the fore in 1896, when plague broke out in India; and in order to prevent the infection spreading to the continent of Europe through the Red Sea by means of the pilgrims to Mecca, the Government of India at the bidding of the authorities in England, adopted various measures of restriction on the embarkation of pilgrims from India, the most harassing of which was detention of the pilgrims for a number of days in a quarantine. As these restrictions were beyond all requirements of the case and were a great hardship on the pilgrims, Sir Ibrahim took a leading part in the agitation for their removal, and his advocacy of the cause brought about the abolition of quarantine detention.

AS A NATIONAL LEADER

By slow and steady work Sir Ibrahim established a reputation as a clear thinker with a firm grasp on practicalities. All classes of people in that mosaic of communities, Bombay, came to recognise him as an indispensable figure alike in the Corporation and the Legislative Council. Nor did the Government place less reliance than the people of his Province in his judgment, and they conferred on him the title of C. I. E. in 1907 and in 1911 he was knighted.

Engaged as he was in the busy commercial and civic life of Bombay, all his political propaganda was done quietly and unostentatiously. Whenever possible he used to attend the sessions of the Moslem League, the Congress, the Industrial Conference, the Moslem

Educational Conference and kindred gatherings. At political meetings in the city of Bombay itself he always took an active part. Even as early as 1904 when the Congress met at Bombay he was elected to a Committee of that body to consider its constitution. All through the stormy period of 1907-10, when the bulk of the Mahomedans held aloof from the Indian National Congress, Sir Ibrahim lent his support equally to the League and the Congress. In 1911, during the Congress week at Allahabad, under the advice of Sir William Wedderburn and His Highness the Aga Khan, a representative conference of Hindus and Mahomedans was held to consider measures calculated to bring about a complete understanding between the two communities on all subjects. A small Committee was appointed, of which Sir Ibrahim was a member, as a result of this conference, but it did not advance matters. Meanwhile, events in India and abroad helped to bring vividly to the mind of the Mahomedan community the necessity of effectively organizing themselves for their future advancement. In March 1913 at their Lucknow sessions, the Moslem League adopted the ideal of Self-Government for India, and made the first approach towards an *entente* with the Congress. This was due to the patriotic efforts of the progressive section of the Mahomedans headed by his Highness the Aga Khan. Then differences arose between the active workers of the parent League in India, represented by Messrs. Mahomed Ali and Wazir Hassan, and the branch League in England, for which Mr. Ameer Ali claimed independence. The fight was the eternal one between progress and stagnation. In Sir Ibrahim was found a safe mediator, and he was elected President of the Moslem League sessions at Agra in December 1913.

The address he delivered created a sensation at the time. It was held that it could have equally well been delivered from the presidential chair of the Indian National Congress. The TIMES OF INDIA, described it as a "breath of inspired commonsense in a somewhat highly charged atmosphere"; the LEADER of Allahabad opined that it well sustained his reputation for ability and independence; the BOMBAY CHRONICLE wrote that he spoke "with sobriety and wisdom, evincing a grasp of his subjects that reflected the highest credit on his sagacity, public spirit and patriotism."

Nothing hesitating or halting he commented freely on many things in a broad survey of the entire political situation. He devoted a considerable part of his address to a discussion of the Balkan War and the foreign policy of Great Britain and its effect upon Indian Mussalmans. He turned to the Cawnpore Mosque affair and recommended for the future "extreme caution in the matter of firing upon mobs when breach of the peace was apprehended," and urged the adoption of a definite policy by Government of appointing an independent commission of enquiry, including an Indian element, into every act of firing, in order to provide a wholesome restraining influence upon the official charged with the responsibility of taking life, and at the same time to create confidence in the public that careful and independent enquiry would be made after exercise of such power by the official. With straightness and force he declared his political faith :

> I think we should not be true to our Motherland, if we did not strive to attain a high standard of progress on democratic lines. I am one of those dreamers who firmly believe that given a sufficiently long spell of British rule in India, we are bound to become united as a nation in the real sense of the term. When that time arrives (as it is sure to do) we shall have qualified to rule the country ourselves and Self-Government will be absolutely assured to us . . . I have called myself a dreamer, and you are welcome to regard me as such if you like, but this I tell you, that I have profound faith in the realization of my dream and it depends upon you to exert yourselves to fulfil the destiny which is inevitably yours. No country such as India can remain for ever under foreign rule, however beneficent that rule may be, and though British rule is based on beneficence and righteousness, it cannot last for ever.

He discouraged all signs of disunion and preached advance as if under military discipline on lines settled after free discussion. "India," he said, "is our motherland, our proud heritage, and must in the end be handed over to us by our guardians......The Hindu and the Mahomedan are two brothers, sons of the same Mother Hind and in a state of minority." He made a spirited, eloquent and far-sighted appeal for Hindu-Moslem unity, in the following brilliant passage :

> Every one must recognise that no form of Self-Government is possible in India unless the two principal communities, the Hindu and the Moslem, are closely and conscientiously united. What can be a nobler aim, a loftier goal, than to endeavour to secure India united ? Once we become genuinely united there

is no force in the world which can keep us from our heritage; without such union the Indians will have to wait indefinitely for the realisation of their fondest hopes. Instead of having differences and dissensions amongst ourselves at the present time on matters of remote realisation, I would earnestly appeal to all true sons of India to concentrate all their energies, all their talents, on the consummation of ensuring a united India. Then we might leave the future to take care of itself, full of hope and full of confidence. If the sister communities devote their energies and concentrate their efforts on the realisation of such an ideal in a spirit of reasoned compromise, all our difficulties will crumble away and India will rise phoenix-like from the ashes of discord and struggle to a fresh and robust life full of promise and full of hope.

IN THE IMPERIAL LEGISLATIVE COUNCIL (1913-18).

At the close of 1912, Sir Ibrahim sought election to the Imperial Legislative Council. Strong in his popularity with all communities, he decided to seek the suffrage of the non-official members of the Bombay Legislative Council, who had the right to send two representatives to the Imperial Council. There were three candidates in the field, Mr. Gokhale, Sir Ibrahim Rahimtoola and Sir Vithaldas Thakersay. The final voting was a cause of general surprise. It was expected that Mr. Gokhale and Sir Vithaldas Thakersay would get the seats, with Sir Ibrahim a strong runner-up. But Sir Ibrahim headed the poll with Mr. Gokhale a strong second and Sir Vithaldas Thakersay a strong runner-up. He was elected for the second time by the same constituency to the Imperial Council in 1916.

In the Imperial Legislative Council, between 1913 and 1918, for a period of five years he did valuable work of immense good to the country at large. His wide knowledge of commercial life in

Bombay and his thorough study of Indian finance and currency helped him to play the part of critic during the Budget time. In his criticism of the Budget he always took the popular view. During his first Budget speech he attacked the idea that a large surplus in the Budget was any indication of the country's prosperity. "Indian Empire Trading Company," he said, "may congratulate itself on such a position, but not a Government." The railways in those days were paying the Government of India a huge revenue. He maintained that in addition to providing large sums of money as was being done for extension of railways in the country, a portion at all events of that large revenue should be earmarked for encouraging inter-territorial trade in India itself, by reducing the rates for carrying goods manufactured in one part of India to another; and he pointed out that the policy of railway companies of charging specially low rates for long distances from ports were helping imported goods to the detriment of indigenous manufactures. He advocated the early establishment of a gold currency. During the subsequent Budget sessions he stressed the need for financial autonomy for the Provinces, subject to a fixed contribution by them to the Imperial Government (a system similar to the one adopted under the Reforms of 1919); urged the grant of fiscal autonomy for India and advocated the policy of industrial development. He opposed the policy of constructing railways out of revenue surpluses and railway profits as against canons of sound finance as they were tantamount to indirect taxation.

When the Indian Companies Act was on the anvil in 1914, he sought to protect the ignorant shareholders by moving an amendment to provide that the majority of Directors of a Joint Stock Company should be persons who were not members or employees of the firms of managing agents, but unfortunately the amendment was lost. Those who are familiar with recent manipulations in the Bombay share market can well understand the force of Sir Ibrahim's remarks then: "if they (members or employees of the firm of managing agents) obtain control as directors they will manipulate the market with the knowledge they obtain of the daily working of the company."

He also made effective contributions to the debate on the Bank failures, and always ranged himself with the popular party in the course of the discussion of the Press Act and the Defence of India Criminal Law Amendment Bills.

His most enduring work in the Imperial legislature is, however, in the sphere of India's commercial and industrial progress. It was due largely to his efforts, at any rate it was on his initiative, that the three important Commissions which have helped to shape the India Government's policy in regard to industries, railways and tariff, were appointed. The Industrial Commission, the Railway Committee and the Fiscal Commission resulted from the strenuous efforts he had made in the direction of industrial progress and fiscal autonomy. A resolution which he had sent in in 1913 that the power vesting in Parliament in fiscal matters should be transferred to the Government of India was disallowed. In March 1914, he moved a resolution recommending to the Governor-General-in-Council to consider the desirability of the policy in regard to State railways being one of management by Government instead of by Companies. Sir William Clark, the then Commerce Member, accepted the resolution on behalf of the Government, and the appointment of the Indian Railway Committee was announced by the Secretary of State in Parliament on the 1st November 1920. This Committee was equally divided in its opinion as regards the policy of direct State management, but the chairman, Sir William Acworth, was one of those who recommended it. It is on the basis of this Report that the Government of India have now finally decided to take over under their direct control the lines now managed by the G. I. P. Ry. and the E. I. Ry. companies.

Ever since his election to the Imperial Legislative Council he had been attempting to move a resolution recommending effective measures for the industrial development of India. At last in 1916 he succeeded in moving the following resolution :

This Council recommends to the Governor-General-in-Council to be pleased to appoint a Committee of officials and non-officials to consider and report what measures should be adopted for the growth and development of industries in India.

He put fiscal autonomy for India in the forefront of his demands; then tariff protection, grant of bounties and subsidies; State guarantee of certain rates of interest on capital invested in private industries and provision of special expert staff to carry on research work and to institute detailed enquiries into the possibilities of successfully initiating and establishing new industries in India and supply expert advice for the development of existing industries. He suggested that Government should consider what means should be employed for securing a sufficient supply of skilled labour; what special railway facilities in the matter of rates and otherwise were needed; and whether any special measures were necessary to attract capital and secure banking facilities. He quoted the opinion of the London Chamber of Commerce—the foremost commercial body of free-trade England—that "the strength of the nation lies in our power to produce our requirements from our own soil and our own factories". He emphasized:

> India cannot always remain an open market for the manufactures of other countries. She earnestly desires to gradually reach a position of one of the foremost manufacturing countries in the world, a position which her resources make it easily possible to attain............India will not be satisfied with the position of a trusted dependant, but claims the rights and privileges of equal status in the Imperial partnership............India has her own economic needs and requirements as much as the Dominions and she claims perfect freedom to pursue such fiscal policy as may in the opinion of her Government and her people be best suited to her conditions.

Sir William Clark, the then Commerce Member, in accepting the resolution announced that Government were taking steps to appoint a Commission, but that the question of fiscal autonomy and tariff protection would not come under the terms of reference of the Commission, as the constitutional issue of fiscal autonomy for India was a topic outside the Government of India's purview, and one on which they were not entitled to express an opinion, while the question of protection in India was not one that could be considered during the War and apart from the determination of the fiscal relations of the Empire within herself and with the outer world, which at that time it was intended to deal with as a whole after the War. This was like asking the Commission to play Hamlet with the Prince of Denmark left out. Most of the points made in Sir Ibrahim's speech have been accepted by the Indian Industrial Commission.

In 1918, when the late Mr. Montagu and Lord Chelmsford were touring India with a view to formulate their proposals for carrying out the promise given in Parliament of gradual development of Responsible Government in India, he struck a new note and presented them a memorandum urging the grant of fiscal autonomy for India and the application of a policy of protection for the development of her industries. The argument he put forward was novel: with the efflux of time, India's military and naval requirements would increase, but with a policy of free trade there was no possibility of improving the national wealth of India so as to enable her to provide the additional revenue that would be required. He wrote:

> There are many causes which have led to the present poverty of India. In my opinion one of the principal causes is the policy of free trade which has been imposed upon India by England. . . . . . India produces from her soil a super-abundant supply of raw materials of various kinds and has an enormous demand for manufactured goods. Its natural advantages for development into a manufacturing country are great. It ought not to be difficult with the unrestricted powers of the Government to organize means to bring about the industrial development of India which will result not only in supplying to a large extent her own requirements, but also enable her to export her manufactured goods to other countries. For this purpose full fiscal autonomy is necessary. . . . . The effect of such measures will not only be to provide increased revenue from the Customs, but with the growth and development of industries, as a result of scientific tariffs and Government assistance, the country will grow rapidly prosperous and the tax-bearing capacity of the people, which has been over-reached by War taxation, will provide ample margin for securing additional revenue for the many purposes of the State.

PRESIDENT OF THE INDIAN FISCAL COMMISSION.

By a despatch dated the 30th June 1921, the Secretary of State intimated to the Government of India that His Majesty's Government accepted the principle recommended by the Joint Select Committee on the Government of India Bill that the Secretary of State should as far as possible avoid interference in India's fiscal policy when the Government of India and its legislature were in agreement, and that any such interference should be restricted to safeguarding the international obligations of the Empire or any fiscal arrangements within the Empire to which His Majesty's Government were a party. A Commission, called the Indian Fiscal Commission, was accordingly constituted and its personnel, with Sir Ibrahim as the

President, was announced on the 7th October 1921. The Commission submitted its Report on the 6th July 1922 subject to a dissenting minute by a minority of five, including the Chairman (Sir Ibrahim). It may be mentioned here that a definite attempt was made by the Commission to bring in an unanimous Report, but without success. While agreement was reached on all points where it was possible to do so, differences arose between free traders converted to protection under necessity and protectionists who believed in their creed. The reasons which led the minority to write a dissenting minute are summarised by them thus:

(a) The main recommendation has been hedged in by conditions and provisos which are calculated to impair its utility.

(b) In places, the language employed is half-hearted and apologetic.

(c) We are unable to agree with the views of our colleagues on Excise, Foreign Capital, Imperial Preference and the Constitution of the Tariff Board.

It is impossible in such a short sketch as this to summarise the recommendations of the Commission, but a few extracts from the dissenting minute might usefully be quoted as showing the main lines of difference:—

We are unanimous in recommending that a policy of protection should be adopted. Our disagreement arises from the fact that the policy of protection recommended by our colleagues is qualified by the words "to be applied with discrimination along the lines of the Report." We do not know of any other country in the world, including the British Dominions, which have so qualified the policy of protection. While it is perfectly relevant for the Commission to indicate the lines on which protection may be worked in the initial stages, the recommendation of the policy should be clear and unequivocal. While our colleagues recommend "a policy of protection to be applied with discrimination along the lines of the Report" our recommendation is that a "policy of protection" should be adopted in the best interests of India. This policy has not only the unanimous support of the people of India, but is on the same lines as it prevails in all other protectionist countries of the world.

While we agree that the policy of protection should be applied with discrimination, we do not think that any qualifications or limitations should be made a condition precedent to its adoption. We recognise that in the efforts to attain a prominent position in the industrial world, India will have to pay a price. The economic well-being of India which we aim at in the tariff policy which we recommend cannot be obtained without making a sacrifice. It is for this reason that we agree that the policy should be applied with discrimination. The discrimination with which we agree is intended to minimise such sacrifice as far as possible consistently with reaching the goal which we are putting before the country. We do not subscribe to the condition that such discrimination should be "along the lines of the Report." The conditions laid down in the majority Report appear to us to be stringent, and will entail considerable delay in giving effect to the policy which we have unanimously recommended and will not produce adequate results. We share the concern shown in the Report for the interests of the consumers, and we agree that the policy should be applied in such a manner as to reduce the burden on the consumer to the minimum necessary for the purpose of carrying out the object in view. In the present economic condition of India, limitations in the interest of the consumers are necessary, but we anticipate that if immediate effect is given to the policy we recommend, India will begin to grow economically prosperous within a reasonable period of time. It is therefore necessary to make it clear that while the policy of protection should endure till the goal is reached, discrimination must vary according to the circumstances for the time being and should not be applied rigidly along the lines indicated in the Report. We may point out that while we want India to rise to a commanding position in the matter of her industrial development under the policy of protection, our colleagues anticipate as a result of the qualified policy which they recommend that "India for many years to come is likely to concentrate on the simpler forms of manufactured goods." A policy which is likely only to lead to this result for many years to come is not and cannot be acceptable to the people of India. In all protectionist countries, the Government and the Legislature as representing the people regulate the application of the policy of protection in a manner most suitable to local conditions and circumstances,

and there appears to us no reason why the discretion of the Government of India and the Indian Legislature should be fettered in any way. The records of the Provincial and Central Legislatures conclusively show that non-official members have vied with one another in pressing on the attention of Government the interests of the masses. We can, therefore, confidently leave the interests of the consumers in the hands of the non-official members of the Indian legislature who are representative of large and varied interests. We would, therefore, recommend that the application of the policy of protection should be regulated from time to time by such discrimination as may be considered necessary by the Government of India and the Indian legislature.

In consequence of the recommendations of the Commission, the Government of India announced in the Legislative Assembly in February 1923 their acceptance in principle of the proposition that "the fiscal policy of the Government of India may legitimately be directed towards fostering the development of industries in India." The first fruit of this policy has been the Indian Steel Protection Act of 1924 which was intended to save the infant steel industry of India from annihilation by powerful competitors abroad.

The Legislative Assembly has recently shown unmistakably that as regards the question of cotton excise and foreign capital, it is the minority view that it favours. Thus the representatives of the country in the Imperial Legislature have accepted the principles recommended by Sir Ibrahim and his colleagues of the dissenting minority of the Fiscal Commission.

AS AN ADMINISTRATOR (1918-23)

When in the beginning of 1918, Sir Mahadev Chaubal retired from his Membership of the Government of Bombay, the choice fell on Sir Ibrahim to fill that vacancy. This choice was as much a tribute to Sir Ibrahim's eminence in public life and reputation for statesmanship as it was evidence of Lord Willingdon's (the then Governor) capacity for discernment of men and things. When giving an account of his five years' stewardship to the Legislative Council in March 1923, Sir Ibrahim revealed the secret feeling that had animated him throughout his career in this exalted office:

> Honourable members are aware that it was under the Minto-Morley Reforms that Indians were admitted for the first time into the executive government of the Provinces and of the Imperial Government. In those days there appeared to be a feeling that these posts should not be open to men in political and public life; but that they should be reserved for men who may have done conspicuous service in other directions. When I was invited by His Excellency Lord Willingdon to be a Member of his Council, a new precedent was created, and for the first time in this Presidency a man in public and political life was invited to be associated in the inner circles of the administration. I could only look upon it as an experiment and felt that it was a call upon me to justify the selection in the interest of the large class of public workers to which I belonged............A distinction has sometimes been made between service of the public and public service. I have now had an opportunity of serving in both these capacities. I have been in the service of the public since the time I joined the Bombay Municipal Corporation in 1892, and I have now had the privilege of being in public service for the last five years; and I can tell you this, that so far as I am concerned there has been no distinction between the two positions which I have occupied. I have always felt that I am a servant of the public. Whether I am on the non-official benches or on the official benches, I have tried my humble best to be a true servant of my country.

The thick screen of official secrecy prevents a full view of Sir Ibrahim's work in the inner chambers of Government. But the following is the tribute paid to him by the then Governor Sir George Lloyd during the course of an address to the Legislative Council in February 1923.

> My honourable colleague is now the only Member of my Council who was in office when I took charge of the administration, and throughout the difficult years that have followed, both I and my Government have constantly profited from his quick intellect, his ripe experience of public life, and the knowledge he has gained of public feeling at moments of difficulty. This Council will lose a leader of unusual ability and of conspicuous power of debate. All these qualities, so conspicuously possessed by my honourable colleague, will make him indeed difficult to replace, and in the deliberations both of this House and of my Executive Council their loss will be most seriously felt.

It is impossible to say whether it was fortunate or unfortunate for India that Sir Ibrahim's advice as a non-official was lost to the nation during the troublous days of the Non-Co-operation movement; but there can be no doubt that his compromising genius must have provided means to the Government of Bombay to deal with the problems in a spirit of statesmanship without any recourse to repressive measures.

As an administrator he initiated policies and directed and controlled their operations, A Civilian who was closely associated with him during his period of office wrote to him after he (Sir Ibrahim) retired:

> I feel that I have lost a friend as well as a guide and I shall miss you in a great many ways......I hope I shall hereafter be able to put into practice the lessons in practical wisdom that you have taught me.

Before the introduction of the Reforms of 1919 he held charge of the portfolios of education and local self-government. In the sphere of local self-government he gave extensive powers of election to municipalities and local boards and introduced that piece of beneficent legislation, the Village Panchayats Act of 1920. The principal features of the measure are but a partial evidence of Sir Ibrahim's faith in popular wisdom. It is essentially democratic in its nature. Under the Act adult male suffrage was introduced in the villages for the first time in the history of British rule in India: the panchayats were wholly elected, except for the village *patil* who became a member by virtue of his office: and for the first time, the control of local bodies was transferred from the revenue officers of Government to district local boards.

We have seen how Sir Ibrahim raised the standard of free and compulsory education in the Bombay Legislative Council so early as 1901. During his term as Member of Council he had the pleasure of seeing two Bills regarding free and compulsory primary education getting embodied into law. Before he became Member of Government, Mr. V. J. Patel had piloted through the Council a Bill to authorise municipalities (not Bombay City) to make primary education compulsory in their areas, the additional expenditure incurred by the municipalities being equally shared between them and Government and in deserving cases Government being free to give more. Within a year of his becoming Member Sir Ibrahim introduced the Bombay City Primary Education Bill, which enabled the municipality of Bombay city to apply free and compulsory education both for boys and girls, throughout the city, or in any of its parts or sections, Government agreeing to contribute half the additional expenditure which the municipality might incur over and above what they were spending in 1918. The second Bill was the one introduced in the Council by the Minister Dr. Paranjpye, which provided for the application of compulsion throughout the Presidency.

As an administrator he put into practice the principles he had preached as a non-official. The new system of auctioning liquor shops introduced in 1917 had added materially to the resources of the Government. Sir Ibrahim took advantage of this condition of the finances and mapped out a programme of expansion of primary education and vigorously pursued it until he handed over charge of the portfolio to the elected Minister in 1921. Within a few months of his assuming charge of office in 1918, he accepted a resolution moved by the Honourable Mr. Upasani urging the Government to take steps to open as far as possible one primary school at least in every village with a population of 1,000 and over.

By March of 1919, the policy was settled by Government as a whole that there should be as far as possible at least one primary school in every village which had a sufficient number of children of school-going age to fill it. It is common knowledge now how well he prosecuted this policy. Within three years of his administration, at the end of which he handed over charge of the Education portfolio to the elected

Minister, he had converted a budget of Rs 1,06,00,000 for education into a budget of Rs. 1,82,00,000. While pursuing the cause of primary education he realised the equal necessity of promoting secondary, higher, collegiate and technical education, and expansion under these heads was also pushed forward with vigour.

After the introduction of the Reforms when Education and Local Self-Government were made Transferred Subjects, Sir Ibrahim was entrusted with the Revenue portfolio. The administration of this subject is, as is well-known, full of technical difficulties, but Sir Ibrahim proved equal to the task.

As senior Member of Council he was for two years Leader of the Bombay Legislative Council. On the 15th March 1923, a day or two before his final relinquishment of office, the Bombay Legislative Council passed the following resolution:

> This Council places on record its expression of deep regret at the great loss it has sustained by the retirement of the Honourable Sir Ibrahim Rahimtoola, Kt., C. I. E., owing to the expiry of his term of office as a Member of the Government of Bombay, of the sense of high appreciation of the valuable services he has rendered and the conspicuous ability with which he has discharged his duties as a member of this Council, as the Leader of the House and as an Executive Council Member of the Government of Bombay.

All sections of the House, Indian and European, official and non-official, Hindu, Mahomedan, Parsi and Christian, vied one with another in paying their tribute of praise to Sir Ibrahim's abilities. The whole Council then entertained him to a dinner. To mark their appreciation of his services the Government conferred on him the title of K.C.S.I. in June 1923.

AS PRESIDENT OF THE LEGISLATIVE COUNCIL

It was Sir Ibrahim's intention to seek election to the Legislative Assembly after his retirement. But suddenly in May 1923, two months after his retirement from the Executive Council, came the sad news of the demise of Sir Narayan Chandavarkar, the nominated President of the Bombay Legislative Council. At the earnest request of Sir George Lloyd, the then Governor, Sir Ibrahim accepted the Presidentship of the Legislative Council. In October 1924 the Legislative Council expressed their appreciation of his able stewardship by passing the following resolution:

> This Council records its warm appreciation of the able discharge of the arduous duties by the Honourable Sir Ibrahim Rahimtoola, K. C. S. I, C. I. E., of the office of nominated President of the Bombay Legislative Council which he held for over a year and a quarter and during which time he won the esteem and respect of both—the official and non-official—sides of this House by his fairness, patience and reasonableness and guided its deliberations with a view to the growth of the Legislature on responsible and democratic lines.

Members of all parties bore testimony to his judicious impartiality and fair-mindedness. The resolution was moved by Mr. A. N. Surve, the leader of the non-Brahmin party. Mr. M. R. Jayakar, the leader of the Swaraj party, also paid a glowing tribute to him.

The Honourable Sir Maurice Hayward, the Leader of the House, said:—

> "I do not think it is necessary for me, Sir, to enlarge on what has been so well and fully expressed by other honourable members, but I do think that we are fortunate in having secured

the services of one endowed with so much courtesy, tact and with such wide experience of men and things......But we do recognise even though we do not share the heavy duties of having to sit here all the time like the President, we do however realize and recognise to the full the great patience which our President has exhibited and the impartiality and the independence which are so necessary for the position of the President.

Sir Ibrahim's term of office as nominated President terminated on the 18th of February 1925. In response to an unanimous desire prevalent among all sections of the Legislative Council, Sir Ibrahim was nominated by His Excellency the Governor as a non-official member of the Council with a view to his eventual election as its President. It is a tribute alike to his commanding personality and his universal popularity that when the nominations were announced on the 19th February not a single rival candidate was nominated by any member of the House. And to-day Sir Ibrahim fills the honoured position of the first elected President of the Bombay Legislative Council.

P. 337

SAHIBZADA AFTAB AHMAD KHAN

Sahibzada Aftab Ahmad Khan.

SAHIBZADA Aftab Ahmad Khan was born in May, 1867 in Kunjpura, District Karnal. He comes of the very respectable family of the Nawab of Kunpusa an account of which is given in the famous book of Colonel Massey entitled "Families of Note." Sahibzada's father, the late Nawab Gholam Ahmad Khan, was a great enlightened Mussalman and at a time when the teaching of English was condemned as heretical by a coterie of disgruntled Moulvis he had the courage and the vision to send his son to Aligarh. In 1878 Sahibzada was admitted to the school and was one of the youngest boys of his class. During his very early childhood his precocious habits marked him out as a promising youth and soon rivetted the attention of no less a personality than the venerable founder of the institution himself who began to evince a paternal care in the activities of the young student.

CAREER IN ENGLAND

After prosecuting his studies successfully at Aligarh till 1891 Sahibzada went to England and joined the Cambridge University. His special subject was history, and specially the growth of the British Constitution; and he took his B. A. with honours in this subject. While at Cambridge, he contracted an abiding friendship with General Smuts of South African fame who was his class-fellow. Among his other class-fellows and contemporaries were Sir Hari Singh Gour, Mr. Abdullah Yusuf Ali and Mr. Aravindo Ghosh—General Smuts and Aravindo Ghosh—an ill-assorted crew indeed—men who have "ridden the whirlwind and directed the storm."

A GOOD SPORTS-MAN

Sahibzada during his academic life has been a keen sportsman, and he captained the football and the cricket team in his early college days. He rightly united in himself the two striking attributes of good intelligence and good physique. Possessed of a handsome face and a robust constitution he would win laurels in the field of sports; while, on the other hand, he would command the applause of his fellow-students by his eloquence in the Union. He was the first winner of the Harold Cox Speaking Prize which is the best coveted prize in Aligarh.

A SPLENDID SCHEME

The Duty Society of the Muslim University is an organisation which needs no introduction to the readers of this book. It has up to this time advanced more than 6 lakhs of rupees to poor and needy students, a large number of whom, it is gratifying to note, are now occupying responsible positions in the various walks of life. It must redound to the credit of this institution that it has afforded equality of opportunity to many a brilliant student who would have remained in comparative obscurity but for its help It is a matter of supreme satisfaction to Sahibzada to witness the efflorescence of this child of his creation. For, while still a student, he grandly conceived the idea of the Society and founded it. Its existence was kept as a secret from Sir Syed Ahmed Khan and when it had commenced its activities it came as a pleasant surprise to the great Founder.

THE INFLUENCE OF SIR SYED

Soon after his return from England Sahibzada Aftab Ahmad Khan settled at Aligarh at the suggestion of Sir Syed and began his practice at the local bar. Within a comparatively short time he secured a lucrative practice and by dint of sheer ability and perseverence held a distinguished position in his profession. But his real interest lay elsewhere. Quite a young man, Mr. Aftab Ahmad Khan fell under the influence of Sir Syed whose personal magnetism was such that he attracted around him a number of workers, young and old, and imparted to them something of his own faith and spirit. Mr. Aftab Ahmad has times out of number publicly acknowledged the deep debt he owes to Sir Syed to whom he was especially attached by ties of high regard and the desire to learn. Mr. Aftab Ahmad Khan had the good fortune to be associated with him as a zealous learner, and being ardent, impressionable and receptive, he has been able to profit by the influence of that remarkable personality.

Sahibzada identified himself closely with the educational renaissance of the Mussalmans and within three years of his return from England he was elected a Trustee of the late M. A. O. College in 1897. He was also elected the Honorary Joint Secretary of the All-India Mohamedan Educational Conference from 1905-17. And it is an open secret that the real work of that stupendous and once live organisation was actively conducted by Mr. Aftab himself. In 1904 he was appointed Trustee-in-charge of the Building Department and the beautiful Mosque with its attractive domes and minarets, the Lytton Library, the Mumtaz House, the Union Club, the Minto Circle and, last but not the least, the Conference Office pay a mute tribute to his artistic taste and skill.

Mr. Aftab Ahmad Khan was also elected a member of the United Provinces Legislative Council during the pre-Reform days; and in that capacity he did much solid work for a greater dissemination of education among the Indians.

In 1898 the whole nation went into mourning on account of the death of that great Prince of Educationists, Sir Syed Ahmed Khan. The Muslim leaders of thought wanted to perpetuate his memory in a suitable manner; hence, they organised a Sir Syed Memorial Fund. Mr. Aftab was elected its Secretary and did yeoman service for the consummation of this scheme. He made an extensive tour of the country and achieved phenomenal success in his efforts. The College, during the life-time of the founder had fallen into heavy debt on account of the flagrant embezzlement of one of its employees. Mr. Aftab and his Committee thought that it was their first duty to wipe out this disgrace and with this end in view they utilized a major portion of their collections to clear away the arrears.

AT THE INDIA COUNCIL

Sahibzada was offered the membership of the India Council in 1917. He gave up his lucrative practice at the bar, and joined the India Council. While there, he did great service to his country by criticising some of the reactionary proposals of the Government. His fearless and independent advocacy of the Khilafat Problem was chiefly responsible in persuading the late Mr. Montagu to advocate its integrity. It is a well-known fact that Sahibzada's relentless and inexorable criticism of the Treaty of Sevres, and his strong note helped the cause of the Khilafat immensely in England.

He was subsequently appointed a member of the Lytton Committee where he helped greatly in the formulation of its report and its recommendations Sahibzada has dedicated himself to the cause of education and of Muslim education in particular. When he returned from the India Council, people thought he would resume his practice. He felt that his vocation lay elsewhere; he returned to his 'first and last love'—Education.

ALIGARH UNIVERSITY

Soon after his return from the India Council he was elected the Honorary Vice-Chancellor of the Muslim University, Aligarh, and his Herculean efforts to reorganise the institution on a sound basis have evoked widespread approbation from the members of his community and others. Indeed his work as the Vice-Chancellor of the Muslim University has already borne a remarkable result. He has once for all knocked on the head the party strife which had become an unpleasant aspect of higher Aligarh life. Sahibzada's next step has been to concentrate his energies on the creation of a healthy atmosphere at this place and in this connection he has taken upon himself the onerous duty of looking personally into all things, even things of a very trivial nature. This has naturally led to some misunderstanding. Sahibzada's volcanic energy and his vigilant attentions have, however, wrought a wonderful change in the working of the institution. The frigidity of his address and the seeming stiffness of his demeanour towards his subordinates has unfortunately conveyed a totally erroneous impression of his temperament. For, the clearest vindication of his character lies in his immense popularity with the students who find in him a true successor of Sir Syed. He is not too big for them, he mixes with them freely, inquires about their grievances, if there be any, and seriously tries to remedy them. In fact Sahibzada possesses a very tender heart and if he is at all stiff towards his subordinates it is due to a higher sense of duty, to the feeling that the interests and the integrity of the institution should be held high above all the petty amenities of social life.

PUBLIC PRONOUNCEMENTS

Sahibzada has been thrice called upon to make a public declaration of his educational creed, as the President of the Provincial Muslim Educational Conference, Bengal, held in Calcutta in 1911, the All-India Muhammadan Educational Conference held in Aligarh in 1923, and the Provincial Muhammadan Educational Conference, United Provinces held in Allahabad in 1925. All his addresses are marked by breadth of vision and boldness of statesmanship.

As a speaker Sahibzada is at his best when he thunders forth in his mother-tongue. Even at such an old age he possesses powerful lungs which many a young man might envy. He also possesses the cogent force of an advocate, with the glowing fervour of an orator.

A word as to the views of the Sahibzada on matters political and social. He has never been a member of the Congress; but notwithstanding this fact he is a staunch believer in its ideals and it is his firm faith that the regeneration of India can only be brought about by peaceful methods of constitutional evolution. His heart beats in unison with the creed of the advanced Liberals. In matters social Sahibzada is a conservative; still he does not want the continuance of the many effete superstitious practices prevalent in modern Muslim homes.

Mr. Aftab Ahmad has been, in his various speeches and addresses to the student community, exhorting them to cultivate a true spirit of self-sacrifice and he has been impressing upon them the necessity of a broader mental outlook and a broader vision. The solid foundations of liberty must rest upon individual character which is the only sure guarantee for social security and national progress. It is this energy of individual life and example acting throughout society which would constitute the best practical education of Indians. Education in action, conduct, self-control, it is these which tend perpetually to renovate mankind.

In one of such speeches delivered in Urdu he said:

> A healthy activity of individual freedom and yet a collective obedience to established authority, the unfettered energetic action of persons, together with the uniform subjection of all to the national code of duty, perseverance in purpose, faith in the Almighty, and a spirit of conduct, these should be our ideal.

ADULT EDUCATION

The problem of adult education has hardly been seriously tackled either by the politicians or the Government in India. It is a problem the solution of which rests on the right interpretation of the term 'education.'

The demand for a greater increase in technical training and a drastic improvement in the method of imparting it is a welcome sign. To make a man a real master of his craft is to go a long way towards educating him. When he is conscious of his ability to make a worthy contribution to the business or industry in which he is engaged, his fine ambitions are awakened, and his social instincts, making for the service of the country are developed. Technical education may be an instrument of this liberal culture. Vocational education may be, and ought to be, a noble and inspiring process. A man who works in wood or metal may find kinship within the world if he learns whence and how his material comes to him, what is the history of his craft; only the secret of beauty lies in the perfect fashioning of the humblest piece of work with a view to its complete fitness for its destined use, and how his own task touches and affects that of many other people in widely different spheres. The addition of such knowledge to a scientific training in the use of his materials and the handling of his tools will make him a valuable member of society and not merely an indispensable unit of production.

Some one has rightly said that the essence of democracy being not passive but active participation by all in citizenship, education in a democratic country must aim at fitting each individual progressively not only for his personal, domestic, and vocational duties, but, above all, for those duties of citizenship for which these earlier stages are the training ground. It is higher mental training which will bring born leaders to the front. It raises the standards of those whom it moulds. It solves automatically some of the acute social problems. 'Knowledge comes, but wisdom lingers' if practical judgment and matured common sense are not developed and exercised. Referring to this problem of adult education in India Sahibzada Aftab Ahmad Khan remarked:—

Gentlemen, the importance and application of the principles underlying this movement to the needs and circumstances of India must be obvious to all of you. With only six or seven per cent. of literates how long are we to wait for the product of our schools and colleges to uplift the people as a whole? At this rate not only generations but centuries would be necessary for spreading education and enlightenment throughout the people, of the kind and on the scale such as are becoming common in Europe, if we are to depend upon our existing schools and colleges alone. In no country, therefore, is there such an imperative need for adult education as it is in India. Please remember that mere compulsory primary education, even if it can be provided in all parts of the country, will not wholly serve the purpose, as the object of adult education is not only to give elementary education but to equip individual members with the necessary qualifications of citizenship. The real question is: how to do it?

In England the lead was taken by the Universities, and now the work is carried on by voluntary associations. This is one of those questions in the examination and solution of which all creeds and communities in India may usefully join. There are Hindu, Muslim, Christian, Sikh, Parsi and other communal organisations carrying on their respective educational propaganda and programmes but is it not time for all of them to combine and co-operate in the consideration of those aspects of this problem which are common to all of them? Various departments of Government have been in charge of your education in all its branches, for generations, and the Missionary organisations have been doing most useful educational work in all parts of India, for more than a century. There are Hindu, Sikh and other conferences and associations which have been serving the cause of their education for a long time. This Conference has been promoting the cause of Muslim education now for nearly forty years. All of these have acquired experience and possess useful knowledge about the real condition and requirements of the various communities which form the Indian people. Do not the common interests of the country demand that, so far as is possible and practicable, all such efforts and activities be co-ordinated, so that the fruits and lessons of the past experience gained by all may be available for the people as a whole. Such co-operation can also prove to be of immense use in the consideration and elucidation of the question as to how education can be made to help the cause of national unity, for education is a force which can be exploited both for Uni n and disunion. Education is now a transferred subject and therefore both the official and non-official agencies may now freely combine to make the best use of this great national asset. I hope and trust that this suggestion will receive the consideration it deserves."

HINDU-MUSLIM UNITY

Sahibzada is a warm advocate of Hindu-Muslim Unity. He never lets slip an opportunity of impressing the vital necessity of this *entente cordiale* between the Hindus and Mussalmans which in his opinion is sure to foster a true and lasting spirit of nationalism. Referring to this problem of Hindu-Muslim Unity Sahibzada says:

I have always been a sincere advocate of Hindu-Muslim Unity as it is essential for our best interest in this country. But this is not a thing which can be had for the asking. It needs conscious and honest efforts on the part of both the communities concerned. How are we to test the sincerity of either side? In my judgment the real test of a Muslim's sincerity lies in his making India the centre of all his worldly interests and aspirations, and in his exclusive devotion and loyalty to the cause of his motherland which, in effect, means co-operation with and support of the Hindu majority in all that is essential for the attainment of India's highest ideal. And the real test of a Hindu's sincerity is his genuine sympathy with and practical support of all that seeks to remove or reduce the cause of Muslim ignorance and poverty. In the best interests of our Motherland the cause of Muslim education and economic recovery should form an important item in the national programme of India. For, nothing will promote national unity and solidarity so much as the enlightment and prosperity of the backward portion of our people. I fully endorse the view expressed in the Calcutta University Commission Report that "In the new movement of the Muslim community towards higher education there lies the presage of an intellectual unity which would lessen, if it might not obliterate the breaches caused by ancient divisions and by deep differences in cultural traditions. A great equality in point of culture might strengthen the forces which make for harmony and co-operation between the two main sections of the Bengal population............"

FEMALE EDUCATION

The problem of female education is gaining ground day by day among the enlightened members of the Muslim community. But the heartless aping of Western manners has naturally created a revulsion of feeling towards enlarging the scope and field of this aspect of education. Sahibzada with the true instinct of a veteran sounds a tocsin of alarm and says:—

> While approving no arbitrary restriction upon the kind of knowledge or culture which our women should acquire I entirely agree with those which deprecate the assimilation or adoption, by our girls, of these artificial and explosive tastes, habits and ways which are the outcome of irrational imitation of European system of life.

RELIGIOUS AND SECULAR EDUCATION

Sahibzada in his various addresses and speeches has been laying special stress on the religious background of a thoroughly secular education but he feels none-the-less that the study of Western culture is essential for our future progress. Referring to this aspect of Muslim culture and theology in his presidential address to the 36th Session of the All-India Muhammadan Educational Conference held at Aligarh he remarked:

> This brings us, gentlemen, to the most important and vital aspect of the subject, as the controversy to which Sir Syed's scheme gave rise, and which agitated the community for about a generation in the latter part of the last century, involved the most fundamental issue upon the right determination and realisation of which depends the whole future of our community. After all the storm and stress to which I have referred, it would not have been necessary at this time of the day, to revert again to this subject now, but during the last few years events have occurred and reactionary forces have arisen which render it important to examine once more this crucial question. I am quite prepared to admit that

those who opposed Sir Syed's scheme were perfectly sincere in their defence of the old system which they regarded as the best for Muslim education. It may also be fairly said that both they and Sir Syed desired to produce true Muslims, but they materially differed in their conception of the type and characteristics of a true Muslim. It is obvious that the problem of Muslim education cannot be separated from Muslim Theology, and that the fundamental principles of Islam should constitute the foundation upon which our educational edifice should be raised. But Sir Syed did claim that it was his scheme which really fulfilled this condition.

Gentlemen, without going into the merits of this controversy let us try to understand the educational aspect of the position taken up by Sir Syed which, as I understand it, may be summed up as follows. He believed that whether we were Muslims, Christians, Hindus or of any other persuasions, our success and happiness in all branches of this life depended, apart from chance or accident, upon our spiritual, mental and moral, and physical equipment. * * * Under the system followed in the old institutions, the souls, minds, moral instincts and vital forces of the rising generations of the Mussalmans were deprived of all that was refreshing in the fruits and achievements of the phenomenal progress which mankind had made during the last three or four hundred years. As a result all the natural springs of spiritual, mental, moral and physical vigour had become clogged, choked, and dry, and, as an inevitable consequence, material power and prosperity also declined and disappeared............

Sir Syed felt it to be his duty to shake and rouse them from their fatal delusion, and wake them up to a sense of reality so as to bring them face to face with the actual hard facts of the situation which confronted the Mussalmans in India and elsewhere. He persistently urged that the system of education pursued by the Mussalmans during the last few centuries was largely responsible for their present condition, and consistently urged the absolute necessity and importance of modern sciences, arts, and literature which were practically banned under the old system.

The Mussalmans had been the torch-bearers of civilization in the West. One has only to look to the pages of Draper * to verify the correctness of this assertion. The achievement of the Mussalmans in the various branches of arts and sciences was a marvel to

* Draper—Intellectual Development of Europe.

an intolerent Europe immersed in darkness. Discussing this question in the course of his address the Sahibzada said:

Gentlemen, it is not only material wealth that we let foreigners to exploit, but we have also lost most of the intellectual heritage which had been left to us by our great ancestors. Books and works of art which embodied the immortal intellectual and cultural achievements of the Muslims of the past are now to be found not at Delhi, Kabul, Teheran, Constantinople, or Cairo but in London, Paris, Vienna, Berlin, New York, Washington etc. And it is an undoubted fact that the Oriental scholars in London, Paris, Berlin and other Western countries know much more about our intellectual and cultural past than any one in the Islamic world. Thus our ignorance and negligence have deprived us both of God's gifts and our own inheritance.

THE AIM OF A MUSLIM'S LIFE

What should be the aim of a Muslim's life? This is a question on which volumes of literary Jeremiad can be compiled by stereotyped Moulvis and old-fashioned people. But it redounds to the credit of Sahibzada that he has very crisply suggested the ideal of a Muslim's life in the two principles of *Abdiat* and *Niabat-i-Elahi*. He preached the same gospel in 1911 as the President of the Provincial Muhammadan Educational Conference in Bengal and he reiterated the same belief in his address in 1923. In this connection he said:

It seems to me that the aim of a Muslim's life may be deduced from the two basic principles of *Abdiat* and *Nayatbat*. In the first place Islam demands from us such a perfect faith in an eternal, merciful, and beneficent creator as involves a complete submission and surrender of our ego or self. Having acknowledged God, in the opening words of "Sure Fathna'—"Praise is due to Allah, the Lord of the worlds"—as deserving of all praise, He being the creator of everything conceivable, we give up once for all every claim to self-praise or egoism in any shape or form, and thus learn to realise the true relation which exists between God and man. We recognise not only our own helplessness and nothingness, in relation to the creator, but of everything else in this universe. In terms of actual conduct. *Abdiat* means complete victory over self, control over passions, humility, simplicity and service of humanity. Such faith and convictions constitute the principle of *Abdiat* which is a standing safeguard against all those human weaknesses which proceed from egoism and which inevitably lead, not only individuals but even great nations, to their fall.

But mere faith and belief, however devout and sincere, is not enough. *Aml-e-Saleha* is an essential and integral part of our *Eman.* In order to grasp the full scope and significance of *Aml-e-Saleha* in Islam we should know man's destiny and mission in this world in pursuance of which he has opportunities which have been placed at his disposal by Providence.

COMMUNAL REPRESENTATION

Mr Aftab is a warm advocate of the policy of communal representation. But he wants that the pursuit of this policy should not be exploited for raking up religious quibbles and animosities, on the other hand, it should hold towards the formation of a community of sentiments and ideals towards the creation of a common national outlook by a judicious and honourable principle of compromise.

THE MAN

Sahibzada Aftab Ahmad Khan had the honour of being the Vice-President of the India Council. Soon after his return from England when he had finally severed his connection from that consultative body he was nominated a member of the Council of State in 1925.

A few hours' company with the Sahibzada will impress one with the type of character he possesses. No one can listen, even casually, to his conversation without appreciating the full manner, full both of dignity and of courtesy, the utter freedom from pomposity, formality, and self-assertion; but one often finds that agreeable dash of genuine cynicism which enlivens the flavour of his conversation.

Sahibzada enjoys a robust health, and takes a pretty long walk every day. His indefatigable energy, his burning enthusiasm for every work makes him more active than many a young man. He has wonderfully defied old age, and kept it at bay. His physical and mental powers are as alert as ever. He is a force making for the ennobling of character and the purity of ideals. May he live long! Amen!!

P. 353.

SYED HUSAIN BILGRAMI

SYED HUSAIN BILGRAMI

DR. SYED HUSAIN BILGRAMI, Nawab Imad-ul-Mulk, who is now in his eighty-third year, is affectionately called the Grand Old Man of Hyderabad. He richly deserves this honour. Half a century of public service in different departments has earned for him well merited recognition. Nor have his services been confined to Hyderabad where he has been a popular and familiar figure. The first Mussalman Member of the India Council, he impressed Lord Morley, the Secretary of State for India, by his knowledge and judgment. His has been a life of varied activity and he enjoys to-day the peace that comes of a well filled and honourable career, marked by the esteem and affection of his countrymen. Judged by the volume of his public work Dr. Bilgrami deserves an honoured place among the Eminent Mussalmans of India.

The biographical sketch that follows and the critical appreciation of his writings and speeches throw a flood of light on the volume and variety of Dr. Bilgrami's work. They are taken from a recent collection of Dr. Bilgrami's ADDRESSES, POEMS AND OTHER WRITINGS, to which they are prefixed.

I. BIOGRAPHICAL SKETCH*

Syed Husain Bilgrami (afterwards Nawab Ali Yar Khan Bahadur, Motaman Jung, Imad-ud-Daula, Imad-ul-Mulk, C.S.I.) was born at Sahibganj, Gaya, in the year 1842. He belongs to an old and well-known family of Syeds of Bilgram. The family are said to have come to India with the Conqueror, Muhammad Ghori, as long ago as the commencement of the 7th century of the Hijri or the 13th century of the Christian era, the date of their settlement at Bilgram being contained in the chronogram "Khudadad" which gives the date 614 Hijri. They have thus been settled there for over seven hundred years. His father, Syed Zainuddin Husain Khan, was a Deputy Collector and Magistrate in Bihar, he and his elder brother Syed Azamuddin Hasan Khan Bahadur being the two first Muhammadans to have held that post.

Syed Husain's earlier education and bringing up were undertaken at home where he studied Arabic under a learned *Moulvi*. In those days among the better class of Muhammadans, the arts of wrestling, swordsmanship, and archery were considered the necessary accomplishments of a gentleman, while the standard of horsemanship was so high that, as a supreme test, the pupil was required to ride and control spirited horses without saddle or bridle and

---

* This biographical sketch from the pen of Edith Bilgrami is prefixed to a recent volume of "Addresses, Poems and other Writings" of Dr. Bilgrami.

to bend them to his will. These and other exercises, inclusive of indigenous games of an active and manly nature, Syed Husain took part in, thus laying at an early age the foundation of a strong and robust constitution which has helped to maintain him in sound mental and bodily health throughout his long life.

At a tender age he lost his mother. This was his first experience, as a child, of death, and the impression it made on his young mind was so profound that he appears never to have shaken it off afterwards. The emotions roused by this loss, suffered as it was at the most impressionable period of life, supplied many years later the inspiration for one of his English poems.

At the age of 14, his Arabic tutor having left him, his father commenced teaching him English. He was afterwards sent to live with his uncle, Syed Azamud-din Hasan, at Patna where he went to school, and afterwards to a school at Bhagalpur, not far from Madahpura, where his father had his headquarters as Deputy Collector and Magistrate. He was finally sent to Calcutta where he joined the La Martiniere College, going a few months later to the branch school then known as the Hare Academy where he matriculated, securing a first class. This success earned him a scholarship with which he entered the Presidency College where he again took a first class two years later in the First Examination in Arts. But in the third year his College course was interrupted owing to his father taking him to Bilgram for the purpose of matrimony. Thence he returned a few months later after his marriage only to find that he had lost the whole of his third year of instruction at the College. He nevertheless went through the course and sat for his degree examination at the end of his fourth year in the College securing for the third time in succession a class and standing very high in the University in the order of merit.

Already a mature scholar of Arabic, Syed Husain had by the end of his College career acquired a mastery over the English language that is given to few Indians to attain. At the same time his great love of books led him to read widely—a practice which he kept up for more than half a century, thus becoming one of the best read men of his time. Nor did he read merely. As a writer too he was gifted with that faculty for clear and terse expression which lends a peculiar grace and charm to his prose and verse.

But greater far than any acquired attainments, is the innate nobility of spirit and integrity of character that runs in his blood, being the heritage of his ancient race, fostered further by the strict bringing up given him by his father, which has made him what he has always been—a man of lofty principles and high ideals with a strong sense of duty and unimpeachable uprightness and integrity coupled with a simple, almost puritanical religious faith.

In 1868 therefore, at the age of about 26, Syed Husain was well equipped both mentally and morally for entering upon a successful career. Young as he was, his proficiency in Arabic secured him a chair of Professor of that language at Canning College, Lucknow. At the same time by his merit as a writer of English, he was put in sole charge of the LUCKNOW TIMES, a bi-weekly organ of the Talukdars of Oudh. About this time took place the interesting controversy about the project of a canal, known as "the Sarda Canal," in Oudh. The Government of the day were keen on constructing the canal which the Talukdars for various reasons believed to be opposed to their interests. The case for the Government was strongly advocated in the columns of the "Pioneer" by a civilian who was a powerful writer and a friend of Syed Husain's to be opposed in the BI-WEEKLY LUCKNOW TIMES in brilliant articles from the pen of Syed Husain. The issue of the controversy was entirely in favour of the latter, and the Talukdars had the satisfaction of seeing the abandonment of the project they disliked.

In 1872 the great Sir Salar Jung, Minister of the Nizam, happening to visit Lucknow met Syed Husain and felt greatly attracted to him and cordially invited him to come to Hyderabad, which the latter did the next year, 1873.

The rest of Syed Husain's career is bound up chiefly with Hyderabad. The surname "Bilgrami," it is interesting to note, was adopted by Syed Husain at the suggestion of Sir Salar Jung. He became Private Secretary to the great Minister and in that capacity played a prominent part in drafting or revising the letters that the Minister from time to time addressed to the British Government regarding the Berars, and which helped greatly the cause of the Nizam. He accompanied Sir Salar Jung on his memorable mission to England where the Minister was greatly "lionised" and feted by the best society. Syed Husain Bilgrami had during this trip the honour of meeting and speaking with Queen Victoria and also of meeting other distinguished people like Disraeli, Gladstone, Lord Salisbury, John Morley and others.

Syed Husain Bilgrami subsequently became Educational Secretary in Hyderabad and also Director of Public Instruction. He further held for a time the post of Private Secretary to the Nizam and other high and responsible posts, finishing, after his retirement, by becoming Adviser to the third Salar Jung, the young grandson of his friend and benefactor, the great Sir Salar Jung, who was for a short period Minister. During his long service in the State extending over nearly fifty years, Syed Husain acted at various times as tutor to the late Nizam, His Highness Mir Mahbub Ali Khan, as also tutor to His Exalted Highness the present Nizam when he was Heir Apparent, and likewise to the Sahibzadas, his sons. He received for his services to the State at various times, the titles of Nawab Ali Yar Khan Bahadur, Motaman Jung, Imad-ud-Dowla and Imad-ul-Mulk, as also the C. S. I. from the Government of

India for his services to the British Empire of which more will be said in what follows.

But it is to his work as an educationist that the State owes its great debt. For with the exception of the Osmania University and the new Girls' school, which are recent institutions, practically all the other educational institutions in Hyderabad owe their existence to Syed Husain Bilgrami. For instance, fifty years ago, there existed no facilities in the State for the education of the upper classes in Hyderabad. At the instance of Syed Husain Bilgrami, a new school was started under highly competent teachers—this was the Madrasa-e-Aizza which is still in working order. Also a High School was started which soon rose to the rank of a College with Dr. Aghornath Chattopadhya, a man of science, as its Principal. This College eventually became the "Nizam College" and was provided with a highly paid European staff. By order of Sir Salar Jung, the "Murshidzadas" or the relatives of the Ruler of the State, who were hitherto brought up without any proper education, were compelled to go to the Madrasa-e-Aizza, stipends or scholarships being granted to them as an encouragement, and large and well-appointed bullock carts or "nibs" employed for their conveyance to and from the school. The education of women had its due share of Syed Husain's attention, and about the year 1885 a Girls' High school was founded, being probably the first institution of its kind for Muslim girls in India. Here a well qualified staff was appointed and Arabic and Persian as well as English were included in the curriculum besides such subjects as needlework and domestic economy. The strictest purda arrangements were made within the premises and special covered conveyances provided for bringing the pupils to school. At the same time industrial education was not neglected. Recognizing the importance of manual and industrial training, Syed Husain Bilgrami caused three Industrial Schools to be founded at the three principal centres of local industries, namely, Aurangabad, Hyderabad and Warangal. These institutions did most useful work in helping to revive declining industries. In order to encourgage oriental learning and scholarship the Dar-ul-Uloom or Oriental College was founded which during its existence had a most competent staff and produced many good scholars of Arabic. The State Library was also started by Syed Husain Bilgrami. originally as a repository for valuable old Arabic books. Afterwards a large collection of English and Persian books was added on, and the Library forms to-day one of the best institutions of its kind in India. One of the aims of Syed Husain was to purchase and republish such of the rare and valuable books in the Arabic language as were in danger of extinction. For the furtherance of this aim he founded with the cordial support of Sir Salar Jung, the Dairat-ul-Maarif, a society for the preservation and publication of old and valuable books. This Society, of which he is still the head, is to this day carrying on its operations and has done invaluable service to oriental learning and culture by editing and publishing, and thereby saving from loss or extinction many works of great literary, historical and even scientific value. The work of the Dairat-ul-Maarif has now been recognised in several countries in Europe where learned collaborators are coming forward to help. The Central Normal School for the training of teachers also owes its origin to Syed Husain Bilgrami.

Nor was his fame as an educationist confined to Hyderabad alone. He was twice elected President of the Muhammadan Educational Conference, on both of which occasions the addresses delivered by him from the chair form not only models of literary excellence but also contain educational and moral advice of great value. The Government of India in recognition of his educational experience and great ability, appointed him on the Universities Commission of 1903. He had already been a member of the Legislative Council and a C. S. I. In 1907 Lord Morley, the Secretary of State for India, selected him as a Member of the India Council, he being the first Muhammadan to sit on that Council. He however resigned his place before the end of his period owing to ill health. He retired from Hyderabad service in the end of 1907 on his appointment to the Secretary of State's Council, but on his return from England he was appointed Adviser to the third Salar Jung during the latter's short term of office as Minister.

Syed Husain Bilgrami has never been a "politician" in the vulgar sense of the word. He but rarely stepped into the political arena, and whenever he did so, it was only to assist his community in orderly progress. Thus the Address of the Muhammadans to Lord Minto in 1906 which he drew up marked one of those rare occasions when he came to the assistance of his community in matters political. It was an epoch-making document which secured the recognition for the first time of the rights of the Muslims a distinct and important community.

Similarly, during the World War, when there was danger of Muslim loyalty being shaken owing to Turkey having jointed the enemy, and His Exalted Highness the Nizam conceived the far sighted and statesmanlike plan of issuing a manifesto to them as a Muslim Ruler in order to steady them and to induce them to remain staunch in their fidelity to British Rule, it was to Nawab Imad-ul-Mulk (Syed Husain Bilgrami) that His Exalted Highness turned for the drawing up of the famous manifesto. H. E. H. the Nizam's advice came in the nick of time and had a most salutary effect on the Muhammadans. The manifesto was worded in a way that appealed to the best sentiments of the Muhammadans and succeeded in calming them completely. This was the last and perhaps the most signal service rendered by Syed Husain Bilgrami no less to H. E. H. the Nizam than to the British Empire.

For the rest, it may be said that it is not only by what he has *done* that the value of Syed Husain Bilgrami to his country and to his community may be gauged, but also by what he *is*. To-day he is the relic of what was best in a past generation which gave birth to men of greater force of character than modern conditions seem to be capable of producing. He stands for unwavering truth, justice, uprightness and sincerity in a world where these virtues are but lightly valued. Amid the sordid struggle that surges all round him for pelf, for power or for preferment, he stands head and shoulders above the common crowd, calm, serene and peaceful, unaffected by these selfish passions. He is the one entity to whom those who aim at high ideals in life can still turn for inspiration and guidance.

II. A CRITICAL APPRECIATION *

NAWAB Imad-ul-Mulk Syed Husain Bilgrami has, of late years not been so much in the public eye. His weak health and advanced age—, he is nearly 84 now—have forced him into retirement. But there was a time covering nearly a half-century —a pretty long period in the life of an individual— when the foremost among the leaders of Muslim thought in this country looked to him for counsel and support.

Syed Husain Bilgrami is essentially a scholar and an educationist. Politics was never his forte. He was drawn into its vortex by pressure of events rather than choice. Even then it was not as an active participant in the political struggle that he appeared before his country; it was more as a detached onlooker, counsellor, and a disinterested friend of its people. Only on two occasions, does he appear to have gone out of his way—first, when he addressed his memorable letter to Sir Syed Ahmed, cautioning him not to be enticed into the Congress politics of the day but to conserve all his energy for concentration on the education of his community—next, when he drew up the famous joint memorial to Lord Minto on the eve of the Minto-Morley reforms demanding special representation for Muslims on the Imperial and Provincial Legislative Councils.

* From Prof. Syed Abdul Latif's Foreword to Mr. Bilgrami's "Addresses, Poems and Other Writings.

The attitude which these and a few other writings of his suggested to the Indian Muslim community at several critical moments in their political life has in no small measure been responsible for their activity during the last two generations. That attitude, it may be observed, has not always found favour with his Hindu compatriots and even a few among his own co-religionists. A careful and dispassionate examination will, however, show that there is much in his standpoint that needs the earnest consideration of everyone, whatever the nationality or creed, who has the interest of this country at heart.

The instinct of self-preservation in man is a powerful impulse. He may in a moment of weak benevolence be carried off his feet by catchwords and shibboleths, but when crises arise in individual or national life and bring realities into play, he is invariably disillusioned. The instinct of self-sacrifice may indeed be very strong in him but when he is made to realise that it is being exploited by a clever comrade for his own selfish ends, he lets the instinct of self-preservation assert itself violently. The writings of Syed Husain Biligrami will reveal to the reader the working of this human trait. In his private and official life he has always been serviceable to one and all, be he a Hindu, Muslim, Christian, or Parsee. Never has he been known to have sacrificed merit on any racial or religious ground. But in matters political, his advice has always been: "Equate yourself to facts."

He has held that without a heartfelt unity among the different sections of the Indian population, India can never hope to command respect from others and secure her proper place in the comity of nations. Says he, addressing a gathering of his co-réligionists in 1896:—

> The different races among whom we live in India are children of the same soil and should therefore be like brothers to us and it is our duty to live with them in brotherly love and amity; their success is our success; their failure our failure: they are naturally our friends and supporters whom it would be suicidal to alienate from us by any act of our own; it would, indeed, be both bad morals and bad policy.

With this expression of genuine friendly feeling towards the sister communities of India, there always went a strong conviction that true and lasting friendship in politics necessarily implied the preservation of one's own identity. The memorial to Lord Minto brings this idea to the forefront. He does not believe in lip-loyalty to any particular political creed or in unity feverishly attempted on paper to prevent a high-souled patriot from starving himself to death. Unity of hearts is what he asks for, and he makes it clear that that is impossible as long as the numerically, and economically the stronger of the two leading communities of India, namely, the Hindus, create new and newer differences by dwelling more on the seamy than on the bright side of the present or past of the Indian Muslims. On this aspect of the inter-communal life of India, the Syed Sahib is most outspoken. And looking at the chequered relationship that exists at the present between the two sections so soon after the vociferous demonstration of love and friendship on either side, who can say that the consistent attitude of Syed Husain Bilgrami is not without its meaning to the people of understanding in either camp? When the hearts do not beat in unison, when one of the two parties is always on the alert to profit by the other's good-will and forbearance, there is bound to be a reaction and the result is that life becomes limited; the thought of self asserts itself, and becomes a creed. That seems to be the reason why some of the political speeches of Syed Husain Bilgrami are such as they are.

The educational addresses are of a different character. They indeed, were almost all of them primarily intended for consideration of his own community and dealt with their immediate needs. In discussing them however, he has given expression to views which are of universal application. The Syed is one of those very few living Indians in whom are harmoniously blended the knowledge and culture of the East and of the West. His attitude in educational matters, therefore, deserves the respectful attention of the exponents of both the Western and the purely Eastern systems of training. He has no sympathy with those who are disposed to idealise and idolise secular training at the expense of religion. He emphasises the claims of intellect as well as of the spirit with equal force. Religion without the searchlight of modern thought will cease to be a powerful factor in human progress. And purely intellectual training divorced from religion is but a soulless culture.

"Bread-earning," says he, "is unfortunately a necessary pursuit, but manhood is not nourished on bread alone; the spirit also has to be provided with good wholesome food. But not only is manhood not nourished by bread alone; it is neither books nor bread that is needed for the body; but what is really healthful for the whole man is a training that will, as I have said before, lead us to clean living and high thinking This is the essence of culture, for what after all is life worth if it is lived as the animals live it in the gratification of mere physical needs or in migrations from the blue bed to the brown."

Says he again:—

We Muhammadans have received a nobler and more sacred inheritance than our secular literature and learning, namely our God and our religion, and were our children to forget these in the turmoil of worldly pursuits however desirable, they shall surely perish, since a people who have abandoned their God and their conscience are like sailors who have lost their moorings and are floating adrift on a tempestuous sea without pilot or rudder.

"True education," says he in another place, "should teach us to distinguish truth from falsehood and draw valid conclusions from the occurrences of daily experience; it should discipline all our faculties: it should make us acquainted with the best that has been said on the topics of importance by the wisest of former generations: and fit us to bring this knowledge to bear on the practical conduct of life: it should inspire us with a burning desire to be ever moving onward, ever taking a step in advance; it should teach us to be sincere in our daily life and considerate of others; it should bring us up to exalt public good above our own, and to respect others as the most natural corollary of respecting ourselves.

Since these last words were addressed to its promoters, the M.A.O. College, Aligarh, has grown into a statutory University, and it is a matter for serious consideration, how far its courses of study are made to conform to this simple and yet great ideal of education.

Apart from their contribution to thought, the speeches of Syed Husain Bilgrami have a literary value of their own. To any reader of them, particularly of his incomplete but masterly translation of the Quran into English it will be obvious that he has a style which, in the polish and purity of diction, and the elegance and precision of expression, can be favourably compared with that of any writer of English that modern India has ever produced.

His poems, all lyrical in character are interesting reading. Nearly half of them are sonnets; some written in the Petrarchan form, some in the Shakespearean. In these, as well as in other songs, the writer has shown a mastery over the technique of English verse which is, indeed, surprising. One hears in them the echoes of the famous English poets, the "Nature's Pontiff Priest," "The Blind Bard of Mars," and of him "Who heard the stars still quiring to the young-eyed cherabim." A line like:

> Time laughed and would not hear the song.

—coming at the end of every stanza of his beautiful poem "April in Upper India" reminds us of Spenser's:—

> Sweet Thames! run softly till I end my song.

which occupies a similar place in "Prothalamion." There is in his poems a lyrical element so true, so sincere, and so apparently spontancous that one hardly fails to note that the ring in them is the ring of a born poet. The only regret is that they are so few.

Syed Husain's has indeed been a scholar's life. Few with the opportunities he has had in his official career would have so successfully stood the temptation to live in the glare of publicity. Lesser minds, men of inferior stature—disturbing elements at best in politics and in literature—have so often frantically striven to win popular applause and even official recognition. Strangely, these go not infrequently to such men. The Syed Sahib, however, has always risen superior to his environment and considerations of ignorant worldly preferment, and has sought, like a true scholar, all the honour that he deserves in the consciousness of having lived a righteous and useful life.

During the last ten years, he has lived in retirement in his retreat, " Rocklands, " raised under the shadow of a rocky hillock which hangs over on one side, the restless Fatheh Maidan, and, on the other, the serene reservoir of Husain Sagar. As a link between the past and the present, with the suavity and serenity of the silent and deep waters behind him and the genial warmth of youth so often displayed on that royal field of tournament before him, with his back to the Great Rock, facing heroically the onslaughts of advancing years lives this sage of Hyderabad supported by his loving and devoted wife a scholar herself, a centre of quiet domestic happiness to his progeny and an object of reverence to many like the writer.

JUSTICE SHAH DIN

THE late Hon'ble Mian Muhammad Shah Din came of a family of historic interest residing near the famous Shalamar Gardens at Lahore, and still enjoying the distinction of being the hereditary custodians of that brilliant specimen of the architecture of the days of Shah Jahan. To quote from a well-known book :—

> The ancestor of the family was Muhammad Ishaq, the founder of the village Ishaqpur, the site of the Shalamar Gardens Muhammad Yusuf, fourth lineal descendant of Muhammad Ishaq, gave the site of the village of his ancestors to Shah Jahan in conformity with the wish of the Royal Engineer, whose choice for the site of the garden had fallen upon that flourishing village. In lieu of the village, the Emperor granted Muhammad Ishaq the site of the present village of Baghbanpura, the headquarters of the family. This won Muhammad Yusuf the favour of the Royal family, and his son Muhammad Fazil was sent to the Deccan on important duty, where he rendered services which secured him the title of Nawab from the Emperor Aurangzeb. Fifth in descent from Nawab Muhammad Fazil was Mian Qadir Bukhsh, the grand-father of the subject of this brief sketch. He was a profound Arabic and Persian Scholar, a physician, and a poet. He distinguished himself in another sphere in the reign of the Sikhs when at the desire of Maharaja Ranjit Singh, he learnt the art of gunnery under French Military Officers and wrote a book in Persian on the subject called Miftah-ul-Qila.

The Persian inscription on a gun, cast in the fort of Lahore, quoted in Syed Muhammad Latif's book mentioning the name of Mian Qadir Bakhsh, is of interest in this connection. The translation of the inscription is as follows :—

Under orders of His Gracious Majesty the Singh Sahib, the Crown Head of the Khalsa, the King Ranjit Singhji (may his dignity last for ever) this gun, belonging to Diwan Lala Moti Ram and Ram Lal, was completed in the blessed fort of Lahore, under the superintendence of Mian Qadir Bakhsh, in 1881. The name of the gun is "Fateh Jang." The work of Muhammad Hyat.

Descended from ancestors who combined refined intellectual tastes with lives of physical activity, for which those days afforded so much scope, Mr. Shah Din was pre-eminently a man of intellect, and his triumphs were mostly confined to the intellectual arena. The healthy influence which during more than a decade of public life he exercised on his countrymen and co-religionists had been derived mainly from mental and moral strength. His education and culture, more than anything else, led him on to the pre-eminent position he occupied in educational circles. In the Councils of the Punjab University he was quite a power, and his voice on educational questions commanded wide respect.

EARLY CAREER

His career as a student from his early school days till his return from England is one of considerable interest. Born in 1868, he received his early education in the Vernacular Middle School in his own village, where he stood first in the Lahore District in the Middle School Examination. In this School he got that thorough grounding in Urdu and Persian literature and that taste for indigenous poetry which characterised him and furnished striking contrast to the majority of England-returned gentlemen in whom high intellectual culture in the language of the West means absolute want of sympathy with the literature of their own land. In the High School young Shah Din continued the promise of his early days, and in the Matriculation Examination headed the list of successful candidates in the Province in the subject of English. Here it is of some interest to remark that his elder daughter later earned a similar distinction in the University. This distinction would have proved fatal to his chances in life, if he had yielded to a suggestion of taking up employment. By reason of his proficiency in English he received through his Head Master an offer of Translatorship under Government, but he had the good sense not to interrupt his studies prematurely and resisted this offer. He pursued his College career successfully and got his B. A., degree in 1887 from the Government College, Lahore, standing high in order of merit.

STUDIES IN ENGLAND

In *November* 1887, Mr. Shah Din proceeded to England to study for the Bar, as a member of the Middle Temple. For this new field of studies he showed as much aptitude as he had done for literature, and won three lecture prizes awarded by the Council of Legal Education in Roman Law, Jurisprudence, International Law, Constitutional Law, and Constitutional History. He also gained the Campbell-Forster Prize and a Scholarship from his own Inn. He was called to the Bar in *June* 1890.

LEGAL CAREER

Soon after his return to India he won a name in the Punjab as the rising man in the Lahore Chief Court, and was counted till his elevation to the Bench among leaders of the Chief Court Bar. He held for sometime the office of Assistant Legal Remembrancer to the Punjab Government, a position to which no other Indian had been appointed in the Province before him. He was appointed a member of the Punjab Legislative Council in 1908 for a term of two years and was re-nominated in 1905 but had to resign his seat in 1906, owing to his appointment as an Additional Judge of the Chief Court. He reverted to the Bar in *August* 1907 and was appointed a third time a member of the Punjab Legislative Council, but again had to resign his seat in 1908 on re-appointment to the Chief Court.

PUBLIC LIFE

His connection with public life began in England where, in conjunction with a few other Muhammadan young men from India, he founded in 1889 the Anjuman-i-Islam, London, which for many years did very useful work and became a recognised institution. The Anjuman was the first institution of its kind in the British Isles, and Mr. Shah Din held the office of its Vice-President till his departure from England. The work thus begun by him in England, of influencing the Muhammadan community through educated young men was taken up in earnest immediately on his return to Lahore, where by means of two eloquent addresses, one delivered to a large audience in the Lahore Town Hall, and another before the first anniversary meeting of the newly founded Young Men's Muhammadan Association, he established for himself the position of a "guide, philosopher and friend" to the numerous young men who might seek his help or guidance. He was elected President of the Association, a distinction which he continuously enjoyed, and in which capacity he came in personal and intimate touch with many of the rising generation, influencing and being influenced by them, and thus creating a large following of friends and admirers. Some of those who came in contact with him as students, and in whose progress and advancement he took lively interest, passed out of their Colleges into active life in the course of time and became men of influence in their own station and a source of strength to him, in whom young Muhammadans rightly recognised a leader of firm principles and strong convictions, whose public and private life furnished a laudable example of devotion to duty, of patriotism and of purity.

EDUCATIONAL ACTIVITIES

His connection with the greatest educational movement of Upper India, represented by the M. A. O. College, Aligarh, and the Muhammadan Educational Conference was both intimate and wholesome; and the College will long remember the services which he rendered to the institution in order to extricate it from difficulties that arose after the deaths of Sir

Syed Ahmed Khan and Principal Theodore Beck. At the Educational Conference of December 1893, he read a learned and instructive paper in English on "The Education of the Mussalmans in the Punjab," which was widely appreciated for the many useful and practical suggestions it contained. A keen-sighted leader like Sir Syed Ahmed Khan soon recognised in Mr. Shah Din one of the rising men of the Punjab even at that state of his career, and honoured him by suggesting his name for the distinction of President of the Conference for 1894. He was the first to preside over the deliberations of that representative national assembly while yet only twenty-six and he discharged his responsibilities as President so well as to win commendation from the Sage of Aligarh and many of his learned colleagues. He was elected a Trustee of the Aligarh College in 1896 and was till his closing years one of the most influential members of that body. In *December* 1913, Mr. Shah Din presided a second time at the Twenty-seventh Session of the Muhammadan Educational Conference held at Agra. His Presidential Address on that occasion was considered by all competent judges as one of the best contributions to the existing literature on Muhammadan Education in as much as it contained most valuable suggestions on many of the complex educational problems, especially affecting the future advancement of the Muhammadan community. The high intrinsic value of Mr. Shah Din's Presidential Address may well be appraised by the fact that

P. 377.

JUSTICE SHAH DIN

the then Lieutenant Governor of the Punjab quoted very largely from that address in the speech delivered by him in 1914 on the occasion of laying the foundation stone of the New Islamia School outside Bhati Gate, Lahore.

WORK IN THE PUNJAB UNIVERSITY

Sir Dennis Fitzpatrick nominated Mr. Shah Din a Fellow of the Punjab University in 1893, and in 1895 he was elected a Syndic, a position which he held for about ten years. He was for several years Secretary of the Law College Committee, of which the President was the Vice-Chancellor, which controlled the affairs of the Law College, the sole institution for teaching Law in the Province. He also acted for some years as Secretary of the Standing Committee for the preparation of approved vernacular books, which had been constituted by the Senate with the object of encouraging vernacular literature by means of translations from English, and the production of original works in the vernacular. He also represented the Punjab University on the Punjab Text Book Committee for several years and took an active part in the Departmental Educational Conference in the Punjab.

LITERARY ATTAINMENTS

Mr. Shah Din's lectures on literary, educational and legal subjects, as well as his speeches on questions of social or religious reform, have been published in different magazines and newspapers and reviewed very favourably by the Press in this country. He was himself in touch with journalism. During his stay in England he used to contribute frequently to the journal of the National Indian Association and occasionally to other periodicals. A series of very readable letters from his pen depicting in beautiful and picturesque language the beautiful natural scenery of the Lakes District, of Wales and of Scotland, appeared in the CIVIL AND MILITARY GAZETTE in *September* and *October* 1890, which displayed remarkable descriptive powers, a well-developed aesthetical faculty, and a wonderful command of English idiom. These were followed up later by a series of graphic letters from the valley of Kashmir, which were widely read and admired. Another contribution to legal studies was a paper on Miss. Sorabji's scheme of legal relief for *purdah* ladies, which was read under the auspices of the Punjab Law Society, of which he was a prominent member, and which did good work under the distinguished presidency of Sir Lewis Tupper.

Mr. Shah Din was also an Urdu poet of no mean order and though he could spare very little of his time to devote to the Muse and that only by way of pastime or amusement, some of his literary contributions to the MAKHZAN (the then leading Urdu monthly) excited considerable admiration and enthusiasm. As evidenced by some of these poems he attracted to his side and influenced such well-known Urdu poets and writers as Iqbal, Abdul Qadir, Nairang, Ijaz, etc. A collection of his poems has lately been edited and published by his only son, Mian Bashir Ahmad, Bar-at-Law.

POLITICAL ACTIVITIES

Until the year 1894 the Muslim leaders headed by the late Sir Syed Ahmed Khan concentrated the whole of their attention and energies in promoting the spread of education among the Indian Mussalmans. About that time the idea of taking part in the political life of the country began to take root in their minds and an Association called the Anglo-Muhammadan Defence Association of Upper India was started, with the late Mr. Syed Mahmood and Mr. Theodore Beck as Joint Secretaries, to represent Muslim interests with headquarters at Aligarh. Mr. Shah Din along with certain other leading gentlemen represented the Punjab on its Council and when subsequently the late Nawab Mohsin-ul-Mulk organised an All-India Muhammadan Deputation, with His Highness the Agha Khan as its head, to represent the claims of the Muslim community regarding their representation in the Legislature and Public Services, Mr. Shah Din was one of its prominent members. Our readers will remember that this Deputation waited on His Excellency the Earl of Minto at Simla on *1st October* 1906 and the recognition of Muslim claims in the Minto-Morley Reform Scheme was the result of its efforts. The idea o starting an All-India Muslim League emanated during the various meetings which took place on that occasion and its final constitution was adopted at a meeting held in *March* 1908 at Aligarh under the presidency of Mr. Shah Din. The Punjab Branch of the All-India Muslim League was organised about the same time and Mr. Shah Din was elected as its first President which position he held until his appointment as the Judge of the Punjab Chief Court towards the end of 1908.

ON THE BENCH

From that year right up to the time of his death in 1918 Mr. Shah Din was a Judge of the Chief Court, Punjab and it was acknowledged on every hand that he had been an acquisition to that Court. He performed the duties of his high office with such marked distinction and success that the Governor-General-in-Council was pleased to sanction his appointment as Chief Judge *sub-protem*, during the absence on leave of Mr. Justice Rattigan—the first time that an Indian was appointed to that high office in the Punjab.

His sense of self-respect, his independence as an Indian Judge, his good treatment of promising junior lawyers, his masterly judgments on disputed points of law will be long remembered by both the Bench and the Bar.

CONCLUSION

There was hardly any non-sectarian public movement or organisation in the Punjab with which Mr. Shah Din's name was not associated, while his share in the success of several movements for the advancement of the Muhammadan community was truly remarkable. The cause of social reform and of the moral uplift of the Muhammadan community was dear to his heart. On several occasions, he faced and overcame violent opposition in his own tribe and elsewhere in order to abolish many pernicious social customs, which were responsible for the economic ruin and the moral degradation of his community. In this task he had often to sacrifice his own comfort and peace of mind; he was misunderstood and sometime even misrepresented by people who happened to differ from him. But this did not deter him from what he considered as the most important task of a leader of men in a period of transition and reform.

He was a strong advocate of higher female education and he and Sir Mahomed Shafi were the first Muhammedans in the Punjab to send their daughters to be educated in Queen Mary's College at Lahore. He believed that while Indian boys and girls should acquire knowledge, both Western and Eastern, in the proper proportion, while they should discard antiquated customs that were sapping the foundations of their social and national life, they should, at the same time, retain those elements of their ancient culture which formed the real essence of the modesty and stability of Oriental nature. In short, conservative by temperament, he was yet a believer in liberal education and liberal ideas. He had in his nature the invaluable gift of balance of judgment. His insight into men's nature was as remarkable as his foresight in the affairs of life. He was reserved and quiet, but whenever he expressed his estimate of a man's character or gave his advice in vital matters, his pronouncement was almost invariably justified by later events. Always ready to learn, he stuck to his principles in the vicissitudes of life. His seriousness and earnestness were almost proverbial in the circle of his friends and acquaintances and his presence always inspired them and even the general public with feelings of respect.

He was extremely regular in his personal habits. Although he had a weak constitution, he managed by his regularity and regard for health, to work hard to the end of his days in apparently sound health. He used to get up early, long before sunrise, have a brisk morning walk by himself and be back home in time to get ready for the day and do some work before going to Court.

In addition to his legal work and occasionally preparing his speeches and lectures, he found time to read English literature, particularly devoting his attention to philosophical subjects, to study Arabic regularly with a Moulvi and to go through Urdu books on Islamic history and theology. But towards the end of his days, he had little time left for such intellectual hobbies, though when he could now and then spare an afternoon he would preside over a Mushaira (contest of poets) or sit at home listening to a song of Hafiz, Iqbal or Saroor, sung by a young member of the family or to some book on "New Thought." Or again he would exhort the young men of the family to cast off their lethargy, to prepare a speech or a lecture, to organize a reform movement, in short, to do something useful and not let their lives be wasted in idle speculation or worthless grumbling. Though of a philosophical turn of mind, his life was, from beginning to end, one of action and work. He was truthful, courageous and always mindful of his responsibilities. He disliked pomp and show, discouraged social functions that entailed unnecessary waste of money, deprecated the use of strong or empty words, insisted upon frugality, simplicity and perseverance as qualities that the Mussalmans stood most in need of. The late Syed Muhammad Latif, the historian of the Punjab, aptly remarked in his book, " he (Mr. Shah Din) is a gifted man of literary genius, and his English attainments are very high. As a public speaker his speeches have excited universal admiration, and as a writer he has shown considerable aptitude. In him young Punjab may feel a just pride. Though still quite a youth, his manners are so polished, and his behaviour is so polite and pleasing that he is endeared to and respected by all his countrymen."

These words of the historian of the Punjab written in 1892 were amply illustrated and his judgment fully justified by the achievements of Mr. Shah Din in the different fields of social, intellectual and civic activities throughout the twenty-seven years of his public and official life. He died on the *2nd July* 1918 at the age of 50 years and 3 months. His death was universally mourned by all classes and communities and it was acknowledged on all hands that the province had suffered an irreparable loss in the death of a man, who besides being an excellent speaker, a brilliant writer, and a thoughtful judge, was also an indefatigable worker in the cause of education and social reform and possessed a character and a personality which profoundly influenced all those who from time to time came into contact with him.

SIR MAHOMED IQBAL

SIR MAHOMED IQBAL

IQBAL was born at Sialkot in 1877. He is descended from an ancient family of Kashmir Pandits, some of whose descendants are now living in Kashmir with the family name of Sapru. The fore-fathers of Iqbal embraced Islam about 200 years ago out of sincere devotion to a Saint, and even to-day there are strong Sufistic tendencies that mark the members of his family to an admirable degree. It may be said that Iqbal, as a true descendant, has inherited the religious fervour of his ancestors along with the noble qualities of mind.

The parents of Iqbal never thought that the boy would become in future the pride of the whole family, nay, the pride of the whole nation. There was nothing extraordinary about him to mark him out from the children of his place. He was sent to a Maktab along with other boys and after some time his education began in an elementary school. His success in the 5th standard won him a scholarship. He finished the middle school course and the scholarship he got in recognition of his merit made it easy for him to take to the entrance examination.

His success in the entrance examination opened to him the field of higher studies. The ambitious young man could not stop with the laurels he had already won in the school. He joined the Scotch Mission College, Sialkot, for his collegiate course. One thing happened at this time, which, perhaps, is the chief factor in his life to prepare him for his future greatness. His acquaintance with Moulana Syed Mir Hasan, who was a very profound Arabic Scholar of his time, exercised over him an imperceptible influence in creating in him a noble devotion to Islamic culture and ardent appreciation for the literature of Islam. Iqbal, after finishing his course in Sialkot, joined the Government College, Lahore, where he graduated with distinction and a medal.

Iqbal was extremely fortunate in his friendship with Moulana Syed Mir Hasan at Sialkot. Even in Lahore good fortune followed him in the person of the well-known Mr. Arnold. Mr. Arnold had been working in the Aligarh College, but, as though by fortune, he was entertained in the Government College, Lahore, while Iqbal was a student there. He found him a promising young man and gradually made him his friend. He was no more the master of Iqbal but an experienced friend who took pleasure in his company. He once remarked about him that he really made his master wiser. Iqbal then took his M. A. degree, the highest degree of the University and received a medal for standing first among all the students.

After his M. A. Examination he was appointed lecturer in History and Philosophy in the Oriental College, Lahore. He subsequently became Assistant Professor in English and Philosophy in the Government College, Lahore. He was held in high esteem for his knowledge and ability by the College authorities, and his position there gave him many excellent opportunities to carry on his literary pursuits. His charming manners soon won him the heart of his students, but Iqbal's ambition to find out truth by means of higher studies could not allow him rest satisfied with his condition. The liberal-mindedness of his brother at last helped him in realising his ambition to go to England, where he remained for three years in Cambridge pursuing his research. The University of Cambridge conferred upon him a very high degree in Philosophy, and his thesis on Persian Philosophy presented to the University of Munich in Germany obtained for him the degree of Ph. D. After his visit to Germany, he returned to London and passed his law examination at Lincoln's Inn. He also joined the London School of Economics and Political Science with a view to study Sociology and Politics. By this time Iqbal became a renowned man. His reputation secured for him for a short period of 3 months the place of Professor Arnold in the London University. He acted there as the Chief Professor of the Arabic Language.

While in service in Lahore, Iqbal was restless for the acquisition of knowledge and his passion had found outlet in various researches. The atmosphere of the place was too incommodious for his high imagination, and his soul needed a wider scope for development which was destined to make him one of the greatest poets of the age. The vast and numerous libraries of the different Universities in Europe and the influence of some of the best thinkers had afforded him an opportunity to develop such intellectual power as afterwards captured the imagination of the whole world. The greatness of Iqbal consists in his powers of writing as well as of speech. It is given to few to be masters in both arts. He made himself conspicuous while in London by his lectures on Islam and won the approbation of the critical public. One cannot but admire his ability when one remembers that he returned to India at the early age of 32 honoured with diplomas and degrees. Iqbal's English life brought him into close contact with Dr. Nicholson.

The conversation was so delightful that the distinguished Professor felt a strong desire to meet this talented Indian again. Luck brought them together once more, and the admiration felt for the brilliant young man resulted in Dr. Nicholson's translating years after Iqbal's return to India his Persian Poem Asrari-Khudi into English. It is not often that Indians capture the fancy of eminent men of letters in Europe.

It was a memorable evening in the month of *July* 1908 when Iqbal was publicly entertained after his return from England by his friends and admirers in Lahore. It was indeed a very warm reception, mingled with feelings of pride and joy, pride for the reputation which he had already earned at home and abroad, and joy for having once more one of their own in their midst after a separation of three years. Their hearts were eagerly waiting for the opportunity to see the Muslim poet who had left his impressions on some of the great European minds, and blessed was the occasion.

Iqbal is one of the great learned poets of the world. His thirst for knowledge could not keep him satisfied with what he acquired in India by means of the University education and research, but it was the chief cause for making him endure the troubles of voyage and denying to himself the pleasures of home. His tour in the various countries was really a necessity for the realisation of his strong desire. A hero, says Carlyle, appears in the world according to the needs of the time, and Iqbal is undoubtedly a hero of his time in the field of inspired poetry. What he says about Shakespeare applies to himself with equal force :—

> Beauty is the mirror of truth, and heart the mirror of Beauty ; but the beauty of thy language is a mirror of the human heart.

To better understand the nature of his inspiration, it is necessary that we should consider the circumstances which have surrounded the Mussalmans of India and the effects they have produced upon them. The establishment of the British Rule brought them into close contact with a new civilization. They were no longer left to themselves, but at every step the influence of Western ideas was apparent. The spirit of freedom showed itself in every department of life and this spirit resulted in the terrible shaking off of the chains of the bigoted and orthodox Mullas. The study of English literature became a favourite pursuit. The traditional songs of the Urdu and the Persian poets, singing of love and wine could no longer attract the youth of the country. Shakespeare, Byron and Tennyson had a greater hold upon their hearts than Insha, Dard or Ghalib. Society was being reconstructed on the new principles of liberty and freedom, and it was no longer considered profane to read the English language or touch the English books. In fact there was the manifestation of free spirit everywhere, ending in a general revolt against the old order of things and a devotion to the Western civilization. The old order, as Tennyson says, has changed to give place to the new.

The West was considered to be the storehouse of all worthy knowledge. The development of science and the progress of the Western Nations presented to the rising generation of the Indian Muslims a very intimate relation, and their minds could not be brought to accept whatever was presented to them. Free thinking became the chief feature of the society, and it worked itself out in finding reasons for what they were used to believe on testimony. The effect of this renaissance or the revival of learning was marked in every aspect of life. Society, Literature and Religion came under its growing influence.

Never in recent history has a great power had such difficult administrative problems to solve, but a crowd of officials of exceptional ability achieved wonderful results. By inaugurating the system of education on Western lines they thoroughly prepared the soil for a mighty transformation. It opened a new era of political opinion in India. It set the people yearning towards a new heaven and a new earth. The nation arose like a sphinx from its ashes to reclaim its rights. The liberal tenden-

cies of the Western literature manifested themselves in the emancipation of the spirit overlaid with the dust of centuries. These were the tributary fountains that, as time went on, swelled into the broad confluence of our own times.

A Voice from the East.

The Aligarh movement whose destinies were in the hands of the great Sir Syed Ahmed Khan was the chief factor in creating an atmosphere suitable for the time. His thoughts and speeches had stirred the souls of the Indian Muslims, who began to avail themselves of the opportunities presented by him in learning more and more about Western ideals. He gathered round him the best intellects of the day, among whom prominently stand the great figures of Hali, Nazir Ahmed, Muhsin-ul-Mulk and Zuka-ùllah. The untiring efforts of Sir Syed Ahmed Khan and his companions in organising education on Western lines and infusing into the hearts of the young men of the country a new spirit are really admirable, considering the desired effect they produced in awakening their souls. Hali admits the influence of English literature upon his powers. His poems were not inspired by the traditional love and the wine, but by his ideal to depict the truth about nature and human life. *The Ebb and Flow of Islam* is Hali's best production which pictures to its readers the past and the present of Islam and inspires the present generation to action and progress along with the other nations of the world.

At this stage came in the humorous Akbar who in his simple but effective manner depicted the shallowness of modern society and the blind enthusiasm of the rising generation in following the Western ideals. His humorous writings did more than pave the way for Iqbal by criticising the influence of the materialism of the West. The importance of Hali and Akbar among poets can be best understood by realising the struggles of the Indian Mussalmans during the period of transition. The fall of the Moghul Empire had brought on them an atmosphere of inactivity and slumber. Their greatness was lost and from the position of rulers they became the ruled. They were tired of the themes of love and wine, and every sign indicated that they had fallen a victim to exhaustion. British Rule in India was established on a firmer basis after the great Indian Mutiny. There was peace in the country after that outburst of discontent which was the chief reason for the unfortunate part played by the Mussalmans in the event.

The Western ideals held the minds of the people at large, but it was not a healthy influence. The devotion to the Western civilization resulted in nothing permanent except the blind imitation in thought and deed of the West. The heart was stirred no doubt, but the energy was running in materialistic channels. Every where there was the leaning to materialism. It may be said that the general effect was only negative in its nature in that it destroyed the prejudices in favour of the traditional ways of thinking and ended in a revolt against them; but there was nothing positive left in its place. The period produced much ephemeral literature which is not worth the name. Hali and Akbar appeared on the stage with their full force expressed in their writings to set the society on a permanent basis. It is here that one feels the importance of these two great men. They admired the awakening in India and viewed it with sympathy, but the materialistic tendencies it was creating among young men were condemned by them. They showed that progress without religion is impossible.

Hali and Akbar, as *Z*ulfiqar Ali Khan says in his "A Voice from the East," paved the way for the genius of Iqbal. The elaborate history of the times throws much light on his work and a knowledge of it is essential to understand the inspiration of the poet. The two great poets showed the greatness of the early Mussalmans as due entirely to the influence of Islam and touched upon the hollow tendencies of the West. It was given to Iqbal to show in a more definite manner the materialism of Europe and its dangerous consequences on one side and the place of religion on the other as a result of mature thinking and experience. He moved in the West with some of the best men of Europe and watched for three years the havoc which the spirit of freedom played among the European Nations not under the healthy influence of religion but the devitalising influences of the materialistic tendencies.

By his education and travel Iqbal is the best person to speak about the West as well as the East. The genius of Iqbal found its expression in poetry. He may be considered undoubtedly to be one of the great men who are needed to interpret the East to the West and the West to the East and bring the two civilizations to a meeting point. Iqbal's message is no more confined to India. It is addressed to the Nations of Europe in as good a manner as it is done to the nations of India. Moulana Shibli rightly said that he would occupy the chair of Hali and Akbar when they would be no more, and the philosopher-poet of India has justified the prediction of the Moulana to a remarkable degree. He studied the different aspects of the growing materialistic tendencies prevalent in the West and has come to certain important conclusions which formed the back-ground of his poetry. Great poets are born, not made. The truth of this familiar saying is illustrated by the early life of Iqbal. Even from his college days signs of his genius have been shown to the world by his early but successful attempts at writing poetry. We have referred to the influence of Moulana Syed Mir Hasan on his mind while he was a student in the Sialkot College. He had genius for the appreciation of literature and the tuition of the Moulana Saheb in the Arabic and the Persian languages assisted him very much in expressing his own mind in verse.

It was the time of Musha'iras (the meetings of the poets) when every one who had something worth expressing in the form of poetry had an opportunity to give to the public the product of his imagination and poetic fancy. Iqbal was one of the poets of his place. Dagh was the famous poet in India at this time of his life. He became a teacher of His Highness the Nizam of Hyderabad, which added very much to his reputation. He was lending his helpful hand as a man best fitted for the purpose out of his experience, to such of the poets as were unable to go to him but carried correspondence about the correction of their own lines. Iqbal was one of them. Very soon Dagh found out that the young poet was a genius.

After all there were very few slips in his poems as early as that period that made the experience of Dagh correct them. He told Shaik Abdul Qadir when he met him in the Deccan that he had the proud privilege of correcting some of the early writings of Iqbal and talked about the young poet in terms of admiration. Iqbal's days in the Lahore College are more noted than his days at Sialkot from the point of view of his literary pursuits. In Lahore he very soon became the star of the poets' gatherings. The two lines which he wrote on one of the occasions won him a very great admiration.

> **Divine grace gathered the dew drops**
> **of memories from my forehead taking them to be pearls.**

Zulfiqar Ali Khan writes :—

> **In the midst of a huge and admiring audience Iqbal could be seen standing on a dais reciting the verses in sweet tunes which exacted applause and occasioned an indescribable enthusiasm. I was a witness of this scene several times when amidst a tempest of acclamation Iqbal was carried away almost fainting through an effort to meet the greedy demand of the cultured audience.**

But it is none of these poems that accounts for the reputation of the poet or shows his genius. They serve no other purpose than indicating merely how his greatness was slowly expressing itself in that early age. There are three stages in the development of Iqbal's poetic mind, leaving aside the outburst of imagination in his College days, and each one of them is marked by a distinct period of time. The first period ranges from 1901-05; the second, from 1905-1908 and the third from 1908 to the present moment. The world should wait to see the future expression of his thought and find out what it will mean. It has been pointed out that the relation between Dagh and Iqbal did not continue very long. Iqbal no doubt took by means of his correspondence the assistance of Mirza Dagh, but his influence was not very great. He admired Mirza Ghalib, the last great poet before the renaissance and followed his example in the art of expression. The lines of Iqbal are as difficult as the lines of his real master, though separated much from each other by the time. As Umrao Singh expresses in his foreword to *A Voice from the East*, "future ages will read more sense into his words as expressions as we find in other languages which have remained stationery, and future generations will understand him better than we do." He is perhaps in this respect like Browning, the English poet. Iqbal perhaps unconsciously reveals himself in his works and his remarks on Ghalib apply to himself in an equally good manner. He writes about Ghalib in his tribute to the great poet:

> **Thou art a complete spirit of the body of the literary men,**
> **And ornament of the Assembly but still hidden from it.**

The fact is that Iqbal's ideas are too deep and too subtle to be easily understood. One has to read the lines twice before comprehending the poet's meaning. He does not present us with cut and dried systems of philosophy. "I am afraid," he once declared, "I have no philosophy to teach. As a matter of fact I hate systems of philosophy nor do I trust principles or conclusions of philosophy. No man has condemned human intellect more than I, *i.e.*, as applied to ultimate realities of religion. No doubt I talk of things in which philosophers are also interested. But with me these things are matters of *living experience and not of philosophical reasoning*."

Iqbal's first poem to be published was "The Himalaya Mountains" which appeared in the MAKHZAN, the famous literary magazine of Northern India. The Editor of this magazine persuaded Iqbal, who was very shy and unwilling to publish it, to give him permission to do so. It was fortunately the first Number of the Journal that appeared in April 1901. From that time onwards, every month it contained one poem of his till he went to England. It seemed as though there was a spontaneous flow of his poetic imagination. The reputation of Iqbal by this time travelled far and wide and there was constant demand for the Professor at the time of the Anniversaries of Associations and especially those of the Anjuman-i-himayth-i-Islam, Lahore.

"The Himalaya Mountains" which is an invocation to the great mountains, is inspired by modern thought. It is full of ideas of patriotism that touches the heart of the people in a very beautiful manner. One of his poems "The Cry of the Orphan" which he read at the time of the Anniversary of the Lahore Anjuman is full of pathos for the forlorn condition of the Mussalmans. It appeals to the spirit of the Prophet of Islam for the amelioration of his followers.

Some of the best poems of Iqbal of the first period are so popular that they find a place in the books that are prescribed for the several University Examinations. "Himala" (The Himalaya Mountains), "Gul-i-Rangin" (The Coloured Flower), "Parinday-ki-Faryad" (The Cry of the Bird), "Sham à Wo Parwana" (The Lamp and the Moth), "Ek-Arzu" (One wish), "Tarana-i-Hindi" (Song of the Indians), "Chand" (The Moon) and "Kinari Ravi" (Beside the Ravi) are some of them. All the poems are in Urdu and very beautifully written. Their names themselves suggest to the mind of the reader that they do not deal with wine and the traditional love but with the natural aspects of the Universe. We find in them a better and a more imaginative intellect than what the poems of Hali, which are to a very great extent destitute of poetic imagination and are no more than prose poems, can make us understand about the writer. They are written in simple language and with much grace and ease.

O Lámp! why dost the Moth love thẻe,
And sacrifice his restless life,
Thy graceful ways keep him as unsettled as the mercury
What principles of love hast thou taught him?
In death he finds peace,
What eternal life is there for him in the light?
His prayer is to fall before thee;
There is the fire of love even in his little heart.
(*Sham à Wo Parwana*).

My way is not to pluck thee from the branch;
'tis the work of they that see the external beauty, alas!
These hands do not seek to oppress,
Nor am I the heartless gardener,
I care not for problems of science
But see thee with the eye of a bul bul.
(*Gul-i-Rangin*)

The earth and heaven were new worlds for me
And the embrace of mother a world itself;
The slight movement outward the pleasure of my life;
And my own speech the meaningless words,
If I cried in my childish pain
The shaking of the door bolt gave me pleasure.
(*Ahad-i-Tifli*).

Thou (reason) knowest the secret of life
But I (love) see it with my eyes;
Thy concern is about the outward, and external
But mine about the inward and hidden;
Knowledge is from thee but love of God is from me,
Thou seekest God, but I manifest the Creator.
(*Aql awr Ishq*).

The Garden is not full of music
Whose blossoms do not give the sweet smell of brotherhood.
I strongly wish for nearness,
And the nearness of the deep and the billows makes me wonder,
(*Sadai Dard*).

Thou seekest (moon) the meaning which I too do,
Thy light is the moonlight,
But mine is my love.
Thou hast no parallel in thy world in beauty,
And I am alone here
The ray of sun is thy death
And the sight of eternal beauty makes me unconscious.
(*Chand*).

Thou thinkest that there is God in stones,
But to me every particle of the dust of my country is a god.
Shakti, and shanti are in the songs of a bhakthi
And real worship is in love.
(*Naya Shuwala*).

> **Thy little heart is wondering at the sight of the lamp,**
> **Perhaps this is the recognition of something seen before,.**
> **The lamp is a ray of light but thou art a complete light,**
> **It is naked in the world, but thou art hidden.**
> **(*Bacha awar Shama*).**

The second period of Iqbal's poetry begins from 1905 and ends roughly with 1908, the period of his life in England. We have seen in a detailed manner the influence of Western civilization on the life of the poet. It will perhaps be interesting to know that during his stay in England he was almost on the point of giving up writing poetry altogether, but for the encouraging advice of his friend, Arnold. He expressed his determination to Abdul Qadir the Editor of MAKHZAN, who happened to be there at the time, but thanks to the advice of the Professor, the world has been allowed to see the genius of the poet more and more.

It is in this period too that he showed his preference to the Persian language, fascinated by the richness of the language to express his thoughts on Sufism.

The poems of the second period mark an advance in the poet's thoughts about life. It is no longer an imaginary play in the main with nature as it was in the first period, but imagination is made to serve the purpose of expressing his thoughts on more serious subjects.

" Muhabhat " (Love), ' Haqiqat-i-Husn ' (Truth of Beauty), " Payam " (The Message), " Visal " (Bliss of oneness,) " Koshishi Na Tamam " (Imperfect trial), " Payam Ishk " (The message of love) and Gazlyath are some of the poems of the second period. Their very names as those of the first period are suggestive of the contents.

My message is different from the message of others,
As different is the way of speech of one overcome by the pain of love.
Thou hast heard the cries of the bird in the cage,
But hear the different cry of the bird that flies high.
(*Address to Aligarh students*)

My friends, the movement of the world is life,
And this is an old truth;
Rest is impossible,
For in rest there is death.
(*Chànd Awr Sayyaray*)

The streams strongly wish for rivers and rivers for the deep;
And the billows for the moonlight,
Find out the secret of life from Khizar
—everything lives by imperfect attempt.
(*Koshishi Natamam*)

Man of the West! the country of God is not a shop;
What thou takest to be real is a counterfeit coin;
Thy civilization will bring about thy death,
As the nest that is built on a delicate branch cannot last long.
(*Payam*)

The third period of his thought begins from 1908, the year which marked his return to India after his contact with Western civilization, and continues to the present moment. It is the best so far in his life, considering the two great works the world has seen from his pen in the Persian language. He returned to India with matured thought and definite conclusions that have found expression in them. His minor poems in Urdu have also been written during this time and they naturally indicate a loftier tone of thought. The names of some of them may again suggest what they stand for. "Mazhab" (Religion), "Kufro Islam" (Islam and heathenism), "Muslim awr-Talimi Jadid" (Mussalmans and the new education), "Khizari Rah" (The guide of the Path), "Tulu-i-Islam" (The rise of Islam), "Shakespeare, Shikwa and Jawabi Shikwa" (The complaint and its reply), "Jawanan-i-Islam" (Young Mussalmans), "Asiri" (Slavery) etc. are the more important of them. But the most important are his Shikwa Jawabi Shikwa and Khizari Rah. The first two poems are the complaint to God and the reply of God about the pitiable conditions of the Mussalmans, and the third deals with a discussion between the poet and Khizar. These three poems* in Urdu give us some of the main ideas of Iqbal about the deplorable condition of the Mussalmans and the means to bring them back to their former greatness, and his interpretations of life, love and Government.

> Thy mercy of old is no more seen,
> What is it that thy old love has passed away?
> Why is the wealth of the world not found in the Muslims
> Thy power is unlimited.
> Thy will creates bubble of water on a desert
> That the traveller deceived by the mirage may satisfy the thirst.
> Strangers are rediculing us and there is disgrace and helplessness,
> Is it the reward for our dying on thy name?
>
> (*Shikwa.*)
>
> We are prepared for bestowing mercy but none seeks it;
> And we are prepared to show the way but none is a traveller;
> There is general training but there is no worthy metal;
> There is no real earth out of which the true Adam can be created,
> If there is a seeker, we give him greatness,

* *N B.*—Some of the lines translated are not in the order in which they appear in the poems. They have been picked up here and there wherever there is the unity of thought. The same principle has been followed with regard to other translations that appear in this sketch.

And a new world to the seekers of it,
Nation is from religion—and no religion, no nation
And if there is no love towards one another, there is no real world.
They (early Muslims) were honoured because they were Muslims,
But you have lost your respect in giving up Kuran.
(*Jawab-i-Shikwa*).

Life is above the fear of loss or the desire of gain
Measure it not by thy to-day and to-morrow;
For it is eternal, ever passing and always young,
Create thy world if there is a desire to be one of the living;
And life is the secret of man.
Thou art nothing if only a heap of dust
But if perfect, a sword that never misses its aim.
The democracy of the West is the old musical organ of despotism.
Behind whose screen there is the song of a Kaiser.
'Tis crushing in the democratic garment
Which thou takest to be a real thing.
The passionate speech of the members of peace associations
Is nothing but the fight of the wealthy.
(*Khizar-i-Rah*).

The more important still are his Asrari-Khudi and Ramuzi Bikhudi (both of them present the continuity of one theme) and Payami Mashriq which are indeed the greatest of his works as has already been mentioned. "The first of them "Secrets of Self" has been translated into English by Dr. Nicholson. This poem may rightly be called the world poetry or the world music meant for all times and all climes.

"It is a unique piece of literary art," says Sir Zulfiqar Ali Khan. He adds:—

It establishes a new system of character training. It formulates a philosophy which will produce saviours of a misguided world. What flavours and forces do we not find mingled in it? It has fire and courage which make the soul restless. It directs thought into new channels. It inspires self-confidence in palsied wills to climb ice and frowning heights. In a fascinating style he deals with the whole problem of 'man,' his life and attempts to forge a new destiny for his people by preaching reversion to the vigorous but simple life of the early Moslems based on the teachings of the Prophet.

The dynamic philosophy of Iqbal inculcates the vital principle of developing the latent forces inherent in man, "in order that the radiant and commanding personality may find manifestation, the travail of humanity being a necessary preliminary"

'Tis the fate of moths to consume in flame,
The suffering of moths is justified by the candle.
The pencil of the self limned a hundred to-day
In order to achieve the dawn of a single morrow.
Its flames burned a hundred Abrahams
That the lamp of one Mohammed might be lighted.

There are three features of the education of the self to become what it can in all its manifestations: (1) Obedience, (2) Self-control and (3) Divine Vice-regency.

Endeavour to obey, O heedless one,
Liberty is the fruit of compulsion.
By obedience the man of no worth is made worthy,
By disobedience his fire is turned to ashes
Whoso would master the sun and stars,
Let him make himself a prisoner of law.
The wind is enthralled by the fragrant rose,
The perfume is confined to the naval of muskdeer
The star moves towards the goal
With head bowed in surrender to a law.
To burn unceasingly is the law of the tulip
And so the blood leaps in its veins.
Drops of water become a sea by the law of union
and grains of sand a Sahara.
Do not complain of the hard nature of the Law
Do not transgress the studies of Mohammed.

The second important feature of the development of the self is self-control. The following lines of the poet, though they lose much of their poetic charm in translation, best represent what he means.

He that does not command himself
Becomes a receiver of commands from others,

So long as thou holdest these staff of
"There is no God but He" —
Thou wilt break every spell of fear,
One to whom God is as the soul in his body
His neck is not bowed before vanity,
The profession of faith is the shell,
But prayer is the pearl,

There is lastly the feature of the perfection of the self, evolved by hard and open struggle out of the first two necessary conditions. This perfection alone confers upon man his fitness to become the vice-regent of God on earth which of course is his birth right.

He wakes and sleeps for God alone
He teaches age the melody of youth,
And endows everything with the radiance of youth,
To the human race he brings both the glad message and a warning.
He gives a new explanation of life
A new interpretation of this dream.
His hidden being is lives' mystery,
The unheard music of life's harp,

The self is divine and unlike what the science of the West reduces it to be, no better than a mechanism and a prey to circumstances. Islam has made man the lord of the creation, and unless one develops the hidden secrets of one's self, there is no justification for us to call ourselves so.

It is this dynamic philosophy of Iqbal that has won him the highest admiration of some of the great men in the English speaking countries. "Payami Mashriq" (The Message of the East) written in the style of the poems of Goethe, the German poet, is the latest work of the great Indian poet. There are three main parts of the book. The first part, Ruba'iyath deals with some of the philosophical interpretations of important problems of human life, such as eternity, manifestation of God, desire and the effects of desire in the world, love and reason and their influence on man, change and materialism. Some of the allied problems such as life, the world of action, wisdom and poetry are dealt with in the second part, and there are beautiful poems on the greatest men of Europe such as Schopenhaur, Nietzche, Hegel, Bergson, Goethe, Tolstoy and Karl Marx. This part consists of "The Message to the Wise of England," "Tavern of the English" and "Address to England." The last part of the book comprises Ghazals that have been written in the style of Sa'di, Naziri, Urfi and Ghalib as a token of the poet's admiration of the masters of literature. The Ruba'iyath in "The Message of the East" begins with a tribute to love.

> **An inward passion lights my heart, my eyes**
> **That see the world are filled with tears of blood;**
> **A foolish stranger he to life's deep truth**
> **Who sadly sees in love a mind diseased.**
> **By love the desert turns to garden fair;**
> **The smiling flowers do get their pleasing smell;**
> **A shining ray that breaketh through the dark deep,**
> **The fish from which doth get the guiding light.**
>
> **Love painteth red the tender tulip petals,**
> **And lo our life with anxious recklessness.**
> **Nor all do have the treasure of love,**
> **Nor 'tis in tune with all, the tulip grows on hearts**
> **That are by passion burnt and spotted all, but never on**
> **Badakshan's fireless stone.**
> **The man hath made the sweet music of love,**
> **Who himself a secret hath made the secret out.**

In fact this forms the central theme of his message that has found its expression in his songs.

Iqbal laments very much the materialism of Europe, destitute of spiritualism that is born of true religion and real love of God. Man is no better than a mechanism and this conception of the Western mind is at the bottom of the miserable consequences and the commercialism of the European Nations.

Happy the man whose wisdom makes him see
Reasoning is Satan's but love is man's.
To seek through reason, ways of love
Is seeking through light the sun,
Real life is change,
The world doth change at every step, nor
With one form stops,—there is a constant change;
Thou art to-day if as the day that passed,
In thee thou hast no fire of changing life.

Nothing is permanent in the world, if at all there is permanence, it is the permanence of change.

Life is characterised by the strong desire to live,
Behold the world what joy is there in life,
Each atom's heart is filled with eager wish,
To live, and the blossoms smile with triumph fair,
When breaking through the tender branch of the tree.

These lines of the poet express in a very beautiful and effective way the great principle of life. It does not consist in the desire to annihilate the self as some of the Eastern philosophies maintained, for the self is as eternal as God.

The self's beyond our morn and eve, and none,
Doth know its hidden origin; but hark,
This Khizar taught me now a worthy truth,
The deep is never older than the billows.

To understand the nature of self is the primary duty of every man. It is ridiculous if he is a stranger to his own self, but the poet sounds a note of warning that the self is not amenable to the discursive reasoning which mechanically divides it.

The human mind soars high and speaks with heaven,
Alas thou knowest not thy own self so near,
For once on self like seed thy eyes be fixed,

That brings from down the earth the needed fruit
To know life's truth like burning flame and heat
The self should not be divided but
To see thyself there is needed a friend's eyesight
Look not at the self as a blind stranger.

Knowledge is acquired by doubts, but faith alone can make action possible in the world. Scepticism is not a good friend in the field of deed. The poet himself admits in his "Asrari-Khudi," how he experienced scepticism about the universal problems during some part of his life:—

Seeketh thou thy knowledge of the things to grow
To doubts a victim be, but if dost wish
The real deed to do, thy faith makes strong
Seek one, see one and be one.

It is interesting to find out that Iqbal's philosophy about change, eternal nature of the self and his hatred of discursive reasoning (but not reason) possesses close resemblance to Bergson's ideas about them. Bergson fights very vehemently in his "Creative Evolution" against the mechanistic conception of the self.

The resemblance between Iqbal and Goethe, though they are separated by time and distance, strikes the mind of the student of literature. It has already been pointed out that Iqbal's "Message to the East" was written in the manner of the German poet. It was a very troublesome time when Goethe lived. There were evident marks of degeneracy among his countrymen but his inspired imagination worked their salvation. Very much similar is the voice of Iqbal in India. His inspiring thought has shown to Indian Muslims the futility of Western materialism and made them devoted to religion and the things of the spirit. They are little by little influenced by his noble appeal for action and spirituality which alone can give them a place as a nation in the world. But the message of Iqbal is not confined to India. It is as much a message as to the Westerners themselves to the Indians who have come under the Western influence. His emphasis on the love of God in his later writings has made some men believe that he is drifting once more to the traditional Sufism, as understood by the ordinary mind which ends in inactivity and annihilation of the self. In fact it was this conception of Sufism that brought on him the uproar of men of the old ways of thinking, that in his Asrari-Khudi where the Self is everything, he is preaching the doctrine of egotism. Such men are now perhaps rejoicing that Iqbal can once more be claimed by them; but this is a mistake. The love he preaches is not antagonistic to the principles of self he depicted in Asrari-Khudi for in that case there is nothing but a contradiction but it is surely a harmonious blending with it. He says, " Carry this message from me to the old Sufis that I am that brave man who realises through self the Creator."

There is activity and there is life. The Self is eternal and the manifestation of God is through the self. Life is full of dangers, but all should be brave for the sake of perfecting the self and bringing out its latent treasure. Love of God and religion are the two means to attain this noble end. Iqbal has thus carried on the work of Hali to perfection.

His poems breathe sincerity. He feels for the abject position of his countrymen and every line of what he writes is poetry in the sense that it is inspiring. It illumines the mind of the reader and brings him to the knowledge of his self. We meet in his writings with neither unnecessary praise of some of the poets of an earlier day nor the traditional talk of beauty. He finds in nature the expression of eternal power and for him as for Keats beauty is truth and truth beauty. Some of his poems are in very easy language. His difficult poems do not betray an effort on his part. He is as spontaneous in the latter as in the former. It is the genius of Iqbal that he talks with grace and ease in the Persian language as he does in the Urdu tongue. Iqbal received his inspiration from nature and history. His genius freely makes use of them. He gracefully draws upon nature for similies and metaphors, which make his poems lively and illuminating in the highest degree. Some of them are very charming by nature of their simplicity, and impressive in an extraordinary way. Iqbal is an out and out nationalist and his poems also sound a pan-Islamic note. In fact it is one of the chief features of Islam that takes in its hold the Muslims of the whole world.

A glance at the poems of Iqbal makes it clear that there is charming variety. One feels as though he is reading the works of some of the modern poets of England. The poetical works of Iqbal side by side with the "Dewan" (poems) of any one of the poets before him make the point very clear. There is not only variety of topics, but also variety of form—Ruba'iyath, Mussaddas, Masnavi, Qita'a Ghazal, but all made use of with his natural ease and charm. The poet's inspiration does not wait to be twisted into one particular form; but it expresses itself freely in the words of the moment, full of harmony and music. The variety of form even in one poem in some cases indicates the natural and spontaneous expression of the poet's thoughts as they rise up in his mind. Some of his longer poems, dealing with the lofty themes bring to our minds the grandeur of Milton's poetry. They carry with them the full soul force of the poet and create in us an emotion that makes us forget ourselves. His power of depicting nature is marvellous, though perhaps his greatness is in his "study of man." There is in him the eye of the poet combined in a happy manner with the eye of the Eastern philosopher marked by its spiritual insight.

He takes pleasure in quoting in his poems verses from great masters of literature. This is generally done in his Persian poetry. Sometimes part of one line and sometimes the whole of it is quoted, the poet completing the part in the case of the former, but the quotation seems so harmonious with the poem that it is difficult to understand that it has not been written by him, but by some other hand.

Iqbal has no faith in modern democracy. It represents to him nothing but the oppression of the poor by the rich. There is behind it the influence of commercialism, which is the result of the materialistic proclivities of European nations. It is in fact slavery but not genuine freedom and shows the least respect to the divine self of man. It is sacrificed to serve the selfish ends of the wealthy classes, the real rulers in the name of democracy. Hence the painful misery which bursts out in a revolt. True freedom must give scope for the development of the self. Submission to one who is inspired by religious feeling is better than submission to the heartless many. People have begun to realise the danger of the doctrine of the survival of the fittest in its application to the relation between man and man, and its unethical implication after the Great War. America has unfurled the banner of revolt against that favourite doctrine in bringing about State interference wherever it is preached. Is the faith of the great poet then unsound not based upon facts but on imagination? Some of the translations in the book show to the reader how he thinks about the problem. He says in *The Message of the East*:—"My days in the English tavern came back to my mind. The cup was more shining than Alexander's and the cup bearer had a prophetic eye, but it did lack the enthusiasm and love of Khaleel and Khaleem, which were devoured by the careless thought."

Iqbal is essentially the poet of the future. As a writer in the ALIGARH MAGAZINE aptly says:

He paints the past to contrast it with the present, and thus pave the way for the future. The greatest charm about him is that he is not a dreamer or idealist, but is a realist, and combines in himself the poet, the reformer, the leader and the practical man of the world. He does not teach us simply to think but to act. To sum up he has rejuvenated the old, roused the lethargic, raised the fallen, inspired the dispirited, strengthened the weak, emboldened the cowardly, elevated the humble, cured the ailing, electrified the inert, invigorated the enervated and enlivened the lifeless.

So lives amidst his glories the philosopher-poet of India, the pride of the world and an inspired messenger to all the nations. It may not be far off when his great works will be translated in every language and he will find a loving welcome in every country. For already in Afghanistan, Persia, and Turkey, in England, Hungary and other European countries his reputation is rapidly spreading. And of late his powerful and vitalising poems have cast a spell over the minds of those who have come in direct contact with the Muse of Iqbal.

Sir Muhammad Habibullah

A SCION OF THE CARNATIC FAMILY

THE Hon'ble Khan Bahadur Sir Muhammad Habibullah, K. C. I. E., Kt. is a son of the late Mr. Aushukh Hussain Khan Saheb, a scion of the famous and ancient Carnatic family. He was born on September 22, 1869, and after completing his education in the "*Zilla*" High School, Saidapet, prosecuted his studies for law for which he had an ardent liking, and joined the Bar at Vellore in July 1888. He soon attracted the attention of the authorities, and was appointed to the various honorary offices open to the Non-Officials in the mofussil.

LEADER OF THE VELLORE BAR

For a period of 13 years he commanded an extensive practice as a Vakil and was recognised to be the leader of the Bar. He laboured much for the welfare of the public; and in 1901 he devoted all his attention to public affairs to the entire exclusion of his legal practice, and thoroughly acquainted himself with the administrative and legislative details of Local Self-Government. He was elected as Non-Official Honorary Chairman of the Vellore Municipality in July 1895 largely through the suffrages of his Hindu brethren on the Council. In this capacity for a period of three years he guided its affairs, with consummate tact for administration.

MUNICIPAL AND ADMINISTRATIVE WORK

After giving up a very lucrative practice at the Bar, he accepted the office of Secretary of the Municipality in September 1901 and despite the great personal sacrifice involved thereby continued in that Office until September 1905, when he was made its paid Chairman. He was specially chosen by the authorities for these Offices as, before he became the administrative head of the Municipality, its affairs had been in such a notorious state, that the Government had found it necessary in the interest of the tax-payers to dis-enfranchise the Municipality in 1900. From the year 1905 till 1919 for a period of over 14 years, he filled the Office of Chairman and showed remarkable industry, zeal and public spirit in the administration of the Municipality. It was during this period that the town secured the benefit of a protected water supply, which eradicated the scourge of cholera to which the city fell a victim every year, as also a Drainage Scheme. He was able to launch these schemes by wise and judicious handling of the finances of the Municipality. He laboured hard to improve the amenities of life in the town and was very keen on improvement schemes for which he was able to obtain appreciable financial aid from Government. He was no less responsible for bringing into existence an up-to-date Hospital in the place of an old and ill-adapted building which served the purpose. He brought about numerous other improvements in the city and it is no exaggeration to say that it was due to him that Vellore was recognised as a model Municipal City. A full-size oil painting of Sir Muhammad, which was unveiled by the Hon'ble the Chief Minister to the Madras Government in 1923, adorns to-day the Lakshmanaswami Town Hall of the City as a reminder of his beneficent activities.

HONOURS AND GOVERNMENT RECOGNITION

In recognition of his disinterested devotion to public weal a certificate of Honour was awarded to him by the Government in 1897 on the occasion of the Golden Jubilee of Her late Majesty Queen Victoria and the title of "Khan Bahadur" conferred upon him in 1905. As the Vice-President and President of the Vellore Taluk Board and subsequently as Vice-President of the North Arcot District Board he earned a reputation for administrative capacity and was in 1917 elevated to the position of the first Non-Official President of the District Board, North Arcot. As an active and vigilant member of the pre-Reforms Legislative Council from 1909 to 1912, he shared in the discussion of many important questions concerning his electorate and was noted for the courage of his conviction. He was regarded as the best orator on that body next to Sir Arthur Lawley, the then Governor of Madras. It is noted to his credit that he was elected to the Madras Legislative Council by a mixed electorate consisting of mostly

P. 417

HON. SIR MAHOMED HABIBULLAH

Hindu voters, representing North Arcot, Chingleput and Nellore Districts. Such was his popularity among the Hindus that they vied with one another in giving their votes to him, in preference to other rival Hindu candidates.

He attended the Coronation Durbar of H. I. M. King George V in December 1911 as the guest of the Madras Government, and was one of the few who was chosen for that rare privilege of paying homage to His Majesty on the occasion of the Coronation. He had also the honour of being presented to the King Emperor at the Royal Court held at Calcutta after Coronation.

In his Council work, as in other fields of public activity, there was not a single Committee or Conference convened by Government, in which his participation had not been secured nor was there any administrative or legislative measure of importance in which his advice was not sought by the Local Government and the District authorities showing the great regard in which his views were held by them.

AS MEMBER OF COUNCIL

It was in the year 1919 that his exceptional merits found suitable recognition when he was appointed by that sagacious and shrewd statesman Lord Willingdon as Temporary Member of the Executive Council during the absence of the Hon'ble Sir P. Rajagopala Achariyar on leave for 6 months (July 1919 to January 1920) and in that capacity he held the port-folio of Local Self-Government with credit. On the expiry of this period, in view of his wide knowledge and long experience of Local and Municipal Administration, he was nominated as expert member to steer the District Municipalities Bill through the Legislative Council.

MADRAS CORPORATION

In April 1920, he was appointed as Commissioner of the Madras Corporation and was the first Non-Official to be chosen to that Office under the Madras City Municipal Act of 1919. In June of the same year he was the recipient of the title of C. I. E. in recognition of his meritorious services as Temporary Member of the Executive Council which His Excellency publicly acknowledged in his speech at Vellore, in reply to the address of the Municipal Council.

BACK TO THE COUNCIL

On the introduction of the Reforms in December 1920, he was appointed permanently to the position of Member of the Executive Council and took his seat on December 17, 1920. He held charge of the Revenue port-folio and inaugurated far-reaching reforms in the Land-Revenue Administration of the Presidency. By his frequent tours, he came into touch with the land-owning and agricultural classes and studied the problems affecting their welfare at first hand. He endeared himself, in particular, to the people of the Ceded Districts by his sympathetic and humane famine measures during the years 1921 to 1923 which were suitably acknowledged by the representatives of these

Districts in the Legislative Council. Although Sir Muhammad assumed charge of the most important port-folio in the Provincial Government without any previous training or experience of the intricate and complex problems of Land Revenue administration, yet it must be said to his credit that he left the Department with an impress of his efficient, tactful and sympathetic management of its affairs.

He has always held independent and authoritative views on all matters of administrative import. He gave valuable evidence before the Royal Commission on Decentralization and the Islington Public Services Commission and was appointed as the Provincial representative of the Indian Reforms Committee.

Further honours were in store for him. A Knighthood was conferred on him in June 1922.

MEMBER OF THE VICEROY'S COUNCIL

Sir Muhammad was a member of the Royal Commission on Superior Public Services in India presided over by Viscount Lee during 1923-24 and he contributed not a little to the Commission's main recommendations on Indianization and Provincialization of Imperial Services. He returned in March 1924 for a few months, as Senior Member and Vice-President of the Madras Executive Council; and in December 1924 was elevated to H. E. the Viceroy's Executive Council as Member for Education, Health and Lands to fill the place vacated by the Hon'ble Sir Muhammad Shafi. He has been since appointed as Pro-Chancellor of the Delhi University. In June 1924 he was made a K. C. I. E. It is confidently anticipated that he is destined for further honours and distinctions at the hands of His Majesty the King Emperor.

A POPULAR OFFICIAL

He is a 'persona-grata' with the people of Madras. On the eve of his departure from Madras in December 1924 to Delhi, there were numerous public demonstrations and entertainments, to give expression to the feeling of esteem and affection in which he is held by the Europeans, Hindus, Muhammadans and Indian-Christians alike. At a public dinner given in his honour on the 18th December 1924 at the Moore Pavilion, Madras, responding to the toast to his health proposed by the learned Chief Justice Sir Murray Coutts-Trotter, and seconded by the late Sir P. Thyagaraya Chetty, the Hon'ble Sir Muhammad made a characteristically eloquent, modest and graceful speech, instinct with a feeling of deep attachment to the Province of his birth. After expressing his grateful thanks for the honour done to him, he concluded:—" Of course on an occasion like this when I am leaving my old friends, my familiar environments, the fields of labour where I have toiled and moiled, and all that is near and dear to me in this Province, to take up a position of responsibility by no means less than the one that I now fill, in a place where I have yet to make friends, to environments with which I have yet to become familiar, I feel seized, as it were, by a certain degree of trepidation. But the consolation that I feel on an occasion like this is that my friends are encouraging me, while I am yet at the threshold of that office. They are assuring me of their continued goodwill towards me. They give me the hope that, wherever I may be, I can always rely upon their comradeship, their cordial relationship with me and their help and assistance. And above all, I have got also this consolation that when I am going, I do so with the pride that my friends who are wishing me good-bye to-day, elated probably by the fact that I have not so far disappointed them in my performances, are wishing me godspeed in my new sphere of work. May it be that that Providence which has given me until now strength, courage, health and life to shoulder the responsibilities which had fallen upon me, will continue to give me the same courage, the same fortitude and the same common-sense, so that I might shoulder those future responsibilities also with courage and firmness! Can you not imagine, my friends, with what a heavy heart I go? But let me assure you that although I am going to what may be regarded as the heights of Olympus, the Madras Presidency will still continue to occupy a warm corner in my heart. Further this Presidency being not only my land of birth, but also my first and foremost love, will continue to demand from me special attention. And I can assure you that whenever opportunity offers itself, or rather to be quite plain with friends, I shall create opportunities as often as I possibly can, I will try to see my friends often and enjoy a warm shake of hands with them.

I am afraid I cannot at this juncture say anything as to what I will do or will not do in my future position. At most, I am now Member-designate of the Viceroy's Executive Council. I have not yet entered upon my duties, and I shall therefore not venture to make any promises as to my future performances, but will only rely on your confidence that in my present and past careers I have not disappointed the expectations of my friends, (Hear, hear). I rejoice in the fact that by my accession to the Viceroy's Executive Council, Madras shall have the honour of claiming a majority on that Council. That, indeed, is a gratification in which Madras may well indulge. And I fervently hope that when I come back after laying down the reins of my future office, I shall still have the pleasure of knowing that I have not disappointed my friends." (Loud cheers).

An eloquent speaker and a trenchant writer, gentle and alert in appearance, catholic and large-hearted, highly thoughtful and cultured, known alike for his devotion, courage, sympathy and insight, this distinguished nobleman enjoys in a pre-eminent degree the respect and confidence of Government and the love and affection of the people, as it is given to few in the illustrious roll of public men in India. As an administrator and statesman, he has made a name; and as a premier Muhammadan nobleman of India, he is held in universal esteem.

Referring to his public career the TIMES OF INDIA, Illustrated Weekly, dated 23rd January 1923, in the course of a brief review, paid a tribute to him with something of a prophetic insight, in the following words:—

"An accomplished speaker, courageous in his convictions and sympathetic in his outlook, he has made his mark as an administrator and statesman; and not yet has he reached the pinnacle of his political career."

From a seat in a Municipal Council to one in the Cabinet of the Indian Empire, the record of this distinguished public servant is a shining example to every public worker and patriot. In the words of the Earl of Rosebury—"These great men form the pedigree of nations; and their achievements are their country's title-deeds of honour. The dark mass of humanity passes to the grave, silent and unknown. It is these men, who stand forth and mark the march of generations. Here stands one who embodies honest faith, honest toil and honest devotion to duty."

Sir Abbas Ali Baig

SIR ABBAS'S ANCESTORS

MIRZA ABBAS ALI BAIG, who succeeded Syed Husain Bilgrami to the India Council, comes of an old military family, who trace their descent back to those sturdy sons of the mountains, the Chaghatais, who under their illustrious clansman, Mahomed Zahiruddin Baber, overthrew the Pathans and established their dominion in India in 1526. Mr. Baig's ancestors came down with the Imperial Army to the Adilshahi Kingdom of Bijapur, when it was wrested by the Moghuls from the feeble grasp of Sikander Adil Shah, and one of them, Mirza Imam Ali Baig, was in command of the Bijapur forts just before the establishment of British Sovereignty in the Deccan. Mr. Baig's father was a Commissioned Officer in the British Army and fought under the British flag in the Afghan, Sikh and other wars, and in the Mutiny, and had his breast covered with medals.

THE MIRZA'S EARLY CAREER

Mr. Baig received his education at the Wilson College, Bombay, where he held a Senior Scholarship throughout his career. He graduated in 1878, topping the list of successful candidates from his college. In January 1882, Mr. Baig was appointed

Deputy Educational Inspector for Muhammadan schools in the eleven districts of the Central and Southern Divisions of the Bombay Presidency. During his tenure of office, Muhammadan education received a great impetus, the number of schools nearly doubling in three years' time. Schools for girls were established at the more important centres of Muhammadan population, and the training of teachers was placed on a sounder basis.

AS DEWAN OF JANJIRA

In March 1886, his services were lent by Lord Reay's Government to the Janjira State to serve as Dewan to Nawab Sir Sidi Ahmed Khan. When he took charge of his new post, the State treasury was quite empty, and corruption and mismanagement were rampant in almost every department of the administration. His administration was characterised by vigour and efficiency, both unknown so far in the annals of that maritime State. Every branch of the administration was reorganised; the finances of the State were placed on a sound basis; municipalities and dispensaries were established in all the principal towns; the Victoria Water Works, which have so greatly improved the health of the capital town, were started; the number of schools was increased; and, though several vexatious imposts were abolished, the revenue was considerably augmented. Year after year the administration received the warm commendation of the British Government, and when Mr. Baig relinquished his post in 1889 on being appointed a

Statutory Civil Servant by the Marquis of Lansdowne, the State Treasury had a balance equal to a year's revenue, and the State was considered to be quite as well administered as any part of the adjoining British territory.

A BOMBAY CIVILIAN

On his admission into the Statutory Civil Service, Mr. Baig was posted to Thana, where he served for three years with distinction as Assistant Collector and Magistrate, passing all his Examinations with credit, and heading the list at the final test before his confirmation in the service. In 1892, he was transferred on special Political duty to Kathiawar to serve on the Prabhas Pattan Commission. In 1893 he acted for a brief period as a Presidency Magistrate in Bombay, and in June of the same year he was appointed Oriental Translator to Government. In 1901, the post of Reporter on the Native Press and Registrar of Native Publications was merged in his office. He became soon after Secretary to the Civil and Military Examination Board and to the Central Committee for Departmental Examinations. Mr. Baig was appointed a Fellow of the Bombay University in 1887 and a Justice of the Peace in 1894.

The designation "Oriental Translator" does not perhaps convey an adequate idea of the multifarious responsibilities devolving on this official in Bombay. He had, in addition to his other duties, to assist the Political Department in all ceremonial matters, such as

Durbars, State visits etc., to advise the authorities as to the social status of the native gentry desirous of entering the portals of Government House for attending certain social or State functions, to report on the eligibility of the aspirants for presentation to Royalty or the Governors, and to serve as the medium of communication between the representatives of the King-Emperor and those of the Native Chiefs who were not familiar with English. He had also to report on the entire Native Press of the Presidency, and to extract the essence of all Press criticisms on the policy and measures of Government and to condense the grievances of the ryots for such action as might be called for. Needless to say that these extremely delicate functions call for the exercise of exceptional tact and judgment, as any lapses from the strictly right course might give offence to the susceptibilities of the public or arouse the disapproval of the authorities.

Mr. Baig is known to have satisfactorily discharged all the duties of this onerous office during the period of eleven years he was in charge of it. He worked very hard during the last visit of His Majesty as Prince of of Wales to India.

AS DEWAN OF JUNAGADH

His services were lent to the Junagadh State, in 1906, where he was serving until his appointment to the India Council in 1910. That State during his Dewanship made good progress. Within the quinquennium he was privileged to be at the helm of affairs there, he evolved order out of confusion, prosperity out of impending bankruptcy and initiated progressive schemes in all directions. As a writer who examined the conditions before and after the Mirza's four years' Dewanship of the State truly pointed out: "He inaugurated progressive schemes in every direction. Large schemes of irrigation were tackled and, as a consequence, the area under cultivation was greatly extended and larger crops insured. Scientific conservation of forests was begun, and over 50,000 trees were planted by the road-side. Railways, roads, bridges, water-works, markets, and hospitals were built or projected. Impetus was given to industrial life. The annual value of trade rose from Rs. 4,000,000 to Rs. 11,000,000. The prosperity brought about by these economic measures enabled the Dewan to increase the annual revenue from Rs. 1,900,000 to Rs, 3,200,000. Mirza Abbas Ali Baig did not hoard the surpluses that accrued, but spent them upon building public works and upon extending education."

"I have been looking," said H.E. Sir George Clark, the Governor of Bombay, when he visited Junagadh, "into the Administration Reports of Junagadh and I cordially congratulate Your Highness upon the position to which you have raised this important State. The facts speak for themselves. In all that implies thoughtful care for the happiness and advancement of the people, there has been steady progress. The results are plainly to be seen in a prosperity which nothing but exceptionally bad seasons could check. The growth of the cultivable lands and the increase of production under well and canal irrigation are most noteworthy, while the development of trade to the extent of an average annual increase of 33¾ lakhs is an example of prosperity for which it would be difficult to find a parallel. I am specially glad to know that there is now an organised Forest Department. Unquestionably the rainfall of parts of Kathiawar has been diminished by reason of indiscriminate cutting and the conservation of forest areas on scientific lines is essential, although we find it very difficult to make our people realize the fact. The surpluses of a revenue that proved a record last year are being expended on public works of permanent utility and are exactly calculated to advance the health and happiness of the people, while the feeder railway, which I am to have the honour to open to-morrow, will promptly stimulate trade and agricultural development. A fair future lies before Junagadh under the beneficent rule of Your Highness. All that His Highness owes to the wise and beneficent administration of Mr. Baig."

IN THE INDIA COUNCIL

Though the Mirza was a successful administrator in two Native States as well as in British India and was very popular with those immediately concerned his name was not familiar to the rest of India. Indeed, when in 1910 he was suddenly appointed by John Morley to take the place of Mr. Bilgrami on his Council, the appointment was by no means much favoured. Commenting on the appointment the

PIONEER wrote: "Until the other day it would have seemed passing strange that anyone on hearing of an appointment to the Council of India should have to stop and ask who the Member was." Evidently John Morley's intention was to preserve the balance between Hindu and Mahomedan in his Council. That a Mahomedan should be appointed for the place vacated by Mr. Bilgrami was understood in the then prevailing temper of Muslim thought in India. But the public desired that the Secretary of State should have the benefit of a Councillor selected from among the more prominent public men, in the wider arena of Indian public life. Why go to an obscure native State and for an officer in the routine of the services? In the Mirza's case however the experiment proved a success principally because of his own exceptional abilities. THE TIMES OF INDIA welcomed the appointment and congratulated the Secretary of State on his choice of "so able, experienced and independent a representative" of the Mahomedan community for his Council. And events fully justified the choice. For during the seven years that he spent in Whitehall—the last year as Vice-President of the Council—Mirza Ali Baig championed the Indian cause against traducers and reactionaries. In persuading the Secretary of State to go ahead with progressive measures, in winning the acquiescence of civilian colleagues with pronouncedly reactionary opinions, he brought to play all the tact and experience he had gained in the Native States. He could be firm, fearless and independent and at the same time tactful and courteous. For several long intervals, says one who knew him, Mr. Baig was the only Indian on the Council, and his strong and persistent advocacy of the Indian cause was of exceptional value. Not unoften he was opposed by a solid phalanx of Anglo-Indians on the Council but he continued to exert his influence though in a minority.

"Mirza Abbas Ali Baig's presence at the India Office was particularly useful during the last three years, when grave questions affecting India's destiny arose for consideration and settlement. Among these problems were the Indian demand for Self-Government, the Indianisation of the higher branches of the Administration, the partnership of India in the British Commonwealth of Nations on a footing of complete equality, the abolition of indentured labour, and the treatment of Indians in the Self-Governing Dominions."

Those services naturally won him the regard and esteem of his countrymen. Nor were the Government unmindful of his great work on the Council. For, soon after his retirement from the India Council, after serving his full seven years' term, His Majesty the King bestowed on him the insignia of a K.C.I.E.

A FINE SCHOLAR

Sir Abbas is a fine scholar of Persian and is acquainted with eight Oriental languages. The Glasgow University in recognition of his scholarship conferred on him in June 1912 the Degree of LL.D. in *causa honoria.*

LADY BAIG

The present Lady Baig, for Sir Abbas married a second time, is a cultured and accomplished lady who has taken part in some social and humanitarian activities of her husband. One who knew her writes: "Lady Ali Baig's presence in London, gave British women the opportunity to come in contact with one of the most cultured of Indian women. She is a progressivist in thought, speech, and action, vitally interested in movements of reform, and withal a devoted wife and mother and a careful housewife."

P. 433.

MAHOMED ALI JINNAH

Mahomed Ali Jinnah.

BIRTH

MR. MAHOMED ALI JINNAH was born on Christmas Day 1876, at Karachi in a rich Khoja trading family; he has always felt proud of his native city. In his speech on the resolution for the abolition or reform of the Council of the Secretary of State for India at the Indian National Congress held at Karachi in Christmas 1913, he said: "You do not know what pleasure it gives me to stand in this platform in this city of Karachi where I was born, where I have found by my side, after my arrival in this city, personal friends with whom I played in my boyhood."

SCHOOL

Mr. Jinnah was the eldest son of a rich Khoja merchant; and he was consequently reared up in affluence and fondled by the members of his family: one might very easily have become a spoilt child under these circumstances. But young Mahomed Ali exhibited an extra-ordinary passion for study. He was, very early in life, put to school and sent to the local Madrassah; from the Madrassah, in due course, he went to the Mission School whence he appeared for the Matriculation Examination of the Bombay University.

EARLY INFLUENCES—GOKHALE

From his boyhood Jinnah developed a passion for his religion and his motherland. His ambition was to be considered one of the Faithful and at the same time one of India's worthy sons; to put it shortly, he was anxious to earn the sobriquet, "The Muslim Gokhale". Gokhale was Jinnah's early model. In moving the resolution for a memorial to Gokhale at a meeting held in Bombay in May 1915 soon after Gokhale's death, he said:

> We mourn the death of Mr. Gokhale so deeply with the rest of India that I have no words at my command to adequately express our deep sorrow and grief. He was respected by the Mahomedans and the Hindus alike and trusted by both He had endeared himself to all India by his single-mindness of purpose, the earnestness and zeal with which he worked and his absolute devotion to the cause of India as a whole. He was of late looked upon as an all-India man if such an expression is permissible. He was a great political Rishi, a master of the finances of India and the greatest champion of education and sanitation. He was a fearless critic and opponent of the measures of Government and the administration of the country but in all his action and utterances he was guided by reason and true moderation. Thus he was a help to Government and a source of great strength and support to the people.
>
> One of the greatest lessons that his life and work teach us is the example of what one single individual can achieve, how powerfully and materially he can help and guide the destinies of his country and his people and from whom millions can derive true lead and inspiration.
>
> Personally I have had the honour of being one of the colleagues of Mr. Gokhale in the Imperial Council for some years and to me it was always a matter of pride and pleasure to listen to him and often follow his lead.
>
> Mr. Gokhale has left millions behind him to mourn his death but to millions his life and work will be a source of education and inspiration, especially to Young India. Once addressing the students in England, he advised them to keep their faces towards India always, no matter where they were and worked, like the Japanese who always has his face towards "Nipon."

In these words of Mr. Jinnah we notice what a great influence Gokhale had on his early life. Of Mr. Jinnah also it might be said that he was a fearless critic and opponent of the measures of Government and the administration of the country, but that in all his action and utterances he was guided by reason and true moderation which was Gokhale's. And like Gokhale, Mr. Jinnah is an all-India man. He is an Indian first and a Mussalman only afterwards; or rather, as he himself put it in the course of the discussion on the Indian Finance Bill this year (1925) in the Imperial Legislative Assembly:

> I never was a candidate and I am not a candidate for any post. .....I, sir, stand here with a clear conscience and I say that I am a nationalist first, a nationalist second and a nationalist last.......I once more appeal to this House, whether you are a Mussalman or a Hindu, for God's sake do not import the discussion of communal matters into this House and degrade this Assembly which we desire should become a real national Parliament. Set an example to the outside world and our people.

IN ENGLAND

After matriculating at the Bombay University Jinnah went in 1892 to England to study for the Bar. He was scarcely sixteen and there is a picturesque portrait in words about his appearance then—"a tall thin boy in a funny long yellow coat." In England, he joined the Lincoln's Inn and kept his terms. In due time he was called to the Bar and he returned to India as a Barrister in 1896.

During his stay in England he came under the magic influence of Dadhabhai Naoroji and had the good fortune of taking his first lessons in politics from that veteran patriot. Dadhabhai was then the president of the London Indian Society and he acted as the guide, philosopher and friend of the Indian students in England; young Jinnah soon attracted his attention. Under the leadership of Dadabhai Jinnah developed a sound sense of political values and a genuine enthusiasm for fair play which were the outstanding features of Dadhabhai Naoroji's patriotism. It is no wonder that Gokhale noted his worth and said that Jinnah had true stuff in him and that freedom from all sectarian prejudices which would make him the best ambassador of the Hindu-Moslem Unity.

THE LONDON INDIAN ASSOCIATION

His five or six years' stay in England as a student induced him to take an active interest in the welfare of Indian students there and he never forgot them in his later annual visits. He did his best to make himself acquainted with the feelings of the Indian students, as he said on the speech he made at the public meeting held in the 28th June 1913 at the Caxton Hall, Westminster. He felt the need for an Association and at that public meeting he moved a resolution to the following effect:

This meeting of the Indian students in the United Kingdom resolves that a central society called the London Indian Association be formed with the following aims and objects. (1) To maintain and foster unity and to strengthen and encourage friendship between the Indian students in the United Kingdom by providing various opportunities for social intercourse and interchange of thought and ideas by holding *(a)* debates and discussions on various subjects of interest, *(b)* social gatherings and *(c)* by acquiring a clubhouse; (2) Provided that this

association does not take any part in actual and administrative politics.

In the course of his speech on that occasion he said:

The position of the Indian students in this country is one without a parallel The Indian student class is typically representative of the best the country can produce. They are, so to speak, the custodians of the reputation of India. Unfortunately just now, so far as the British public is concerned they have not a good name. Instead of conducting themselves merely as students and learning all they can of the civilization which the British people had taken centuries to build up they are tempted to use strong language in political questions. I will remind you that you are scarcely competent as yet to deal with the political problems presented by our country. Nobody appreciates more than I do the honesty of purpose or the patriotism which has induced you to do what you have done; but it is time that you seriously consider your position.

You might ask me what the proposed association is going to do. We are in the first place going to get rid of the exclusiveness which is the outcome of having many different clubs and societies. We are going to develop the opportunities for a wider national outlook.

To-day, in India, the men who were taking the most active part in politics are men who were educated in England and have returned home to serve our country. By all means mix with the English people and make friends among them. But make it your first duty while you are here to meet and understand your own countrymen. It is your presence in England that gives you an opportunity of coming in contact with others from all parts of India.

In conclusion, he pointed out that they must give the Government no cause to take precautionary measures, that they must observe a high code of honour and morality, that they should abandon strong language and hysterical ideas and become earnest workers and serious thinkers and that when they go back home they must become great missionaries in the cause of Progress.

We may be sure that Mahomed Ali Jinnah in England as a student conformed to these principles which later on he laid down for the guidance of the Indian students; nor need we doubt that he utilised his stay in England to come into close contact with the people from different parts of India.

RETURN TO INDIA

Jinnah returned home to find his family involved in financial troubles. He was denied the welcome of a comfortable home and the easy affluence in which he had lived when he left for England. The advantages of fortune were denied to the young barrister and Jinnah had to struggle through somehow during the lean years at the Bar. After three years of struggle and difficulties, Jinnah secured through the kind offices of an old friend of his family an introduction to Mr. Macpherson then acting Advocate-General of Bombay. Mr. Macpherson was kind and extended to the young Indian the privilege of reading in his chambers—an unprecedented thing in those days for a European Barrister to do. Occasional briefs now came to him and found him ready to utilise them in winning and building up a reputation for legal learning and powerful advocacy. Gradually Jinnah rose to power and to a leader's position at the Bar. In 1906 he was enrolled as an Advocate of the Bombay High Court. To-day Mr. Jinnah occupies an envied position at the Bombay Bar and commands a very extensive and lucrative practice.

AS A LAWYER

As a lawyer Mr. Jinnah is considered a very able and powerful advocate on facts and is respected as an authority on questions of law. In the debate on the Transfer of Ships Restriction Bill in particular and generally when questions of law were raised Jinnah always commanded a respectful hearing both in the old Imperial Council and in the new Legislative Assembly.

EARLY POLITICS

Mr. Jinnah has, from the very beginning, been a staunch Congressman; his own political views have been shaped by association with Gokhale, Dadhabhai Naoroji, Surendra Nath Banerjee and Chitta Ranjan Das. Speaking in the Legislative Assembly, he said:—

> Sir, I might say that I learnt my first lesson in politics at the feet of Sir Surendra Nath Banerjee. I was associated with him as one of his followers and I looked up to him as a leader. He commanded the utmost respect of a large body of people in this country and of my humble self. Sir, as far as Mr. Das was concerned, he was a personal friend of mine. I have enjoyed his hospitality and he was one with whom I worked for many years.
>
> On this occasion I should like to say this; that these were leaders in this country for whom the Muhammadans had the greatest respect; and they commanded the confidence of the Mussulmans as much as any Mussulman leader. Sir, the only lesson I feel that we might draw from the careers of these two great men is this: that in *Unity lies Salvation.*

THE AMBASSADOR OF UNITY

And Jinnah was pre-eminently fitted to be the 'Ambassador of Unity.' For though he represented purely communal constituencies both in the old reformed Council and in the New Legislative Assembly, he has always enjoyed the confidence of Hindus and Muslims alike.

And no wonder. For he belongs to a Khoja trading family; the family trait brought in its wake cosmopolitan views of life and an intimate acquaintance with the Parsi community. A 'Khoja' inherits by birth the virtues of both Hinduism and Muhammadanism; 'Hindu by race and Moslem by religion' as Sarojini Devi put it. He had the courtly and pacific demeanour of a Hindu combined with the virility and strength of purpose characteristic of a Moslem. And he married a daughter of Sir Dinshaw Petit, a Parsi magnate of Bombay; the marriage did not mean a deviation from orthodox Muhammadan religion; for the faith permitted a marriage with a lady professing an alien religion. But the marriage brought in relief his cosmopolitan outlook. While like a true Khojah he retained the faith and the enthusiasm of a convert to Muhammadanism, his faith was rooted in the soil of true Indian nationalism.

A MOSLEM LEADER

Though certain orthodox Moslems looked askance and considered him outside the pale of orthodoxy, Mr. Jinnah, both in his inner life and in his outward conduct has proved himself a true believer as will be evident from the following extracts from his speech.

There is one word more, Sir, before I finish. I do not think it is necessary to mention these things really, but one is forced into this lest one may be misunderstood. But for the present state of the Mussalman community and in some quarters in particular, I do not think it is necessary for any Mussalman to say that he would not do anything either in this Council or outside this Council which is likely to prejudice the interest or the cause of his community. I, Sir, yield to none in that respect. If this Bill (The Elementary Education Bill introduced by Gokhale) had been referred to a Select Committee and I wish it, if certain requirements were not embodied in this Bill by the Select Committee to safeguard the Mussulmans and if this Bill would have come before this Council without those requirements which I think will be necessary in the interest of the Muhammadans in the present state of the condition of the people in this country, I would have been the first to oppose that Bill until and unless those requirements were incorporated in the Bill. But that is not the question, that is not the point before the Council to-day. Therefore I will only rest content by saying this : that if this Bill were referred to the Select Committee and if this Bill did not provide for certain requirements and modifications which I think are just in the interests of the Mussulmans, I would certainly then be the first to oppose it.

And take this passage from his speech on the Indian Shipping (Second Amendment) Bill.

Sir, I am one of those men who do not mind vilification or misrepresentation. Any man who enters into public life takes it as in the day's work that you are vilified and you are misrepresented. But that is not going to prevent us on the floor of this House from doing our duty according to our convictions. Now, Sir, as the Honourable Sir Muhammad Habibullah has said, if I thought that this measure was against the tenets of our religion, I certainly would not be a consenting party to it. Then if we are satisfied that it is not against Islam or the interests of Islam and the community, what is the next question that we have got to consider in this House? On the merits, is this Bill a beneficient Bill or is it not? That is the next question.........Well, Sir, I am satisfied that it is for the benefit of my community and therefore I have no hesitation in giving my assent to this Bill.

Passages like this may be multiplied from his speeches wherein he expresses it as his first article of faith that the Mussalman should not deviate from the tenets of his religion ; and even a consideration of what is beneficial to the Moslem community comes only afterwards.

It is this attachment to Muhammadan religion and Muhammadan law that inpelled him to sponsor the Wakf Validating Bill in the Imperial Council in 1913, sitting as a special member for an extra term for that purpose. Wakfs are religious endowments made by a Muhummadan ; and under the

Muhummadan Law and religion, a wakf can be validly created for the benefit of the family of the author of the wakf. But the Privy Council, contrary to the accepted interpretation of the Muhummadan Law, decided that such a wakf is invalid if the ultimate benefit to the public is really illusory. Motives of public policy may support that decision and probably the decision on the whole might have been a blessing to the Moslem community. But Mahomed Ali Jinnah felt that public policy ought not to be the test. There must be no deviation from the Law. In the speech he made in support of the Bill he said:

> What we have got to do is to administer the Muhammadan Law to the Mussulmans, and therefore to introduce the question of public policy which is foreign to the Islamic jurisprudence, to my mind is outside the question; and therefore, there is no such thing as public policy of any kind, so far as Muhammadan jurisprudence is concerned to which the provisions of this Bill are in any way opposed. I therefore give that simple answer to that point.

COUNCIL WORK

Indeed his position as a true Moslem leader has been so unchallenged that we find him repeatedly returned as a Muhammedan Member from Bombay ever since the first Imperial Legislative Council of the Morley-Minto Reforms. In the Council Hall he never brought in communal strife; but at the same time he watched jealously and saw to it that the fact of the Moslems being in a minority was never used against their interests. And he never allowed encroachments on the interests of the Moslems, their laws and their religion. The result is that his work has been much appreciated. As a nationalist he made effective speeches on the Elementary Education Bill, the Indian Criminal Law Amendment Bill and Transfer of Ships Restriction Bill. His speeches on the Police Administration, on the working of the Indian Railways and on the Budget are clear and to the point and constitute powerful attacks on the ways and methods of the bureaucracy. We may cite some passages as examples.

ELEMENTARY EDUCATION BILL

In the course of his speech on the Elementary Education Bill, he said :

I regret very much that some of my countrymen are opposed to this Bill. Well, Sir, it is our misfortune that there should be this difference of opinion. One thing I can assure this Council of, however, and that is this : that a great and overwhelming majority of my people are with me. When I was speaking on the Marriage Bill the other day, I frankly and openly admitted that I was supporting a minority, that the majority of my people were opposed to that measure. But my innermost convictions were in favour of that measure, and I felt it my duty to support the motion. In the same spirit, I ask those who are opposed to this Bill to concede to me that a great majority of my countrymen, Hindus and Mussulmans, are in favour of and support this Bill. That being so, Sir, I have a double satisfaction not only my innermost convictions are in favour of this Bill which shall always be the first and foremost consideration with me either in opposing or in supporting a measure, but I have the additional happiness that even the opinion of my countrymen, of the majority of them is in favour of it.

The brilliant manner in which he tore the arguments of Sir Harcourt Butler (who opposed the Bill) to shreds deserves to be carefully read alike for its cogeney and eloquence.

THE CRIMINAL LAW AMENDMENT BILL

Jinnah has pointed out in the course of his speech, that a frank and independent criticism of the Government or the measures of the Government is the duty of every member of the State. But he believed that there was a certain amount of misguided enthusiasm in the country; enthusiasm which was subversive of law and order. Therefore in connection with the Criminal Law Amendment Bill he said:

I wish to express that nobody condemns in stronger terms the misdeeds of which a long list was given us a few minutes ago by the Home Member. I also wish to express that every attempt on the part of my countrymen to undermine the authority of the Government and to disturb law and order deserves, in my opinion, the strongest condemnation and the highest punishment. These men have a desire to undermine the authority of the Government; these men who have a desire to disturb law and order, are in my opinion, the highest enemies of my country and my people. They are to-day doing the greatest harm to the cause of India.

THE PRESS ACT

Mr. Jinnah has no sympathy for the revolutionary. He does not despair of reforming the Government and if he has moods of despair, he does not even then think the less severely of the anarchists and the revolutionaries who seek to undermine the Government.

His abhorrence of anarchism and the revolutionary led him to support the Press Act and in the same speech he justified his attitude in the following words:—

I remember, Sir, in 1910, when the Press Bill was introduced at Calcutta, much as we felt that a severe blow was going to be dealt at the liberty of the Press, much as we felt that our most prized liberty *viz*, the liberty of the Press was going to be curtailed, our hands were tied, our mouths were closed by the misdeeds of some of the misguided men who belong to our country, and we, almost as a body of non-official members, realised and felt that the Government was bound to take certain measures to maintain order and law; and reluctant as we were, we felt that, although we were losing what we prized most, *viz*., the liberty of the Press to a certain extent, we not only supported it but we supported it with every power that was in our possession.

Then referring to the conditions of the time (April 1913) he said:

On this occasion I feel that having regard to the history of political crimes, my hands are tied, my mouth is closed and my countrymen who are responsible for these deeds are responsible to-day for the position which I occupy in the Council at this moment.

And he uttered a grave note of warning to the misguided anarchists:

Let those men who still have these misguided ideas, let those men who still have these hallucinations realise that, by anarchism, by dastardly crimes, they cannot bring about good Government; let them realise that those methods have not succeeded in any country in the world and are not likely to succeed in India. Let those men realise, before it is too late and before they bring their country into a position which may be regretted by every patriot who feels for and loves his Motherland; let them realise that those are not the methods.

In the remaining portion of his speech, he discusses the legal aspects of the Bill and ends thus:

With these remarks I have no alternative but to support the principle of the Bill and I trust that it will emerge from the Select Committee in a manner that will not go beyond the English law and that the safeguard I have indicated will be provided for.

ATTITUDE TOWARDS GOVERNMENT

Mr. Jinnah once said in the Imperial Council: "Sir, I believe in criticising the Government freely and frankly; but at the same time that it is the duty of every educated man to support and help the Government when the Government is right." It was in pursuance of this policy that he did not oppose the Press Bill, and the Criminal Law Amendment Bill.

It was in the same spirit that he welcomed the Indian Defence Force Bill. The same spirit animated his speech at the public meeting held in July 1917 in Bombay to pass a vote of confidence in Lord Hardinge.

> Why was it, he asked, that even now India was willing to bleed white without a murmur? It was because they had a Viceroy who shared in their sorrows and who shared in their joys, who understood the hearts of the people of this country and who held liberal and generous ideas about their national progress.

The following passage indicates what, in Mr. Jinnah's opinion, is right for the Government to do.

> My Lord, if you want India to care for your Government, to stand by you, to co-operate with you, what we want is that the spirit of the Government should be Indian (no matter whether the personnel is foreign or Indian) and that on occasions when the interests of India are likely to suffer, when any injustice is going to be done, our Government and those who are at the head of the Government should stand up for us and speak for us as any Indian would do.

HIS WORK IN THE OLD IMPERIAL COUNCIL

We have so far considered the activities of Mr. Jinnah in the old Imperial Legislative Council, how he was a nationalist first and last and how he supported all progressive Bills like the Elementary Education Bill and Civil Marriages Bill, how he stood by the Government as he felt himself in duty bound to do in the passing of the Press Act and the Criminal Law Amendment Act, how in the midst of his nationalist activities he did not forget his duty to his constituency but watched jealously lest the Mussalman interests should suffer at the hands of the majority and the Moslem well-being overlooked. We need not add that when the question of Primary Education came up again before the Imperial Legislative Council five years after Gokhale's Bill was thrown out, Mr. Jinnah fought both on principle and for the sake of Gokhale's revered memory for the grant of free and compulsory primary education.

Before passing on to consider Mr. Jinnah's relation with the Congress and the Moslem League and the Home Rule Movement and the present Legislative Assembly where he is the leader of the Nationalist party we might usefully consider certain subsidiary matters.

MR. JINNAH AND THE STUDENTS

From the time when he was an Indian student in England, Mr. Jinnah kept a continued interest in students and in education. He was never tired of addressing students and advising them. Delivering the inaugural address at the Bombay Moslem Students' Union in February 1915 he emphasised firstly the value of discipline and secondly of self-reliance; and he said:

> Then again one of your chief objects should always be co-operation, unity and goodwill, not only among the different sections of Mahomedans but also between the Mahomedan and other communities of this country. As citizens, you would have to share the burden of work, when your student days are over, with other communities; and it would be therefore better if you started at the earliest possible opportunity to try to understand the other communities; that would be the surest way of progress in this country. There was one thing which must be realised by every thinking person as essential. If progress was to be made it would not be by dissensions. Unity was absolutely essential to progress.

Lastly, he always insisted on advising that students should not take an active part in politics; but he also urged that they must take an interest in and understand politics; for, in India, politics had become the life-blood of the people and it was therefore no use shutting their eyes to it.

Mr. Jinnah also fought for the removal of restrictions on admission which English educative centres imposed on Indian students. He took a prominent part in the agitation for simultaneous examinations for the Indian Civil Service; he fought for and obtained new openings for educated Indians; and he welcomed the Indian Defence Force Bill on this account.

Mr. Jinnah does not object to a foreign personnel in the Government; he does not want to exclude Englishmen from the Indian Civil Service or from India. What he, with the rest of his politically minded countrymen, fights for is equal treatment; equal opportunities for service being given to the Englishman and to the Indian. What he objects to are the three monopolies that the Englishmen enjoy in India (1) the monopoly of power in the administration of the country (2) the monopoly of commerce and (3) the military monopoly.

AS A CONGRESSMAN

From the beginning Mr. Jinnah was an ardent Congressman. His early influences ensured that; he attracted considerable attention at the Calcutta Congress of 1906 at whose historic sessions Dadhabhai Naoroji, as President, enunciated the ideal of Swaraj for India. Mr. Jinnah was then acting as Naoroji's private secretary. He had been regularly attending the 'big meetings' every year. At this Congress he made his maiden speech on family wakfs about which he put up such a fight later on in the Legislative Council.

ALL-INDIA MOSLEM LEAGUE

Being a Congressman, the narrow sectarianism which actuated the Moslem League in its inception kept Jinnah away from participation in it. But his sympathies were in favour of the Mussulmans and their forming a League to advance themselves and their country. At the request of the League (which showed a great respect for Mr. Jinnah even when he kept out of it) he attended the Conference of Hindu and Moslem leaders at Allahabad convened in 1910 under the presidency of Sir William Wedderburn. Doubtless, he worked for Unity even then, although the times were not favourable. But the times changed and with it Moslem opinion. In 1912 there was a conference of Muslim leaders at Calcutta to consider the remodelling of the constitution of the All-India Moslem League "on more progressive and patriotic lines." Its secretary went on an extensive tour gathering Moslem opinion. And in December a special council meeting of the League met to consider proposals at which Mr. Jinnah was invited to be present and to render help although he was outside the League; His Highness the Aga Khan presided and an entirely new constitution was drafted which was ultimately enthusiastically adopted at the Special Sessions of the League at Lucknow on the 22nd March 1913. At this Lucknow meeting, Mr. Jinnah, still an outsider, gave his invaluable though informal support to clause D of the new constitution which materially embodied the Congress ideal of "attainment under the aegis of the British Crown of a system of Self-Government suitable to India through constitutional means by bringing about a steady reform of the existing system of administration, by promoting unity, by fostering public spirit and by co-operating with other communities for the said purpose."

The year 1913 marks an era in Mr. Jinnah's life. Already he had sat three years in the Legislative Council. This year, he introduced and successfully piloted the Wakf Validating Bill. For the first time a Bill introduced by a private member became law. He displayed during the progress of the Bill great powers as a tactician and debater and his powers in effecting unity were brought into play. Now that the League had a new constitution, he was persuaded by its sponsors, Mohamed Ali and Syed Wazi Hussain, to join it. He was enrolled as a member in autumn 1913; the enrolment was to him a sacrament. His sponsors were required to make a solemn preliminary covenant that loyalty to the interests of the Muslim League and the Muslim interest would in no way and at no time imply even a shadow of disloyalty to the larger national cause.

WITH GOKHALE IN ENGLAND

About the middle of April 1913 Mr. Jinnah left for England in the company of Gokhale for a long holiday. But there could be no holiday for the active and energetic minds of Gokhale and Mr. Jinnah. As Mrs. Sarojini Naidu guesses with characteristic poetic vision and accuracy, " the Arabian stars and the Egyptian waters keep record, doubtless, of their mutual hopes and dreams for the country of their devoted service." And once in England, Jinnah could not keep idle. He founded the London Indian Association. He fought for the removal of the restrictions on Indian students. He made a study of the working of the India Council. When he again returned to England in 1914 as a member of the Congress Deputation concerning the reform of the India Council, this study was particularly useful.

REFORM OF THE INDIA COUNCIL

For, by this time, he became a full-fledged Congressman taking a prominent part in every Session. At the Congress session at Karachi in 1913 he moved for the abolition of the Council as then constituted and its reconstruction on sound and progressive lines. His chief suggestions were (1) that the salary of the Secretary of State for India should be placed on the English estimates (2) that the independence of the Council should be secured by providing for election by the members of the Legislative Councils in India, and (3) that the character of the Council should be advisory and not administrative. In commending the resolution for the acceptance of the Congress he remarked that the then constitution of the Council made the Secretary of State a greater Moghul than any Moghul that ruled in India. He pointed out that the objection to the existing constitution was that the Council consisted of men with settled opinions, that there was no place for the representation of the views of non-official Indians and that the Council unduly interfered with the details of the administration. He emphasised this opinion in the Agra Session of the Moslem League at about the same time. And in the speech delivered by him in London at the party given to the Congress delegates by Sir William Wedderburn, he strongly criticised the proposed portfolio system and fought for seats in the Council to be filled up by election from India. He expounded the Congress proposals on this matter in clear and unambiguous terms and strongly supported them by a statement to the LONDON TIMES criticising the Bill introduced by the Secretary of State.

> I cannot but say that the provisions contained therein are most disappointing and I feel sure that that is how the people of India will receive it; what hope can measures like this inspire in the people of India who are working forward to bigger and more substantial reform in time to come when in matters such as the reform of the Council of the Secretary of State for India which is after all more advisory in its character than anything else, the just proposals of the Deputation appointed by the Indian National Congress have not been accepted.

THE BOMBAY PROVINCIAL CONFERENCE

The untimely death of Gokhale in 1915 stirred Jinnah into greater political activity. He was chosen as the President of the All-India Moslem League which met at Lucknow in the Christmas week 1916. At about the same time (October 1916) he presided over the Bombay Provincial Conference at Ahmedabad. Already Mr. Jinnah was looking ahead for the Reforms. In the course of his Presidential Address at Ahmedabad he said :

> Granting that there is peace, prosperity and efficient administration in the hands of the civil servants is that any reason that the control the management and the administration of the affairs of our country should for ever be continued as a monopoly in the hands of a bureaucratic Government .. ...Is that any reason why the commissioned ranks in the Military and Naval Services should be closed to the sons of India? Is that any reason for denying to Indians the right to join the Volunteer Corps and for continuing the application of the Arms Act?......... The first question that arises is whether this system of administration conducted by the Civil servants who are neither under the control of or responsible to the people who pay their salaries can any longer continue. It is said that they are responsible to the Secretary of State for India and that the Secretary of State for India in his turn is responsible to Parliament......Is it possible or natural as a rule for members of Parliament to grasp or grapple with questions affecting the internal administration and progress of India? When it was found that that was not possible in the case of Australia, Canada and South Africa, with few millions of population, would it not be miraculous if they continued to manage successfully the affairs of India by Parliament sitting in London?

Mr. Jinnah is nothing if he is not constructive and clear ; and in this address he mapped out the form of administration he would like to set up in his Province, embodying the principles of devolution and decentralization.

COMMUNAL ELECTORATES

And then he passed on to consider the need for separate electorates :

> To most of us the question is no more open to further discussion or argument as it has become a mandate of the community. As far as I understand, the demand for separate electorate is not a matter of policy but a matter of necessity to the Mahomedans who require to be roused from the coma and torpor into which they had fallen so long.

And after pleading for Unity and concerted action by the Hindus and the Mahomedans he ended with this peroration :

In conclusion, let me tell you that after all a great deal depends upon ourselves. Hindus and Mahomedans, united and firm, the voice of the three hundred millions of people vibrating throughout the length and breadth of the country will produce a force which no power on earth can resist. India has, I believe, turned a corner. She has passed through great sufferings and borne them patiently for centuries. There is now a bright and a great future in front of her. We are on a straight road; the promised land is in sight. 'Forward' is the motto and clear course for Young India. But in the onward march, we must be circumspect, and never lose sight of the true perspective before us. And Wisdom and Caution should be our watchwords.

ADDRESS TO THE MOSLEM LEAGUE

The Moslem League Address followed closely on this speech. He spoke of India's loyalty to the Empire ideal.

What India has given in the fellowship of service and sacrifice has been a free and spontaneous tribute to the ideals of the great British Nation, as well as a necessary contribution to the stranger of the fighting forces of civilisation which are so valiantly rolling back the tides of scientifically-organized barbarism. In this willing service of the people of India there has been no distinction of class or creed. It has come from every part of the land and from every community with equal readiness and devotion. In this service there has been no cold calculated instinct at work. It has sprung from a clear compelling sense of duty and moral sympathy and not from any commercial desire to make a safe political investment. India's loyalty to the Empire has set no price on itself.

After considering "a few of the baseless and silly generalities in which the advocates of the existing methods of Indian governance indulge freely and provocatively when the least menace arises to the monopoly of the bureaucratic authority and power," he emphasised that India was fit for freedom and that she is determined to convince the British Empire that she is fit for the place of a partner within the Empire and that nothing less would satisfy India. He went on to point out the spirit of

Unity that actuated the Hindus and the Mussulmans. There was a simultaneous sitting of the Congress and the League at Bombay in 1915. There was a simultaneous sitting again at Lucknow in 1916. How much of the credit for this Unity is Mr. Jinnah's is obvious from this passage from his League Address in 1916:

> The simultaneous sessions were brought about with no little labour, anxiety and trouble. I do not wish to go into past controversy but I venture to say that the session of the All-India Moslem League at Bombay will go down to posterity as peculiarly interesting in its results............The League rose phoenix-like, stronger, more solidified and determined in its ideals and aspirations, with added strength of resolution in carrying out its programme............The main principle on which the first All-India Moslem political organisation was based was the retention of Moslem communal individuality strong and unimpaired in any constitutional readjustment that might be made in India in the course of its political evolution. The creed has grown and broadened with the growth of political life and thought in the community.
>
> I have been a staunch congressman throughout my public life and have been no lover of sectarian cries, but it appears to me that the reproach of separation sometimes levelled at Mussulmans is singularly inept and wide of the mark when I see this great communal organisation rapidly growing into a powerful factor for the birth of United India. A minority must above everything else have a complete sense of security before its broader political sense can be evoked for co-operation and united endeavour in the national tasks; to the Mussulmans of India that security can only come through adequate and effective safeguards as regards their political existence as a community.

So much in justification of the communal spirit of the Muhammedans. We have an inkling that Mr. Jinnah's own views are different, for he says:

> Whatever my individual opinion may be, I am here to interpret and express the sense of the overwhelming body of Moslem opinion of which the All-India Moslem League is the political organ.

THE CONGRESS LEAGUE SCHEME

Then he spoke of the Congress-League scheme in moulding which he took an active part, and of the need to have a Bill drafted by constitutional lawyers as an Amending Bill to the Government of India Act. Mr. Jinnah was one of the nineteen members of the Imperial Legislative Council who submitted the famous Memorandum on the Reforms and a new constitution. His part in this and in the Congress-League Deputation to England to effect changes in tbe proposed Montford Reforms and his evidence before the Joint Committee are not dealt with here as they form part of the general movement for reforms. He said in his address:

> I was one of the signatories (to the memorandum of the nineteen members) and I would urge upon you to follow them (the proposals) substantially so far as fundamental principles are involved in those proposals; those demands were formulated by responsible men who owe duty to the Government and the people alike as 'chosen representatives' and not in a spirit of bargaining; those demands are the minimum in the strict sense of the word.........Co-operation in the cause of our Motherland should be our guiding principle.

It is by these active steps in the cause of Unity that Mahomed Ali Jinnah earned the sobriquet of "the Ambassador of Unity." As early as 1913, Mr. Jinnah said "we have now reached the active stage when we realise that we must co-operate with one another for national work." Ever since, he had worked to bring about a union between the League and the Congress, between the moderates and the extremists. He was in turn a Congressman, a Moslem Leaguer and a Home Ruler and President of the Bombay Home Rule League:

I wish to say why it was that I joined the Home Rule League. When representations were made and resolutions passed year after year by the National Congress, when their demands were pressed last year in that carefully drafted memorandum of the 19 members of the Imperial Council, it was said that that was only the demand of a few educated agitators and lawyers, but that the masses were not ready for any such reform. It was to meet that attack, which was made in this country as well as in England, it was to remove that misrepresentation that they resolved that they should be an educative propaganda, and that they should reach the masses and put the verdict of the masses not only before the bureaucracy but before the democracy of Great Britain. (October 1917, at the Allahabad Home Rule League.)

He moved for the adoption of the Congress-League Scheme in the Calcutta Congress and ably defended it against criticism. He also seconded the Self-Government Resolution in the same Congress. He had already in 1915 issued appeals to Moslem leaders to attend the simultaneous sessions in Bombay. The following is from his appeal:

I wish to state with the greatest emphasis that there is no truth in the baseless statements made in some quarters that any responsible Mahomedan leader thinks that the League should be merged into the Indian National Congress. But conference in collaberation, if possible, is the object, and what objection is there to this course?

IN THE ASSEEBLY

With the advent of the Reforms Mr. Jinnah found himself in his proper place in the Legislative Assembly, and there he organised the Nationalist party. He took an active part in the debate for the grant of full Self-Governing Dominion status to India and supported Pandit Motilal Nehru. A passage from his evidence before the Joint Committee was cited to him where he said in answer to a particular question:

We have no other method to suggest. Dyarchy fits in more with the order of things as they exist at present in India and it can be justified on the ground that it is for a transitional period.

Mr. Jinnah replied " my proposal was that there should be dyarchy in the Central Government also—" and he added: " We have realised, Sir, that dyarchy has failed."

THE REFORMS REPORT

Mr. Jinnah found an excellent opportunity to emphasise these views in an authoritative document. He was one of the Members of the Reforms Enquiry Committee presided over by Sir Alexander Muddiman. The publication of the Report in March 1925 was an important stage in the history of the reform movement in India. The Majority Report signed by the President and four others upheld the present system and suggested some trivial modifications in the Act with a view to pacify the national demand which was becoming insistent. While the Minority Report which was signed by Sir Tej Bahadur Sapru, Sir P. S. Sivaswami Iyer, Dr. Paranjpye and Mr. Jinnah boldly put the case for dropping dyarchy altogether. The signatories pointed out :—

In our opinion, the system of Dyarchy was during the first three years everywhere worked in the Legislatures by men most of whom were professedly its friends and who, generally speaking, tried to work it in that spirit of reasonableness which is referred to by the majority of our colleagues, and it is no exaggeration to say—indeed this is also the testimony of several local Governments which we have quoted above—that generally a spirit of harmony and co-operation prevailed between the Legislature and the Executive notwithstanding the fact that the atmosphere outside was for sometime markedly unfavourable. The Indian Ministers and members of Executive Committee also, upon whom new opportunities of service were conferred, appeared to us to have been with the sphere of their Executive duties, equally eager to work the Constitution in the same spirit of reasonableness, and yet differing from the majority of our colleagues we have been forced to the conclusion that the pre-

sent system has failed and in our opinion it is incapable of yielding better results in future.

AN INDIAN SANDHURST

In his Budget speeches he effectively criticised the Government policy, especially in the matter of the Army. He was perhaps in his best form in attacking the bureaucracy in respect of its Army policy. In Feb. 1925 a resolution was moved in the Assembly urging the Governor-General-in-Council to take early steps for starting a well-equipped Military College in India. Mr. Jinnah's speech on this occasion made a profound impression on the House as well as on the Government. In a series of searching questions and cross examination he strongly criticised the Government's delay in taking steps to Indianise the army. He went so far as to question their *bona fides* with regards to their promises of early concession to the legitimate military ambitions of Indians. It was in fact this speech that made the appointment of the Skeen Committee inevitable.

NOT A WRECKING PROGRAMME

In his speech upon a discussion of the demands for grants in the Assembly, Mr. Jinnah made the position of the Nationalist party clear (11-3-1924). He said:

I want to make it clear further that the Nationalist party here in this House do not stand for any wrecking programme. In this Assembly, we stand to pursue a policy and a programme of a constitutional character. We shall pursue that policy and that programme until the last stages of the constitutional struggle are exhausted. There is no idea in the mind of the Nationalist party to resort to civil disobedience. There is no idea in the mind of the Nationalist party that we want revolution. There is no idea in the mind of the Nationa-

list party that we are going to carry on a campaign of non-payment of taxes.

Mr. Jinnah fought for protection to Indian industries in the Assembly even when it affected the interests of the city of Bombay which he represented.

I say I am not going to be guided by my own city that I love...... ...I have got here as a Member of this Assembly to consider the larger and national interests; and that is the one consideration which weighs with me in this Assembly and I hope that is the only consideration which will always weigh with me. Certainly, I would be the first to assist Bombay if I could, but not at the expense of larger interests.

He supported the motion for the unconditional release of the Gurudwara prisoners.

THE LEE REPORT

Mr. Jinnah's independent attitude to political questions was never more explicit than in his protest against the Lee Report. He recognized the work and worth of the Superior Services in India but protested strongly against the extravagant claims of the Services, claims which are incompatible with the policy of Indianisation besides being a heavy drain on the finances of India. At the same time he urged that his own community should have an equal opportunity to serve the administration. In supporting the Resolution of the Assembly on the Lee Commission Report he said:

Speaking on behalf of my colleagues here who would agree with me, the Muhammadans do not desire anything else but their just and fair share and their proper rights and I feel confident also that there is no Hindu Member in this House who would for a single moment grudge to the Mussulmans their just and fair rights; and I am glad that the Home Member has also recognised that in his speech.

THE BENGAL ORDINANCE

Mr. Jinnah opposed the Bengal Criminal Law Amendment Bill in very strong terms. He never minced his words in his criticism of the bureaucracy.

It is nothing else but a disgrace to any civilised Government to resort to a measure of this character.............I repeat without fear of contradiction that when the Ordinance was promulgated by the Governor-General it was condemned universally by the people of India. That Ordinance has not expired yet. It could be in force for six months only. In the face of public opinion, the obstinacy of the Government has gone to this length, that instead of coming to this Legislature they take shelter under the local Legislature. They go to the Bengal Council, what did they find there? The Legislature of Bengal rejected the Bill; and how was it enacted? It was enacted by a process of certification, a certification which required the assent of his Majesty. And here I may say that I am shocked that such an abhorrent measure, that this abomination should have been placed on the table of the British Parliament and should have been allowed to pass the scrutiny and the resentment which ought to have been shown against this measure; I am one of the greatest admirers of the British Parliament, but when the British Parliament has come to this, I think I am entitled to say that certainly it has lost the title of Mother of Parliaments which it claims..........Why is it that we show this resentment? Why is it that we are opposed to it so much? Why is it that it goes against our grain? The reason is a very simple one, and it is this—that by this measure you are not giving any protection to the innocent, that the innocent are likely to be persecuted, that this is an engine of oppression and of repression of legitimate movements in this country and it has been abused in the past and there is every likelihood of its being abused in the future.

Speaking on the Ordinance he had already pointed out the danger in clear terms:

I owe allegiance to the King Emperor. What do I get in return for it, what do I claim in return for it? Protection of my liberty, my life and my property. My liberty should not be taken away without a judicial trial in a proper court where I have all the right to defend myself, Under this Ordinance, if I were a citizen of Calcutta, I should have to transfer my allegiance to Mr. Tegart the Commissioner, because he is the only man who can give me protection and not His Majesty's High Court or His Majesty's Courts.

Mr. Jinnah took an active part in the discussion on the Special Laws Repeals Bill, on the Indian

Finance Bill, on the Maternity Benefits Bill and supported the resolution for the establishment of a Supreme Court for India. And whatever might be his views on the political problems of the day, whether he supported a Bill or attacked it, whether he moved or opposed a resolution or debated on questions of public importance with the Government or with the Swarajist party he always took an independent attitude in the interests of the country according to his lights.

BOMBAY REPRESENTATIVES' CONFERENCE

It is this transparent sincerity of purpose and candour of utterance, this willingness to consider and to pay regard to the opinions of others and to adopt them as his own when he was convinced, this toleration for people with other views that characterised the part he played in the Bombay Representatives' Conference and in all his other enterprises as the "Ambassador of Unity". A full report of the proceedings of the Conference of Representatives has been published and it shows what a great part Mr. Jinnah took in it for the sake of promoting Unity and for presenting a united demand.

MR. JINNAH'S MOVE FOR A NEW PARTY

In the Assembly, we have seen that Mr. Jinnah took an independent attitude, sometimes voting with the Liberals and sometimes with the Swarajists. He found he could not go with either Party completely and he invariably found himself the leader of a centre Party. In the closing weeks of 1925 the Swaraj Party was torn with dissensions arising out of what was known as the Tambe controversy. The Party split itself in twain, some favouring responsive co-operation and others swearing by obstruction. At this time Mr. Jinnah was endeavouring to effect a coalition of all or most of the existing Parties, or, if that was found impossible, to create the nucleus of a new Nationalist or Central Party, which might in course of time, attract to itself Swarajists on the Left, and Liberals on the Right. Mr. Jinnah, accordingly, convened a meeting to consider this question and made every effort to bring about a new Party. He made the following statement on the formation of a common party in the country:

My own opinion is that a party, on the lines of the Independent Party in the Assembly, should be formed, outside, in the country, because I know that a large bulk of opinion in the country does not approve, either the policy and programme of the Swaraj Party and what is its practised policy or the programme of the Liberal Party and what is practised by them. I strongly hold that the time has come when a definite organisation should be started, which will stand midway between the two, so that we may level up the Liberals, and level down the Swarajists. Until the public at large realise that, at present it is the only feasible and practicable way open, I fear the Government is not likely to be affected. As I have already said, empty and impotent threats will only give the Government a handle to resort to reactionary measures and a ruthless policy of repression under the name of 'law and order.' The only use that we can make of the legislatures is, 'to create strong and powerful Oppositions to the Government. Standing there as the people's party and backed up by the people throughout the country, we must carry on our struggle inch by inch. In the meantime, we must organise and train up our electorates not necessarily as framed under the rules of the Government of India Act, but our natural electorates.

AS A SPEAKER

Mr. Jinnah is not yet past middle age. He has not completed his fiftieth year. He has had a bright career and a more brilliant one awaits him. He has, in the words of Mrs. Sarojini Naidu 'the triple assets of a magnetic presence, an impressive delivery, and a voice which while lacking in volume has an arresting timbre.' He has 'the cogent force of a brilliant advocate.' and at round table conferences, his genius finds the fullest scope; 'his extraordinary powers of persuasion, his luminous exposition, his searching argument, and his impeccable judgment' are revealed at their best when he sits in committee.

SIR ABDUR RAHIM

Sir Abdur Rahim.

BIRTH AND BOYHOOD

SIR ABDUR RAHIM was born in September 1867; his father was Moulvi Abdur Rub, owner of a *Zamindari* in the Midnapur District in Bengal; his grandfather, besides being a *Zamindar* had also been a Deputy Collector, a very big office in those early days. Young Abdur Rahim came of a rich and highly cultured family, and we can trace in Sir Abdur Rahim an inheritance of scholarship from his father and his grandfather. Young Abdur received his early education in the High School, Midnapur, whence he matriculated. On matriculating, he joined the Presidency College at Calcutta. He had a brilliant career at College and took his Bachelor of Arts, Degree, with first class honours before he was twenty years old. His studies at the University did not stop on his becoming a graduate. He continued his post-graduate studies in English Literature and passed the M.A. Degree Examination 'first among the first classes' of his Presidency.

After such a brilliant career at the University young Abdur Rahim left for England to qualify himself for the Bar. Once he decided to study for the Bar, the Begum of Bhopal's foreign scholarship for Law was naturally awarded to him. He joined the Middle Temple and was called to the Bar in 1890.

AT CALCUTTA

He returned to India at the end of the same year and was duly enrolled as an Advocate of the Calcutta Bar. He decided to practise in the Presidency Town. While in England studying for the Bar, he had made a special study of both Muhammadan Law and Criminal Law. He had decided to be a Mussalman jurist, studying the original texts and text-books in Arabic or Persian and the Fatẃahs of the Mogul Emperors; and he had also decided to build up his practice at the Calcutta Bar as a great criminal lawyer. One characteristic feature of Sir Abdur Rahim is evident from this; that he always considered deeply and looked far into the future and made his decisions early and kept to them in his later life. In the course of three or four years he had built up an appreciable practice and attracted the attention of the Government as an able and learned lawyer conscientious in the discharge of his duty. He was consequently appointed as Deputy Legal Remembrancer, the first step in the ladder of service which led him to the high place of a Membership in the Executive Council of the Governor at Fort William, Calcutta. The position of Deputy Legal Remembrancer he occupied for about eighteen months. Then he resumed practice once again and on the Appellate side of the Calcutta High Court he soon achieved distinction as an able advocate and a sound criminal lawyer. Consequent upon the reputation he had for scholarship in criminal law and its basic principles he was appointed as the Presidency Magistrate for the northern division of the City of Calcutta —an office not usually bestowed upon Indians. Here, too, he achieved distinction and a name and was considered a capable and conscientious and at the same time a very civil and polite Magistrate. This position he occupied for about three years (1900 to 1903) but the Bar attracted him again and he reverted to practice in 1903. He resumed his old place as a thriving practitioner on the Appellate side appearing mainly in criminal cases.

TAGORE LAW LECTURES

But ever since he studied for the Bar, Sir Abdur Rahim had been utilising his leisure hours in studying the Muhammadan Law at the fountain head. He developed a thorough mastery of the original sources and when in 1907 he was appointed as the Tagore Law Lecturer on "Muhammadan Jurisprudence" everybody who knew him felt that the choice was peculiarly apt. And their expectations were more than amply justified. The lectures that he delivered in 1907 were published in book form in 1911 after he had become a puisne Judge of the High Court at Madras.

The book is of great value not only to the busy practical lawyer who usually looks upon Muhammadan Law as an arbitrary collection of rules and dicta based on no intelligible data; but also to those who, though not directly interested in the study of law or its science, wish to understand the true basis and character of the principles which inspire and guide the lives and conduct of the Muhammadan Sunnis, that is, the followers of the four schools of law (the Hanafi, Maliki, Shafi and Hanbali) who form the bulk of the Muhammadan population of the world. The book is invaluable also to the student of historic and comparitive jurisprudence as revealing the contributions of the Muhammadan jurists to the science of law.

The chapters relating to "constitutional law and administrative law" and to "the law regulating relations between Muslims and Non-Muslims" are original contributions to legal literature and are of great usefulness in these days when attempts are made for bringing about an amity between the Hindus and the Mussalmans in India.

In the concluding portion of the book he points out the duty of Muslims in a non-Muslim country which throws a flood of light on the present situation:

> As I have had occasion to point out, the Muhammadan law generally speaking, has two sides. In its worldly aspect, it is enforcible by the Court, and in its spiritual aspect, it affects the conscience of every individual Muslim. The head of the Muslim State can obviously enforce Muhammadan laws only within his own jurisdiction. A Muhammadan living within the territory of non-Muslims is required to conform, as far as is practicable for him to do so, to the rules and injunctions of the Muhammadan law and religion If he violates them, he incurs religious guilt and when he finds that he cannot stay in a particular non-Muslim country with safety of person and property nor discharge his religious duties there, he is expected to retire to his own State. If such a person finds that the non-Muslim Government actually interferes with his property and reduces his children to slavery or suffers it to be done or is guilty of other similar acts of oppression, he would be justified in interfering with the lives and properties of the non-Muslim inhabitants of the place. The reason is that the Government itself of the country of his adoption must in such circumstance be held.

to have been guilty of treachery towards him for he could not have resided in an alien country without its express or implied permission and it is always lawful for a Muslim according to his law to repel oppression. But otherwise, he must forbear from interfering with the non-Muslim Government and inhabitants of the country of his adoption as that would be an act of perfidy on his part which the Law absolutely forbids.

Mr. Abdur Rahim's Tagore Law lectures revealed his vast erudition and classic scholarship and paved the way for his promotion; when the Madras High Court wanted a Muhammadan Judge and no competent Mussalman was found in that Presidency, the choice easily fell on him. And although consequently Bengal lost one of its best men for a decade and more the Madras High Court vastly gained by his acquisition to the Bench.

AS A HIGH COURT JUDGE AT MADRAS

When Mr. Abdur Rahim was appointed as a Judge in July 1908, he was not much known to the legal world though his Tagore Law lectures on Muhammadan Jurisprudence had been delivered only sometime before. An eminent Calcutta Judge introduced him to the Madras Presidency as a scholar and gentleman rather than as a lawyer. But soon after he assumed charge of his office he earned for himself a high reputation as a sound judge endowed in abundant measure with patience and decision, industry and independence, qualities that in the main go to make up a successful and popular Judge. It is no disparagement to him to say that he lacked the legal condition or familiarity with case law which some of his colleagues possessed. But his robust common sense, his firm grasp of basic principles, and his unflinching determination to render impartial justice marked him out as one of the most notable of Indian Judges during recent years. A keen eye to broad features and probabilities combined with a due sense of proportion in dealing with the details of a case made him an excellent Judge in the hearing of regular appeals. He had the right perspective in criminal cases, the slender links in the case of the prosecution rarely escaping his searching vigilance. Justice Abdur Rahim did not confine himself to a mere interpretation and administrating of the law. He felt that in India, at least, it was the duty of judges to comment upon the legislative enactments brought to their notice, wherever they infringe the fundamental rights of the people and to focus public opinion and the attention of the Government by such comment with a view to secure the fundamental rights by proper legislative amendments. The following extract from his Judgment in the matter of "New India Printing Works" is an illustration in point:

That generally speaking, the terms of the section (§ 4 Press Act) are extremely wide and comprehensive cannot be doubted. They vest the Local Government with a discretion so large and unfettered that the keeping of printing presses and the publication of newspapers become extremely hazardous undertakings in the country. A press may be devoted to the printing of most useful and meritorious literature or other publications of an entirely innocent and non-controversial nature, yet it will be liable to forfeiture if any matters printed in such a press are considered by the Government to be objectionable within the meaning of the Act.........

Similarly, a newspaper may be consistently staunch in its loyalty to the Government, its general policy may be above all reproach, the sincerity and *bonafides* of the intentions of the Editor may not be liable to question but if any letters or other writings were let in, may be through carelessness, which come within the scope of any of the clauses to § 4, the Government may at once without any trial or even a warning forfeit the security and in this way ultimately put an end to the newspaper itself. That the influence of a periodical on the public life of the country is on the whole decidedly beneficial need be no bar to the Government's action. The Local Government, it may be, assumed, will not indiscriminately exercise the power which it possesses under this enactment; but the vesting of such unlimited power in the Executive Government is undoubtedly a serious encroachment on the freedom which the press in India enjoyed before the passing of the Act.

Mr. Abdur Rahim came to Madras as a Judge in 1908; in 1912 he went out as a Member of the Public Services Commission; on that occasion the MADRAS WEEKLY NOTES said:

Justice Rahim will not be with us in the High Court on its re-opening after the Christmas leave. He is drifted to a place of greater usefulness on the Public Service Commission. On the Bench he has earned a name for impartiality and independence of character and has maintained its high traditions. If occasionally he has exhibited a temper we have felt he was not responsible. On the whole, we are sorry we are losing even temporarily one of our ablest and most independent Judges.

The same Journal wrote in welcoming him back as a Judge in 1915:

We are glad to welcome Mr. Justice Rahim back to his permanent place in our High Court. During his absence many changes in the personnel of the High Court have taken place. His Lordship is now the senior puisne Judge and his return is very opportune. There is great need of his independence now that even Sir C. Sankaran Nair has been taken away from our High Court. We are sure his English sojourn will enable him to maintain the dignity and prestige of the High Court all the better. He would have noticed that in England, as in all civilized countries the judicial power is an independent and sacred element and that the legal profession plays a very important part.

OFFICIATING CHIEF JUSTICE

Justice Rahim was Officiating Chief Justice from July to October in 1916 and for the same period July to October in 1919; and it was hoped, before his appointment in Bengal was made, that he would be a permanent Chief Justice of Madras. From what we knew of him as Officiating Chief Justice, we have no doubt he would have filled the place with dignity and prestige, with independence and integrity.

EXTRA JUDICIAL ACTIVITIES AT MADRAS

Now, we will briefly refer to his extra-judicial activities in Madras.

Outside the domain of law, he took an abiding interest in educational matters. He was for many years a member of the Senate of the Madras University and also of its Syndicate. He delivered the Convocation Address of the Madras University as well as of the Mysore University both of which afford us an insight into his progressive and liberal views. He was the President of the Reception Committee of the most influential conference of the Muslim theologians of India, known as Uudwat-ul-Ulama in the year 1916. He was also the President of Majlis-ul-Ulama, another Conference of Muslim theologians held in Tanjore in the year 1917.

Before he came to Madras, he was instrumental in starting the Muslim League and he took an active part in shaping its constitution. He was a member of the All-India Deputation which waited on Lord Minto at Simla in the year 1904. He was a trustee of the Aligarh University and of the Madras Muhammadan Educational Association and of the Anjuman. He was the President of the Board of Visitors in the Madrasa-y-Azam and the Government Muhammadan

College at Madras. He was also the President of the Cosmopolitan Club, Madras.

In all fields of activity, whether legal, political, communal, social, educational or industrial, Sir Abdur Rahim has evinced a great interest and has always fondly cherished the desire of bringing about a spirit of thorough unity in aspirations and achievements between the Muslims and Hindus of this great land.

EARLY HONOURS

Mr. Abdur Rahim, as he then was, was granted II class Kaiser-i-Hind Medal in recognition of his public services as early as 1908. He was and is a loyal subject of the Crown. In the course of a speech delivered by him in Madras sometime before the Coronation Durbar which, he said, was held in order to "enable them (*i. e.* Indians) to realise that they were no strange inhabitants of an outlying dependency but occupy a place of dignity and responsibility in the Great Empire." He added:

"I am one of those who firmly believe that the connection of India with England is for the great benefit of both; and I feel sure that the Imperial visit will strengthen that connection by bringing into play feelings of mutual respect and cordiality both between the English and the Indian on the one hand and between the different communities on the other."

MADRAS CONVOCATION ADDRESS

Soon after his arrival in Madras, he was made a Fellow of the Madras University and was selected for the honour of delivering the Convocation Address on

31st March 1910. His address is a welcome departure from the usual stereotyped form, a departure which was emphasised by the Convocation Address of Mr. V. Krishnaswami Ayyar in the succeeding year. He is a firm believer in the good work done by the modern Indian Universities. In answer to a criticism, that these Universities turned out godless men he said:

In the Colleges maintained by the Government, you have not, it is true, been instructed in the tenets of any particular religion. But unless the epithet 'godless' is to be used in some special sense, it cannot be a true description of the effect which your education must have had on the moral and spiritual sides of your nature. I do not think it is possible at the present day to assert that the well-recognized code of morals and good conduct has no hold upon a man of culture, unless it be associated in his mind with a particular religious sanction. I admit, however, it would be a matter of serious concern if the teaching of our schools and colleges tended to sap the religious beliefs of our young men. But I feel sure that if I were to assert that you are not good Hindus, Christians or Muhammadans by reason of your having had the best modern education which is available in the Presidency, you would, one and all, repudiate the charge. So far as Hinduism is concerned, I think it is a fact too palpable to be ignored that English education has either led to, or been concomitant of, its revival.........In a matter like this, I should be inclined to regard the phenomenon in the light in which the educated Hindus themselves regard it. According to them it is but a reversion to the religion of the Vedas, the Upanishads and the Gita, and I believe many European thinkers confirm them in this view. As regards the Muhammadans, who have been educated under the present system, I know they yield to none of their co-religionists in their devotion to the teachings and ideals of Islam.

From his enthusiastic picture of the influence of home life on the Indian students, we can form a good idea of the influence of his own home life on his scholastic career.

I will just tell you what the home life is of a young man in a well-regulated Muhammadan household, of which I can claim to speak with some knowledge. Every Muhammadan child has his ears filled with the cry of "God is great and there is no God but God" the God who to him is the embodiment of the highest perfection; he is taught not to begin any work or duty of the day or any undertaking of life, great and small, but in the name of "God, the kind, the merciful"; he learns to thank the Almighty whenever his efforts are crowned with success and to trust in Him all the more if he fails; to bend the knees of devotion every now and then, each day; every day he repeats and pores with loving reverence on the words of the Koran, whose divine eloquence has an abiding place in every Muhammadan's heart, he is brought up to find the keenest pleasure in the practice of the most rigid self-denial for one month in each year, and the practice of charity and kindness towards his neighbour is impressed upon him as a legal duty and a high spiritual privilege. Thus brought up, a Muhammadan youth can be trusted never to swerve from his faith. And I may fairly assume that a Hindu boy at home is similarly trained in the practice and tenets of his own religion.

He further pointed out that the religious beliefs are not shattered when a Muhammadan or Hindu youth with such training and teaching is introduced in the lecture-room of his college, into regions of science, philosophy and poetry. "He does not think that the scientist, the philosopher and the poet have any thing better to teach him of the inner meaning of life than Mahommed, Buddha or Sankaracharya. He does not find that the teachings of his spiritual master is in any way inconsistent with the discoveries of science or the speculations of philosophy. He seeks to reconcile the two and is at least himself satisfied that he has done so. He eagerly avails himself of all the results of the modern movements of thought in order to justify his belief in his own religion."

Sir Abdur Rahim refutes the idea that the present generation of educated people is irreligious nor does he believe that the movement owes its strength to the Westernised education.

The natural and inevitable result was a quickening of India's intellectual life, but English schools and colleges would have been of little avail, if the new impulse has failed to arouse an adequate response in the religious sympathies of the people. Some resistance it was bound to encounter from that blind force of bigotry which lurk in every society; but the great minds of the time soon caught the Western idea, and having infused it with a religious purpose scattered it broad-cast in the land. The great service which English schools and colleges have rendered is to introduce into the country a knowledge of the technique of modern arts and sciences. But all that I am concerned to point out is that the desire for progress which is now so marked among the people was not created by English schools. It was generated by the mere contact with a progressive civilization. It could not helped.

M. E. CONFERENCE

Justice Rahim's keen interest in the problems of education in this country and of Mahommedan education in particular justified the choice of the Presidentship of the All-India Mahommedan Anglo-Oriental Educational Conference, in its twenty-ninth sessions held at Poona in December 1915. The responsibility attached to that office have always been great and was specially onerous on that occasion. He was expected to guide the community in arriving at a decision on the difficult question of a Muslim University which faced them at that time. Mr. Rahim managed the situation ably and with great foresight and considerable statesmanship. In his Address, he emphasised on the need of Government help in these words:

Gentlemen, at one time much controversy existed on the respective duties of the Government and the people with reference to education. In my opinion, this is not a matter to be dealt with in the abstract. Education is a fundamental necessity of a community in all its grades. It must be met by whichever agency or agencies are capable of meeting it In some countries, the people are in a favourable position to organise and look after their children's education, in some directions perhaps even better than the Government In other countries, such as India, where the Government commands larger resources and a more effective organization than what can be supplied by private efforts, the burden of educating the people has primarily to be borne by Government. I do not wish to suggest that the people themselves or such of them as are in a position to undertake this civic duty are at liberty to consider themselves relieved of the obligation. All that I mean is that to the extent the people are unable to help themselves in this respect, the Government is expected to come in and supply whatever is needed. It is primarily the duty of the parents to educate their children; but parents who are themselves illiterate or poor cannot be expected to fulfil that obligation. Hence the most thoughtful men among the people have found themselves driven to look principally to the Government to undertake the national organisation of education and I believe the Government has been realising more and more vividly every day the responsibilities of the situation; to whichever field of education we turn, the tract which lies waste and untouched is immeasurably vast in comparison to what has been yet taken in hand. And to my mind it would be a barren discussion to consider the relative degree of importance which should be assigned to the different departments of education. The aim in view should be to develop the various energies and talents of the people to their fullest measure; and a little reflection will tell us that the object cannot be achieved, unless education in all its different faculties and forms is vigorously pushed on—elementary. secondary and higher education, scientific, literary and artistic, professional and industrial, technical and commercial education of the masses—of boys as well as of girls.

Referring to Mr. Gokhale's Bill he said:

Unfortunately it came to nothing; I am afraid public opinion, which at the time was not very well instructed, did not express itself with sufficient clearness and definiteness. Since then, however, opinion has in this connection grown with remarkable rapidity so that at the present day there is an universal demand for free and compulsory education. As practical men, we do not expect that such a measure can be applied all at once throughout India. But there can be now no difficulty whatever in accepting the principle and enforcing in selected areas.

He always emphasised the need for education in Urdu, at least for the Mussalmans:

> With a few exceptions, it is the desire of Muhammadans all over India that the vehicle of primary education should be Urdu, which is not only looked upon as a national language but is practically the only vernacular through which it is possible to impart instruction in the tenets of their religion or in those moral and civic duties which among the Muhammadans are best enforced by the sanction of religion.........Wherever there is a demand for Urdu schools it should be met, and in other primary schools there should be facilities for giving instruction in the fundamentals of Islam to Muhammadan boys.

In the course of the address, Mr. Rahim urged the need for a combination of training in some useful industry with instruction in the three R's; for the encouragement of the continuation classes to prevent a relapse into illiteracy; and for the proper organisation of a service of popular preachers and lecturers, for it is through the Ulemas that we can best reach the masses. He also pointed out that the state of the community in the matter of secondary education is so depressed that nothing but special remedies will ameliorate the position; and he added: "the education of any portion of a community, if it is a favour at all, is a boon to the entire people, and I cannot think of anything more mischievous or foolish than to cry down measures which may be found necessary to advance education among such portions of the nation as may have lagged behind on the apprehension of communal favouritism."

Emphasising the position of the vernacular in higher education, he said:

> Until our own languages receive some recognition as the medium of higher education, the development of advanced branches of knowledge in the country must necessarily be slow.

While pointing out the difficulties that beset Government help, he used this telling illustration: "Among lawyers, the saying is current that the troubles of a litigant begin when he has obtained a decree and seeks to execute it. Similarly, it would seem that the troubles of the Indian public commence when any large measure of reform, after it has been formulated, is brought to the stage when it has to be carried out"—a proposition which is true not only of Indian education but of Indian politics also.

INTEREST IN STUDENTS

Sir Abdur Rahim had always a soft corner for the Indian students; and he realised their many difficulties and sought to remove them. He protested vehemently against the raising of the standard required of them in their examinations. "The conviction is growing stronger every day" he said "that under the new regulations the Indian boys are made to do far more work than is good for their physical or mental growth. It is a fact that by the time the educated Indians reach an age when intellect generally attains full maturity and experience ripens, they are mostly incapacitated from any strenuous work by same fatal ailment....I feel sure that if an enquiry were instituted on this subject, facts would be forthcoming showing that we are confronted with something like a national danger...... It is true now-a-days more attention is paid to outdoor games and physical training. But here again it must be remembered that intense physical exertion is not a remedy for the evils of mental overstrain. In fact the two when combined may often result in a greater harm."

With equal vehemence, Sir Abdur Rahim protested against the enhanced fees which bar the doors of the University to the real student who is generally poor. "In the East," he said, "learning has never been considered as a privilege of the rich. In India, one inherent feature of the old indigenous system was the provision of special and abundant opportunities to poor students. Under the new conditions of life, that system has been swept out of existence, and if its provision for the poor students is not generously reproduced under the new regime, I have great fears that the fame for learning and higher culture which India has always enjoyed from the very dawn of history will soon be lost to her."

Sir Abdur Rahim, consequently, advocates a generous system of scholarships which will extend right through the primary, the secondary and University stages. "We are also in need of liberal scholarships to help competent students to go through the various professional and technical courses and the opportunities which our young men have of completing their general professional or technical education in Europe and America, ought not to be allowed to be restricted."

Finally, Sir Abdur Rahim emphasises the need for organized endeavour:

Time has arrived when we must organize our efforts on a far larger and more comprehensive scale than hitherto. In every Presidency town we want a central organization which will be in a position to look after the education of the community by means of local agencies throughout the Presidency. There should be different sections dealing with particular branches of education. In every large city committees must be formed. There must be Branch Associations in District towns and sub-divisions extending at last to every village.

MYSORE UNIVERSITY ADDRESS

It is this need for organization and co operation that Sir Abdur Rahim emphasised once again at the Convocation Address delivered by him at the University of Mysore on the 10th October 1919. He said that it should be a distinct and direct aim of the educational institutions to train students in the art and methods of organization and co-operation. One means of doing this is by paying special attention to the promotion of corporate life and activities in schools and colleges and in the University.

To the graduates he pointed out the sacred path of duty:

I have often felt that the full significance of liberal education is not always well grasped in this country. Nothing indeed can be more pathetic than to meet men who have received University education, unable to rise above their cramped surroundings, who are afraid to think and act for themselves, whose minds are enchained to the unrecallable past, men with no adequate perception of the great forces which are shaking the destiny of the world and with no desire to adjust themselves to the changed times. . It is the sacred duty of men educated in a modern University to undertake the essential task of social reformation.

The passages that follow, regretting the absence of such liberal movements in India, the utter pessimism of the present day leaders and the attitude of complacency and satisfaction with the existing order of things that some of them assume, and pointing to the fallacies of the statement that what was good for our fore-fathers was good enough for us and to the good points of intelligent imitation, constitute a brilliant defence of social reform.

In this Convocation Address, he again reiterated the three main planks in his scheme of educational reform; scholarships, special help for backward classes and adequate pay for the teachers.

"A proper and adequate system of scholarships, in my opinion, should indeed be in the forefront of the educational programme throughout."

"Effort must be made to give equal chances of education to all communities and castes and not to allow the educational opportunities to be monopolised by the most active and the forward. At the same time, the state would itself be a heavy loser if it failed to encourage intrinsic worth or talent simply because it happens to be more common in one community rather than in another."

"The educational service should be at least as well paid as any other service and it should be assured as an honoured status."

These views on education he had already given adequate expression to in his dissenting minute attached to the Report of the Public Services Commission.

PUBLIC SERVICES COMMISSION

It is not within the scope of this short sketch to consider the merits of the dissenting minute nor is it necessary now for practical purposes to consider what Sir Abdur Rahim's views were on particular problems; suffice it to say, that the minute has become a political document of great value by reason of the transparent candour and the forceful advocacy which characterises it. His defence of the Indians has become a classic:

> No one who lives in India and knows the people can fail to perceive that a vast welding force has come into existence. It may be safe to assert that whatever undesirable significance the caste system may have had in the past, the educated classes of Hindus would at the present day regard it as an undeserved and cruel aspersion of their character to have it suggested that they do not sympathise with the uneducated masses or would not deal fairly with them in the discharge of their official duties.
>
> Further, it must be remembered that care for the poor so definitely enjoined by all the religions of the East, has developed in the Indian character generally almost an overflow of charity and generosity; while the new movements have helped largely to divert much of that fund of philanthropy into more regulated channels.
>
> The keynote of the attitude of Mussalmans, is the same as that of the others, a demand for a more intimate and more extensive association of the people with the administration and a complete removal of disabilities.

Answering the stale charge that Western-educated Indians do not reflect the views or represent the interests of the many scores of millions in India he says:

> So far as the views of the latter on any of the matters in dispute or of an allied character are concerned it is impossible to imagine what opinions they are in a position to form so long as they are allowed to remain, as at present, in their illiterate and appallingly ignorant condition. As for the representation of their interests, if the claim be that they are better represented by European Officials than by educated Indian officials or non-officials, it is difficult to conceive how such a reckless claim has come to be urged. The inability of English Officials to master the spoken languages of India and their different religions habits of life and modes of thought so completely divide them from the general Indian population that only an extremely limited few possessed with extra-ordinary powers of intuitional insight have ever been able to surmount the barriers. Such knowledge of the people and of the classical literatures as passes current among the European Officials is compiled almost

entirely from the data furnished to them by the Western educated Indians; and the idea of the European officials having to deal with the people of India without the medium of the Western educated Indian is too wild for serious contemplation. It would be no exaggeration to say that without their co-operation the administration could not be carried on for a single day.

With the educated Indians, on the other hand, this knowledge is instinctive and the ties of religion and custom, so strong in the East, inevitably make their knowledge and sympathy far more intimate than is to be seen in countries dominated by materialistic conceptions It is from a wrong and deceptive perspective that we are asked to look at the system of castes among the Hindus more as a dividing force than as a powerful binding factor; and the unifying spirit of Islam, so far as it affects the Muhammadans, does not stand in need of being explained; while in all communities the new national movement has received considerable accession of impulse from the lessons of such arguments as are hinted at in the majority report.

Looking back to past history, India, until the disruption of the Mogul Empire, always produced men of high administrative talents, and at the present day in the more advanced native states, wherever opportunity exists, Indians are successfully bearing the burden of the entire administration; some of them achieved notable distinction, such as Sir Salar Jung and Sir T. Madhav Rao. It should also be noted that a fair proportion of these men were originally in the British Indian service but only found an adequate opportunity for a full play of administrative capacity when they were appointed either as Ministers or heads of departments in these States.

Speaking of the English recruits to the Indian Civil Service, he says:

There can be no doubt that the offers which Indian services ordinarily get proceed mostly from candidates of average attainments and rather limited outlook, more or less obliged by circumstances to seek for a living in a land which otherwise does not evoke much enthusiasm in their breasts. We cannot look with confidence to recruits of this type as a body to supply the higher order of administrative talent which alone can enable a foreigner to understand the real forces at work in the very complex conditions of modern India and to guide them with sympathy. I have no hesitation in recording my opinion that the country in its present circumstances cannot safely or fairly be called upon to accommodate more than a very limited number of English officials of this class.

Contrasting the Indian and the English official he observes:

An English official is so far as he represents a high level of Western knowledge and training, has a sincere and earnest desire to help the cause of progress combined with an aptitude for adopting Western methods to the changing conditions of an ancient oriental country, and above all a determination to deal justly not merely between one Indian and another but what is more politically important and far more difficult between conflicting Indian and English claims which constantly crop up in various forms, has a very useful career in India and will always be welcomed by competent Indian public opinion. A few such men will considerably strengthen the bonds between the Government and the people; on the other hand an English official of a lower type or with lower ideals would at the present day be felt as an anachronism and prove a fruitful source of political friction.

Then Sir Abdur Rahim goes on to point out how an English Official at his best is but a bird of passage in India, how "he is expensive to train, expensive to employ—two men, roughly speaking, being required to do one man's work—and is a dead loss to the country when he retires." "Even supposing" says Sir Abdur Rahim, "that he initially brings to his work some superior qualifications, still the balance of advantage must in the nature of things be heavily on the side of the Indian official." For, the Indian official has a value to the country far greater than is to be measured by the actual output of his daily routine work; he becomes a centre of further growth.

And again, he boldly and clearly states the Indian point of view:

The point of view from which the majority of the commissioners and myself have approached the question of employment of Indians are substantially different, the question they have asked themselves is, what are the means to be adopted for extending the employment of Indians. But the proper standpoint, which alone in my opinion furnishes a satisfactory basis to work upon, is that the importation of officials from Europe should be limited to cases of clear necessity, and the question therefore to be asked is, in which services and to what extent should appointments be made from England......The general policy to be kept in view is that the public service of India should be recruited for in the country itself.

Sir Abdur Rahim, among other things, advocated simultaneous examinations for the Civil Service, protested against high judicial and executive posts including Lieutenant-Governorship being reserved for the Civil Service; and in the field of education, he urged the exclusion of all professional chairs, whether in the ordinary Arts Colleges or in special institutions like the medical colleges, from the cadre of any service. He pointed out that to fill these appointments, for which men of original powers of mind and thought with distinguished work to their credit are wanted, it was obviously inexpedient to confine their choice to the limited personnel of a service. He recommended that for all such appointments the practice should be to secure men of achievement wherever found for the more important subjects of study and research, and that the state should offer them such reasonable terms as will be suitable in each case. He similarly condemned the policy of communal representation in the superior services.

Generally speaking, the principle which has commended itself to me, and which is in accord with practically unanimous opinion of representative Indians of all communities and provinces, is that it is as inadvisable as it is unsound and unnecessary to emphasise the question of communal or provincial representation in the superior services. The personnel required for these services must be possessed of the highest qualification available and any narrow contraction of the area of recruitment should be avoided.

These extracts from Sir Abdur Rahim's dissenting Minute are sufficient illustrations of the admirable manner in which he put up a strenuous and vigorous fight single-handed against the influences of the bureaucracy and of the Britishers in India and for the sake of the political and material advancement of India.

MUDDIMAN COMMITTEE

In his evidence before the Muddiman Committee, Sir Abdur Rahim stated the results of his experience as a Member of the Executive Council of a premier province:

> As I have been a member of the Bengal Government from the commencement of the Reformed regime, I propose to put down the results of my experience in my own words......I venture also to assert that any step of a retrograde or reactionary tendency would be in direct opposition to unanimous Indian opinion and gravely intensify political difficulties. There could be no doubt that the demand of Indian public opinion, as voiced by many of the influential, thoughtful and responsible exponents of such opinion, is for the immediate grant of an entirely autonomous and Responsible Government in the Provinces and a considerable introduction of responsibility in the Central Government

But, unfortunately, Sir Abdur Rahim took the view that this large question was not within his purview or that of the Committee and added that even if it were he should before supporting the demand wait until a genuine experiment has been made in Responsible Government for the life of two more councils in the "transferred subjects." He wanted to see how far the electorates and their representatives were able to realise their responsibility when thrown entirely on their own resources. To that end, Sir Abdur Rahim suggested an immediate separation of the purse and a revision of the Meston Award. He recognized that the Government must reckon upon the possibility of there being always a party in the Council which would be impatient of the pace by which the British Parliament might regulate the development of responsible government in India and might even adopt measures of wholesale obstruction in order to achieve their object. But he was convinced, after a careful study of all that had happened and was happening, that if the Legislative Council were made *genuinely* responsible for the administration of the transferred subjects—on whose proper and adequate administration depends so largely the well-being and prosperity of the people—no party can for long persuade the people not to make the best use of the opportunity. Consequently, Sir Abdur Rahim proposed: (1) There should be a separate purse for the transferred departments with a separate Financial Secretary. (2) The nominated and ex-officio members are not to vote on "transferred subjects." (3) The interference of the Governor in the administration of the "transferred subjects" to be limited to cases in which he is of opinion that such interference is called for in the interest of law and order. (4) All question of policy relating to the "transferred subjects" should be settled by the Ministers themselves. (5) Special constituencies should be done away with. (6) A greater devolution of responsibility to the local legislature and the local Government in provincial matters is necessary. (7) And the Meston Award should be revised. These recommendations reveal two things. (1) Sir Abdur Rahim still retains his strong independence and judicial temperament in spite of his experiences as Member of the Executive Council. His Note reads more like a calm dispassionate judgment than a warm vehement advocacy of the cause of the progress of India towards Responsible Government. (2) Sir Abdur Rahim continues as when he was a High Court Judge, to be out of touch with popular opinion and popular feeling and does not consequently make adequate allowances for such opinion and feeling in his suggestions for reform. This is a matter for regret. As he himself points out :

> The present convention or etiquette which debars the Members of the Executive Council from all political activity in the country must be abandoned, for I am sure that if they adequately helped the Governor in the task of educationing public opinion by explaining to the public every now and then the measures and policies of the Government, this will not only remove many misunderstandings but enable the people to realise the extent of co-operation that is possible between Europeans and Indians under the present system.

Such a course will at the same time educate leaders like Sir Abdur Rahim out of their aloofness and consequent mis-interpretation of public opinion and will serve to render them useful exponents of public opinion to the Government and stronger advocates of the Indian cause than they are at present.

Sir Abdur Rahim's recommendations were summarised in the 'Majority Report' of the Muddiman Committee who follow his opinion that except by some form of dualism, it was not possible to afford an equally valuable training towards Responsible Government in India and still to safeguard those conditions on which Government depends. The 'Minority' in its separate Report merely noticed that Sir Abdur Rahim took a different view from Sir Surendra Nath Banerjea's and Sir P. C. Mitter's who said that "Dyarchy should go as quickly as possible, not because it has been a failure everywhere but because public opinion apparently does not want it" and that "apart from the inherent defects of Dyarchy" its failure to fulfil the expectations of the people had made it so unpopular that it could no longer be run as a democratic institution. The result of Sir Abdur Rahim's aloofness and dispassionate judgment apparent in his Note was that neither Report accepted his recommendations which however just and necessary from an absolute point of view entirely ignored the problems of Indian sentiment and popular opinion.

M. A. N. HYDARI

BIRTH AND EDUCATION

MAHOMED Akbar Nazarally Hydari was born in Bombay on the 8th November 1869. He inherits the living traditions of a prosperous home, whose gates were ever wide open for the needy and whose atmosphere was elevating with religious ardour. His Arabian ancestors seem to have come to Bombay in the pursuit of business. They were simple, God-fearing Mahomedans, shrewd and adventurous businessmen. They kept up their relations with Arabia, even after they had built up large concerns in Europe and the Far East. They early recognised the benefits of English education. The maternal great grandfather of Mr. Hydari had sent his sons to study in foreign lands and they afterwards became successful in various walks of life. Mr. Hydari's father himself made six voyages to China where he developed large business interests. The boy was put to school and very early in his scholastic career was initiated into English and Latin. At the age of 14, Mr. Hydari passed his Matriculation and he took his B. A. Degree with University Honours when he was only 17. His education was principally at St. Xavier's College, where the Jesuit Fathers evinced warm interest in his progress. The austere simplicity, the spirit of sacrifice, and the love of service which marked his subsequent career may partly be traced to this association with the noble Fathers. Mr. Hydari was, from his school days, fired with patriotism and an intense love of India as his Motherland. He used to attend political meetings when a boy and take part in debates on Indian topics. Herbert Spencer was his favourite author, and made a durable impression on his mind; giving him a power of clear analysis, an eye for details, and an eagerness to forestall and provide against criticism. He became a devotee of self-discipline and clear thinking. In his family circle, his uncle, the late Mr. Justice Tyabji and Haji Najmuddeen Tyabjee the famous Oriental scholar took particular interest in him and gave a wholesome direction to his mental activities. Mr. Hydari was, later on, married to Haji Najmuddeen's daughter.

OFFICIAL CAREER

Mr. Hydari began his official career in February 1888, in his 18th year. He appeared for the competitive examination for the enrolled list of the Indian Financial Department and passed with distinction. He was posted successively to Nagpur, Lahore, Calcutta, Allahabad and Madras, and wherever he was posted, he did excellent constructive work, especially in the field of Education. He was then appointed in the Indian Finance Department on special duty as Examiner of Government Press Accounts, a post which afforded him opportunities to visit various parts of India. He submitted the results of his investigation with practical suggestions regarding the expenditure on Government Printing and incidentally on Stationery and devised a new scheme of Press Accounts which is still in force. The Government while accepting the report, created a Controllership of Stationery and appointed Special Commissions presided over by Mr. Crawley and Sir William Meyer successively. Apart from this maiden achievement, those early travels in India afforded to the patriotic young man the opportunity of personally seeing and studying men and affairs in various parts of his Motherland. The knowledge he thus gained was of great value when years afterwards he was called upon to handle more important problems. They showed him the appalling illiteracy in the country and inspired him with a longing to dispel it and let in the light. Thenceforth he applied himself to the study of Educational Systems and visions of educational reform enlivened the hard figures of Finance. The late Mr. Gokhale asked Mr. Hydari to join the Servants of India Society but the path he was to follow was, perhaps, predestined and Mr. Hydari's services were secured by His Exalted Highness the Nizam. He also at that time began to show his deep love for the arts, especially painting. Though an accomplished Financier Mr. Hydari does not estimate the status of a nation only by rupees, annas and pies. He looks to its achievements by the brush and pen. The arts are the real treasures of a nation. This attitude of his is responsible for a fine collection of original paintings and old prints which has earned the approbation of many competent critics and which has now been given as a loan collection to his native city of Bombay. At Hyderabad he used his good offices to restore and preserve the frescoed caves of Ajanta and it is largely to his efforts that the Hyderabadis owe their Archæological Department, which has done splendid work.

IN HYDERABAD

In October 1905, the Hyderabad State recquisitioned his services as Accountant-General. Mr. (now Sir) George Casson Walker was then in charge of the Finance and Mr. Hydari was invited to assist him. It was the period of transformation for the State Finances. The old order of things was giving place to modern, scientific organisation. Two years later he was appointed Financial Secretary; and from April to October 1907 he was called upon to take independent charge of the entire Finances of the State, while Sir George Casson Walker was on furlough in England.

The creation of a Famine Reserve, the appointment of an Educational Advisor to survey the present position and future programme of Public Instruction, the development of the Mahbubia Girls' School on special lines which make it probably the best school of its kind in India, the institution of Hyderabad Civil Service Examinations, and the recommendation to secure Sir M. Visveswarayya to draw up a scheme of flood protection, drainage, and city improvement works are some of the good things for which Mr. Hydari as Financial Secretary, was mainly responsible. Of Mr. Hydari's work during these years, his chief himself said in his farewell budget note :

"It remains to mention briefly what results the Financial Department have to show for their past year's work, in which Mr. A. Hydari of the Indian Finance Department has taken a prominent and effective part for the past five years as Accountant-General and then as Financial Secretary. The expenditure has, certainly, been brought under more effective control so far as local conditions permit and the Finance Department is now, generally, allowed its say in such matters of administration as obviously concern it."

AT THE HOME OFFICE

The need for a well-informed man, calm and collected was keenly felt in the administration and the Nizam's Government transferred Mr. Hydari, in July 1911, to the Home Office as Secretary to Government in the Judicial, Police and General Departments. Apart from the general direction he gave to the policy of various departments under his charge, his administration was marked by solid work of a constructive nature. In the Judicature prompter disposal of cases, especially extradition cases, was effected. The magnificent buildings of the High

Court were planned and finished during his tenure of office. The re-organization of the Medical Department, encouragement to Doctors with special qualifications, help to the Leper Asylum of Dichpalli, reform of plague measures, the construction of permanent health camps and the improvement of the Unani Medical Department are among the fruits of his enlightened policy. But it is in the Educational Department his achievements are most noteworthy, supported by the zeal of the present enlightened ruler to promote learning and all else that may contribute to the welfare of his subjects. A firm believer in education, Mr. Hydari saw in his new office something like a special mission for which he was chosen. The expansion of Public Instruction in all grades, which followed, is phenomenal. Before Mr. Hydari became the Education Secretary the Government grant was only a little above 10 lakhs. It is 72 lakhs now. The Government schools and scholars in the pre-Hydari epoch were, in round numbers, 900 and 60,000 respectively. To-day they are 4100 and 250,000, But that is not all.

THE OSMANIA UNIVERSITY.

The crowning glory of his Education work is the establishment of the Osmania University and the Translation Bureau. Mr. Hydari had been thoroughly familiar with the various attempts at Indian National Education in the past. The Bengal Scheme of National Education did not live long; Mrs. Besant's Central Hindu College turned out a communal institu-

M. A. N. HYDARI

tion; the Gurukul stood as a severe Sectarian Gymnasium; in all these, the old boundaries were merely shifted, never crossed. In no scheme of Education, if it is truly national, Mr. Hydari asserts, should the student be cut off, at any stage, from the living springs of his own mother-tongue, and English should be an organic part of his cultural equipment. The one nourishes his young talents to develop into independent expression, the other opens out to him wider horizons of thought and culture. Mr. Hydari gave practical proofs of his beliefs in the Osmania University. He boldly transgressed the customary bounds of Indian Education, by making the vernacular the medium of higher instruction. By so doing he effectively did away with the unnatural environment and alien character of Education in our institutions, facilitating a progressive continuity and living unity of the domestic life and public instruction of a student; and furthermore relieved the student from a lot of the mental load that involved in mastering a foreign tongue, the energy thus released strengthening his powers of assimilation. It is Mr. Hydari's strong belief that the most impressionable period of a student's life should not be left without religious instruction. The mere development of intellect will narrow down a man's outlook into materialism and starve, if not stifle the feeding roots of virtue and restraint *i. e.*, religion. But he does not advocate bare religious instruction, divorced from human culture and association. Life and culture are, for him, a lovely landscape bringing into relief the light and beauty of religion, a true understanding of which is alone productive of wide toleration.

THE CRITICS

There seems to be a good deal of misunderstanding with regard to the scope and meaning of the Osmania University. The University is, no doubt, a new and bold departure, nonetheless deliberate. The authors of the scheme knew well what they were doing and so had no misgivings. They appreciated the simple truth that the vernaculars are the blood-vessels of the national body and that no growth is possibly sustained unless they are rendered vigorous for the purposes of assimilation. To tune the language of the people into a vehicle of higher thought may seem like an ambitious dream in India to-day, but the idea is natural and scientific. The authors of the Osmania University believed that it would triumph through inherent truth and the ruler who chartered the experiment had the vision to perceive that truth. It was Mr. Hydari who conceived and in loyal obedience to his Sovereign, worked out the scheme of the University and the Translation Bureau whose duty is to translate and produce all the necessary text-books in Urdu, and even to invent fresh terms—in all its details, and his scheme, worked out in many anxious days and nights, has nobly stood the crucial test of practice. It is sometimes argued that this University is a retrograde movement opposed to modern culture, and that it is an attempt to revive the old, dead superstitious cult of the East. Nothing could be further from the truth. The University is, indeed, a new departure in the annals of Indian Education, but, far from being opposed to modern scientific methods, it seeks to introduce those methods into India's inmost life and thought; in short, to make them Indian. The promoters of the scheme are no impatient idealists. For them the present is the real. They are not dwelling in the past, or in a dreamy future. Their aim is twofold. First to carry the torch of modern learning and culture to the very villages of India, and secondly to reform, if not, to revolutionise the ultra-literary character of University studies, on sound productive lines suited to the special genius of the country. To achieve the former they had to rely on the vernaculars, and to achieve the latter they had to encourage technical and scientific studies. It is too early to proclaim complete success, but any one with eyes can see that fine results have been achieved. The future historian of Indian Education will no doubt record the foundation of the University as the dawn of a new era and estimate the benefits it carried to the State and country and he cannot fail to praise the energy of Mr. Hydari, the practical author of those benefits. Mr. Hydari works for the cultural unity of India as the precursor of inter-communal amity and racial harmony. He has often passionately maintained that the educated youth are the proper plough-men and the College hostels the proper fields for the cultivation of unity. Mr. Hydari always insisted upon a healthy hostel accommodation as a necessary part of the equipment of Educational institutions. It will be remembered now, in this connection, he criticised the scheme of the Central Hindu College whose doors were shut against the Mohammedans. He also strongly opposed a movement for sectarian Universities in an article on the proposed Muslim University which he contributed to THE EAST AND WEST. That article brought on him a certain amount of unpopularity amongst his own cc-religionists, especially the Aligarh School. That feeling, however, has long died away. Mr. Hydari has been a Trustee of the M. A. O. College since 1908, and was received with enthusiasm in the College when he visited it in 1913. His own words at Calcutta in 1917 will amply bear this out:

> I need not remind you how in the earlier days of the Conference, the idea of a Mohammedan University had filled one with fear, that the already too great emphasis on caste and creed that has been the bane of our land, might thereby be further accentuated. The new spirit has, however, inspired me with confidence that the Hindu and Muslim Universities will work in a spirit of common understanding, co-operation and love, devoting themselves to the development of all that is finest in their own particular culture; yet ever mindful of the one aim, that the collective tribute brought by the streams of the Hindu, Buddhist, Iranian, Muslim and Christian civilizations to be laid at the feet of our common Mother is made the richer and the more fruitful so that the message of India to the world might be Catholic, Universal and all-compelling. It is only if these institutions are worked in this spirit that they will be able to justify themselves.

Mr. Hydari has all along been opposed to the mixing of politics with education just as he was opposed to a policy of mendicancy. In this connection he was able to render signal services to Indian Muslims when in 1920 he and Prince Hamidullah of Bhopal, at the head of the moderate party among the Trustees of Aligarh, defeated the attempt of the Ali Brothers to capture the College for the Non-Co-operators.

With an open mind, Mr. Hydari has read and re-read the bitter history of the National Education movement in India. The Bengal Council of National Education disappeared as soon as the anti-Partition politicians were propitiated. Mrs. Besant's National Institutions applied for Government affiliation simultaneously with the close of the Home Rule campaign. The state of the National Schools, born of the heat of the N. C. O. movement, is still fresh in memory. In the light of these historical events it is now possible justly to appreciate the clarity of vision and strength of conviction with which Mr. Hydari fought against the Ali Brothers in the Aligarh affair, and suffered misunderstanding from many of his best friends.

Rarely can the work of a great educationist be adequately weighed and measured in his lifetime. Mr. Hydari's energy and enthusiasm, the silent labour of innumerable hours which he has devoted to India, the sometimes heart-breaking and always hard battles he has had to fight against prejudice, blind conservatism and weakness, are not the kind of news that generally meets our eyes beneath bold headlines in the papers, inspiring journalistic panegyrics. The results of a sound educational policy can only be judged by its results in the succeeding generation. For a critical and impartial judgment, therefore, of Mr. Hydari's work in Hyderabad and outside Hyderabad, we must wait for several years, though we have no doubt of the general tenour of the verdict. Mr. Hydari's own claims are very modest:

> Do not, I pray you, regard this movement, or movements of this kind (Osmania University), as, in any way, separatist or provincial or sectarian. They are based upon the first principles of National self-respect, reverence and respect for your cultural traditions which are not the insidious enemies but the strongest supporters of a National Evolution. "To be attached to the sub-division," as the greatest of political philosophers, Burke, said: "to love the little platoon we belong to in society is the first principle, and germ as it were, of public affections It is the first link in the series by which we proceed towards a love to our country and to mankind."

This "Novel experiment" as H. H. the Aga Khan called it, has now been going on for nearly six years with increasing success. Facts have dispelled the misgivings which were felt by some upon its first foundation and its supporters are encouraged by the growing enthusiasm of the staff and students and the generous recognition which the University has justly won not only from the people of the State, but also from the educational world outside. The Dacca University has made Mr. Hydari one of its Honorary Members on account of his eminent services to Indian education, a distinction as uncommon as well-merited; while the Universities' Conference elected him President of the Inter-University Board, a unique honour. In December 1925 Mr. Hydari was invited to deliver the Convocation Address of the Punjab

University. Mr. Hydari's address was full of observations embodying his experience in many spheres of the needs of higher education in India.

FINANCE PORTFOLIO

In February 1920, Mr. Hydari reverted of his own account to British service and was posted as Accountant-General, Bombay. But his services were again requisitioned by His Exalted Highness the Nizam in June 1921. He took over from Mr. R. I. R. Glancy, I. C. S. who reverted to the British service, the Finance Portfolio with a seat in the Executive Council—the position he at present occupies. Controlling the entire finance of the State Mr. Hydari, now, seems to be anxious to effect such reforms as will give the Exchequer a permanent balance and a productive tendency. His scheme of Deparmentalization of Finances has great potentialities and deserves much wider notice than it has obtained. On the one hand it minimises the chances of speculation in the Departments and conduces to the formation of Reserves without which the productive branches cannot be financed and developed, whilst on the other hand a fair share of autonomy is granted to the local officials to work out their plans without undue haste or delay. The critic will not fail to perceive that this is a means to a definite and foreseen end. It is paving the way for an automatic adjustment of the State Treasury when large financial undertakings such as the State management of the Railways and the like are accepted by the Government. He has already revised the classification of the heads of receipts and expenditure and drawn up proposals to prevent the payment of British income-tax on Railway earnings; he has ear-marked special reserves for the stabilization of Osmania Sicca Exchange and paper currency, and has planned a detailed scheme for the expansion of co-operative credit and agricultural improvement. Mr. Hydari, as a shrewd business man, raises no storms. He has effected these reforms without any noise. His Exalted Highness the Nizam has graciously recognised his work which has added to the fame and honour of the State and has bestowed on him the title of Nawab Hydar Nawaz Jung Bahadur. Mr. Hydari has also been appointed by His Exalted Highness to a seat on the Railway Board, London, as an Official Member —a coveted privilege which no Indian has ever before attained. It is hoped that he will continue his services to the State till the great questions of Railways and other development works are satisfactorily solved.

SOCIAL ACTIVITIES

His social and educational activities date from the very beginning of his service. He realised from the very first that without a real and solid rapprochement between the Hindu and Moslem communities progress on truly national lines was impossible. In an essay which he wrote some 17 years ago he says:

> I can conceive no nobler work to which an Indian can consecrete himself than that of cementing the hearts of the diverse races and nationalities of our vast continent into a

solid and united whole, bound by a union that is not merely a superficial one, or that merely enables the Hindu and the Mussalman, the Parsi, and the Christian to regard each other on sufferance or even with a species of benevolent neutrality, but a living and active union, whereby they come to look upon each other as brothers working for the cultivation and progress of their common heritage.

The spectacle of Hindu-Moslem unity is fortunately an everyday occurrence now but in April 1903, when the Hindus of the United Provinces gave him, on his transfer to Bombay, a farewell party as a mark of the affection of their community towards him, it was something of an event. This same appeal for comradeship between the different sections of the Indian Commonwealth runs through most of his speeches and is also expressed in his actions and in his friendships. In his Presidential speech before the 21st All-India Mohammedan Educational Conference held at Calcutta, he voiced the same appeal with a beautiful richness of imagery:

It will not be the growth but the death of Indian Nationalism if the Mussalmans of India fail to be impressed by the greatness of Asoka, Chandragupta, or filled with pride and joy at the immortal frescoes of Ajanta and the sculptured monuments of Ellora, or fail to derive fresh inspiration from the glorious songs of Jayadev and Tukaram, or find food for deep and satisfying thought in the discourses of Sri Krishna and Gautama the Buddha. It will not be the growth but the death of Indian nationalism, if the Hindus are not filled with pride at the architectural splendours of the Moghuls and the Adil Shahis, at the political achievements of great rulers like Sher Shah and Akbar, at the fine heroism of noble queens like Chand. Sultana and Nur Jahan, at the liberal statesmanship of devoted ministers like Mahmod Gawan and Abul Fazal, at the wide learning of scholars like Al-Beruni and Faizi or at the inspiration of poets like Amir Khusru and Ghalib. It will be a sad day indeed if the minds of Hindus and Mussalmans alike are not stirred with the high and noble aims of the Viceroys like Mayo and Ripon, of administrators like Munro and Elphinstone, of friends of India like Fawcett and Bright, of Missionaries like Hare and Miller. For, all these and many more, whether Hindu, Mussalman or Christian, loved India and worked for her.

In his labours for female education and female emancipation, he found a constant and staunch supporter in his wife. He married in 1893 the daughter of the late Mr. Haji Najmuddin Tyabji, a great Arabic and Persian scholar, and head of the old and well-known firm of Tyabji and Co. Mrs. Hydari was the first Moslem lady in the Bombay Presidency to give up *purdah;* her example has since been followed by many other Mohammedan ladies. Her services in connection with the disastrous floods of 1908 earned for her the then unique distinction for a lady, of the Kaiser-i-Hind medal of the first class, and her relief work in the plague and influenza epidemics will long be remembered. Mr. Hydari said before the First Hyderabad Educational Conference:

> That country can never be educated or progressive whose women are steeped in ignorance, however enlightened the men may be It is as if the body-politic were suffering from hemiplegia, half sound and half paralysed. If the mothers who give our children their first lessons in life—lessons which must inevitably influence their entire future—are devoid of education, how can we be sure that when the children go out of their hands they will be blessed with real education and morals?

He said in 1917 at Calcutta:

> It has been well said that while the education of a boy helps him only, the education of a girl lifts a whole family to a higher stage of mental and moral (and may I add physical) life.

And once again at Vaniambadi quoting Dr. Lungen of Frankfort he said:

> Let us now begin to pay the debt of centuries. To the grace and personal charm of women let us add the charm of a trained intelligence, let us remove the bandage from their eyes and lead

them to the fountain of knowledge that they too may have their share in the gathered wisdom of the ages, that they may despise empty frivolity and idle chatter, and may learn to know the highest and most inspiring of all human pleasures, the joys of mental achievements.

To these views he has been able to give practical expression during his tenure of the Educational Secretaryship at Hyderabad. To mention but one instance the Mahbubia Girls' School which is acknowledged to be one of the model Girls' schools in India was the idea of Sir George and Lady Casson Walker and Mr. & Mrs. Hydari—an idea which, by the generosity and help of His Exalted Highness the Nizam, has found fulfilment in the present school.

Taking a live interest in all forms of intellectual and social activities, no man of letters, Indian or European, fails to find a ready welcome in his house or calls for his help in vain. Such is the man Mr. Hydari whose life we have attempted to portray in these brief pages. His work is a worthy monument to his love of his country.

THE ALI BROTHERS

IT is our object to record within the short space at our disposal the life of one who has played no inconsiderable part in recent Indian politics, *viz.*, Moulana Mohamad Ali. It is indeed very difficult to write a life of Moulana Mohamad Ali without referring now and again to the life of his valiant brother Moulana Shaukat Ali. They are always known as the Ali Brothers and not so much as Shaukat Ali and Mohamad Ali. We shall content ourselves in this sketch to deal more with the life of Mr. Mohamad Ali.

PARENTAGE

The Ali Brothers belong to an Indian State. Their paternal ancestors however, were originally the residents of Moradabad. Moulana Mohamad Ali's grandfather, Ali Baksh Khan was a man of means. He succeeded in securing a decent post in the Rampur State. He was the right hand man of Yousuf Ali Khan, the Nawab of Rampur. During the Great Indian Mutiny of 1857 he was of great help to the British. For his loyal services, Khani Samar was awarded the grant of a large rent-free Jagir in the Moradabad district. Mohamad Ali's father Abdul Ali Khan also held a high office in the Rampur State. Abdul Ali Khan died of cholera very young leaving a widow of 27. At the time of their father's death Moulana Shaukat Ali was a boy of 2 years and Mohamad Ali a baby. The boys grew up under the personal care of their mother. Their education was the sole object of her life.

EARLY EDUCATION

The young widow took up the education of her sons in her own hands. In the face of great opposition and against the wishes of her relatives she sent the boys to Aligarh where they got their early education in the Collegiate School and they completed their Arts course in the Aligarh College. Bi-Amma, as the mother of the Ali Brothers was called, spent her all in bringing them up. They grew up under her personal care. She lived with them and guided them even during their internment at Chindwara. Her love for Islam was greater than her love for her dearest sons. She was always prepared to sacrifice even their valuable lives in the cause of Islam, if such a sacrifice was deemed necessary.

AT OXFORD

Both the brothers were very popular in Aligarh. They were always held in high estimation among their fellow students. One or other of the brothers would be at the head of any movement that was started in the College. After a brilliant career in Aligarh, Maulana Mohamad Ali went to England and joined the Oxford University. He was in Lincoln's Inn for four years from 1898 to 1902. He was not a very successful student in Oxford, since his energies were diffused in many interests. He devoted much of his attention to literary subjects, so much so, that he failed to secure a place in the Indian Civil Service.

MOULANA SHAUKAT ALI

Moulana Shaukat Ali, well-known in Aligarh and amongst his numerous friends as Bare Doda, the elder brother, was very popular in the College. He was a great sportsman. His favourite game was cricket. On several occasions he captained the College Eleven and won victories at All-India Cricket Tournaments. He was one of the best Cricketeers of his day.

After taking his Degree from Aligarh, he joined service, for he had to support his beloved "Mohamad" at Oxford. Although only a couple of years older, he treated his younger brother like his son. One could see the proud smile on the face of 'Shaukat' whenever Mohamad Ali made a stirring speech. It was Moulana Shaukat Ali who supplied the heart to the Non-Co-operation. Even in the early days of the movement Mr. Gandhi discerned the greatness of this 'big man' and had implicit trust in him. It was largely the support that Mr. Gandhi received from Shaukat Ali, that encouraged him to launch the Non-Co-operation movement in the country. It was to a very large extent Moulana Shaukat Ali who was responsible on the Muslim side to have brought the workers of the two communities together. It has always been a marvel to the people how a man with such a big personality could be so active. There is hardly any place in India which he did not visit during his travels spreading the gospel of non-violent Non-Co-operation. Wherever he went he made such intimate friends, who could not help loving him. His large heartedness and sincerity befriended him to one and all.

• His love for his brother and his implicit faith in his 'chief' are proverbial. He is a man of action and has made very few speeches indeed. Whenever he spoke, his utterances were frank and fearless. In the course of their trial at Karachi the brothers challenged the authority of the Court by frequent interruptions. Their love for Islam and their country is so great that they were prepared to sacrifice their precious lives.

Both Shaukat Ali and Mohamad Ali readily made the sacrifice for Islam and their country. It is believed that Moulana Shaukat Ali devotes most of his time in *namaz* and reading of the *Quran*.

IN BARODA CIVIL SERVICE

To turn now to the younger brother, Mohamad Ali returned to India in 1902 and joined the Baroda Civil Service. It is an irony of fate that Mohamad Ali should have served in the opium department of the Baroda State. So long as he was in the State service, he worked hard and was zealously devoted to his work. He carried out many reforms. The stoppage of the land oppression was a boon to the poor. He discharged his duties most efficiently and won the admiration of the Maharaja who treated him with marked kindness.

For a man like Mohamad Ali the State service did not afford sufficient scope. It was too narrow. He had high ambitions and wanted to serve his community. With this object he took leave for two years and started the famous weekly the COMRADE in Calcutta.

LITERARY ACTIVITIES AND "THE COMRADE."

He contributed to journals like the TIMES OF INDIA, the HINDUSTAN REVIEW and the SPECTATOR. His article on "Thoughts on the Present Discontents" received great praise from Lord Minto. His articles on the Minto-Morley Reforms brought about a long discussion between him and the late Mr. Gokhale. Mohamad Ali's articles were very humorous and learned. He was endowed with humour which one has seen at its best in the "Gup" one of the most interesting features of the COMRADE. Mohamad Ali had made up his mind to be a Journalist. He declined the Prime-Ministership of Jaora offered to him at this time by the Nawab of Jaora State and Sir Michael O'Dwyer.

He started the COMRADE in Calcutta, but when the seat of the Central Government was transferred to Delhi, he also removed his office to the new Capital in September 1912, Although he had not undergone any training in journalism, he conducted his weekly with remarkable ability. In a short time his

MR. MAHOMED ALI AND HIS BROTHER

weekly became very popular. His object in starting the paper was to serve his community and "to bring about better relations between race and race and the rulers and the ruled. His aim was to obliterate the line of demarcation between the two." He always advocated Hindu-Muslim unity through his paper.

His COMRADE grew to be more and more popular throughout India. Even the officials were subscribing till its very candour and frankness made itself distasteful to them, and they dropped off when it began to fight India's battles.

THE MUSLIM LEAGUE

Mohamad Ali was amongst the founders of the Muslim League in the year 1906. The object with which the League was started was to safeguard the interests of the Muslim Community and to promote the feeling of loyalty to the Government. The League could not be allowed long to remain in the quagmire of narrow politics. The liberalising influences which had been at work at Aligarh brought themselves to be felt on the creed of the League. They could not allow the community to lag behind any other community in the field of politics. At the Lucknow session of the League held in 1913, they adopted "the attainment of Self-Government for India, along with the other communities" as its creed. Thus the Muslim League also was brought in line with the Indian National Congress which has been labouring for the same ideal for a long time.

HIS ACTIVITIES BEFORE INTERNMENT

Ever since the Aligarh College was started fifty years ago, it has been the intention of the promoters of Muslim education to establish a Muslim University, where the gospel of free enquiry could be preached and which could be a second Cordova or Baghdad. Even so early as the year 1873, Justice Mahmood, the celebrated son of the worthy father Sir Syed Ahmed Khan drew up a tentative scheme for the Muslim University. It was premature and the idea had to be given up. But later on Moulana Mohammad Ali and some others revived the idea and worked for it.

They along with H. H. the Aga Khan went about the country popularising the idea and collecting funds.

THE HAMDARD

Mohamad Ali realised the value of journalism, but to reach the masses a vernacular daily was deemed necessary. He started the HAMDARD in Urdu. It was very popular, so much so that in a short time it secured a circulation equal to that of four or five of its vernacular contemporaries. Its popularity was fatal, for the Government suppressed it just before the internment of the brothers.

THE CAWNPORE MOSQUE AFFAIR

The greatest of Mohamad Ali's early achievements was in connection with the unfortunate Cawnpore Mosque incident of 3rd August 1913. For the purpose of constructing a road the Municipality of

Cawnpore found it necessary to acquire a portion of the Machlibazar mosque premises. The Mutawallies (trustees) gave their consent and in spite of great opposition the portion of the Mosque was demolished in the presence of a posse of police. It was an insult to Islam and a sacrilege according to Islamic Law. Protest meetings were held all over India, but to no purpose. The Hindu press co-operated with their Muslim brothers. The manner in which they carried on the agitation was praiseworthy. The Mussalmans of Cawnpore assembled in a meeting at the Idgah and after the meeting they went to the mosque and hundreds of them including many youngsters began to heap loose bricks, symbolic of the re-construction of the demolished portion. The police apprehended danger. It was all in their imagination. To justify their apprehension a large force of police arrived on the spot and fired on the agitated mob and bayonetted them. Many arrests were made. Mohamad Ali carried on a strenuous agitation through his paper against the sacrilege perpetrated against Islam. He trusted to the sagacity and wisdom of Sir James (now Lord) Meston, the Lieutenant-Governor of the Province for a solution of this problem.

When he failed to move the authorities in India, he and Syed Wazir Hasan proceeded on a deputation to England. There they addressed meetings and had interviews with the leading people. The ignorance of the British people regarding Indian affairs was shocking. The most deplorable incident was the misunderstanding between these young patriots and Mr. Amir Ali. In spite of all these disadvantages they achieved creditable results. They interviewed Sir James La Touche, the ex-Lieut. Governor of U. P. and a member of the Secretary of State's Council. This interview was largely responsible for the Viceroy's intervention in the matter, his visit to Cawnpore and the ultimate settlement of the question to the satisfaction of the Muslims.

THE ALL-INDIA MEDICAL MISSION

The accounts of the sufferings of the Turks during the Balkan War and the utter lack of medical aid to the wounded soldiers, moved Indian Muslims to action. Large sums of money were sent. Moulana Mohamad Ali and Dr. M. A. Ansari organised a Red Crescent Mission to Turkey in 1912 which rendered yeoman's service.

DELHI AFFAIRS

The way in which he identified himself with the masses and fought for their interests made him the idol of the people in Delhi. One of the most intricate problems which seemed difficult of solution was the wholesale strike of the Butchers. They were stubborn in their demands. It was Mohamad Ali's intervention that brought about a satisfactory settlement.

He took more and more interest in the politics of his community which grew more and more virile, courageous and self-assertive. He worked zealously and untiringly for the advancement of his community and for a democratic spirit among them. Young men with really democratic ideals took the place of the old. They brought their community out of its isolation and thenceforward began to participate with the other communities in national work.

HINDU-MUSLIM ENTENTE

It is no doubt true that he devoted his time entirely to the uplift of his community. But he was not a mere communal worker and a hater of non-Muslims. He never ignored the claims of other communities, when he fought for those of his own. "No friendship," he once wrote "can endure long that is not based on mutual confidence and respect." In his lecture to the students of the Benares University, he is reported to have said that if Hindus became true Hindus and Muslims true Muslims all the friction would disappear in a moment. To-day we do not find two better and stauncher advocates of Hindu-Muslim unity than the Ali Brothers.

HIS EDUCATIONAL IDEALS

Mr. Mohamad Ali had always definite views on education as on several other subjects. He condemned the present system of education in un-ambiguous terms and put in a strong plea for national education in the truest sense of that expression. "A national system of education" he said, "can only be evolved on *national lines*, and in accordance with the inspiration of *national* hopes and genius. The control and direction of higher education must be in the hands of the Indians themselves if India is to grow through unity of purpose and training to a vigorous and complete national life."

The national Muslim University at Aligarh is as far as possible worked on these lines.

SPEAKER, JOURNALIST AND POET

There are some Indians whose command of the English language is a marvel to Englishmen themselves. Mohamad Ali is an orator of a high order. He has an impressive and persuasive style. He has a marvellous command of language. His courage is of a high order. He is not much of a tactician. He has a blunt, outspoken manner and is a fierce controversialist, unsparing in his criticism of the adversary. He has rich imagination too which sometimes, as in the case of what he called the "wireless message" from the Mahatma, led him into dubious positions.

Readers of the COMRADE can bear testimony to his abilities as a journalist. His clear, incisive and persuasive style never failed to have its maximum effect on the readers. His criticism of the Government was free from malice. It has always been fearless and frank.

Mohamad Ali is also a poet but not of the type which indulges in 'gul' and 'bulbul.' The style is simple and the dominating feature of his poetry is the practical religion he always preached. The spirit of optimism pervades his poetry. His choice and musical words prophesied a bright future for Islam. With Iqbal he sang of hopefulness and faith. One of the essential characteristics of his poetry is that it appeals to the heart.

TURKEY AND THE GREAT WAR

When Turkey declared War against the Allies, the Mussalmans in India were in a greatly perturbed condition of mind. They owed spiritual allegiance to the Kilafa in Turkey and at the same time had to recognize the political Sovereignty of England over India. In spite of their religious convictions and in a spirit of loyalty to great Britain, Mussalmans fought England's battles in Europe. Mr. Lloyd George's solemn promises to the Indian Mussalmans that nothing would be done to interfere with their religious feelings and sentiments and integrity of the Ottoman Empire were a great relief to them. While Mussalmans were reconciling themselves to the situation the criticisms of several of the anti-Moslem Powers and some English journals against Turkey and the Sultan were trying the patience of many a patriotic Mussalman. The LONDON TIMES was one of the severest critics. Mahomed Ali was in a rage. In his COMRADE, he wrote an article entitled "The Choice of the Turks" in reply to one under the same title that appeared in the LONDON TIMES. In that article he could not help giving a frank and clear expression to the long list of wrongs to which Turkey was subjected at the hands of the European Powers. Mohamad Ali's reply was so complete and powerful that it was too much for the Government to let go without being suppressed.

Mohamad Ali's attitude was always just, and never hostile to the Government. But he loved Turkey the only Muslim power worth the name. The LONDON TIMES took upon itself the duties of the Foreign Minister of Turkey and advised her to remain neutral and warned her against waging war even on Greece. The whole article was provocative and illogical. Mohamed Ali wrote a pointed reply in the COMRADE of 16th September 1914. The authorities in India grew nervous, thought Mohamed Ali was encouraging the King's enemies, and therefore ordered the securities of both the COMRADE and the HAMDARD be forfeited. The Brothers were not given a moment's rest. One trouble followed another. They were not allowed to remain free for long.

INTERNMENT

In May 1915, they were interned. No reason was assigned for their internment. Protest meetings were held all over India, which demanded from the Government the reason for such a procedure. It was in vain. No reason was given. From Mahrauli they were removed to Chindwara. During internment both the brothers made a wide study of religion and world's history. It was there that Mohamad Ali composed the most soul-stirring and inspiring of his national poems. The brothers were interned under the Defence of India Act and that was the only reason. They were considered dangerous to the peace of the country and the Government placed a restraint on their movements. The following appeared in the Administration Report of the Delhi Province for the year 1915-16 under the chapter entitled "Protection."

In the same month (May) was found necessary to intern Mohamad Ali and Shaukat Ali on account of the bad influence which their bitter propaganda against the British Government was having on a section of the Muhammadan Community.

On the 21st February 1917, the Hon'ble Mr. Dadabhoy moved a resolution in the Imperial Legislative Council recommending to the Government of India, a revision of the Defence of India rules, 'so as to provide for the constitution in each province of a special machinery to consider the cases of persons whose movements or actions it is proposed to control under those rules.' On this resolution the Hon. Mr. Mazhar-ul-Haque spoke as follows :—

"......Sir, my own community, I mean Muhammadans, have suffered most in this respect. Men of great influence, men who are looked upon by the entire community with the greatest regard and affection have been interned, and the entire community is absolutely ignorant why they have been interned and what is their fault. If we knew their fault, and if we knew that their cases were examined by responsible officers, perhaps we would not object. We would be sorry all the same but we would not object. Now what is the case? I say—and I feel my responsibility when I say it—that the vast majority of my community is entirely disaffected in this country as regards these internments. I have no hesitation in giving to the Government the names of some Mussalman leaders, and I hope the Hon. the Home Member will note these names, who have been interned and about whom the community feels so much. They are Mr. Mohamad Ali, Mr. Shaukat Ali and Maulana Abdul Kalam Azad. All these men are looked upon with great veneration and respect by the Muhammadans throughout India, and unfortunately their fault is not known. If they are at fault let them be interned by all means; we shall all side with the Government, but for Heaven's sake let us know their fault and the cause of their being interned. If there were any Advisory Committee such as proposed by my Hon. friend Mr. Dadabhoy and my Hon. friend Mr. Chanda and the Committee gave its opinion, I think the whole community would be satisfied; at least they would know that there was strong suspicion or evidence against the people who are interned.

The then Home Member replied to Mr. Mazhar-ul-Haque that they (the Ali brothers) were persons who were 'publicly making speeches and writing articles, and the only question was ' what they were doing, whether criminal offence or not,' was 'likely to be dangerous or prejudicial to the public safety or to excite the populace,' and according to Sir Reginald Craddock, ' you do not require Advisory Committees to tell you that. As he had taken care to remind the Council, ' the wording of the Act itself is not that a man to be interned must necessarily be a criminal, or have committed a criminal offence, but that it should be believed that he has acted, is acting or is about to act in a manner prejudicial to the safety of the country."

The country could never be satisfied with such vague reasons.

The Hon'ble Mohamad Ali Jinnah moved for the release of Mrs. Besant from internment. The Government replied saying :—

The Government of India are prepared to recommend to the Government of Madras to remove the restrictions placed on Mrs. Besant and Messrs Wadia and Arundale under the Defence of India Rules, if the Government of India are satisfied that these persons will abstain from unconstitutional and violent methods during the remainder of the War.

Further,

The Government of India are prepared, subject to the same conditions, to take the same course in regard to other persons upon whom restrictions have been placed under these rules, merely by reason of their violent methods of political agitation.

This reply naturally turned Mr. Jinnah's attention to the Ali Brothers. He asked for their release also. The reply was :—

The Government are already considering the cases of Mohamad Ali and Shaukat Ali and are making inquires in regard to them.

The period between the 5th and 26th September, 1917 is very significant in the history of their internment. On the 7th September, however, Mr. Abdul Majid, Deputy Superintendent of Police, was sent as an emissary from Simla to Chindwara, and he showed to the Ali Brothers the form of an undertaking initialled by Sir Charles Cleveland which as he informed them, the latter desired them to give. It ran as follows :—

Undertaking :—

I shall abstain during the remainder of the War from doing, writing, or saying anything intended or reasonably likely to encourage or assist the enemies of the King-Emperor. I shall also abstain from doing, writing or saying anything intended or reasonably likely to be construed as an attack upon the Allies and friends of the King-Emperor. I also promise to abstain from any violent or unconstitutional agitation which is likely to affect the public safety.

Explanation :—

The abstentions promised above are not intended to cause me to refrain from participation in politics within constitutional limits.

Messrs. Mohamad Ali and Shaukat Ali replied to the Government in the following terms instead of the above:—

Bism-i'-llah-i-r-Rahman-ir-Rahim.

We have always been God-fearing Muslims who accept above all else the commandments of God as conveyed to us in the Holy Quran and the life and sayings of our Prophet. Without prejudice to this faith we have always been law-abiding lovers of our country, opposed to all unconstitutional and violent methods, and, war or no war, this we always desire and hope to remain. Therefore we have no objection to give an assurance, if any is still needed, to the effect that without prejudice to our allegiance to Islam we shall abstain from doing, writing, or saying anything intended or reasonably likely to encourage or assist the enemies of the King Emperor, and from doing, writing, or saying anything intended or reasonably likely to be construed as an attack upon the Allies and friends of the King-Emperor, and that we shall also abstain from any violent or unconstitutional agitation likely to affect the public safety. We understand and base the above undertaking on the clear understanding that the abstentions promised above are not intended to restrict in the slightest measure our freedom to observe all our religious duties as Mussalmans or to cause us to refrain from participation in politics.

A couple of days after this incident the Raja of Mahmudabad went to Chindwara to discuss with the Ali Brothers, the question of their release and he was satisfied with their attitude. He was however, annoyed to find that a C. I. D. had preceded him. It was generally expected that the Ali Brothers also would be released along with Mrs. Besant. Nothing would induce the Government to accept the statement of the Brothers. On the 26th September, Sir William Vincent replied to Mr. Jinnah in the following words :—

Restrictions under the Defence of India Rules were imposed upon Messrs. Mohamad Ali and Shaukat Ali, not merely for violent methods of political agitation, but because they freely expressed and promoted sympathy with the King's enemies thus endangering the public safety. The Government of India have made further enquiries regarding these persons and on a careful consideration of the information and opinions received, and on a re-examination of previous papers, the Government of India are not satisfied that the attitude of these persons has materially changed in this respect, or that these restrictions can be safely removed

These mysterious 'previous papers' made a sudden appearance. They were said to be the two letters written to the Amir of Afghanistan and the well-known Muslim divine of Farangi Mahal, Lucknow. They are described as of a treasonable nature. "In this he (Mahomad Ali) again denied categorically on behalf of his brother as well his own the authorship of, and every other criminal connection with, any such letters and repeated the request that they might be shown to them." They were not shown to them.

RELEASE

The Royal Proclamation of Dec. 25, 1919, evidently secured the release of the Brothers also. The news of their release flashed from one end of the country to the other and there were rejoicings everywhere. They proceeded straight to Amritsar where the Indian National Congress had assembled that year. They were given a fitting reception. To people of all shades of opinion their release was welcome. They thanked the Government for this act of justice. Mohamad Ali made a powerful speech on the resolution of the recall of Sir M. O'Dwyer. He attended the session of the Muslim League, where he supported the resolution for giving the Reforms a trial. This shows the faith he had in the Government in spite of his sufferings during his internment.

What with the forfeitures, confiscations and their long internment the Brothers had sustained heavy financial loss. When they were released many of their friends and admirers proposed to make a present of a substantial purse to them. An influential Hindu-Muslim Committee consisting of leading Indians of all parties was formed for making collections for the Ali Brothers' Purse Fund. But they would not accept the money for their personal use, however poor they may be. They resolved to devote the collections to objects of public utility.

THE ORGANISATION OF KHILAFAT WORK

During the Great War Mr. Lloyd George, the Premier of England had made solemn promises to Indian Muslims who depending upon them went and fought against their brothers in Islam. When the War came to a close, a curious interpretation was put upon the promises evidently to avoid fulfilment. If there was anything that exasperated the Indian Muslims it was this attempt of the British Premier. The pledges were unredeemed and promises were broken.

The Muslim contention was that the *Jazarat-ul-arab* including Mesopotamia, Arabia, Syria and Palestine with all the Holy Places situated therein must always remain under the direct Suzerainty of the Calif. But as a result of the terms of the Armistice, Turkey was deprived of her homelands. Thrace was presented to Greece. Both Great Britain and France divided the Asiatic portions of the Turkish Empire among themselves under the guise of mandatories. A High commission was appointed by the Allied Powers, who to all intents and purposes were the rulers in Turkey, with the Sultan nothing better than a prisoner.

Not only the entire Mussalman population in India but other communities as well were in rage against what was rightly termed as the British Premier's betrayal and while in Amritsar the leading Congress and Khilafat men discussed the situation in the country caused by Lloyd George's doings. They decided to organise the Khilafat work under the guidance of Mahatma Gandhi.

In the middle of January 1920, Mr. Mohamad Ali issued along with his brother a manifesto to the country in the course of which, after formally thanking the public for their sympathy and support, he outlined his future course of action. "We expect to hear from His Excellency the Viceroy in a day or two," wrote Mr. Mohamad Ali and his brother in that Manifesto, "when he would be pleased to receive the Khilafat Conference Deputation and arrangements are in train for the Deputation to proceed to England, Persia, America and Turkey through the kind assistance of His Excellency." They said,

> We trust they will be enabled to start at the latest by the end of this month. Our case is so strong and based so firmly on the solid rock of religion and reason that we should have very little doubt of the success of our mission. No effort will be spared to conciliate Europeans and Americans, and to convince them of the genuineness of our deepest concern for the Caliphate, the Jazarat ul-arab, the Holy Places and the integrity of the Ottoman Empire and of the extreme reasonableness of our demands in relation to these and of the solid mass of entire Islam at our back.

They realised the enormous cost of such deputations but at that time they thought it was the best course to adopt in this agitation.

An influential Deputation of Hindu and Muslim leaders waited on the Viceroy, in Jan. 1920. An address was presented to Lord Chelmsford, setting forth the demands not only, of Muslim India, but of the Indian public as a whole in regard to the Khilafat Question.

The Deputation went on to state significantly, "that the Imperial Government is as much a trustee for Muslim and Indian interests as for the Christian. It is therefore not enough that our sentiments and wishes are placed before the League, but it is essential that British Ministers make our case their own." "Islam," stated the address, "has ever associated temporal power with the Khilafat.

> We therefore consider that to make the Sultan a mere puppet would add insult to injury and would only be understood by Indian Muslims as an affront given to them by a combination of Christian Powers. Whilst, therefore, we must insist upon the pledge given by Mr. Lloyd George on 5th January 1918 being fulfilled, in order to show that we desire no more than the strictest justice, we concede the right of the Allied Powers to ask for such guarantees as may be considered necessary for the full protection of non-Muslim races living under the Sultan.

The Viceroy received the Deputation well and assured the members of his sympathy and promised to do all that was possible of him, to place their case carefully before the Peace Conference.

The result of the Deputation was not satisfactory.

The Government refused to issue passports to the Missions to the Hedjaz, Smyrna, Mesopotamia, Egypt and Persia. They directed their attention to India, where they began organising the Khilafat work. They put themselves in touch with the Central Khilafat Committee of India, got control of it, revised its constitution and rules and placed it on a strong and effective basis.

DEPUTATION TO ENGLAND

The All-India Khilafat Delegation with Moulana Mohamad Ali as the head reached England early in March 1920. At every town they met with disappointment. This did not discourage them. They persevered in their work though they met with little support in England regarding their Mission. There was a strong body of influential opinion in England that the Turks should be driven out bag and baggage from Constantinople and that their sympathy must not extend to any territory in Europe. Mohamad Ali interviewed Mr. Fisher on behalf of the Government, also Mr. (now Earl of) Asquith and a number of leading politicians of all parties. The Delegation received much help from the Labour Party who arranged public meetings at Albert Hall and Kingsway Hall, which afforded an opportunity to place their case before the English public.

Mohamad Ali was discouraged but with his undaunted optimism carried on his work with greater zeal. The MUSLIM OUTLOOK was started in England and ECHO-DE-ISLAM in Paris for the purpose of carrying on continuous propaganda in England and France respectively. The English public opinion was made to recognise the folly of accepting the burden of the Mesopotamian mandate.

Mohamad Ali applied for leave to make representation to the Supreme Council Meeting at San Remo. This was denied to the delegation.

FRANCE AND ITALY

From the beginning he discovered that France and Italy kept an open mind on the Turkish question. These two *Powers* were determined not to force Turkey to accept the cruel terms.

The delegation met 30 French deputies who were very much impressed with the claims of the Indian Muslims. The French Premier in an interview with Mohamad Ali on 12th August 1920, stated that the Sevres Treaty was not final. The noteworthy result of the delegation work in France is that complete revision of the Sevres Treaty was urged even by the Venezelist *Matin.*

In Italy Mohamad Ali had an interview with H. H. the Pope who expressed full sympathy with the Turkish aims and recognised the religious tolerance shown by the Ottoman Turks and their Government and said that the Apostolic Delegate at Constantinople had borne testimony to this in his reports.

Nothing tangible was achieved by the delegation.

Having exploited every source of influence, official as well as non-official, the Press as well as the platform in France and Italy as well as Britain, Mr. Mohamad Ali came to the conclusion that it was useless to rely on the good offices of European Nations to secure the salvation of Muslim requirements.

THE NON-CO-OPERATION CAMPAIGN

Mr. Mohamed Ali along with most other members of the delegation returned to India in October 1920. At a meeting held in Bombay on his arrival he gave an account of his mission in Europe and the only advice that he could then give was to join the Hindus and get freedom for India, on which, he believed depended the freedom of the Khilafat.

While the delegation was busy in Europe, the All-India Congress Committee met at Benares and decided to call a Special Session of the Congress, at Calcutta to consider the Khilafat question.

In June there was an informal meeting of leading Hindus and Muslims at Allahabad. Among the prominent non-Muslims who participated in the deliberations were Pandit Motilal Nehru, Madan Mohan Malaviya, Mrs. Besant, Dr. Sapru, Lala Lajpat Rai and Mr. Chintamani. There was an overwhelming majority in favour of united action and it proposed to resort to an effective method of agitation to get the Khilafat wrong righted.

The Khilafat Committee met and resolved unanimously to accept the leadership of Mahatma Gandhi under whose guidance they proceeded with their work in right earnest.

On June 22, a mainfesto was sent to the Viceroy touching the Khilafat demands and calling upon him to resign his office and lead the Khilafat movement if he failed to move the Home Government to recognise the validity of their demands.

Mahatma Gandhi sent the following message to Mohamad Ali:

Respectful but firm Muslim representation influentially signed announcing resort to Non-Co-operation from the 1st August 1921 if Ministers' peace terms be not revised or if the Viceroy does not head Khilafat agitation now in His Excellency's hands. I have sent my own separate representation explaining my connection with the movement and associating myself entirely with it. In my opinion the vast majority of Muslims and Hindus are behind this great and just agitation for respect of Muslim religious sentiments and for ensuring fulfilment of Ministerial pledges. You may be sure of everything possible being done on this side. I have no doubt that in this great cause God will help us if we will help ourselves.

When it was found that nothing would come out of the manifesto to the Viceroy, the Non-Co-operation campaign was launched on the 1st August in accordance with the determination of Mahatma Gandhi and his associates.

The campaign began with the giving up of titles, honours and honorary offices. Mahatma Gandhi, Hakim Ajmal Khan, and Saraladevi Chaudharani, set an example by renouncing their respective titles. The main items of the Non-Co-operation movement as it was originally conceived included also the boycott of Government Schools and Colleges, Law Courts and the reformed Councils.

In every Province there were several students who gave up their Government Schools and Colleges. Calcutta and Lahore came out first in the race.

The question of liberating the Colleges at Aligarh and Benares from Government control drew the attention of Mahatma Gandhi and Mohamad Ali. As has been seen, the brothers have always been the idols of the students and Professors of the Aligarh College. Mohamad Ali could not long tolerate the control of the Government. Mahatma Gandhi and Maulana Mohamad Ali impressed upon the students the necessity of freeing themselves. They came out *en bloc* on the 13th October. For some time he remained the Principal of the National Muslim University at Aligarh. But the ever growing seriousness of the movement in the country dragged him out of the four walls of the Aligarh College. From this time he fell heart and soul into the movement. He took a leading part in the Nagpur Sessions of the Congress, the Khilafat Conference and the Muslim League. He was the right hand man of Gandhi at these Conferences.

At the Nagpur Congress it was resolved to collect a crore of rupees for the Tilak Swarajya Fund. Mohamad Ali along with Mahatma Gandhi and Maulana Shaukat Ali, went about the whole country in order to make the national resolve effective. In Aligarh, where his influence was great the District Magistrate served on him an order not to make speeches.

THE CHARKA

He attended the All-India Congress Committee meeting held at Bezwada, where the well-known Non-Co-operation Programme was passed. From Bezwada he went to Madras and then to the Southern Districts. At all these places he made powerful speeches, calling upon students to concentrate "all attention on the peaceful revolution, on the bloodless revolution that you are to make in History" and preached the "doctrine of the Charka." He spared no pains in his efforts to fulfil the Bezwada programme, particularly with reference to the Tilak Swarajya Fund, and the Charka.

THE AFGHAN BOGEY

In his Madras speech he made an important statement regarding his attitude towards an Afghan invasion. "If," he said, "any outside power, Germans or Bolsheviks" confirming what he wrote in his letter from Betul jail, "or Turks or any outside power comes to invade our country and its people and to subjugate them we shall not only not assist but we shall consider it our duty to lead the resistance in India (Hear, hear.) We have been made slaves once. We do not want to be made slaves again."

SWARAJYA DEFINED

He presided over the Khilafat Conference held at Erode where in his address he defined his attitude:—

> We want to prove, that it is not necessary to go about making speeches but still carry on the work and correct a Government that is based on tyranny. We want the Government to mend itself. If it will not mend itself, we have got to do it. We give it a chance. It was I who was against declaring absolute independence in the Congress, because I want to give the British Government one more chance. We should honestly give them a chance. We do not want to subvert the Government merely for the sake of subversion. We do not hate the Government because it is foreign and if we had a government of Indians which was equally 'satanic,' we will hate it all the more. That is the work we have got to do.

When we decided at Bezwada that the country was not sufficiently ripe and disciplined to undertake civil disobedience, it was because there were not enough volunteer corps. If you enlist in sufficient numbers the best blood amongst you, the most educated and enthusiastic amongst you, and at the same time exercise self-restraint, Swarajya will come to the nation. Swaraj will come to the Nation when Swaraj has come to the individuals. When self-government is within you, it will be with you. Self-government of the individuals will result in the Self-Government of the Nation. * * * * * * * We want you to go to the fire, and be placed on the anvil so that the leaders may hammer you and you will come out as true steel which will never bend. I want you to be that steel for we have got to face a very big, bold enemy.

It was upon this speech that the Government decided to prosecute him. From the South he proceeded to Northern India where he went from town to town calling upon the people to fulfil the Bezwada programme. The speeches which the Ali Brothers made at these places were considered seditious and incitements to violence. The Government were alarmed. They resolved to put the law rigorously in motion against all those who were considered to have broken the law of the land.

THE GANDHI-READING INTERVIEW

At this juncture came the famous Gandhi-Reading interview brought about by Pandit Malaviya. At this interview, Lord Reading drew the attention of Mr. Gandhi to the speeches of the Ali Brothers as falsifying the view of the Non-Co-operation movement put forward by Mr. Gandhi. These speeches, it was pointed out to Mr. Gandhi, might be construed as subtle incitements to violence, and, scrupulously fair as Gandhi always is, he agreed that such a misconstruction of the speeches was possible. He, therefore, wrote to the Ali Brothers and secured from them a statement repudiating any such intention on their part.

THE BROTHERS' STATEMENT

Our friends have drawn attention to certain speeches of ours, which in their opinion, have a tendency to incite to violence. We desire to state that we never intended to incite to violence, and we never imagined that any passages in our speeches were capable of bearing the interpretation put upon them. But we recognise the force of our friends' argument and interpretation. We therefore sincerely feel sorry and express our regret for the unnecessary heat of some of the passages in these speeches, and we give our public assurance and promise to all who may require it that so long as we are associated with the movement of Non-violent Non Co-operation we shall not directly or indirectly advocate violence at present or in the future, nor create an atmosphere of preparedness for violence. Indeed we hold it contrary to the spirit of Non-violent Non-Co-operation to which we have pledged our word. Bombay 29, May.

This "apology" was an important event in the history of the movement. The Anglo Indian and certain other sections of the Press hailed with joy "the victory of the Government." Although it was not an apology to the Government, yet the statement coming soon after the interview had a depressing effect on the people. The Government of Lord Reading, satisfied with the "apology" gave up the idea of prosecution. The brothers went on undaunted with their work. They were responsible to the people, they said, and not to the Government.

Then came the Karachi Khilafat Conference at which the resolution deciding that it was *haram* for true Muslims to serve the enemies of Islam, was passed. After this Conference, Mohamad Ali travelled along with Mahatma Gandhi in North and North-Eastern India.

ARREST

The collection of a crore of rupees, the introduction of Charkas and the enlistment of members to the Congress alarmed the bureaucracy. In England, the Diehards raised a hue and cry and would not rest satisfied until the Indian leaders were muzzled and their activities put a stop to. They became very powerful, so much so the Government of India was compelled to take action against the leaders. On September 14, Mohamad Ali was arrested at Vizagapatam on his way to Southern India along with Mahatma Gandhi. He was taken to Karachi where the trial took place.

THE GREAT TRIAL

Maulana Shaukat Ali was arrested in Bombay soon after Mohamad Ali's arrest. The other leaders including Dr. Saifuddin Kitchlew and Sri Shankaracharya of Sharada Pitt were also arrested. The same resolution for which they were prosecuted was repeated by thousands of people throughout the country. The Working Committee of the Gongress, as well as of the Hindu-Mussalman leaders issued a manifesto reiterating the Karachi resolution. It was largely signed among others by Mahatma Gandhi, Pandit Motilal Nehru, C. R. Das, N. C. Kelkar and C. Rajagopalachariar. This created a trying situation for the Government. The challenge was too much to be accepted. The trial of the leaders began in October at Karachi. The main charge against them was that of criminal conspiracy promoting enmity to Government and attempting to seduce the troops from their allegiance to the King. The Magistrate committed all the accused to take their trial at the Sessions.

This most exciting and interesting trial opened at Karachi on October 26. Even here the accused confined themselves to addressing the Jury after the case for prosecution was over. There were many irregularities on the side of the prosecution New charges were framed even after some of the witnesses had been examined. However, they abstained from defending themselves in obedience to the Congress resolution. They however thought fit to present elaborate statements in defence of their conduct. Mr. Mohamad Ali said, in the course of his address to the Jury, that he could have swept away the Crown Prosecutor's case, for none of the charges were proved. There was not a single Muslim on the Jury who could understand the Muslim's position. It was not he declared, the Khilafat leaders who were on trial, but the Government who were on trial, since they had set themselves up against the law of God. The Jury, after deliberating anxiously for sometime, returned a verdict of not guilty under the principal charges of conspiracy and seduction of soldiers, but pronounced guilty under the minor charges of causing mischief. On November 1, the Judge pronounced judgment. He agreed with the Jury's verdict, acquitted the accused under the serious charges, but convicted them for the minor offences of causing mischief, abetting offence etc. He sentenced Mr. Mohamad Ali and his brother to two years' rigorous imprisonment. Allah-ho-Akbar was the cry of the anxious crowd when they heard the sentence.

The Brothers' behaviour during the trial called forth many an adverse comment at the time. Their fierce and sometimes petulent and defiant attitude was in strong contrast with the calm dignity and the serene atmosphere that six months later pervaded the trial of Mahatma Gandhi. But Gandhi himself who could see no blemish in his brave and faithful followers attributed their behaviour to their sincerity and their scorn of social niceties.

"FROM A SMALLER INTO A BIGGER JAIL"

Mr. Mohamad Ali was released from prison in August, 1923 after serving his full term of two years. During those two years he was shifted from one prison to another and he spent the major portion of his prison life in Bijapur. From time to time rumours of the Brothers' illness or ill-treatment caused a panic in the public mind and on one occasion it became necessary for the jail authorities to exhibit the Brothers so as to allay public excitement. When one morning in the last week of August Mohamad Ali was suddenly released at Jhansi, thousands gathered round him in an instant to welcome him back to freedom and public life. Addressing the first meeting after the release he said that the so-called freedom from jail had made him very gloomy because he felt that on his shoulders had fallen the great responsibility of his religion and country. In the absence of the great leader Mahatma Gandhi who was dearer to him than his brother Shaukat Ali himself he felt as if he had come out "from a smaller prison to a large one." His first duty to his country was to "search for the key of Swaraj to open the Yerawada jail in which was encaged the soul of India." He said he would move a resolution at the next session of the Special Congress that every member of the All-India Congress Committee and the Working Committee should sign a pledge that he would ever be prepared to sacrifice his life to attain freedom for the country. He said he would be the first man to sign such a pledge.

> **As regards my political views there is absolutely no change. I come out from jail, unrepentent and with the same convictions with which I entered and I have no fear of re-entering it. I stick to the Mahatma's programme of non-violent Non-Co-operation and Hindu-Muslim Unity. If I do not succeed in bringing my fellow countrymen together I shall consider that I have failed in my task.**

DELHI SPECIAL CONGRESS

Though Mohamad Ali came out of the prison, with the same opinions with which he went in, the country had changed considerably indeed from the programne of 1921. Already a strong contingent of Congressmen including some leaders had outgrown the orthodox creed of Non-Co-operation. They stood for Council-entry and obstruction from within. Already the Swarajya party was in embryo, determined to capture seats in the Legislatures and use them to further the cause of the country. Already the Civil Disobedience Committee had begun to doubt the wisdom of civil disobedience and the majority looked to the Councils for any constructive politics in the distracted state of the country. It was at this time that Mr. Mohamad Ali was called to guide the Special Congress at Delhi and he gave a right lead by recognizing the validity of the demand for Council entry and by urging the need above all for unity. But he has always a theatrical way of doing things and he gave full vent to his imagination by exclaiming that he had a "wireless" from Mahatma Gandhi asking him to yeild to the agitation for change in the programme and pave the way for unity. What he meant was but a figurative way of saying that he was doing what the Mahatma would do under the changed circumstances of the country. Of course Mr. Gandhi with such a rigorous code of honour would never have infringed the jail regulations by sending a "wireless." But all the same the effect of this pronouncement was electrical. The intransigent no-changers yielded and the Swarajists came into their own. Though a pronounced no-changer himself, he was one of the first to recognize the wisdom of conceding to the Swarajists the right to carry on their work within the Congress.

PRESIDENT OF THE COCANADA CONGRESS

It is not surprising that Mr. Mahomed Ali should have been chosen to preside over the next Congress at Cocanada. His is one of the longest even among presidential addresses of the Congress which are invariably lengthy. But it was a brilliant and forceful expression of his views and of the part he has played in recent Indian Politics. A large portion of the Address is taken up by a masterly survey of the history of the Indian Moslem movement since the days of the Mutiny. He explained why in the earlier days Moslems stood out of the Congress and how later in the march of events they were naturally led into the great movement.

In putting forward an impassioned plea for the Hindu-Moslem unity, Mr. Mohamad Ali pointed out how most of the disturbances result from trivial causes and how, granted toleration on the part of both the communities, an easy solution might be found for the present difficulties. As part of a programme to secure Hindu-Moslem unity, he suggested the formation of local committees and district conciliation boards, greater and continuous vigilance on the part of Congress organizations and the Press and a readiness to be generous in regard to communal claims for representation in the Services and Local Bodies and in the Legislatures.

He concluded that Swaraj is imperative for Moslems no less than for Hindus and that, if the people organised themselves and steadily prosecuted the Constructive Programme, prepared, if necessary, to face even death, Swaraj is as good as achieved.

Let us resolve to work, and, if need be, to die for the sake of our nation's freedom, and if at the end of a year's honest work this Government does not send for our absent leader to witness

its heartfelt repentance for the past, and to receive the great charter of Swaraj for the future, let us in God's name unfurl without a moment's hesitation the flag of the Indian Republic, India's independent Federation of Faiths. Then friends, you will not find your retiring President so unwilling to break the link that joins him to Great Britain as he is in some quarters suspected to be.

As President for the year it was his task to guide the Congress through the changes and chances of shifting programmes. And the Congress programmes of these days are as changing as the weather. Mr. Mohamad Ali brought to his task a judicial outlook somewhat perplexing to the no-changers. Of the Swarajists to whom he had not always been civil, he said in his address:—

The Swaraj party is there to day, and even though it may be composed of some very dissimilar elements, it is undoubtedly strong enough in numbers to-day and has always been strong in the quality of its leadership. More than all else, it was permitted at Delhi to go to the polls on its own moral and religious responsibility. It has gone there and has achieved great enough success considering what forces were arrayed against it, how short a time it had in which to organise its own forces, and how greatly it was handicapped by the fact that some of its best members were disqualified from contesting the elections owing to their having undergone longer terms of imprisonment than those which do not affect eligibility.

THE ALL PARTIES CONFERENCE

Once again Mr. Mohamad Ali played an important part in the year of his presidentship, in connection with the All Parties Conference at Delhi. In September 1924 Mahatma Gandhi, appalled by the Kohat riots and the failure of his efforts to bring about Hindu-Muslim Unity, took the astounding vow of a 21 days' fast. He was then at Delhi as Mr. Mohamad Ali's guest. Of course there could be no intervention in an affair which to one like Mr. Gandhi is a matter between himself and his Maker. Mr. Mohamad Ali appealed in vain, now in anger, now in tears, but Gandhi was inexorable. "The God who has spared my mother two months ago" wrote Mr. Mohamad Ali in piteous anguish, "will, I trust, also spare me this brother—nay this more than brother to me." Mr. Gandhi safely came out of the ordeal. The immediate effect of this fast was the bringing together of all parties at Delhi to devise methods whereby to prevent further ruptures between the two communities. Mr. Mohamad Ali took a leading and by no means negligible part in this work of Hindu-Muslim Unity. Indeed unity still continues to be his one principal objective. He is not even quite so keen on independence as of old, realising that unity is the key to independence. In supporting the Independence Resolution in the Belgaum Congress he defined his position in these words:—'My position is Swaraj within the Empire and outside if necessary. I am not afraid of going out of the Empire nor am I ashamed at present of remaining within it."